D0260729

Skill Acquisition and Human Performance

ADVANCED PSYCHOLOGY TEXTS

Lyle E. Bourne, Jr.
Series Editor

Advanced Psychology Texts (APT) is a series of intermediate but highly readable textbooks and monographs in the core areas of psychology. The primary objective of the series is to give undergraduate student majors and beginning graduate students in psychology a basis for evaluating the state of the science and a springboard into further guided or independent scholarship in a particular area. Each volume will center on the current issues and the basic concepts of a core content area of psychology. Students who use these books are expected to have some general background in the field. The textbooks take advantage of that background, building it into a sophisticated contemporary understanding of the facts and of the important yet-to-be answered questions. Each text focuses on recent developments and the implication of those developments for future research. Although the emphasis is on psychology as an evolving systematic scientific discipline, applications of basic research findings are also included. Authors have been asked to present clearly and thoughtfully what it is that each subarea of psychology has to contribute to human knowledge and welfare.

Volume 1 Skill Acquisition and Human Performance
Robert W. Proctor and Addie Dutta

SKILL ACQUISITION AND HUMAN PERFORMANCE

ROBERT W. PROCTOR
ADDIE DUTTA

ADVANCED PSYCHOLOGY TEXTS

SAGE Publications
International Educational and Professional Publisher
Thousand Oaks London New Delhi

For information address:

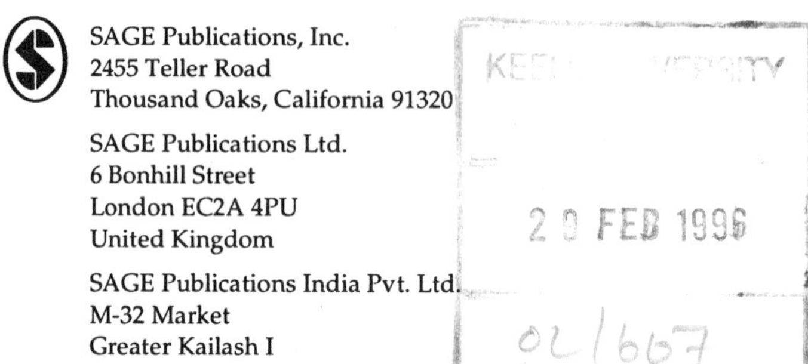

SAGE Publications, Inc.
2455 Teller Road
Thousand Oaks, California 91320

SAGE Publications Ltd.
6 Bonhill Street
London EC2A 4PU
United Kingdom

SAGE Publications India Pvt. Ltd.
M-32 Market
Greater Kailash I
New Delhi 110 048 India

Printed in the United States of America

Library of Congress Cataloging-in-Publication Data

Proctor, Robert W.
Skill acquisition and human performance / authors: Robert W. Proctor, Addie Dutta.
p. cm. — (Advanced psychology texts; vol. 1)
Includes bibliographical references and index.
ISBN 0-8039-5010-1
1. Cognitive psychology. 2. Performance. I. Dutta, Addie. II. Title. III. Series.
BF311.P7474 1995
153—dc20 94-32594

95 96 97 98 99 10 9 8 7 6 5 4 3 2 1

Sage Project Editor: Susan McElroy

Brief Contents

Contents

Preface

Systematic research on skill acquisition and human performance has been conducted since the late 1800s. However, in recent years and across many different areas there has been a dramatic upsurge in the number of studies devoted to some aspect of skill. There are numerous reasons for this increase in interest in the topic of skill acquisition, including the realization that the acquisition of cognitive skill can be studied in much the same way as that of perceptual-motor skill, the development of theoretical frameworks and modeling techniques that lend themselves readily to the topic of skill, the establishment of methods for investigating and representing the knowledge possessed by experts, and the demands for effective training procedures imposed by increasingly sophisticated technology. In this book, we pull together research from a variety of relatively distinct research areas to provide a coherent picture of our current understanding of human skill and of the status of skills research.

The approach that we take in the book is "bottom up." That is, after a historical and conceptual introduction (Chapter 1), we start with studies investigating skill in comparatively simple laboratory tasks (Chapters 2-4). We then consider skilled performance of more complex tasks that impose greater demands on attentional and memorial resources (Chapters

5-7) and examine expertise in specific real-world domains (Chapter 8). In the remainder of the book, we discuss topics of more directly applied relevance, including training, the role of individual differences in abilities, and situational performance-shaping factors (Chapters 9-11). In the final chapter, we summarize the general principles that emerge from our review of skills research and discuss the critical role that computational models play in contemporary research.

We place a heavy emphasis on empirical studies in our treatment of skill. We want the reader to know not only what researchers have concluded about the characteristics of skill acquisition and human performance but also how and why these conclusions have been reached. Throughout the book, we also stress the close relation between theories and data, highlighting in particular the use of formalized models to aid in understanding the underlying nature of skill. In short, we want the reader to gain an understanding of the process by which research on skills is conducted in addition to learning about the current state of knowledge regarding skilled performance.

This book is intended for use in upper-level undergraduate courses and in beginning graduate courses. It is suitable to serve as the primary text for courses devoted specifically to skill or to human performance more generally. Because we cover many of the topics investigated and methods used in contemporary cognitive psychology, the book also can be used along with other books or readings for survey courses devoted to cognitive psychology. Finally, because we are aware of no other book that integrates skills-related research across many different areas of research, as the present book does, we also think that it will be a valuable resource for a wide range of researchers studying human behavior.

We would like to thank Lyle E. Bourne, Jr., the series editor, for inviting us to prepare this text and for his guidance and assistance along the way. We also thank C. Deborah Laughton, our editor at Sage, for her support and advice. Alice Healy and several anonymous reviewers provided detailed and invaluable reviews of some or all of the chapters from which the book has benefited. Finally, we would like to note that this book is a completely joint project of the two authors, reflecting equal contributions of each. Preparation of the book has been a very satisfying experience for us, in part due to the encouragement and feedback that all of the individuals mentioned above have provided.

Robert W. Proctor, *Purdue University*
Addie Dutta, *Rice University*

Historical Overview

Phases of Skill Acquisition and Modes of Performance

Varieties of Skill

Measurement of Skill

Modeling Skill

Summary

CHAPTER 1

Foundations of Skill Research

Skilled behavior is fundamental to all human activities. Skills such as driving, reading, and typing are so common among adults that they can be taken for granted. Yet these skills, and most others, require coordinated processes of perception, cognition, and action. Fairly general definitions of skill in terms of these processes and associated abilities have been offered in the past. For example, Welford (1968) defined skill as being

> concerned with all the factors which go to make up a competent, expert, rapid, and accurate performance. Skill in this sense thus attaches, to a greater or lesser extent, to *any* performance and is not limited to manual operations but covers a wide range of mental activities as well. (pp. 12-13)

In this general view, the processes that go into the development of common, everyday skills also go into the acquisition and performance of more specialized cognitive and motor skills such as troubleshooting equipment failures, operating heavy machinery, and playing tennis.

Evidence is accumulating that skill acquisition and skilled performance share underlying mechanisms across the perceptual, cognitive, and

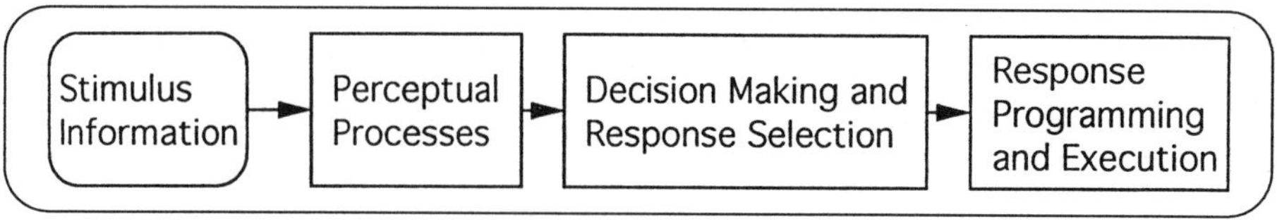

Stimulus Information → Perceptual Processes → Decision Making and Response Selection → Response Programming and Execution

Figure 1.1. Three-stage model of human information processing.

motor domains (Carlson & Yaure, 1990; Rosenbaum, 1987), and we hold that general principles and properties of skill become apparent only when an interdisciplinary view is taken. For this reason, and because we are interested in skill in a broad sense, our coverage of skill is not restricted to any particular area or domain. Where possible, we show how the processes of perception, cognition, and action jointly determine skilled performance across many task types.

Most of the studies that we review in this text fit within the **information processing approach** to studying human performance. This approach assumes that the activities taking place within a person between the presentation of an external stimulus and the observation of an overt response can be studied with behavioral and psychophysiological methods. Typically, distinct stages of processing are assumed, and experimental methods are applied to isolate and study the stages of interest. The simplest framework of information processing, shown in Figure 1.1, distinguishes just three stages: perceptual processes, decision making and response selection, and response programming and execution. This framework typically is supplemented with an attentional system that selects some sources of information for processing over others and a memory system that stores the vast knowledge that we possess (**long-term memory**) and maintains in an active state a limited amount of the information of immediate relevance to the task at hand (**short-term or working memory**).

Specific models differ in the proposed properties of the stages, such as whether or not attention is required for processing, whether particular processes can be carried out concurrently or must be performed sequentially, and the extent to which one process affects another. It has even been suggested that the ordering of the stages should be changed, putting the response stage first rather than last, because our actions also serve as a source of information to guide perception, cognition, and future actions (Flach, 1993). Because the basic goal of most skills researchers is to determine the influence of skill on perceptual, cognitive, or motoric processes, the simple information processing framework consisting of just the three primary stages described above serves well as an organizing framework not only for this book but also for research on skill.

Most of the research on skill has been carried out in laboratory settings, but the same processes involved in the execution of controlled, laboratory tasks are required in tasks encountered every day in the real world. However, everyday tasks typically are more complex, affected by a wider range of variables, and subject to fewer constraints. The competing desires to impose experimental control and to consider a wide range of factors thus trade off in using laboratory versus real-world tasks. For example, the reading of X-ray pictures for medical diagnosis is a skill that develops over many years. Because of its importance, this skill has received considerable study, much of which is discussed in Chapter 8. X-ray diagnosis has been studied naturalistically by comparing the performance of medical students, residents, and practicing radiologists. To gain a fuller understanding of particular factors influencing diagnostic skill, such as prior knowledge of patient anatomy, more detailed analyses have been performed using constrained diagnostic tasks with the subject populations of interest. Because X-ray diagnostic skill depends on basic skills such as visual search and decision making, findings from laboratory studies of these basic abilities have also been applied to the specific problem of medical diagnosis. Thus, as with many other skills, a full understanding of skill in reading X-ray pictures requires an interplay between naturalistic study, the study of constrained tasks within the domain, and basic research.

Historically, the primary focus of skills research has been on perceptual-motor performance (see, e.g., Welford, 1976). This research, both basic and applied, has produced a better understanding of issues such as the way in which actions are selected and coordinated, the different levels of skilled performance, and the conditions of practice and training that facilitate the acquisition and transfer of skill. Over the years, research on skilled performance has expanded to encompass higher-level cognitive skills such as those involved in expert problem solving and decision making. This expanding research base, coupled with the development of sophisticated methods for modeling performance, has resulted in significant advances in the investigation of skill. In this chapter, we review many of these historical developments while introducing terms and concepts fundamental to skills research as well as the basic methods used to study skill and human performance.

Historical Overview

The history of research pertaining to skill begins in the early years of experimental psychology with the publication by Ebbinghaus (1885/1964) of a monograph on learning and memory that, although not directly concerned with skill acquisition, set the stage for the research on skill that would follow. Skill acquisition and performance were subsequently featured in many studies around the turn of the 20th century, with these early studies providing a foundation for later work. Topics most widely studied at this time were the nature of learning curves, transfer of training, and the learning and control of movements.

Ebbinghaus's Contributions

At the time that Ebbinghaus published his monograph, the generally accepted view was that higher mental processes could not be studied experimentally. Given this prevailing atmosphere in early scientific psychology, the breadth and depth of Ebbinghaus's investigations are remarkable. He demonstrated beyond question that it was possible to obtain objective, quantifiable measures of mental processes.

Ebbinghaus himself served as the subject for his experimental analysis of memory. He studied learning and retention of lists of nonsense syllables about which he reasoned that no prior associations would exist. Over a period of several years, he learned many lists of these syllables under different conditions and tested his ability to recall the lists in serial order.

One issue examined by Ebbinghaus was the number of repeated readings of a list necessary to attain a criterion of one correct reproduction of the list—with the unsurprising finding that the required number of repetitions increased with the length of the list. He also established that after a series of nonsense syllables had been learned, one syllable of the series would act as a retrieval cue for other syllables in that series, even when the cued and retrieved syllables were separated by other elements in the original list. The idea that associations are formed between elements that are relatively remote from each other is a feature of many contemporary models of learning and memory.

Ebbinghaus introduced two paradigms that are still used today in memory and skills research. The first of these is **savings**, which, in Ebbinghaus's case, required a previously learned list to be relearned, with the difference in the number of repetitions required for original learning and relearning taken as a measure of retention. Savings is a sensitive measure that can reveal retention of information even when other measures, such as overt recollection, fail to show evidence of learning. The second paradigm is that of **transfer.** In Ebbinghaus's use of this paradigm, one list was learned and its influence on the learning of a subsequent list was examined. Because the relation between original and transfer items can be varied, tests of transfer provide evidence regarding the specific nature of the learning that has occurred.

Through use of the savings and transfer paradigms, Ebbinghaus was able to draw conclusions about the nature of the associations learned, the effects of the passage of time, and the influence of learning schedules on later performance. All of these issues have subsequently received wide attention in skills research.

Early Studies of Skill Acquisition

The advent of the study of skill acquisition can be dated to the work of Bryan and Harter (1897, 1899) on the acquisition of telegraphic language. They bypassed the limitations associated with studying skill acquisition in the laboratory by examining the performance of field operators, noting, "Society has already made for us in each occupation a vast experiment in the development of habits" (1899, pp. 348-349). Bryan and Harter were prescient in their realization that highly skilled behavior develops over many years and that it is sometimes necessary to go into the field to examine the development and nature of expertise.

Telegraphy was a major form of communication at the turn of the century, and the accurate transmission and reception of telegraphic messages were important for the broadcast of news and other current events. In telegraphy, a sender must translate a message written in English into Morse code and rapidly tap a telegraph key, in taps of long and short durations, separated by pauses. The receiver of the code must retranslate the message into English and transcribe the message, typically by typewriter. The speed with which messages are transmitted is limited by the skill of the operators at translating the messages and executing the required physical actions.

Bryan and Harter's initial work focused on differences in performance as a function of level of experience. Among the findings noted by Bryan and Harter were that a minimum of two to two-and-a-half years at the job was necessary to develop the skill necessary for fast and accurate transmission and reception of messages. They also found that rates of receiving varied greatly across operators, that external disturbances had less impact on experts than on novices, and that variability in sending decreased with increasing skill level. Subsequent to their early descriptive work, Bryan and Harter examined the learning curves of several operators. Measurements of performance were taken weekly, beginning with the operators' initial experiences as telegraphers and continuing for up to as many as 40 weeks (see Figure 1.2).

Bryan and Harter's investigations of telegraph operators showed that the sending rate improved more rapidly than the receiving rate but reached asymptote sooner. Eventually, the receiving rate approached or even exceeded the sending rate, so that a skilled receiver could easily handle the most rapid incoming message. Moreover, the sending curves showed continuous improvement with practice up until the point that the asymptote was reached, whereas the receiving curves for some operators showed distinct **plateaus,** or periods during which there was relatively little change in performance. These plateaus led Bryan and Harter to characterize skill acquisition as the development of a **hierarchy of habits.** This hierarchy for telegraphic skill was proposed to involve letters, words, and higher language units. According to Bryan and Harter, receivers are concerned with identifying individual letters during their first few days as telegraphers. Over this period they begin to identify words, and it is words that then become the primary units for the next few months. Only after the letter and word habits have been acquired does the operator fully benefit from the higher-level organization of the language. Thus the plateaus represent periods where a lower-level habit is at asymptote but the next higher habit is not yet affecting performance.

Just as Ebbinghaus's (1885) research set the stage for the investigation of skill by establishing paradigms for measuring learning and demonstrating fundamental learning phenomena, Bryan and Harter's work provided a direct impetus for the systematic investigation of skilled performance. Among other things, Bryan and Harter showed that much could be learned from studying practical skills acquired in the work environment. Importantly, their results suggested that skill acquisition proceeds through distinct phases and that basic elements of a task must become automatic or second nature before higher-level aspects of the task can be mastered.

However, both the finding of plateaus and Bryan and Harter's interpretation of the cause of the plateaus were the subject of considerable debate. In the realms of telegraphy and typewriting, Book (1908) and Swift (1904, 1910) found evidence in support of the notion of a hierarchy of habits as well as some evidence of plateaus in the course of learning. Book

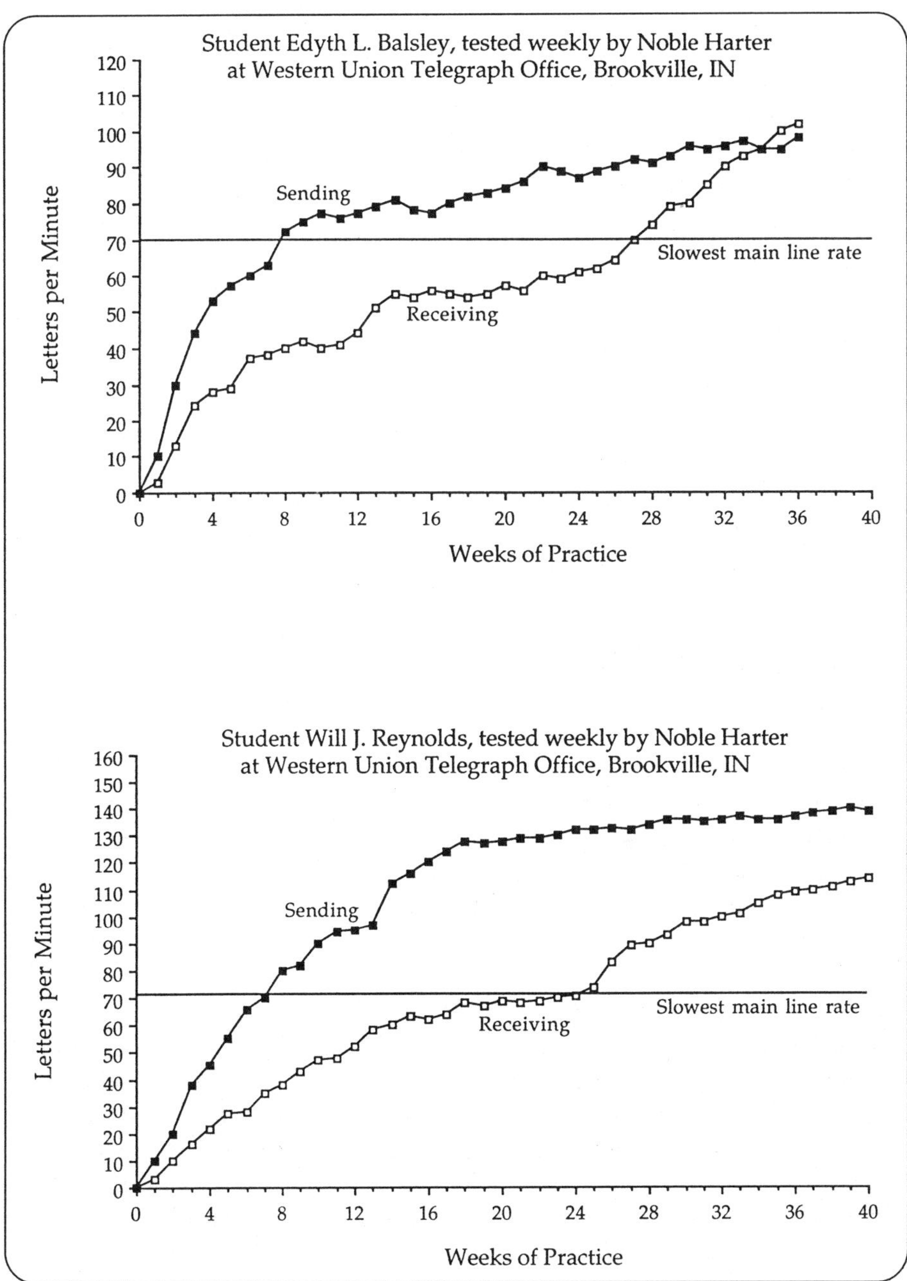

Figure 1.2. Sending and receiving curves for two telegraphers studied by Bryan and Harter.
SOURCE: Bryan & Harter (1897).

attributed these plateaus to lapses in attention and a need to eliminate inefficient habits, not to the nature of the learning occurring at the time. Swift's view was more in line with Bryan and Harter's in that he felt that plateaus represented periods during which habits were becoming automatized. Other researchers have failed to find plateaus in learning (see Keller, 1958), and the study of plateaus is no longer a primary concern among skills researchers. The current view is that plateaus do not represent a necessary stage of learning and thus that the process of automatization does not imply that there must be periods of relatively little improvement in performance.

Another characteristic of improvement with practice, which was described early in the history of skills research, continues to be the focus of research and theorizing. Most tasks have the characteristic that performance seemingly improves indefinitely, with the greatest changes occurring early in practice. When the logarithm of response time is plotted as a function of the logarithm of the number of trials performed, a straight line is the result. Such a relation is indicative of a power function—for example, performance time = (amount to be learned)(number of trials)$^{-\text{learning rate}}$. Snoddy (1926) was the first to conclude that learning could be described as a linear function of the logarithms of time and trials and proposed the following general learning equation: $\log C = \log B + n \log x$, where C is a measure of performance, x is the number of trials or time on task, and B and n are constants. This relation has attained the status of a law—the **power law of practice**—that any model of skill acquisition is expected to produce (Newell & Rosenbloom, 1981).

Several examples of power-law improvement were provided by Crossman (1959). Among these examples is a naturalistic study of operators of cigar-making machines. The number of cigars that had been produced by an individual operator prior to the testing period varied from 10,000 to over 10 million. Crossman plotted the log speed of operation of the machine by the various operators as a function of the log number of cigars that had been produced to date (see Figure 1.3), with the prediction that a straight line would result. Only after 3 million cigars (about two years of practice) did the curve deviate from a straight line, indicating no further decrease in performance time. Moreover, this apparent asymptote in performance time was close to the minimum machine cycle time and thus was apparently due to machine limitations rather than to learning limits.

Crossman provided a theoretical explanation for the observed power-law speedup. In this formulation, when first faced with a task, the operator

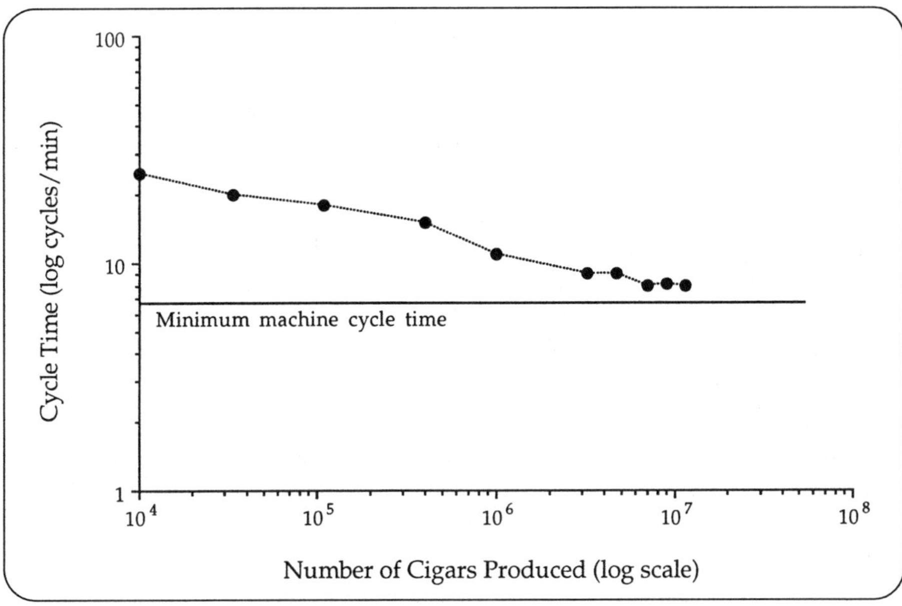

Figure 1.3. Speed of cigar making (cycle time) as a function of practice (number of cigars produced).
SOURCE = Adapted from Crossman (1959).

has many alternative ways of performing it. According to Crossman, "For each trial or 'cycle' he[1] will adopt some particular combination of sensory, perceptual, and motor activities, partly from deliberate choice, partly from habit, and partly by chance" (p. 159). Thus the operator has a repertoire of actions from which particular actions may be selected. As the operator practices the task, a comparison process allows more efficient actions from the repertoire to come to be favored over less efficient ones, producing the speedup. There is some question regarding whether selection of efficient procedures over inefficient ones can occur, and studies will be discussed later in the book that suggest some degree of inflexibility in human performance. However, when tasks are relatively complex and time is available to reflect on performance strategies, it is likely that selection of efficient procedures does occur.

Transfer of Training

In parallel with the research investigating learning curves, researchers also examined transfer of training. Transfer studies evaluate the extent to which experience on one task facilitates or interferes with performance of another task, and the breadth of transferability can be used to distinguish alternative theories of skill or learning. Broad transferability was the key feature of the view called the **doctrine of formal discipline** (see Higginson, 1931), which was popular at the close of the 19th century. According to this doctrine, training in a classical discipline, such as mathematics, can foster the acquisition of general reasoning abilities that are of use in virtually all mental endeavors rather than establishing a collection of specific associations between particular stimuli and actions to be taken. In the early 20th century, investigations that challenged the formal discipline view were reported.

In one series of studies, conducted by Thorndike and Woodworth (1901a, 1901b, 1901c), participants were first tested on their ability to perform a simple task, such as estimating areas of geometric shapes, then were given training on a related task. Following training, the participants were again tested on the original task. In every case, Thorndike and Woodworth looked for evidence of transfer from the training experience to the subsequent performance of the original task. Their general finding was that there was relatively little transfer from one task variation to another. For example, in one experiment, the participants practiced marking words containing the letters *e* and *s*. Although some positive transfer to other letter sets was observed, the magnitude of improvement on different letter sets relative to the initial, pretraining performance with *e* and *s* was considerably less than that on the training set.

Thorndike and Woodworth interpreted their findings as evidence against the view that practice at one task develops a general ability that enhances performance of most other tasks. Based on this and subsequent work, Thorndike developed the view that practice strengthens particular associations between elements within a task. This view has been called the **theory of identical elements** and predicts transfer of training only when two tasks have particular elements in common. The identical elements theory marked a turn away from the doctrine of formal discipline, with its emphasis on general faculties of attention, memory, and the like, toward consideration of habits and associations particular to individual tasks.

The limited nature of positive transfer was captured by Osgood (1949) in his **transfer surface** (see Figure 1.4). Osgood noted three empirical principles that held across most transfer studies: When stimuli are varied and responses are functionally identical, positive transfer usually occurs and is an increasing function of stimulus similarity; when stimuli are

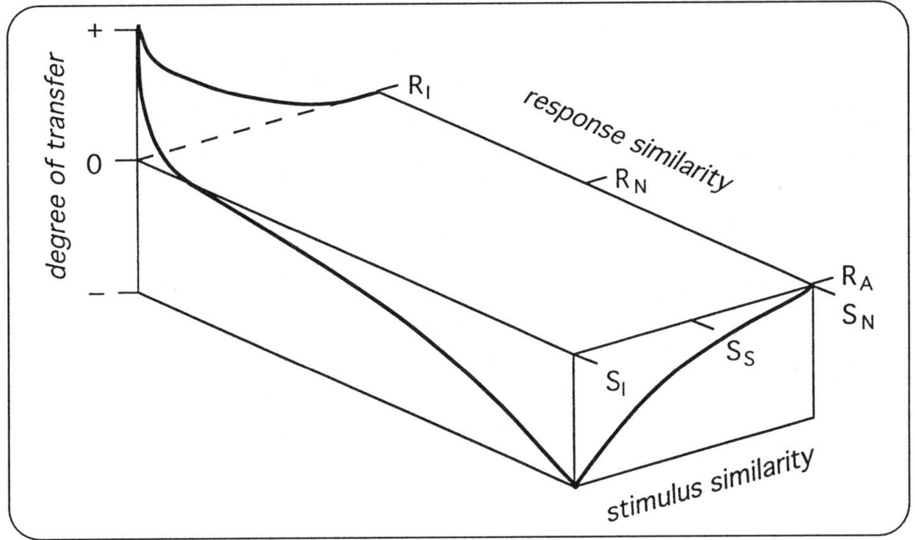

Figure 1.4. Depiction of Osgood's transfer surface. Response similarity is represented on the *X* axis, marked by "identical" (I), "neutral" (N), and "antagonistic" (A) responses. Stimulus similarity is on the *Z* axis, where I represents "identical," S represents "similar," and N represents "neutral." The *Y* axis shows the expected degree of positive or negative transfer.

functionally identical and responses are varied, negative transfer usually occurs and is a decreasing function of response similarity; and when both stimuli and responses are varied, any transfer is negative, with the amount being an increasing function of stimulus similarity and a decreasing function of response similarity. In Figure 1.4, stimulus and response similarity are represented on the *Z* and *X* axes, respectively, and the degree of transfer is shown on the *Y* axis.

As can be seen in the figure, the region of positive transfer is much smaller than the region of negative transfer. In the model, positive transfer is restricted to situations in which both the stimuli and their associated responses are identical or nearly so. Osgood (1949) described the region of extreme negative transfer as "admittedly hypothetical" (p. 140). Although negative transfer is common when learning verbal materials (e.g., Postman & Underwood, 1973), it has not often been found in skills research (Singley & Anderson, 1989).

Skilled Action and Information Processing

Noting that "man is not merely perceptive and intellectual, but distinctly active or reactive" (p. 1), Woodworth (1899) made another major contribution to the study of skill, this time concerning the relation between perception and action. He investigated the initiation and execution of voluntary movement, emphasizing that even relatively simple movements require timing and coordination. In his most extensive study, Woodworth had people draw series of ruled lines of a specified length. He examined the accuracy and variability of the movements executed to make these lines under different conditions of speed stress, practice, fatigue, and sensory control. By comparing performance under these conditions, Woodworth was able to draw conclusions about the relative influence of each factor.

Two major findings that continue to receive investigation stand out. First, when people were required to make the same movement but at different rates (as governed by a metronome), accuracy decreased as the speed of the movement increased. Importantly, Woodworth noted that equal increments of speed did not produce equal increments in the error rate; rather, the function was S-shaped (see Figure 1.5 and the discussion of this speed-accuracy trade-off later in the chapter). Second, Woodworth found that although vision was usually beneficial, its benefits depended on the duration of the movement performed. For movement durations of less than 450 ms, accuracy was no better with the eyes open than with the eyes shut. However, for slower movements, accuracy was better when the eyes were open. These results suggested to Woodworth that visual feedback can be used to guide movements but only if the movements exceed some critical duration so that guidance is possible.

Not only were Woodworth's empirical contributions important, but so were his theoretical ones. He distinguished between two phases of movement control, which he called **initial impulse** and **current control.** Foreshadowing present ideas on the initiation and control of movement, Woodworth (1899) believed that "the first impulse of a movement contains, in some way, the entire movement" (p. 55). This idea implies that a representation or plan (often called a motor program) underlies the intended movement and that the current control phase consists only of adjustments based primarily on visual feedback.

Much of the subsequent research on the control of action has used tasks that require movements of fixed extents or durations. However, many task environments are dynamic and require that movements be adapted to changing goals. Intense involvement of psychologists in the investigation of human performance in these dynamic environments and in the control of dynamic systems arose from the rapid technological advances associated with the world wars.

Many systems, such as a manufacturing process, require an operator to track some aspect of the system and to correct any error. A **tracking task** involves manipulating a control mechanism to reduce the error distance between an element to be controlled and an environmentally driven "track" stimulus (e.g., turning a steering wheel to keep a car on a road). Craik (1948) formulated the view that the operator is an element in the control system. He referred to the operator as a human chain composed of links by which the sensory signal (in this case, the perception of error) is converted into a motor response (in this case, a corrective action). Thus Craik conceived of the human being as an information processor actively operating on environmental information to produce an observable response.

Craik (1948) emphasized a mechanistic approach in which the person's behavior was described much as a machine's would be. In this approach, the questions of interest regarded the human system's "sensory resolving-power, its maximum power-output and optimum loads, its frequency-characteristics and time-lags" (p. 142), and so forth. However, in his 1943 book, Craik emphasized the internal mechanisms of information processing more generally, specifying three essential processes. The first process translates external events into internal symbols. In the second process, the symbols are manipulated and new symbols created through reasoning. The role of the third process is to retranslate the symbols created by earlier processing into either external actions or the realization of a problem solution. These three processes roughly parallel the three stages in the information-processing framework that became popular after Craik's death. Throughout his book, Craik used the mechanistic metaphor and compared reasoning to the approximation of real-world situations by an internal model, a view, called **mental models,** that has had a resurgence of popularity in recent years (e.g., Johnson-Laird, 1989).

Cognitive Skill

One of the most important advances historically was the realization that cognitive skill could be studied in much the same manner as perceptual-motor skill. In his 1958 book, Bartlett made the case that thinking is a high-level skill and should be studied as such. He attempted to extend the study of skill, which had been carried out largely in the perceptual-motor domain, into problem solving and thinking. Bartlett noted that, as with perceptual-motor skills, thinking must be based on information picked up directly or indirectly from the environment and used to satisfy a goal. He also emphasized that expertise is acquired through considerable practice with appropriate feedback. One implication of Bartlett's analysis is that performance on problem-solving tasks can be analyzed analogously to performance of perceptual-motor tasks.

Many of Bartlett's experiments involved what he termed **thinking within closed systems.** This is the solution of problems that have one correct answer, with all the information required for problem solution given. In keeping with the skills framework, Bartlett considered issues such as the transfer of problem-solving ability to new problems and the linking together of a series of solution steps. Bartlett also speculated about the characteristics of thinking in less structured, open systems. He evaluated scientific, artistic, and "everyday" thinking, noting that they differ in many respects. Although Bartlett's work was short on details, it clearly made the case that thinking is a skill that can be studied experimentally.

The type of experimentation advocated by Bartlett was developed and formalized by Newell and Simon (1972). In their now classic book, *Human Problem Solving,* they presented new techniques for describing problem-solving behavior and developed a comprehensive theory of problem solving. Newell and Simon employed modeling concepts and notation systems from the field of artificial intelligence to show that the human problem solver can be described as an information-processing system. Their approach emphasized issues in problem representation and problem-solving strategies. Although Newell and Simon were concerned primarily with problem-solving performance and not the acquisition of problem-solving skill, research directed toward understanding the differences in problem solving across levels of expertise has followed directly from their work. We will have much more to say about Newell and Simon's approach in Chapter 7.

Phases of Skill Acquisition and Modes of Performance

Since the work of Bryan and Harter, it has often been proposed that skill acquisition proceeds through phases characterized by qualitative differences in performance. This view continues to be prominent, even without convincing evidence for the performance plateaus on which Bryan and Harter initially based their distinctions. Moreover, performance differences are observed in the course of well-learned skills when they must be performed in situations that vary in their degree of familiarity, and it is useful to make comparable distinctions between modes of performance across these situations. We describe below three popular frameworks that make similar distinctions between qualitatively different levels of skill.

Fitts's Phases of Skill Acquisition

A very useful and influential framework for skill acquisition was proposed by Fitts (1964, 1962/1990; Fitts & Posner, 1967). Based on his observations that different cognitive processes are involved at different stages of learning, Fitts distinguished three phases: **cognitive, associative,** and **autonomous.** Early in the learning of complex skills, cognitive processes are used by the learner to understand the nature of the task and how it should be performed. The learner must attend to outside cues, the instructions that are provided, and feedback about performance. Because of the heavy involvement of conscious cognitive processes early in learning, Fitts called this the cognitive phase.

After the instructions have been learned and task expectations are understood, the learner enters the associative phase. In this phase, inputs are linked more directly to appropriate actions, and the need for verbal mediation is diminished. Thus error rates decrease, as does performance time. The transition from the associative phase to the autonomous phase is marked by reduced interference from outside demands and the lessening of attentional requirements. When task performance has reached the autonomous phase it is said to be automatic, no longer requiring conscious control. According to Fitts, this automaticity may take months or years to develop and will allow the automated task to be performed concurrently with many other activities.

Even though Fitts distinguished three distinct phases of skill through which the learner passes, he regarded the progression through the phases as continuous. Transition from one phase to the next was predicted to be gradual and not marked by an abrupt shift. Moreover, Fitts argued that the learner may not make the transition to later stages. In his work extending this theoretical framework to training methods, Fitts found that the efficacy of a particular method depended on the current phase of acquisition and that appropriate training methods could reduce acquisition time dramatically. Similar ideas for training have been pursued more recently, as is discussed in Chapter 9.

Anderson's Framework for Cognitive Skill Acquisition

Anderson (1982, 1983) developed a framework for the acquisition of cognitive skill based on Fitts's three phases. In doing this, Anderson considered specific processes and mechanisms underlying performance at each phase, as well as the transition between phases. Anderson usually describes skill acquisition in terms of two stages, **declarative** and **procedural,** which correspond to Fitts's cognitive and autonomous phases, respectively. Rather than postulating a separate associative phase, Anderson describes a process of **knowledge compilation** by which knowledge is converted from declarative to procedural form.

The distinction between declarative and procedural knowledge is fundamental to Anderson's framework. Roughly speaking, declarative knowledge is the body of facts and information that a person knows, whereas procedural knowledge is the set of skills a person knows how to perform. In the declarative stage, instructions and situational characteristics are encoded as a set of facts. These facts must be rehearsed and retained in an active state in working memory to be used by general interpretive mechanisms. As the person practices, **procedures** specific to the task at hand develop that do not require the active maintenance of declarative knowledge about how to do the task. These procedures, also called **productions,** are basically if-then rules: *If* the condition specified in the production is satisfied, *then* the action is carried out. Sometimes, the production specifies something other than an overt action, as when a number is carried when performing mental arithmetic.

Performance continues to improve gradually after the task-specific procedures have been developed and the procedural stage has been reached. This improvement is accomplished through what Anderson (1982) calls **tuning,** which involves refinement of the procedures through processes of generalization (that broaden the range of applicability), discrimination (that narrow the rules to only appropriate situations), and strengthening (that weaken poorer rules and strengthen better rules). One implication of such continuing changes in the procedural stage is that someone who has practiced sufficiently to enter the procedural stage is most likely not yet performing at the level of an expert. Extensive additional practice is necessary to produce the refinement characteristic of expertise.

Rasmussen's Modes of Performance

A third framework relating to skilled performance has been developed by Rasmussen (1983, 1986). This framework deals with different modes of performance in complex task environments. Rasmussen distinguishes three modes of performance, **knowledge based, rule based,** and **skill based,** which he likens to Fitts's phases of skill acquisition. Knowledge-based behavior corresponds to behavior during the cognitive phase, in that performance is guided by verbal mediation and conscious control and depends on a thorough understanding of the system and task goals. However, a major difference between the two formulations is that, whereas the cognitive phase refers to an early stage of skill acquisition, knowledge-based behavior is just the present mode of performance. Rule-based behavior is also guided by conscious control, but in the form of stored rules, much like productions, rather than in the form of knowledge of a system. Skill-based behavior is characterized by "smooth, automated, and highly integrated patterns of behavior" (Rasmussen, 1983, p. 258). When behavior is skill based, it can be said to be automatic.

The major difference between Rasmussen's formulation and those of Fitts and Anderson is that Rasmussen emphasizes that the performer can move between modes of behavior as dictated by task demands, whereas Fitts and Anderson both emphasize skill acquisition as a progression through the stages. The dynamic nature of work and other task environments guarantees that not many skills will be completely automatized. New skills must be acquired and often must be integrated with existing skills. Also, novel situations may be encountered to which performance must be adapted, so that automated responses are no longer appropriate. Consequently, as stressed by Rasmussen, task performance often will involve combinations of the different modes of behavior, depending on situational factors.

Varieties of Skill

In our historical review, we covered many different types of skill. These skills share several critical characteristics in terms of which skill can be defined (see Annett, 1991; Fitts, 1964). First, skill is acquired through practice or training. A defining characteristic of the skills discussed in this book is that they are not innate but must be learned. Second, skilled behavior is goal directed. Skill develops in response to some demand imposed by the task environment on the organism, although some learning may occur that is incidental to that demand. Third, skill is said to have been acquired when the behavior is highly integrated and well organized. Through experience, the components of behavior are structured into coherent patterns. Finally, cognitive demands are reduced as skill is acquired, freeing limited mental resources for other activities. From these characteristics, we derive our definition of skill: *Skill is goal-directed, well-organized behavior that is acquired through practice and performed with economy of effort.*

As stated earlier in the chapter, most skills involve the entire information-processing system. However, at a gross level, skills can be divided into those with primarily perceptual, motor, or cognitive components. For example, the task of crossing out letters used by Thorndike and Woodworth is primarily perceptual in nature. Woodworth's task of drawing lines of specified lengths involves primarily motor abilities. Cryptarithmetic (solving arithmetic problems in which letters have been substituted for numbers and the task is to decide which number each letter represents), popular both with Bartlett and with Newell and Simon, can best be described as a cognitive task. Both within and across these types of skill, it is possible to make further distinctions.

The first such distinction is between **simple** and **complex** skills. People can become skilled at tasks as simple as pressing a specified key in response to the onset of a designated stimulus. When first presented with this task, they struggle to understand the instructions and must attend to every aspect of the task, from motor requirements to stimulus identification and classification. After relatively modest practice, the task is performed with little thought or effort, and performance is fast and accurate. More complex skills, such as proving geometric theorems (e.g., Anderson, 1982), often are made up of multiple components that must be integrated before performance is highly skilled. These skills require more time to develop, and the acquisition time will depend more on the training conditions than it will for simple skills.

Another dimension of variation in skill is defined by the environment in which the skill is performed (Poulton, 1957). A **closed** environment is a predictable environment. Performance in such environments can benefit from expectancies developed from prior experience and can become routinized. For example, in using a keyboard to enter text, we do not have to worry about where the keys will be located from one word to the next and, barring a power failure, the outcome is predictable. **Open** environments are characterized by uncertainty and dictate to some extent how the skill must be performed. A classic example is maintaining altitude in an airplane, where weather conditions can change the required actions from moment to moment. Consequently, skills performed in an open environment must be more flexible than those performed in a closed environment.

Measurement of Skill

As skill at a task is acquired, many changes occur. The goal of the researcher is to determine what these changes are and how they can be quantified. Most obvious are increases in the speed and accuracy with which the task is performed. However, these increases may reflect changes in mental representations or operations involved in task performance, the choice of strategies used to perform the task, or the degree of attentional involvement. A major question is "What differences in information processing underlie these measurable changes in performance?" Methods for answering this question can be divided into performance measures, verbal protocol analysis, and psychophysiological and neuropsychological techniques.

Performance Measures

Most of the experimental tasks used to study skill focus on speed and/or accuracy of performance. For example, the speed and accuracy with which problems can be solved under different conditions would be of interest to investigators of cognitive skill. A motor skills researcher might measure the time to initiate a movement as well as the time to execute the movement and its accuracy. In the remainder of the chapters, many of the research conclusions discussed depend on the interpretation of such measures.

Considering reaction times, means are typically obtained for different groups or conditions, and differences between the conditions are used to make inferences about the complexity of the required processing. However, it is not enough to know only that two conditions differ in reaction time. We want to be able to characterize more specifically the nature of the differences in information processing that lead to the observed reaction-time differences. Consequently, methods have been developed that allow inferences to be made about the stages or processes that contribute to the overall reaction time.

The earliest of these chronometric methods, the **subtractive method,** can be attributed to Donders (1868/1969). To use this method, two conditions are selected that are presumed to differ by exactly one stage or process. The difference in reaction times between these conditions is then taken as the time to complete that stage or process. For example, Posner and Mitchell (1967) had people classify pairs of letters as "same" or "different." Reactions to classify a pair as "same" were approximately 75 ms faster if the letters were identical in form (e.g., AA) than if they were only identical in name (e.g., Aa). Posner and Mitchell proposed that this difference in response times occurred because the former judgments could be made on the basis of the visual information, whereas the latter judgments required in addition that the name of each form be determined. Applying the subtractive logic, they concluded that this additional naming process took approximately 75 ms. Note that application of the subtractive logic, as in this example, depends on the assumptions that the processing stages are distinct and independent and that the insertion of the additional process does not alter the basic task structure.

The **additive factors method,** developed by Sternberg (1969), allows determination of the processing stages involved in task performance. To use this method, the researcher manipulates several factors (i.e., independent variables) and determines whether the factors have additive or interactive effects on reaction time. If two factors have additive effects, they are assumed to affect different stages. If the factors interact, they are assumed to affect the same stage. Usually at least one of the factors manipulated can be logically assumed to affect a particular processing stage (e.g., stimulus clarity most likely affects perceptual processing time). By examining the pattern of interaction contrasts, the underlying processing stages can be inferred (e.g., if the frequency with which a stimulus occurs interacts with stimulus clarity, the effect of frequency can be localized at the perceptual stage).

As with the subtractive method, use of the additive factors method requires the assumption of sequential stages for which the processing associated with one stage must be completed before that associated with the next stage begins. However, it is likely that many processes operate concurrently, and it may be the case that a given process outputs partial rather than complete information (e.g., McClelland, 1979; Townsend,

1974). Despite these limitations, a consistent picture emerges when a set of findings of additivity is interpreted in terms of processing stages (Sanders, 1990).

Another aspect of performance, accuracy of response, also has been used as the primary measure in many studies of skill. Typically, in such studies there is no speed stress for responding, and the task is sufficiently difficult that accuracy is less than perfect. This difficulty may be inherent in the nature of the task (e.g., a problem may be sufficiently difficult that not all people will solve it), or it may be induced by presenting stimuli briefly or under degraded conditions (e.g., an array of letters may be exposed for 50 ms, followed by a masking stimulus). As with reaction times, factors are manipulated and their influences on accuracy are compared to determine the nature of the processing involved.

Although it is often convenient to focus primarily on speed or primarily on accuracy, there are problems associated with doing so. As we mentioned above, it has been known since at least the time of Woodworth (1899) that the speed and accuracy of responding are closely linked. This linkage is in the form of a trade-off between speed and accuracy, such that a person can emphasize one to the detriment of the other. The **speed-accuracy trade-off** function, illustrated in Figure 1.5, shows this relation. As more time is taken to respond, accuracy improves. As noted by Woodworth, this function is S-shaped, which means that only very small changes in accuracy with changes in reaction time occur when responding is already relatively slow or already relatively fast. In any experiment, the possibility must be considered that differences in reaction time or accuracy between experimental conditions are attributable to speed-accuracy trade-offs. If faster reaction times are accompanied by higher error rates, then a speed-accuracy trade-off is implicated, which may imply that the factors being manipulated do not affect ability, but only response strategy. Important to the study of skill is that practice may enable determination by the performer of the optimal setting on the speed-accuracy function (e.g., Rabbitt, 1989) where speed is maximized without undue sacrifices in accuracy.

The approaches described above can be brought to bear on issues of skill acquisition by sampling the performance of learners at different stages of skill acquisition and constructing learning curves that plot reaction time or accuracy as a function of practice. Experimental factors can be manipulated at different points along the learning curve to see whether the processing characteristics of the task have changed with experience. For example, Logie, Baddeley, Mané, Donchin, and Sheptak (1989) had

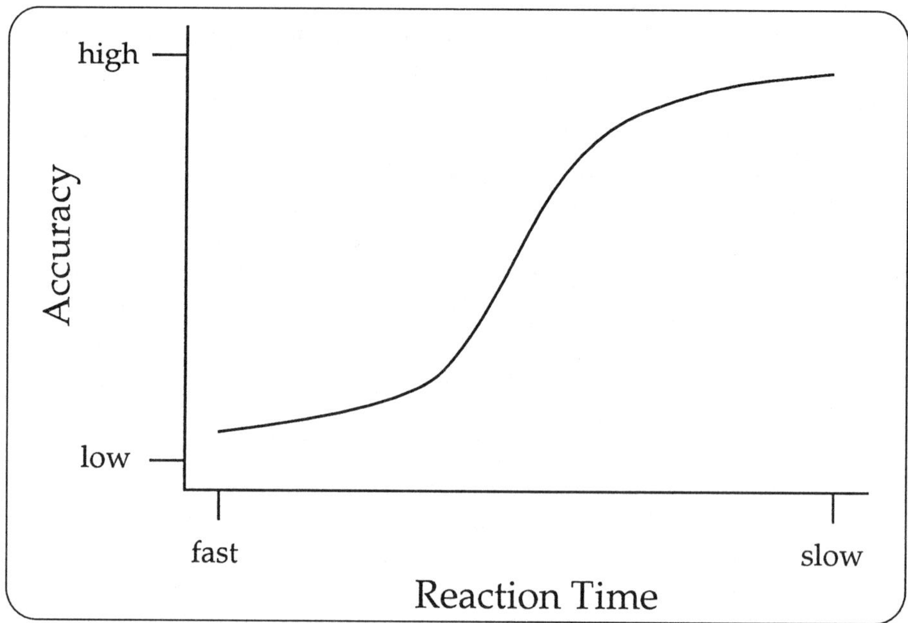

Figure 1.5. A speed-accuracy tradeoff function.

people play a complex computer game, which relied on both perceptual-motor and cognitive skills, for many sessions. To evaluate the way in which processing changed as skill at the game was acquired, various secondary tasks (e.g., tasks requiring paced rhythmic tapping, spatial visualization, or verbal cognitive processing) were introduced at different points during practice and performed concurrently with the primary game task. Paced tapping had only a small effect on game performance early in practice but a larger effect later in practice, which Logie et al. interpreted as indicating that response timing is more crucial to expert performance than to novice performance. Also, whereas both visuo-spatial and verbal secondary tasks interfered with game performance at low levels of practice, the disruption produced by the visuo-spatial task was reduced greatly at higher levels of practice. Logie et al. interpreted this aspect of their results as suggesting that perceptual-motor tracking control is a demanding part of the computer game initially but becomes an automated skill for expert performers.

Besides looking at individual learning curves, curves for different groups can be compared in terms of their respective learning rates and asymptotes. However, caution must be exercised in interpreting learning curves. First, the group learning curves may not be representative of the individual curves. Second, performance measures may also be influenced by transient factors, such as fatigue, that may vary as a function of time. Because of the problem of transient effects, it is important to use additional measures that test retention or transfer to evaluate learning.

As mentioned previously, the logic underlying retention and transfer measures is that if learning has occurred from practice on a task, it should have some durability beyond the experimental session and should affect performance of similar tasks. In retention, performance of the task again is tested after some interval and compared to earlier measures. One measure of retention is the savings score,

$$\%\text{savings} = \frac{P_{\text{original}} - P_{\text{relearning}}}{P_{\text{original}}} \times 100,$$

where P is some measure of performance, such as reaction time or number of errors.

In transfer, practice on a task is followed by a later test that differs in some way from the original task, and performance on this test is compared to that of a control group. There are numerous indices of transfer, all of which evaluate performance of the trained group relative to a control group who received no training (Gagné, Foster, & Crowley, 1948). The most commonly used index is

$$\%\text{transfer} = \frac{P_{\text{control}} - P_{\text{transfer}}}{P_{\text{control}}} \times 100,$$

where P is a performance measure, as defined above.

Verbal Protocol Analysis

In some tasks, particularly those requiring complex problem solving, reaction time and accuracy data can be supplemented with verbal protocol analyses (Ericsson & Simon, 1993). To perform protocol analyses, reports consisting of verbalizations made by the person either during (**concurrent protocols**) or after (**retrospective protocols**) solving a problem or performing some other task are collected and analyzed. Although verbal reports have been viewed with distrust since the advent of behaviorism early in the 20th century, recently they have begun to be accepted as providing useful information.

A framework proposed by Ericsson and Simon (1980) provides a theoretical rationale for the use and interpretation of verbal protocols. According to this framework, the necessary conditions for valid protocols are that (a) participants report the contents of working memory (i.e., what they are thinking about) without interpretation or elaboration and (b) the contents of working memory be verbal in nature, as opposed to pictorial. Only concurrent protocols satisfy the first of these conditions, which cautions against the use of retrospective protocols. Even with concurrent protocols, however, several potential problems exist. First, the requirement to verbalize may interfere with, or otherwise alter, primary task performance. For example, if the task is to determine whether two complex geometric forms shown in different views are the same or different, the requirement to verbalize the actions being performed may interfere with performance of the task. Second, some crucial aspects of performance likely occur without the person's awareness and so would not be verbalized. This can lead to gaps in the protocols because statements such as "I don't know how I know, I just know it," do not provide much insight into performance.

Once verbal protocols have been elicited, they must be interpreted. This can be a major hurdle in the use of protocols as data. Several methods have been developed to deal with the volume and density of these data (e.g., Fisher, 1988). In all of these methods, the experimenter must make decisions about how to code the protocols in terms of a formal language for analysis. Typically, these decisions are guided by an analysis of the task, a theory of task performance, or the hypotheses being tested. Because of the inherent difficulty in coding protocols, most recent methods rely on computer programs to assist the human coder (e.g., Crutcher, Ericsson, & Wichura, 1994; Sanderson, James, & Seidler, 1989). Such computer programs force the coder to focus on one protocol segment at a time and may suggest how a specific protocol segment should be coded. Selection of an appropriate method for protocol analysis is important because the value of the protocols for understanding performance will depend on the method used.

Psychophysiological and Neuropsychological Measures

The measures of human information processing described above are increasingly being supplemented by measures of the electrical and mag-

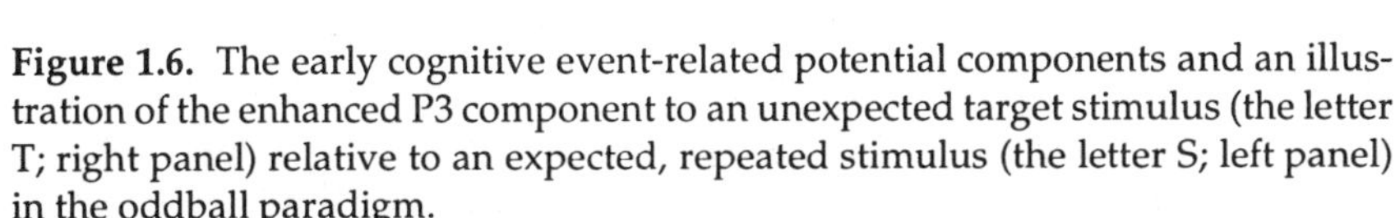

Figure 1.6. The early cognitive event-related potential components and an illustration of the enhanced P3 component to an unexpected target stimulus (the letter T; right panel) relative to an expected, repeated stimulus (the letter S; left panel) in the oddball paradigm.
SOURCE: Adapted from Polich (1993).

netic manifestations of the physiological processes that underlie such processing. The most widely studied of these psychophysiological measures is the **event-related potential,** or ERP, which is electrical activity recorded at the scalp that is time locked to an external stimulus event (see Polich, 1993, for an overview). Typically, the electrical activity at several scalp sites is recorded for many trials and then averaged. With such a procedure, the electrical activity unrelated to stimulus processing is eliminated, and the resulting potentials reflect only the mental events associated with the information processing that is performed.

The magnitudes and latencies of several components of the ERP have been found to be associated with specific cognitive events (see Figure 1.6). These components are designated by the letter N or P, to indicate whether the component is negative-going or positive-going, and a number indicating the serial order in the event sequence. Thus N1 is the first negative-going component. Sometimes, timing in milliseconds rather than serial order is used to designate the components (e.g., N1 is also called N100 because it occurs approximately 100 ms after stimulus onset).

One of the most widely studied ERP components is the third positive component, or P3, which has been clearly linked to one aspect of performance in the so-called oddball paradigm. In this paradigm, one, standard, stimulus is repeated in a series. Occasionally, a different stimulus (the oddball) is presented, and the participant is either to make an overt response or to covertly count the occurrences of the oddball stimulus. A large P3 component is elicited to the oddball stimulus (see Figure 1.6, right side) that is not elicited by the repeated stimulus (see Figure 1.6, left side). Consequently, the P3 component has been interpreted as reflecting processes involved in memory updating (Donchin & Coles, 1988) because only when the oddball stimulus appears does memory need to be updated. P3 amplitude has been found to be affected by cognitive variables, such as whether attentional resources are allocated to the task, and P3 latency is considered to reflect the time devoted to stimulus evaluation. Increasingly, analysis of the P3 component and other components of the ERP is providing evidence about information processing that is not obtainable from performance measures.

Another developing area is the use of neuropsychological studies with brain-damaged patients to clarify aspects of normal cognition (see, e.g., Shallice, 1988). Such studies typically compare performance of patients with specific neurological impairments to that of unimpaired people on a battery of tasks. The basic assumption of these studies is that the information-processing system of the patient has been damaged in some specific way. To the extent that the specific nature of the damage can be determined, evidence about what the impaired person can and cannot do becomes relevant for evaluating models of the intact information-processing system. For example, research discussed in Chapter 6 shows that Korsakoff patients, who are not able to consciously recollect items or events that occurred more than a few seconds previously, show facilitation of reaction times to repeated stimulus sequences much like that shown by unimpaired people. Because these patients have no conscious recollection of the repeated sequence, this outcome implies that awareness is not required for sequence learning to occur.

Modeling Skill

Another way to evaluate human performance and the acquisition of skill is to develop and test quantitative models. Modeling has a long history in psychology, ranging from models of conditioned learning, such as the Rescorla and Wagner (1972) model, to more general frameworks, such as Crossman's (1959) theory of skill acquisition as the elimination of inefficient procedures. Although there are numerous mathematical models that defy any simple classification scheme, the two dominant modeling approaches to be reckoned with in the study of skill are **production systems** and **connectionist models** (also called **adaptive networks**).

Production System Models

Production system models are built from production rules. Each rule is a condition-action pair, for which the condition specifies the situation in which the rule will apply and the action specifies what will be done. For example, Anderson (1993) gives the following as one production rule that might be involved in addition:

> IF the goal is to solve an addition problem and c1 is the rightmost column without an answer digit
>
> THEN set a subgoal to write out an answer in c1

Production systems operate by a cycle consisting of pattern matching, conflict resolution, and production execution. The current contents of memory are first matched to the conditions of the productions. Because the conditions of more than one production may be satisfied, a conflict resolution procedure is invoked to select the specific production to be executed. (Procedures used for conflict resolution vary considerably among alternative production system models.) The selected production then executes, or fires, and the cycle begins anew.

Production systems have several critical features (Anderson, 1993). First, each rule represents a distinct, compartmentalized unit of knowledge, and complex cognitive functioning is achieved by stringing rules together. Also, as illustrated by the example production rule above, the rules can be abstract and thus apply to many specific situations. Finally, because the represented knowledge is in the form of actions to be taken when conditions are met, there is an inherent asymmetry in knowledge. In other words, there is no guarantee that a person who has acquired a particular production will be able to work backwards to recall a condition if the action is subsequently provided as a new condition.

Advocates of production-system models emphasize that production rules seem to capture many of the regularities in human performance across a wide range of situations. In fact, the two most prominent candidates for unified theories of cognition capable of explaining the full range of human behavior, Anderson's (1993) ACT family of models and Newell's (1990) *Soar* family of models are both production systems. However, this generality of the models comes at a cost. It is difficult both to discover which of the many alternative versions of production-system architectures are viable explanations of performance and to demonstrate that a particular model provides a unique explanation.

Connectionist Models

Connectionist models consist of some number of neuron-like processing units and connections between them (see Figure 1.7). Generally, one subset of units, called an **input** layer, represents input from the environment to the system, and another subset, called an **output** layer, represents output from the system to the environment. There also may be one or more layers of **hidden** units, which have neither direct input from nor output to the environment.

In connectionist models, the knowledge or behavior of the system is contained in the connections between the units (see, e.g., McClelland, Rumelhart, & PDP Research Group, 1986; Quinlan, 1991). Each connection has an associated weight that can be zero (i.e., input has no effect), positive (i.e., input has an excitatory effect), or negative (i.e., input has an inhibitory effect). As a consequence, when input from the environment is received, patterns of activity are set up in the respective layers. It is these patterns of activity that represent different states of the system. One consequence of this distributed representation is that connectionist models can continue to function effectively when some of the units are damaged, a property that is called **graceful degradation.**

Many connectionist models have learning mechanisms for modifying the weights assigned to the connections between units. Although different specific learning rules have been used, modifications in the weights typically are based on the reduction of error between the actual output of the system and desired output. Because these models with learning mechanisms allow performance to change as a function of experience, they are applicable to issues in skill acquisition.

It is not our intent in this book to advocate one type of modeling over another. Both specific production-system models and specific connectionist models are discussed when they illuminate a particular aspect of skilled behavior. Although our introductory description of these models has of necessity been sketchy, details of the approaches and of how the models contribute to our understanding of skilled behavior will be discussed in later chapters as particular models are introduced.

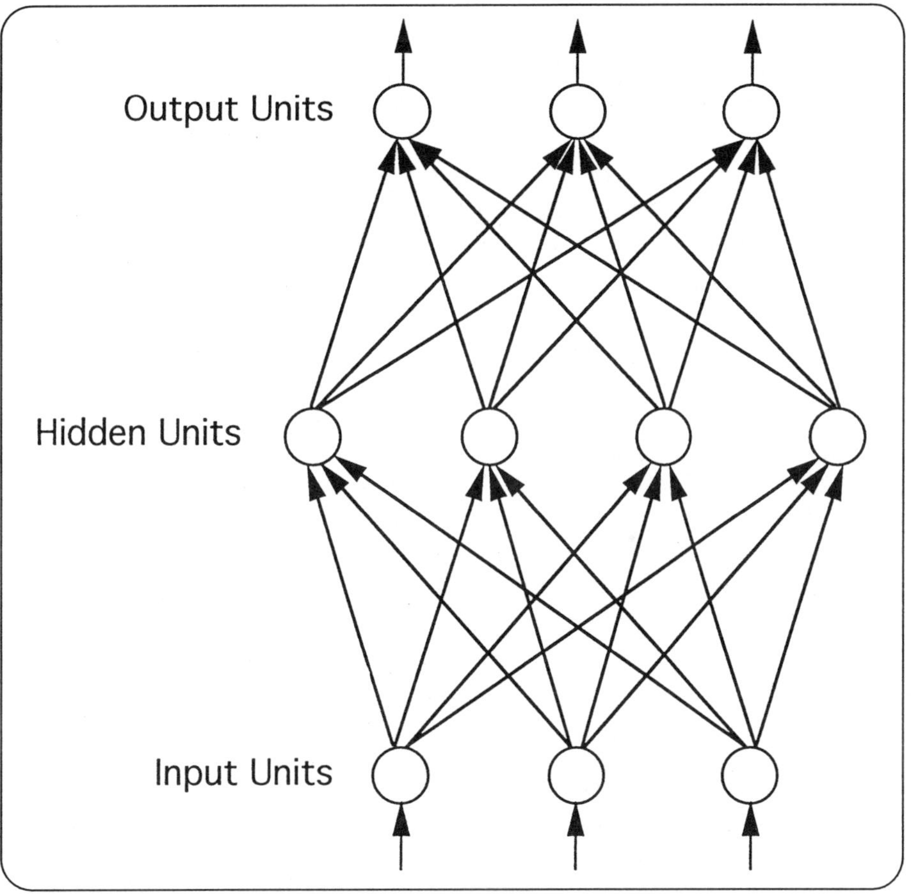

Figure 1.7. A multilayer network in which information from the input units is recoded by hidden units, which then activate output units.

SUMMARY

Systematic research on skill acquisition and skilled performance began late in the 19th century. This initial activity, which encompassed such topics as the description of learning curves, transfer of training, and motor performance, lasted approximately 30 years. A revival of interest in skill occurred around 1945. Since that time there has been an increasing emphasis on the mechanisms underlying skill and on cognitive skill. Many contemporary developments within a variety of disciplines have contributed to the growth of skills-related research in the recent past.

A defining property of skill is that it develops over time, with practice. Initial performance is usually a tentative, rough approximation of the desired action and requires considerable conscious effort. With practice, this initial halting performance gives way to relatively effortless, smooth, integrated patterns of behavior. These modes of performance and the transitions between them are captured by several frameworks. The frameworks can be applied to the acquisition of a specific skill, as well as to the performances exhibited by a skilled individual in different task environments.

Much insight into skill acquisition and skilled performance can be gained by examining performance measures, typically response times and accuracies, and several methods have been developed to refine the inferences that can be drawn from such data. In recent years, verbal protocol analyses have been increasingly used as additional sources of data, and psychophysiological and neuropsychological techniques have been developed that provide new insight into the processes and brain structures underlying skilled behavior. Finally, quantitative models of skill can be used to generate predictions and test assumptions regarding the mechanisms and knowledge structures underlying the acquisition of skill.

Note

1. The operators in Crossman's (1959) cigar-making study were actually all women.

Signal Detection Methods and Theory

Tasks

Perceptual Learning

Searching for Features and Conjunctions of Features

Perceptual Unitization

Procedural Learning

Automatic and Controlled Processing

Summary

CHAPTER 2

Perceptual Skill

When first confronted with a novel perceptual discrimination task, a person's performance is often poor. For example, at a wine-tasting party, it is not uncommon for at least one person to find little difference among the various vintages. After much additional exposure to a variety of wines, that same individual may become a connoisseur, pointing out subtle differences between wines of different regions or years.

The enhanced ability to discriminate between and to classify stimuli based on perceivable properties is a hallmark of perceptual skill. Perceptual skill develops in everyday life (e.g., recognizing "good" melons at the grocery store) and in the work environment (e.g., recognizing defective circuit boards). An example of perceptual skill was reported in a classic study by Lunn (1948), who reviewed the commercially important skill of determining the sex of day-old chicks. The sex organs of male and female chicks of this age appear identical, even to poultry farmers. However, after three to eight weeks of training, and additional experience, an expert sexer can classify up to 1,000 chicks an hour with over 98% accuracy. Although manual skill in handling the chicks is necessary to reach such levels of performance, enhanced visual (and in rare cases, tactual) discrimination of the sex organs is primarily responsible for the improved ability to perform the job.

In this chapter, we focus on perceptual skill. However, when we set out to measure perception, we necessarily involve processes of cognition, especially response selection, and of response execution because responses to stimuli must be collected. The problem is to isolate perceptual factors, and a wide variety of paradigms have been developed for doing this. In the research reviewed in this chapter, the motor requirements are already well learned and thus contribute little to performance improvements. For example, many studies use simple keypress or vocal responses. Such responses are so well practiced that little change in their execution should occur over the course of an experiment. Moreover, because the same response is required across all the different experimental conditions, motoric factors do not systematically influence the experimental outcomes of interest. Controlling for response execution factors still leaves the problem of separating perceptual processes from response selection processes. Fortunately, several methods exist, including the additive factors method of analyzing reaction times described in Chapter 1, that can be used to isolate effects due to perception from those due to response selection.

We begin this chapter by discussing an important method for analyzing accuracy data, **signal detection theory,** that provides a conceptual framework for evaluating many experimental results. Following the discussion of signal detection theory, we describe a variety of tasks that have been used to study perceptual skill with simple and complex stimuli. Subsequently, factors that increase the ability to extract information from the task environment are considered, as is the retention of perceptual skill and its interaction with memory. Attentional factors involved in searching visual displays are then covered, and the possibility that there are qualitatively different modes of processing stimuli is discussed.

Signal Detection Methods and Theory

Perception and response selection co-occur in information-processing tasks, and effects that appear to be due to one may be attributable to the other. This problem can be illustrated with a detection task in which an observer is to determine whether a just detectable 1,000-Hz tone is embedded in a briefly presented burst of white noise. Suppose that the tone is present on half of the trials (called signal-plus-noise, or **signal**, trials) and absent on the other half (called **noise** trials). On a given trial, the observer may be unsure whether the tone was heard or not but still must respond either "yes" or "no." Consequently, some strategy must be adopted for selecting a response on these ambiguous trials.

Assume that three observers, all of whom are equally sensitive to the signal, are tested. One observer might adopt the strategy of responding "yes" when unsure and another the strategy of responding "no" when unsure. The third observer might adopt a strategy for these trials that results in approximately half of the responses being "yes" and half "no." Note that these various response selection strategies could produce large differences in the number of "yes" responses made on signal trials. These differences, which in this example are entirely a function of the response bias dictated by the strategy, could be misinterpreted as reflecting disparities in perceptual sensitivity across the three observers.

To determine whether response selection strategies and not perceptual detection abilities are responsible for observed differences in responding "yes" on signal trials, it is necessary also to consider the responses on noise trials. If an observer is biased to respond "yes" on signal trials, a similar bias should exist on the noise trials because the observer does not know the nature of the trial. If we assume that the response bias is indeed systematic, holding across trial types, we can use the **hit rates** (the proportion of "yes" responses on signal trials) and **false alarm rates** (the proportion of "yes" responses on noise trials) to determine the true sensitivity of the observer. When the hit rate exceeds the false alarm rate, it indicates at least some ability to detect the presence of the tone because the observer indicated that the tone was present more often when it actually was than when it was not.

Signal detection theory formalizes the ideas described above and provides procedures for performing sensitivity and response bias analyses (Green & Swets, 1966/1974; Macmillan & Creelman, 1991). Underlying signal detection theory is the assumption that on every experimental trial there is some amount of sensory stimulation to suggest that the signal may have been present, regardless of whether or not it actually was. The amount of stimulation on a given trial thus corresponds to a point on a continuum of evidence suggesting that the signal event occurred, as depicted by the horizontal axis in Figure 2.1. For any point on this continuum, there is some probability that the particular amount of stimulation came from a signal trial and some probability that it came from a noise trial. Thus the evidence value sampled on any given trial does not indicate unambiguously whether or not the signal was present, but it does indicate

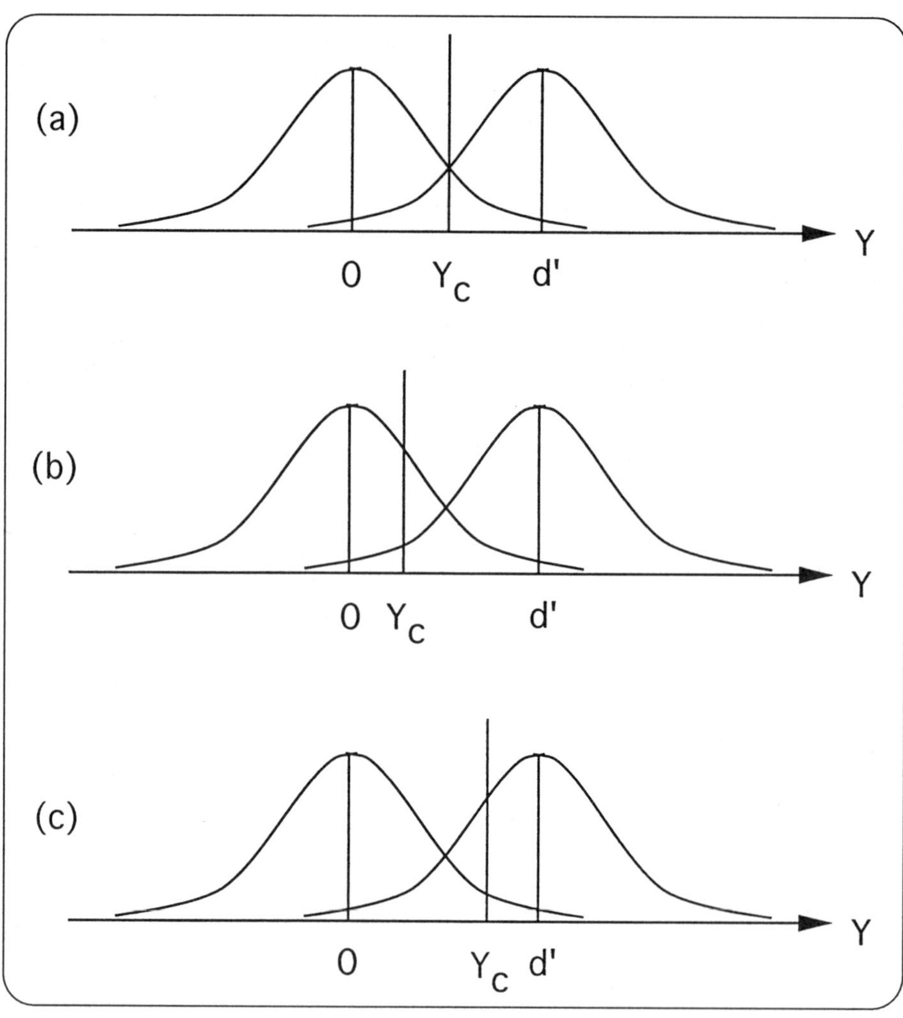

Figure 2.1. Theoretical distributions of noise (left) and signal plus noise (right) on the continuum of sensory evidence, Y. The mean of the noise distribution is denoted 0, and the mean of the signal-plus-noise distribution is denoted d'. Settings of the criterion setting, Y_C, that are unbiased, liberal, and conservative are shown in panels a, b, and c, respectively.

the relative likelihood of its presence. If the signal trials can be discriminated from the noise trials to at least some degree, the relative likelihood that the point was produced by a signal event increases as the value on the sensory continuum increases. In most applications, the probability distributions that correspond with the signal and noise events are assumed to be normal (i.e., symmetric and bell shaped) and of equal variance, and to overlap to some extent (i.e., the observer is unsure on at least some trials whether or not the signal occurred).

Earlier, we spoke of observers dealing with uncertain trials by adopting a response selection strategy. This assumption corresponds to the setting of a criterion (often denoted as Y_c) at some point on the sensory evidence continuum. If the sensory effect of the stimulus is below the criterion, the observer responds "no"; if the effect exceeds the criterion, the observer responds "yes."

When signal and noise trials are equally probable, the optimal criterion setting is at the point on the sensory continuum at which the signal and noise distributions are of equal height (i.e., given that amount of sensory evidence, the two trial types are equally likely; see Figure 2.1a). This is called the unbiased setting, and it implies that an approximately equal number of "yes" and "no" responses will be made. A **liberal** observer would set the criterion to the left of this point (see Figure 2.1b) and would say "yes" more often than "no." A **conservative** observer would set the criterion to the right of the unbiased point at a higher evidence value (see Figure 2.1c) and would say "no" more often than "yes." The bias of the observer can be measured independently of the observer's ability to discriminate the stimulus, allowing comparisons of bias across individuals or conditions. The most commonly used measure of bias is β, which is found by taking the ratio of the height of the signal distribution relative to the height of the noise distribution at the criterion. The criterion can be located quite easily from the hit and false alarm rates, as described below.

The discriminability of the stimulus, and hence the sensitivity of the observer, can be conceptualized as the difference between the means of the signal and noise distributions. A measure of observer sensitivity, called d', can be calculated by subtracting the z score (i.e., the standardized distance of a score from the mean of a distribution) corresponding to the false alarm rate from the z score corresponding to the hit rate. If the two distributions overlap completely, so that the difference between the means is zero and performance is at chance, then d' will be equal to zero. The value will increase as the separation between the distributions increases. This measure of sensitivity is independent of response bias, as evidenced by stable d's regardless of response biases when the conditions of the discrimination are not changed.

Signal detection methods are often used to ascertain whether the primary effect of an independent variable is on observer sensitivity or

An Eye for Kisses

Picking out the perfect Kiss isn't all sweetness and light. Just ask **Steve Bailey.** "Well, some pieces just aren't quite there. They may lean to one side or be too curly on top. They could be flat, pointy or too small. It's my job to catch the defective ones before they head straight for some kid's Halloween bag," the Hershey's inspector told Life. "When someone unwraps a Hershey's Kiss, he has certain expectations. He expects a traditional shape. It should stand up. It should have a smooth appearance. The candy's size—the diameter at its base, which is precisely 15/16 of an inch—can be checked with an official Kiss sizer. But the height and the curl and the . . . essence—well, these are elements that must be measured by a trained eye."

—*Houston Chronicle,* Tuesday, September 21, 1993

Figure 2.2. An example of a detection task in quality control.

response bias. For example, a quality control inspector may have the task of detecting and removing all faulty products coming off of an assembly line, such as imperfect Hershey's Kisses (see Figure 2.2). Suppose that over the course of the day, the proportion of products removed decreased. Assuming that the actual proportion of faulty products remained constant throughout the day, then the change in the worker's performance could be due to changes in sensitivity or bias. By comparing d' and β values calculated on performance early in the day to those calculated on performance late in the day, it can be determined whether the change reflects a change in sensitivity, criterion, or both (see Table 2.1). Determining which of these measures has changed would allow hypotheses regarding the causes of the change to be developed. This example suggests how a signal detection analysis might be used to assess the nature of changes with practice on a task. The amount of practice given would be an independent variable, just as time of day is the independent variable in the example, and its separate effects on sensitivity and bias would be evaluated.

Tasks

Perceptual skill has been studied with many tasks, usually with accuracy or reaction time as the primary dependent variable. The tasks used to study perceptual skill can be classified in part by the type of

Table 2.1 Example Hit Rates (proportion of faulty products removed) and False Alarm Rates (proportion of good products removed) for Early Versus Late in the Day When (a) Sensitivity Decreases, (b) a More Conservative Criterion Is Adopted, and (c) Both Sensitivity and Bias Change

Measure	*Early in Day*	*Late in Day*
Sensitivity change		
Hit rate	0.84	0.75
False alarm rate	0.16	0.25
d'	1.98	1.35
β	1.00	1.00
Criterion change		
Hit rate	0.84	0.47
False alarm rate	0.16	0.02
d'	1.98	1.98
β	1.00	8.22
Sensitivity and criterion change		
Hit rate	0.84	0.60
False alarm rate	0.16	0.10
d'	1.98	1.54
β	1.00	2.20

judgment that is required (see Table 2.2). A **detection** task, such as those discussed in the section on signal detection theory, requires the observer to judge whether or not a stimulus event occurred during a designated interval. The stimulus in this task is usually just barely detectable. The observer is told the type of event to expect and typically must respond "yes" if the stimulus event occurred and "no" if it did not. Alternatively, two or more intervals may be presented, only one of which contains a stimulus, with the observer's task being to indicate in which interval the stimulus occurred.

In a **discrimination** task, two or more stimuli are presented simultaneously or successively, and the observer must indicate whether the stimuli are the same or different, or whether one has "more" or "less" of some quantity. In a **recognition** task, the discrimination to be made is between items that have been presented previously and items that have not been. Like a discrimination task, one of two responses ("old" or "new") would be made. Finally, for an **identification** task, a particular response

Table 2.2 Tasks Used to Study Perceptual Skill

Task	*Judgment*
Detection	Presence or absence of stimulus
Discrimination	Same-different; greater than or less than
Recognition	Old or new
Identification	Identify stimulus with assigned response
Memory search	Presence or absence of target in memory set
Visual search	Presence or absence of target in display

is assigned to each possible stimulus, and the judgment to be made is which stimulus occurred. Often, each stimulus will have a unique response assigned to it. However, it is also possible to have the same response assigned to two or more members of the stimulus set. This latter procedure is sometimes called an **information reduction** task because the number of stimulus alternatives exceeds the number of response alternatives.

Search tasks have been widely used to study perceptual skill and related issues, such as the role of attention in performance. In a **visual search** task, one or more stimuli are designated as possible targets that may occur in a display. On a given trial, a target (i.e., the item to be detected or identified) may or may not be presented along with one or more distractors (i.e., the items to be ignored). Critically, the target can occur in any of the possible display positions. Either detection or identification may be required. In a **memory search** task, a set of one or more items to be held in memory (called the memory set) is first provided. This is followed by the presentation of a single, displayed target item that is to be compared to the memory set. Many studies use hybrid search tasks in which memory-set size and display size are both varied. Other variations of search tasks have been used, differing in such things as the temporal characteristics of the display, the number of items included in the task, the format of the display, and whether the location in which the target occurred must also be specified by the participant.

Perceptual Learning

The wine tasting and chick sexing examples in the introduction to this chapter suggest that the ability to discriminate stimuli increases as a function of experience. What accounts for these effects of practice, and how can they best be characterized? **Perceptual learning** has been defined as "an increase in the ability to extract information from the environment, as a result of experience and practice with stimulation coming from it" (Gibson, 1969, p. 3). The major factor in perceptual skill seems to involve learning features specific to a particular stimulus that distinguish it from other stimuli. As an illustration of featural learning in the acquisition of perceptual skill, we first review a study on a modality—olfaction—that has received relatively little research attention.

In studies of absolute identification, observers must identify a stimulus by, in most cases, giving its name. Desor and Beauchamp (1974) used an odor labeling task to examine the effect of experience on subsequent odor identification. Three individuals were given extensive training with a set of 32 natural odors, such as those of molasses, a musty book, or ivy, until all of the odors were identified correctly in two consecutive sessions. Five days after this initial training, each of the 32 odors was presented three times in random order to be identified again. Whereas initially many errors were made, all of the individuals who received the training achieved the criterion of perfect discrimination and continued to show this level of performance after the five-day retention interval. This finding in itself is interesting because it had been argued previously that the capacity of the olfactory channel, as estimated from the number of odors that could be identified without error, was relatively low (e.g., Engen & Pfaffman, 1960). Thus Desor and Beauchamp's study showed that the number of odors that can be classified accurately increases substantially with practice.

In the Desor and Beauchamp (1974) study, the accuracy with which odors could be identified (i.e., labeled) improved with practice. However, the question remains of whether performance of a task for which labeling is not required would also benefit from practice. One way to answer this question is with a relative discrimination task in which two stimuli are compared on each trial and classified as *same* or *different* rather than a single stimulus being labeled or otherwise identified. As a general rule, performance will be better for relative judgments than for absolute judgments, but it is not immediately obvious that experience would affect relative discriminability because no labels need be learned. However, studies with visual stimuli have shown that relative discrimination accuracy does improve with practice or prior experience with the stimuli (e.g., Pick, 1965; Robinson, 1955), so there is some reason to expect improvement in olfactory tasks, too.

Rabin (1988) examined the influence of experience on the relative discriminability of seven odor stimuli in an experiment in which three types of prior experience with olfactory stimuli were given to different groups of observers. One of the groups receiving prior experience was trained to label the target stimuli, another group performed a profiling task in which each odor in the target set was rated on a list of adjectives, and a third was trained to label a set of seven other odors. The latter group was considered a control group, as was a fourth group that received no pretraining. Discrimination performance was measured using a two-interval, same-different task. The participant sniffed an odor from one jar and then another odor from a second jar and responded as to whether the two odors were the same or different. A measure of discriminability analogous to d' showed that the group that learned to label the seven test stimuli was more sensitive at discriminating the stimuli than was the group that profiled the stimuli. Both of these experimental groups were more sensitive than the two control groups, which did not differ in performance.

One difference between prior experience labeling the stimuli versus profiling them is that the labeling judgments require that discriminations be made among the stimuli, whereas the profiling judgments do not. It is likely that this difference accounts for the greater benefit arising from labeling than profiling when the task is subsequently changed to one in which relative discriminations must be made. That is, labeling forces observers to attend to those features of a stimulus that make it distinctive and unique, thus enabling increased accuracy of discrimination.

If perceptual learning consists of developing the ability to recognize distinctive features, training that emphasizes these features should be more effective than training based on holistic properties of the stimuli. An experimental test of this hypothesis was conducted by Gagné and J. Gibson (Gibson, 1947), who were concerned with the practical problem of training cadets to distinguish among types of aircraft. In the relevant study, two groups of cadets were shown slides of 40 different aircraft, and the type of instruction that they received was varied. In the *total form* group, the instructions emphasized the total form of each plane. In the *feature* group, the instructions emphasized a set of distinctive features for each plane presented. At the end of a 30-hour training period, the feature group performed better on a recognition test than did the total form group. Moreover, the instructors noted that cadets in the total form group persistently asked which features could be used to distinguish similar planes, suggesting that search for distinguishing features is a natural mode of learning.

An even more striking demonstration of the benefit of instructing people about distinctive features was reported by Biederman and Shiffrar (1987). With the help of an expert chick sexer, they determined that the critical region used to distinguish male and female chicks is a region called the bead. For males, the bead is usually convex, whereas for females it is usually concave or flat. Biederman and Shiffrar developed instructional materials that showed schematic diagrams of the beads for males and females, characterizing them as "round or fullish like a ball or watermelon" or "pointed, like an upside down pine tree, or flattish," respectively. When given these instructions, the performance of naive observers at classifying pictures of rare and difficult chick genitalia increased from just above chance to the level achieved by a group of experts. This example illustrates the practical importance of understanding the basis for perceptual skill: In capitalizing on the natural learning mode of identifying and learning distinctive features, a highly effective training method was found.

Searching for Features and Conjunctions of Features

Visual search tasks, where one or more targets are presented among one or more distractors, have been used extensively to study the properties of visual detection and the development of perceptual skill. For example, Neisser (1963) conducted experiments in which the display was a list of 50 alphanumeric strings (see Figure 2.3), one of which contained a target item. When the list was presented, the observer was to begin scanning it from the top down, indicating when the target had been located. The initial finding was that the time to locate the target was an approximately linear function of the location of the critical string from the top of the list. The shape of this function suggests that the strings in the list are scanned sequentially at an approximately constant rate. Neisser also showed that the rate of search varied as a function of the featural similarity of the distractor items to the target. For example, searching for the letter *Q* was faster in a background context of angular letters than in a background context of generally circular letters, suggesting that the participants were searching for the particular features of the letter *Q*.

When long lists of items are scanned, as in Neisser's experiments, eye movements must be made to perceive all of the items. To eliminate the possibility that the linear relation between list position and search time is a result just of eye movements, many researchers turned to the use of a variation of the visual search task in which a small number of stimuli is presented briefly in a way that does not require physical scanning. An effect of context, which initially appeared to rely on properties of the whole stimulus rather than on stimulus features, has been studied using this task variation. The effect is that there is little or no influence of the number of distractor items when the target is a letter and the distractors are digits, or vice versa, even though these stimulus sets contain many of the same features (e.g., Jonides & Gleitman, 1972). This is in contrast to the common finding that responses become slower and less accurate as the number of items displayed increases when search is for a letter target among letter distractors or a digit target among digit distractors. Initially, this so-called **category effect** was taken as evidence that search performance could be based on category membership alone.

However, subsequent research has shown that the category effect is an artifact of the visual composition of letters and digits (Krueger, 1984). That is, digits are more similar to each other on average than they are to letters and vice versa. When featural similarity is equated for subsets of letters and digits, the category effect disappears. This is consistent with Neisser's (1963) finding that search speed depends on the visual similarity of the targets to the distractor context in which they are presented, as well as with findings of Gardner (1973) and others that no array size effect occurs when people search briefly presented displays for targets among physically dissimilar distractors (e.g., the target *T* or *F* in an array of *O*s).

```
EHYP
SWIQ
UFCJ
WBYH
OGTX
GWVX
TWLN
XJBU
UDXI
HSFP
XSCQ
SDJU
PODC
ZVBP
PEVZ
SLRA
JCEN
ZLRD
XBOD
PHMU
ZHFK
PNJW
CQXT
GHNR
IXYD
QSVB
GUCH
OWBN
BVQN
FOAS
ITZN
VYLD
LRYZ
IJXE
RBOE
DVUS
BIAJ
ESGF
QGZI
ZWNE
QBVC
VARP
LRPA
SGHL
MVRJ
GADB
PCME
ZODW
HDBR
BVDZ
```

Figure 2.3. Sample list of alphanumeric strings as used in Neisser's (1963) search task, with the target letter *K*.

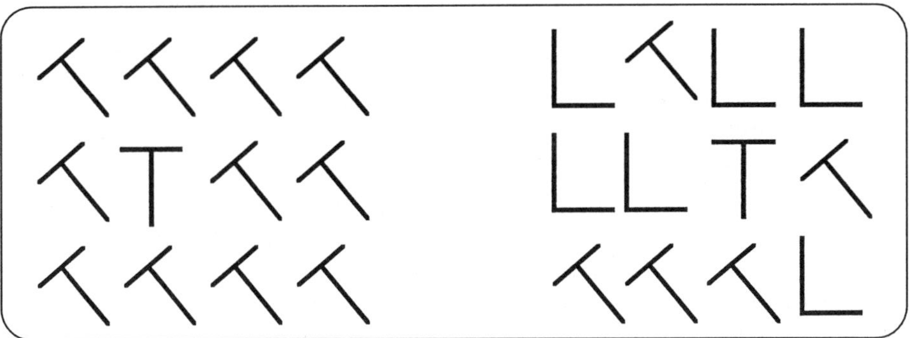

Figure 2.4. Examples of a feature search based on orientation (left) and a conjunctive search based on orientation and form (right).

Treisman and Gelade (1980) proposed that the ability to base search on particular features of the stimuli depends on the nature of the discrimination to be made. Specifically, they found that if a target can be distinguished from distractors on the basis of a single feature (e.g., orientation), detection performance is relatively unaffected by the number of distractors in the display. For example, the task of detecting a vertical *T* in a field of oblique *T*s (see Figure 2.4, left side) is easy regardless of the number of distractors. However, if a target is defined by a conjunction of features (e.g., orientation and form), performance is a decreasing function of the number of distractors. Consider the difficult task of detecting a vertical *T* in a field of oblique *T*s and vertical *L*s (see Figure 2.4, right side). In this case, reaction time increases dramatically as the display size increases.

These basic results and other findings led Treisman and Gelade to develop a **feature integration theory** of attention, according to which individual features are processed preattentively but the integration of features required to detect conjunctive targets requires attention. Thus the detection of single features seems to be the result of parallel processing of the display elements, whereas conjunctive search may depend on the serial search of individual display locations because attention can be directed to only one location at a time. In Treisman and Gelade's model, the display size effect is due to the limited nature of the attentional processes that are required to integrate the features that make up conjunctive targets. When the search can be conducted preattentively on the basis of single features, thus bypassing this limited capacity process, no display-size effects are predicted.

The feature integration account of how conjunctive targets are processed has been challenged and is currently the subject of considerable debate. One challenge to the account was made by Wolfe, Cave, and Franzel (1989), who showed that search for targets defined by conjunctions of three features was less difficult than search for targets defined by conjunctions of only two features. To explain this result, Wolfe et al. proposed that preattentive processes are involved in conjunctive search as well as in featural search, and that triple conjunctions are easier to detect than double conjunctions because there are three preattentive processors (one for each feature) guiding attention rather than two. Double conjunctions would not be expected to yield a similar benefit relative to single-feature search, even though two preattentive processors are involved as opposed to one, because in feature search the responses could be based on the preattentive analysis whereas in conjunctive search this analysis would only guide attention to possible targets. Regardless of the specific account, it is generally accepted that there is a fundamental difference in the processing performed for featural and conjunctive searches.

A study by Yonas and E. Gibson (cited in Gibson, 1969) suggests that preattentive processing of features may also provide a basis for performance improvement in classification tasks. Their study used a set of nine letter stimuli, of which either one or three were assigned to a positive response and the rest to a negative response. On a given trial, a single letter was presented to be classified as rapidly as possible. In the first condition, the letter *E* was the only item in the positive set; in the second condition, *A, O,* and *F* were assigned to the positive response; and in the third, *A, N,* and *V* were the members of the positive set. Importantly, the letters *A, N,* and *V* share a common feature, a diagonal line, and the set of nine letters was chosen so that this feature distinguished this target set from the rest of the letters.

Initially, reaction times for the two three-item sets were equivalent and slower than for the one-item set. However, performance improved more rapidly with practice on the *ANV* set than on the *AOF* set. One person was tested until asymptotic performance was reached. At this point, responding was just as fast for the *ANV* set as for the single-letter condition, whereas the reaction times for the *AOF* set were slower. Thus it appears that the performers were able to use the distinctive diagonal feature to speed their reaction times. This finding is consistent with the view that features can be processed preattentively. In accord with this view, E. Gibson (1969) noted that most of the participants did not report awareness of the common diagonal feature for the *ANV* set.

Perceptual Unitization

To this point, we have seen that features usually are detected more easily than are conjunctions of features and that featural distinctions can be learned and used as a basis for classifying stimuli. However, it is also possible for performance to benefit from features being organized into higher-level units.

Feature Combinations

LaBerge (1973) provided a demonstration of how unitization of feature combinations can facilitate responding. In his relative discrimination tasks, stimuli were familiar letters or unfamiliar letterlike forms (see Figure 2.5), presented in *primary* or *secondary* test blocks. Each trial in the primary test blocks began with a cue that was one of the letters or letterlike forms shown in Figure 2.5. On 75% of the trials, the cue was followed by a target stimulus that was the same as the cue stimulus. A speeded response was to be made on these trials, but not on the remaining 25% of the trials for which the cue and target were different members from the same stimulus set (e.g., both letters). In the secondary test blocks, the cue was a letter from a different set than that shown in Figure 2.5; on approximately 80% of the trials, which were fillers, this cue stimulus was followed by the presentation of another letter that was either the same as or different from the cue, and a response was to be made if the two letters were the same. The remaining 20% of the trials were the critical trials, on which the cue stimulus was followed by a pair of simultaneously presented stimuli (either two letters or two letterlike forms from the sets shown in Figure

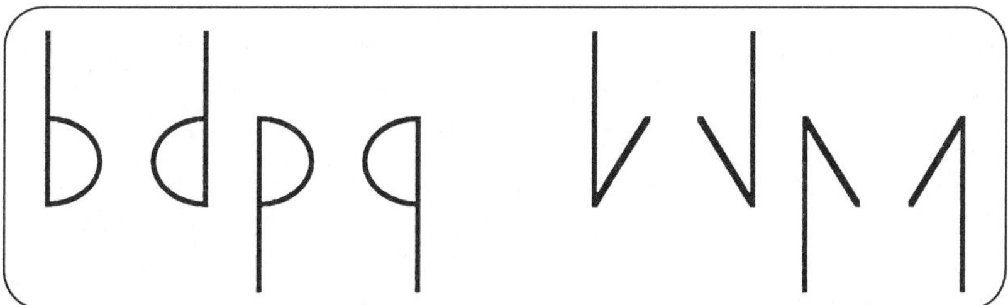

Figure 2.5. Depiction of the letter (left) and letterlike (right) stimuli used by LaBerge (1973).

2.5), and the pair was to be judged as same or different, regardless of the relation of the pair members to the cue stimulus.

LaBerge's idea was that, in the primary test blocks, the features for the letter designated by the cue would already be integrated so that even the unfamiliar, letterlike stimuli would be fully processed, whereas in the critical trials in the secondary test blocks, features in the letterlike stimuli would require integration before the stimuli could be judged. Consistent with this, no difference between discrimination times with the letters or the unfamiliar letterlike forms was found in the primary blocks. However, for the secondary test blocks, when the same-different judgment was made for two uncued stimuli, performance was better with the familiar letters than with the unfamiliar letterlike forms.

LaBerge interpreted his findings in terms of a hierarchical model in which features are analyzed and then integrated into compound stimulus codes. The model allows for automatic integration of the features into the compound codes when the stimuli are familiar, so automatic integration is possible for the letter stimuli. However, for unfamiliar stimuli, attention is required for feature integration. Because the features are integrated into compound stimulus codes automatically for familiar letters, the unexpected occurrence of these stimuli in the secondary test blocks is not as disruptive for them as it is for the unfamiliar letterlike forms. LaBerge showed further that with practice, as the participants gained familiarity with the initially unfamiliar letterlike forms, the difference in reaction time for letters and letterlike forms in the secondary test blocks disappeared, suggesting that the letterlike forms had become unitized.

Additional evidence that practice leads to the unitization of previously unfamiliar forms comes from studies in which people had to judge matrixes composed of filled and unfilled squares, or random polygons of varying complexity, as same or different (Bethell-Fox & Shepard, 1988; Pellegrino, Doane, Fischer, & Alderton, 1991). Initially, reaction times are an increasing function of the complexity of the two forms being judged. However, this complexity effect decreases systematically with practice, suggesting a shift from a strategy based on individual features to one based on representations of the stimuli as whole units.

Interestingly, the nature of the learning that occurs in these tasks is different when the same-different discrimination is easy from when it is difficult. For the random polygons used by Pellegrino et al. (1991), same pairs were constructed for each of several referent forms of varying complexity, and the different pairs were constructed by pairing a referent with one of six mismatching forms derived from it (see Figure 2.6). These

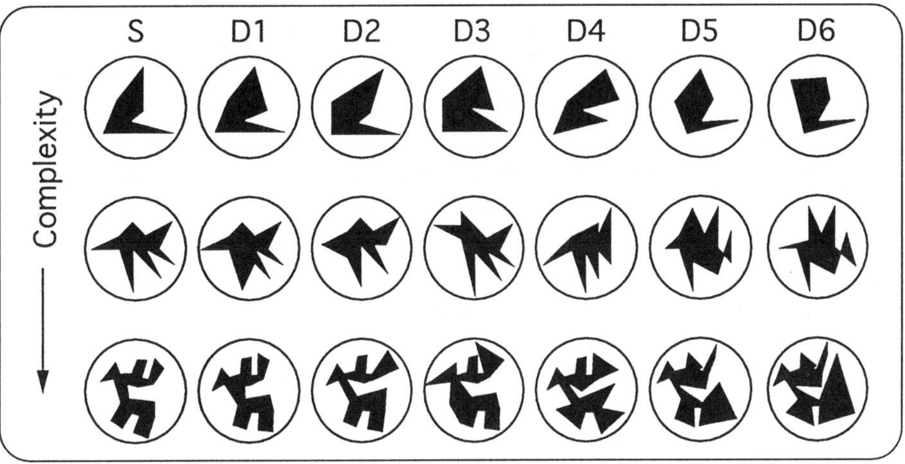

Figure 2.6. A set of forms similar to those used by Pellegrino et al. (1991) for both members of same pairs (S) and for the other member of different pairs (D), with D1 being most similar to S and D6 least similar.
SOURCE: Based on Cooper and Podgorny (1976).

mismatching forms varied in their degree of similarity to the referent, with D1 being most similar and D6 least similar. Pellegrino et al. gave one group of people (the *difficult context* group) eight sessions of practice discriminating the same pairs from the similar different pairs (D1-D3) and another group (the *easy context* group) eight sessions discriminating the same pairs from the dissimilar different pairs (D4-D6). Eight additional transfer sessions were then provided in which both groups were tested with the complete set of same and different pairs (D1-D6).

As might be expected, reaction times for the same pairs were initially much slower for the difficult context group than for the easy context group. The difficult context group also showed a greater initial effect of stimulus complexity, suggesting that the difficult context forced the observers to process the stimuli in greater detail. However, the effects of practice were much greater for the difficult context group than for the easy context group. By the eighth session, the difficult context group showed mean reaction times similar to those of the easy context group and exhibited less of an effect of stimulus complexity. This latter finding suggests that the more detailed processing required for the difficult context group resulted in the learning of more precise representations of the forms.

The transfer data provided additional evidence to support this interpretation. When the complete set of different forms was introduced in the transfer sessions, the difficult context group showed no disruption in performance but the easy context group did. Even reaction times to the same pairs, to which both groups had had equivalent amounts of practice, were slowed for the easy context group in the transfer sessions. This suggests that the representations of the stimuli acquired by practice in the easy context may not have been sufficiently detailed to provide an efficient basis for the same-different discrimination when the more similar different pairs (D1-D3) were introduced during transfer. The general point illustrated by this study, that the context in which a task is practiced determines what is learned, is one that recurs throughout the book.

Word Units

Hierarchical models, such as the one proposed by LaBerge (1973) for the relation between features and letters, have also been developed to explain the relation between letters and words. These models differ in the nature of the interactions that are presumed to occur between letter and word information. A first possibility is that letter information may be passed to word units in a strictly feedforward manner (see model a in Figure 2.7). Another option is that letters and words are represented separately and independently (see model b in Figure 2.7). A third possibility is that information may be exchanged between letter and word units (see model c in Figure 2.7). Two effects, word superiority and pseudoword superiority, suggest that the third model is the correct one (Pollatsek & Rayner, 1989).

The first of these effects, the **word superiority effect,** is that identification accuracy for a single letter is higher when the letter is presented in a word context than when it is presented singly, even though more letters must be processed in the first case. To illustrate this phenomenon, we describe a study by Reicher (1969) that examined letter identification performance under three conditions. In one condition, a word was displayed briefly, followed by a pattern mask. Two letters for the identification task were then displayed above and below one of the letter locations; either of these letters, when combined with the other letters in the word context, would make a meaningful word. For example, if the word *work* was presented, the letters *d* and *k* would be presented above and below the fourth letter position, and the observer's task would be to indicate which of these letters appeared in the word. The second condition was similar but used a nonword composed of the rearranged letters from a corresponding word (e.g., *rwok*). For the third condition, only a single

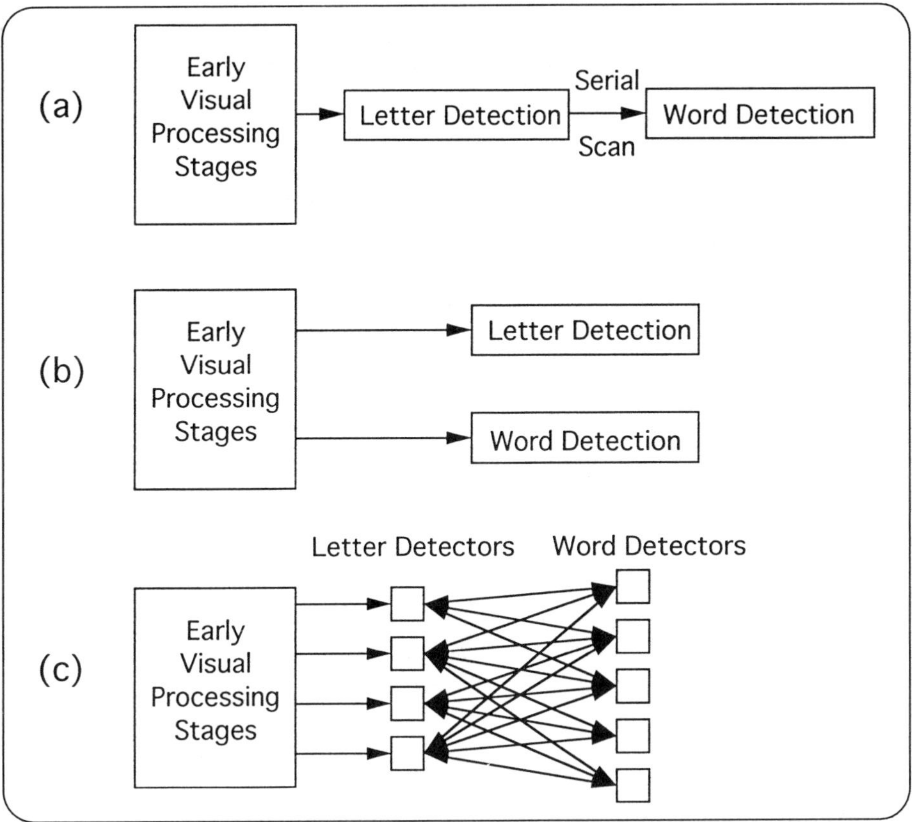

Figure 2.7. Three alternative models for the relation between letter and word units: (a) serial letter model, (b) direct word recognition model, and (c) parallel letter model.
SOURCE: Adapted from Pollatsek and Rayner (1989).

letter was displayed, but it occurred in the position that would have been occupied had the letter been presented in the word (e.g., _ _ _ k). Reicher found that letter identification was more accurate in the word condition than in the other two conditions. That is, performance was better within the word context than without. This surprising phenomenon rules out model a of Figure 2.7, in which word recognition depends on letter recognition but cannot influence it.

The second phenomenon mentioned above, the **pseudoword superiority effect,** rules out models in which letters and words are represented independently. Pseudowords are letter strings that are pronounceable but are not words—for example, *drame.* If letter and word information were represented independently, there should be no benefit of a pseudoword context in a task such as the one used by Reicher. This is because word identification would never occur and so could not benefit letter identification performance. The fact that presenting letters in a pseudoword context also benefits letter identification (e.g., Baron & Thurston, 1973) rules out model b in Figure 2.7 and suggests that there is an interaction between word units and letter units, as in model c.

By its nature, reading of text emphasizes word units over letter units: Skilled readers read words, not letters. Thus reading words embedded in a larger text might lead to performance different from that obtained when reading words in isolation. When text is being read, word units might dominate letter units so that identification of particular letters is actually inferior in the word context. Evidence for this kind of word inferiority effect has in fact been obtained when passages are read for comprehension, as opposed to reading single words just for identification. Healy (1976) originally demonstrated this phenomenon by requiring people to mark instances of the letter *t* while reading a passage at normal speed. Proportionately more occurrences of *t* were missed in the word *the* than in the other words of the passage. Comparisons with control conditions indicated that it was the high frequency of usage in the English language of the word *the* that differentiated performance with *the* from performance with other words. The same result is obtained with other high-frequency-use words, such as *and* and *of* (e.g., Drewnowski & Healy, 1977), and the word inferiority effect is eliminated when the high-frequency-use words are misspelled (e.g., Healy & Drewnowski, 1983).

To explain this disadvantage for detecting letters in correctly spelled high-frequency-use words, Drewnowski and Healy (1977) proposed a **word unitization** model in which processing of text occurs at various levels, two of which are the letter and word levels. With high-frequency-use words, identification at the word level can be completed before identification of the constituent letters. Once identification is complete at the word level, no further processing is given that word. It is as if words such as *the* are processed automatically in the reading of text. An additional factor contributing to the difficulty of detecting individual letters in high-frequency-use words may be that the roles of words like *the* and *and* in the text are structural rather than meaningful (Greenberg & Koriat, 1991). Words having only a structural function may be overshadowed by representations of meaning.

The letter detection disadvantage in high-frequency-use words is a consequence of the extensive prior experience with reading that a person has had before participating in the letter detection task. This observation leads to the question of whether practice on the letter detection task can make the constituent letters more salient, leading to the elimination of the word frequency disadvantage. Healy, Fendrich, and J. Proctor (1990) found that with minimal practice at letter detection in prose passages letter detection accuracy in high-frequency-use words became comparable to that for letters in lower-frequency-use words. This practice effect was still evident when the participants were tested in the detection task after intervals as long as six months. However, this benefit of practice depended on the nature of the practice task. Experience detecting the target letter in random letter strings had little or no impact on subsequent detection of the target letter in prose. Thus prior practice at letter detection was beneficial for detection in a prose context only when the practice was in a similar context.

Unitization or Constituent Processing?

The studies in this section provide evidence for letter units and word units, in addition to feature units. The different levels of units interact in complex ways, with the effects being highly task specific. Moreover, the studies of practice suggest that whatever effect of unitization on task performance is observed, a relatively small amount of practice is sufficient to eliminate the effect. Thus the processes underlying the effects show considerable flexibility. Despite extensive prior experience with the word *the,* for example, a shift in the way the word was processed in the letter detection task was evident in the work of Healy and her colleagues. In this work, it seemed that people could overcome the tendency to process only the unitized word and learn to process the constituent letters as well. In the work of LaBerge (1973), on the other hand, it appeared that people learned to unitize the letterlike forms used in the experiment. Whether or not forms are unitized appears in these cases to be susceptible to task demands and practice.

Procedural Learning

Much research, in addition to Healy et al.'s (1990) work on letter detection in prose, has demonstrated that the operations performed on stimuli while executing a task may have an enduring effect on subsequent performance. A view called **procedural learning** stresses that stimuli are not remembered independently of the operations performed on them

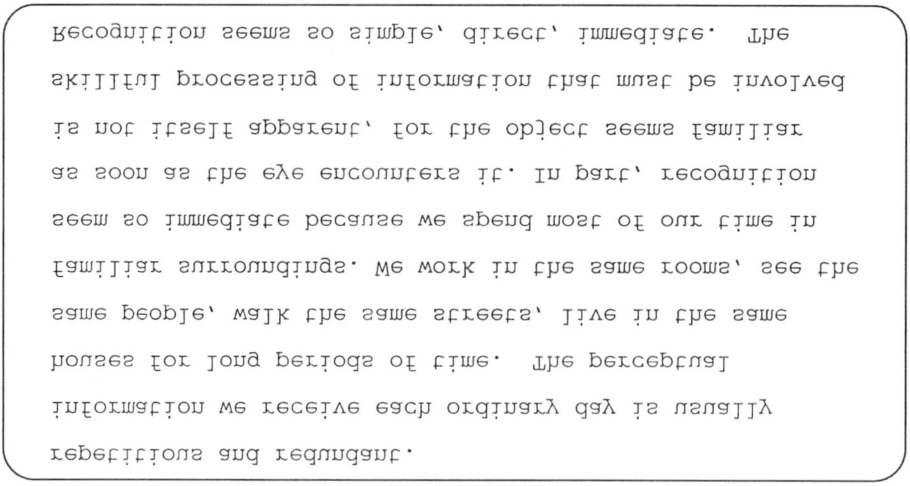

Recognition seems so simple, direct, immediate. The skillful processing of information that must be involved is not itself apparent, for the object seems familiar as soon as the eye encounters it. In part, recognition seem so immediate because we spend most of our time in familiar surroundings. We work in the same rooms, see the same people, walk the same streets, live in the same houses for long periods of time. The perceptual information we receive each ordinary day is usually repetitious and redundant.

Figure 2.8. An example of the geometrically inverted text used by Kolers (1975a).

(e.g., Kolers & Roediger, 1984). Instead, learning is presumed to depend on the processing required during task performance. A major source of evidence for such a procedural view has come from studies of reading.

In literate adults, reading is a highly overlearned skill requiring coordinated processes of perception, cognition, and action. Letter and word shapes must be recognized, eye movements must be controlled to select relevant text, and the meaning of the passage must be extracted. Because of its substantial perceptual component, reading would seem a natural choice for the study of perceptual skill acquisition. However, the degree of overlearning present in the adult population leaves little room for change within the context of an experiment.

To isolate the perceptual aspect of the reading process, an approach is needed for which the words and their associated meanings as well as the syntax remain familiar but the perceptual characteristics are novel. Kolers (1975a) adopted such an approach in his use of geometrically inverted text (see Figure 2.8). In one experiment, participants read 160 pages of inverted text over a period of approximately two months. As might be expected from looking at the text in Figure 2.8, all persons initially experienced considerable difficulty reading the inverted text. In fact, initial reading speeds were from 8 to 22 times slower than normal. With practice, this initial difficulty was to a large extent overcome. Learning followed the familiar power function, and by the end of the experiment the average rate of reading the inverted text was only slightly slower than a normal reading rate.

Kolers (1976) reported the results of retesting some of the persons who had learned to read inverted text 13 to 15 months earlier. Used in the retesting were equal numbers of pages that had been read previously and pages that had never been read. Reading speed for the new pages was somewhat slower than the final reading speed in the original experiment but nowhere near as slow as the original reading speeds had been. In the original study, the initial reading speed was 15 minutes per page, whereas the initial reading speed in the retest was 4 minutes per page. With additional practice, the speed decreased further to 1.7 minutes per page. Moreover, reading speed was approximately 5% faster for the pages used in the earlier experiment than for the new pages, suggesting that more than just general pattern recognition skills had been learned.

The savings in reading speed for the previously read old pages relative to new pages could be due to familiarity with the content of the pages or to experience with the specific graphemic patterns. Other work by Kolers (1975b) supports the latter account. For example, prior reading of sentences in normal orientation did not produce a similar magnitude of benefit on subsequent readings of the same sentences when they were presented in the inverted orientation. Also, Masson (1986) found that transfer of word identification skill for inverted text occurred only when the transfer words had the same letters as the practice words. Specifically, he gave people training at reading 24 word triplets composed from 13 letters of the alphabet. In a transfer phase, the same 24 triplets were tested along with 24 triplets of new words composed from the same letters and 24 triplets of new words composed from the remaining 13 letters not seen previously. The benefit of practice evident in the training phase transferred readily to the new words constructed from the same letters as the words read originally but not to those constructed from new letters. That is, the skill at reading inverted text was specific to the letters that had been practiced.

Placing the locus of improvement at graphical pattern analysis suggests that reading inverted text is primarily a perceptual skill. The differential performance on old and new passages illustrates the specificity of the skill that has been learned. Kolers's results for the reading of transformed text are consistent with the procedural view of learning in which the acquisition and processing of symbols are intertwined (Kolers & Roediger, 1984). In the procedural view, the way in which symbols are manipulated during acquisition forms the basis for their retention, such

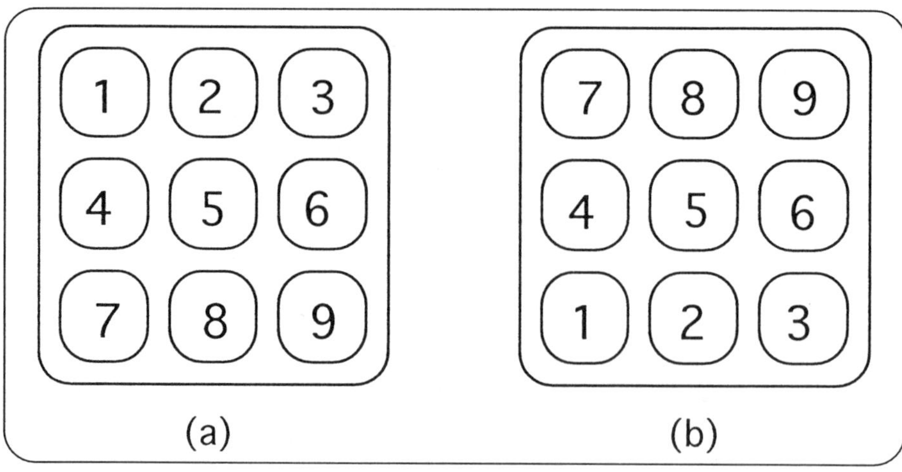

Figure 2.9. Telephone (a) and calculator (b) keypads.

that performance at a later time depends on the similarity of procedures in acquisition and test. The degree of transfer between tasks also is a function of the correspondence of the underlying procedures.

Using the general logic of transfer studies, we can evaluate the relative contribution of perceptual procedures to skill acquisition by keeping the perceptual components the same across the acquisition and transfer tasks, while varying the other components, or by changing the perceptual components while holding the other components constant. Fendrich, Healy, and Bourne (1991) used a transfer paradigm of this type to study the long-term effects of repeating particular stimulus-response sequences in a perceptual-motor task. Their goal was to determine whether perceptual or motor factors were responsible for these effects. Fendrich et al. (1991) used a task in which four-digit sequences were entered on a keypad. Two keypads were used, a calculator keypad and a telephone keypad (see Figure 2.9). Lists of 10 four-digit sequences were presented three times apiece during each of two acquisition sessions. Initially, half of the people used the calculator keypad and half the telephone keypad. In the transfer session, half continued to use the same keypad and half changed to the alternate keypad. For the persons who changed keypads, one fourth of the lists in the transfer session repeated the digits presented during acquisition (the *old digit* lists), one fourth repeated the motor response patterns (the *old motor* lists), and one half did not repeat either (the new lists). For those who continued using the same keypad, half of the lists were old and half new.

Although reaction times were elevated relative to acquisition, both the old digit and old motor lists were entered faster than the new lists, with a tendency for entry of the old digit lists to be faster than the old motor lists. The advantage for the old digit lists was interpreted by Fendrich et al. as evidence for facilitation in the encoding of the number sequences because the motor realization of the responses was different in transfer from that in acquisition. Similarly, the finding of some benefit for the old motor lists was interpreted as evidence for facilitation in the execution of previously practiced motor procedures. Both of these findings can be attributed to partial reinstatement of procedures used during the acquisition phase. Thus, skill in two such different tasks as reading inverted text and entering strings of encoded digits appears to depend on the acquisition of specific as well as general procedures.

Automatic and Controlled Processing

According to the models of skill acquisition described in Chapter 1, the final phase in the development of skill is characterized by smooth, relatively effortless, automatic performance. In this final learning phase, at least some aspects of the task no longer require conscious attention and place little if any load on limited capacity resources. The development of automaticity has gained the interest of many researchers because it seems so important to effective performance. In any job or task environment, it would be of obvious benefit to perform with a reduced processing load (Schneider, 1985). Although the real-world importance of the development of automaticity has often been emphasized, it has been studied most extensively in visual and memory search tasks.

One of the more robust phenomena in search tasks is that when one or more possible targets in an array of distractors must be detected (e.g., look for Z or Q), search time initially is an increasing function of the number of possible targets. Neisser, Novick, and Lazar (1963) examined the effect of practice on such search for multiple targets using Neisser's multiple list procedure, described earlier. In the initial testing session, search for more than two possible target letters took longer than search for only one or two. With extended practice, this difference was eliminated, so that searching for one of 5 or 10 items took no longer than searching for a single possible target. This result suggests that the processing load imposed by the task is decreased as a function of practice so that capacity limitations are overcome.

The practice effect for multiple targets obtained by Neisser et al. (1963) raises questions about the ways in which processing can change and the conditions of practice necessary to obtain these changes. These questions were investigated extensively by Schneider and Shiffrin (1977; Shiffrin & Schneider, 1977), who measured reaction time and accuracy in tasks that involved both visual and memory search for alphanumeric characters. Their basic procedure was to first present a set of one to four possible targets for the trial. A series of task displays was then presented; each of these "frames" had four positions containing either a dot-pattern mask, a distractor item, or a target. Shiffrin and Schneider defined the memory set size as the number of items in the target set and the frame size as the number of frame locations containing targets or distractors. Memory set size, frame size, and the composition of the target and distractor sets were manipulated to examine the nature of processing in these tasks.

Major differences in performance emerged when people practiced with a so-called **varied mapping,** in which the targets on one trial could serve as distractors on other trials (e.g., if the set of targets and distractors was {*A, B, C, D, E*}, *A* could be a target on one trial and a nontarget distractor on the next), as opposed to a **consistent mapping,** in which the complete target set was disjoint from the distractor set throughout the experiment (e.g., of the target set {*A, B, C, D, E*} and the distractor set {*F, G, H, I, J*}, *A* and *B* could only occur as targets and never as distractors, whereas *F* and *G* could only occur as distractors). In their first experiments, letters and digits were used as targets and distractors. For the consistent mapping, the targets were letters and the distractors were digits, or vice versa, whereas for the varied mapping, the targets and distractors both came from the same set of either letters or digits. When people performed with the varied mapping, performance was a decreasing function of memory-set size and frame size. In contrast, when they performed with the consistent mapping, a very small amount of practice essentially eliminated the effects of memory set and frame size.

Schneider and Shiffrin (1977) interpreted the different patterns of results obtained with varied and consistent mappings in terms of a distinction between two qualitatively different modes of processing: **controlled** and **automatic.** Controlled processing, or, in this case, controlled search, takes the form of an attention-demanding, serial comparison process of limited rate. Even after practice, performance with a varied mapping requires controlled processing. In contrast, when practice is with a consistent mapping a different mode of processing, automatic detection, is possible. Detection is said to be automatic when performance appears to proceed without requiring attentional capacity or intentional control. As a result of this bypassing of attentional capacity, the set size effect disappears.

Because of the automaticity that develops, a consistent mapping is beneficial to performance as long as it is maintained. However, as might be expected, automatic detection of particular stimuli can interfere with performance if the required response is different from the one that was trained. Shiffrin and Schneider (1977) demonstrated that this was the case when observers were trained in a consistent mapping condition until automatic detection had developed and then transferred to a condition in which the target and distractor sets were reversed from their original roles. This reversal severely disrupted performance, such that performance was worse than it had been at the start of the original training period. Additional search experiments were conducted in which observers searched for varied mapping targets on one diagonal of the frames, with instructions to ignore the other diagonal. Performance in the varied mapping search task was disrupted when a previously trained consistently-mapped target occurred on the to-be-ignored diagonal simultaneously with the target for that trial. This result indicates that the automatic detection response to previously trained stimuli cannot be suppressed even when it would be advantageous to do so.

Additional research has addressed the exact conditions necessary for automaticity to develop and whether learning of the distractor set occurs. For example, Shiffrin, Dumais, and Schneider (1981) and Fisk, Lee, and Rogers (1991) conducted experiments in which either the target or distractor set was changed following an extensive training period. In both of these studies, strong positive transfer was observed when either the target set or the distractor set was maintained. The finding that an equivalent amount of transfer occurred when the distractor set was maintained as when the target set was indicates that not only processing of the targets but also that of the distractors changes with practice. This result is consistent with a model of automatic attending in which consistent practice increases the strength with which the targets draw attention and decreases the strength with which the distractors draw attention. Untrained items, and items used in varied mapping, are presumed to have an amount of strength intermediate to that of consistently trained targets and distractors. The reason why positive transfer occurs when either the target or distractor set is maintained is that the difference in strength between old targets and new distractors is comparable to that between new targets and old distractors (Shiffrin et al., 1981).

If the role of either the target or distractor set is changed (e.g., the target set from previous training is now used as the distractor set), performance is no different from performance with a completely new varied or consistent mapping (Fisk et al., 1991; Shiffrin et al., 1981). Under these conditions, it appears that performers are successful at reverting to the use of controlled search. The lack of interference from previously trained items under these partial reversal conditions stands in marked contrast to the substantial interference obtained by Shiffrin and Schneider (1977) with complete reversal of the target and distractor sets. However, because of the many procedural differences in addition to the reversal manipulation, it is impossible to determine for sure that the partial versus complete distinction is the critical factor.

Finally, a relative-strength account of the type described above would suggest that graded benefits of consistency are possible. Schneider and Fisk (1982b) obtained evidence for gradations of automatic processing by varying the number of trials in which an item from the target set served as a distractor. If all distractor items can also serve as targets on other trials, the task is the same as the varied-mapping one described earlier. If the target never occurs as a distractor, the task is as with the consistent mapping. As the number of inconsistent trials (i.e., trials on which an item from the target set occurs as a distractor) is varied, the degree of consistency of the mapping is changed. Schneider and Fisk compared mappings with 0 (consistent mapping), 5, 10, 20, and 61 (varied mapping) inconsistent trials. As shown in Figure 2.10, detection accuracy was generally better for the more consistent tasks, and these tasks showed more improvement with practice than did the less consistent tasks. These results demonstrate that consistency does not have to be all-or-none to be beneficial. In agreement with the hypothesis that automatic processing is a function of the relative strengths of targets and distractors, the results also suggest that automatic processing is not all-or-none but occurs to different degrees.

Schneider and Detweiler (1987, 1988) developed a simulation model, in which performance is based on the relative strengths of the targets and distractors, that captures the distinction between controlled and automatic processing. The model is related to the class of connectionist models described in Chapter 1 (see also Anderson & Rosenfeld, 1988), which are loosely based on the characteristics of neurons and their interconnectivity. This relation is evident in that the information processing in Schneider and

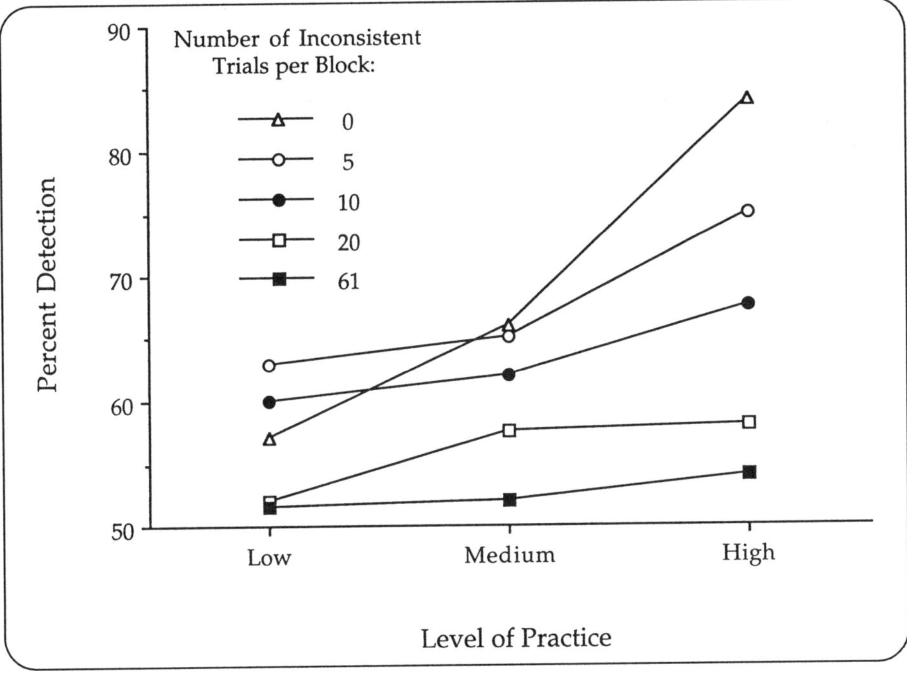

Figure 2.10. Detection accuracy in Schneider and Fisk's experiment as a function of the number of times that items from the target set occurred as distractors (i.e., inconsistent trials) and level of practice.
SOURCE: Adapted from Schneider and Fisk (1982b).

Detweiler's (1987, 1988) connectionist/control architecture occurs in networks of neural-like units, with knowledge stored in the connection weights. The networks are organized into modules, and these modules are grouped into regions (see Figure 2.11). Each module is a modifiable connectionist system that processes only a restricted class of inputs. For example, within the visual region separate modules process features, characters (i.e., letters), and words (see Figure 2.11). The feature module takes as input the pattern of visual stimulation and produces specific features as output. These features are input to the character module, which provides letter output to the word module. The innermost module of each region is presumed to communicate with the other regions through an "inner loop" of associative connections (see Figure 2-11). Thus, for example, the words processed in the visual region are passed via the inner loop to a different region for semantic processing. An important part of the

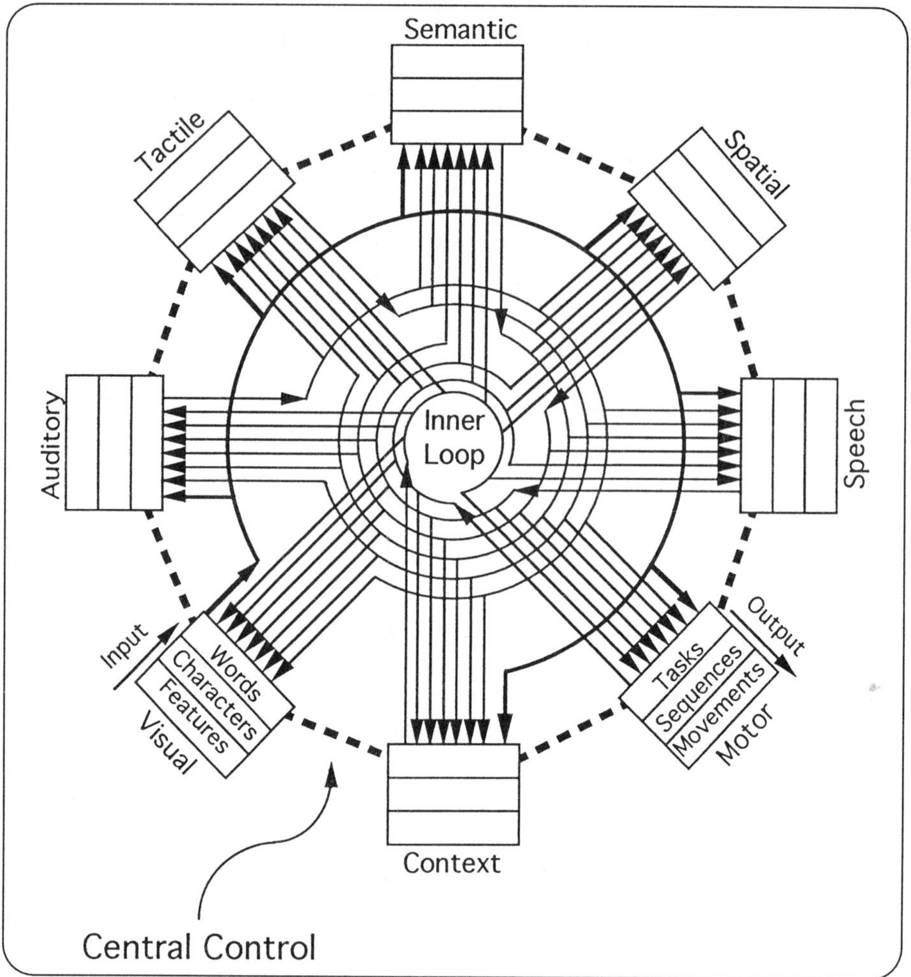

Figure 2.11. Schneider and Detweiler's connectionist/control architecture. The figure shows the regions (visual, auditory, etc.) that are connected by the inner loop and the modules within two regions involved in visual information processing tasks.
SOURCE: Adapted from Schneider and Detweiler (1988).

architecture is a control processing system, which modulates the transmission of information between and within processing regions. Each module has associated with it a control structure, and a central control structure prioritizes the need to transmit between modules, allowing the module with highest priority to transmit through the inner loop.

Information passed out of a module is regulated by attenuation and priority report units within the module and by the control structure (see Figure 2.12). The attenuation unit acts to block the output of information from a module. The priority report unit can in certain circumstances inhibit the attenuation unit so that information can be passed from the module. The control structure acts as a circuit that receives information about the activation of the units in a module via the priority report unit and an activity report unit. This circuit can counteract the inhibitory effect of the attenuation unit when the activation in the module is sufficiently high.

In Schneider and Detweiler's model, controlled processing is processing that is modulated by the control structure. Initially, the attenuation unit acts to inhibit output from its module and the control structure influences the attenuation unit to allow information to be transmitted from a module. The level of activation of the output units is the critical factor in distinguishing controlled from automatic processing. With consistent mappings, connections between input and output units are strengthened such that the output units become highly activated by the appropriate input. When the activation of the output units is high, the priority unit becomes highly activated and overrides the attenuation unit directly, without intervention from the control structure. This bypassing of the control structure defines automatic processing in Schneider and Detweiler's model.

▣ SUMMARY ▣

In this chapter, we have illustrated how people become skilled at making perceptual distinctions. With practice, perceptual judgments come to be made faster and more accurately. In many cases, it is the learning of distinctive features that accounts for these improvements in performance. Unitization of features can also occur, resulting in more efficient processing of stimuli composed of more than one feature, but whether or not unitization will have beneficial effects on performance will depend on the requirements of the task.

The procedures performed on stimuli determine the degree and nature of learning that will occur. Whereas both procedures and specific stimuli can be learned, in many cases the learning of one will be dependent on the learning of the other. Two modes for perceptual processing and task performance, one that requires attentional re-

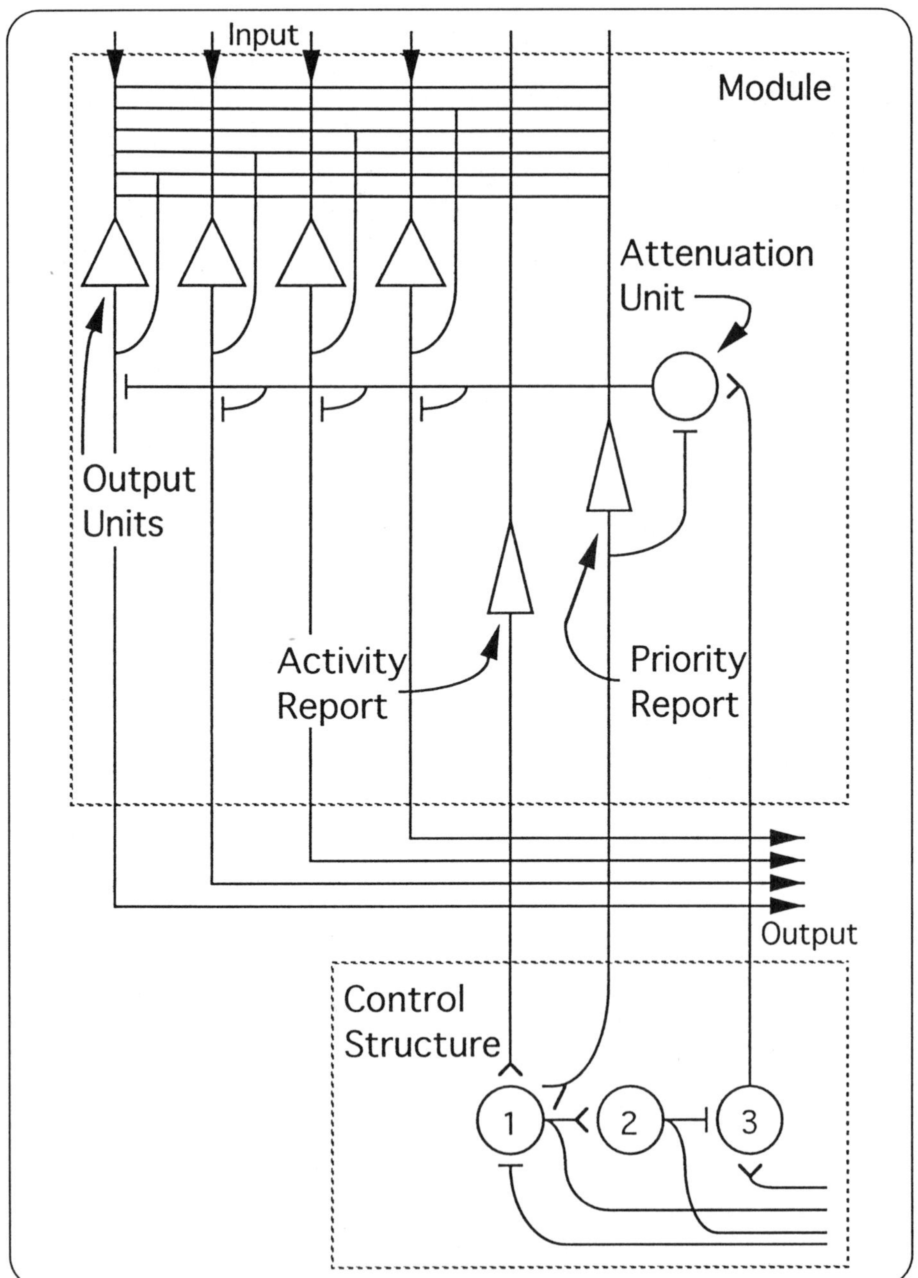

Figure 2.12. The microlevel structure of Schneider and Detweiler's model. Flat connections represent inhibitory influences and reverse arrow-type connections represent excitatory influences.
SOURCE: Adapted from Schneider and Detweiler (1988).

sources and one that bypasses them, have been distinguished. It is widely held that simple, featural discriminations can be made preattentively. More complex stimuli typically require attentional control for their processing. In many tasks, processes that initially require attention become automatized, with automaticity best characterized as varying in degrees along a continuum rather than being all-or-none. Automaticity is an important issue in skill acquisition and has been studied extensively. We will come back to this issue when discussing dual-task performance, training, and the development of expertise.

Response Selection Phenomena

Characterizing Practice Effects

Summary

CHAPTER 3

Response Selection Skill

In the 1992 Summer Olympic Games in Barcelona, controversy arose over the use of a recently developed system for scoring the boxing matches. The system involved five judges, each of whom was equipped with an electronic box used to record responses. In each match, one boxer wore red and the other wore blue. If a judge detected a blow landed by the red boxer, a red button on the response box was to be pressed. Similarly, a blue button was to be pressed if the blue boxer landed a blow. For a point to be scored, three of the five judges had to record the blow within a 1-s interval. In one controversial match, even though each judge had recorded more blows for one boxer, his opponent received more points and won the match. The discrepancy between the judges' individual scores and the point totals likely was a consequence of the restricted time interval during which responses from at least three judges had to be recorded.

In the aftermath of this event, an international boxing official attributed the failure of the scoring system to the judges' slow speed of responding. According to him, "It's the reaction problem that is the problem we have. The machine could work provided people who press the buttons do it instantaneously" (quoted in Schuyler, 1992). Unfortunately, it is well known that people do not have the capability to respond instantaneously.

Besides the time needed for the difficult perceptual discriminations required of the judges, time was needed to select the appropriate response. The need to process and respond to several blows in quick succession made the response selection problem even more difficult than it would have been if one event could have been processed completely before another event occurred. These factors along with the to-be-expected variability in response time should make it clear that many responses by well-intentioned judges would fall outside the 1-s interval.

Although response selection is clearly a factor in complex tasks of the type described above, it can also be studied in simple laboratory tasks, such as sorting cards containing stimulus items into categories or making keypress responses to stimulus presentations. Even in tasks as simple as pressing a left response key with the left index finger if the letter X occurs and a right response key with the right index finger if the letter S occurs, response selection is required to determine which keypress response to make to the identified letter. As in this example, the properties of the response selection process are usually investigated in reaction time tasks for which the alternative stimuli are readily discriminable and the motor requirement is minimal. This is because the major concern is not with the time course or accuracy of stimulus identification or response execution but with the time to determine which response is to be made to the stimulus.

As choice-reaction tasks are practiced, reaction times become progressively faster. In fact, of the many variables that influence choice-reaction time, the variable with the greatest effect is the amount of practice on the task (Rabbitt, 1989). Although perceptual processing may change in certain classes of tasks, such as those covered in Chapter 2, it has been suggested that the primary influence of practice in most tasks is on response selection processes (Teichner & Krebs, 1974; Welford, 1968, 1976). A recent study by Pashler and Baylis (1991a) illustrates the type of evidence that supports this claim.

Pashler and Baylis (1991a) tried to determine the locus of practice effects in choice-reaction tasks by having people practice with one set of symbolic stimuli and then transfer to another set. Different conditions of transfer were used to evaluate the relative importance of perceptual, categorization, response selection, and response execution processes. Stimuli were letters, digits, or nonalphanumeric characters. In one experiment, two members from each of these categories were assigned to left, middle, and right response keys, which were pressed by the index, middle, and ring fingers, respectively, of the right hand. For example, numbers 2 and

7 might have been assigned to the left key, letters V and P to the middle key, and symbols # and & to the right key. After 750 trials of practice, during which responses became considerably faster, two additional stimuli from each category were assigned to their respective keys along with the original stimuli. For each category of stimuli, reaction times were approximately as fast for the new items as for the already practiced items. Pashler and Baylis interpreted this result as evidence against a perceptual basis for the practice effect; if the speedup had been wholly perceptual, it would have been restricted to the original stimuli.

An additional experiment by Pashler and Baylis's (1991a) ruled out a response execution basis for the practice effect by showing little effect on performance of transferring from using the right hand to make the responses to using the left hand or vice versa. Thus performance remained at the practiced level even though the fingers used to respond on the transfer trials were different from those used in practice. Also consistent with the hypothesis that response selection is the process affected by practice, Pashler and Baylis found that when the stimulus categories were reassigned to the response keys for the transfer trials (e.g., if numbers 2 and 7 were assigned to the left key initially, they would be reassigned to either the middle or right key, and so on), there was no benefit of prior practice.

The Pashler and Baylis (1991a) study illustrates the major role played by response selection processes in skilled performance of even simple tasks. The contribution of such processes is much greater in more complex tasks. Understanding human behavior in both simple and complex tasks, therefore, requires an understanding of response selection processes. To facilitate this understanding, we review many of the basic phenomena associated with response selection. In each case, we explore the role of practice in shaping the effects under consideration in an attempt to establish this part of the foundation for skilled behavior.

Response Selection Phenomena

Speed and accuracy of performance are influenced by numerous variables affecting response selection: the duration of the intervals between different events in a task trial, the number of stimulus and response alternatives, the availability of advance information regarding the identity of the forthcoming stimulus, and the assignment of stimuli to responses. The effects produced by these manipulations are quite robust and are

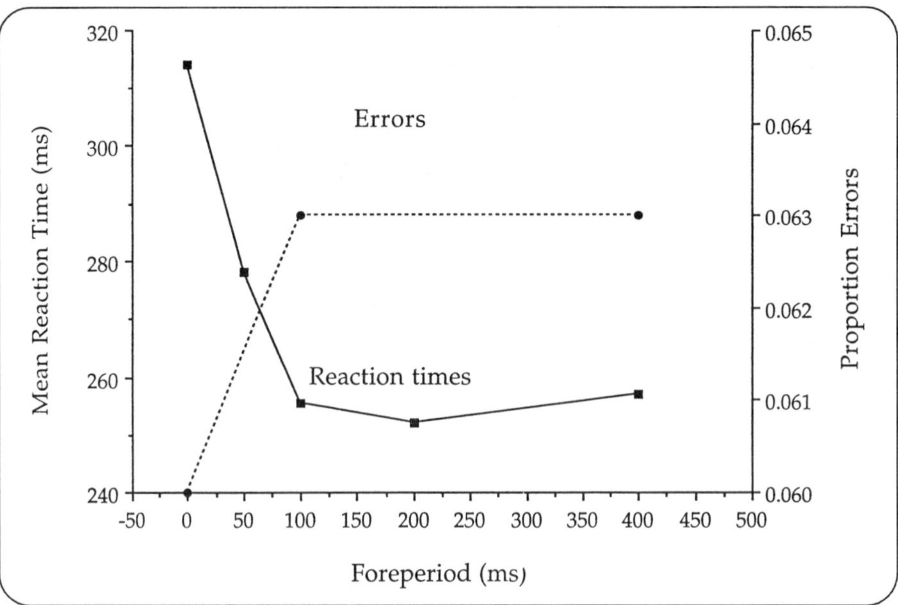

Figure 3.1. Changes in proportion of errors and reaction time as a function of foreperiod.
SOURCE: Based on data from Posner, Klein, Summers, and Buggie (1973).

particularly informative about the relative times at which different aspects of information processing occur.

Foreperiod Effects

One of the factors affecting reaction time to a stimulus is uncertainty about the time at which the stimulus event will occur. When successive trials in an experimental session are separated by intervals of several seconds, reaction times are faster if a warning signal precedes the onset of the stimulus than if the stimulus is presented without warning (e.g., Bertelson, 1967). As shown in Figure 3.1 by the solid line, choice-reaction times decrease as the warning interval, or foreperiod, increases from 0 ms (simultaneous onset) to 150-250 ms and remain relatively fast for intervals of up to about 500 ms. As the foreperiod increases beyond that point, reaction times return to the unprepared level.

It is generally thought that this U-shaped foreperiod function reflects the person's level of alertness at the time the target stimulus occurs (e.g.,

Posner, 1978). The initial decrease in reaction time presumably reflects the time required to develop a high state of alertness. The increase in reaction time that is seen at long intervals reflects a decrease of alertness over the foreperiod due to limits in the ability to maintain an alert state. Increased alertness at optimal foreperiods could possibly have its effect on the efficiency of information processing. If increased efficiency is the operative factor in faster performance, accuracy in the task should be unimpaired. However, in many cases, although not all, the foreperiod function for errors is the inverse of that for reaction times (Bernstein, Chu, Briggs, & Schurman, 1973; Bertelson, 1967; Posner, Klein, Summers, & Buggie, 1973). That is, error rates first increase and then decrease as the foreperiod increases (see Figure 3.1, dotted line).

This inverse relation between reaction times and errors is indicative of a speed-accuracy trade-off (see Chapter 1) and suggests that the efficiency with which the information provided by the stimulus is processed is not being affected, whereas the readiness to act on that information is. It is much as if a response is made on the basis of a less complete analysis of the stimulus when a person is in a state of high alertness than when she or he is not. When arousal is low, identification processes analyze the stimulus for a longer period of time before response-selection processes commence, enabling response selection to be based on better information and leading to slower but more accurate responses.

There has been relatively little investigation of how foreperiod effects are affected by practice, but practice has sometimes been manipulated along with other factors of interest. For example, Sanders (1975) included practice as one of several variables in a study of the effect of foreperiod duration on responses to auditory and visual stimuli. Simple reactions, for which a single response was made to all stimulus events, and go/no-go reactions, for which a single response was made to some stimulus events and no response was executed when one of a different subset of stimuli was presented, were examined. Reaction times decreased across four sessions of practice for both simple and go/no-go tasks, but the amount of practice did not interact with foreperiod duration or with any other variable. The lack of interaction between practice and foreperiod indicates that the foreperiod effect neither increased nor decreased as skill in the task developed. Although Sanders did not examine more typical choice reactions, one implication of his study is that foreperiod effects in general are not reduced by practice. This implication stands in contrast to findings discussed later in this chapter which show that, with practice, people learn to locate the most optimal speed-accuracy trade-off criterion. It is consistent, however, with attribution of the foreperiod function primarily to the level of alertness and preparedness to respond rather than to changes in the strategic control of the speed-accuracy criterion.

Set-Size Effects

Another factor presumed to affect response selection that has robust effects on performance in choice-reaction tasks is the number of alternative stimuli and responses. As a general rule, the larger the set of stimulus-response alternatives, the slower the reaction times. A theoretical foundation for set-size effects is provided by **information theory** (Shannon & Weaver, 1949), which gained wide acceptance in engineering applications in the 1940s and began to be applied by psychologists in the 1950s (Quastler, 1955).

Uncertainty and Reaction Time

Information theory defines the information value of a stimulus event as the reduction of uncertainty conveyed by that event, where uncertainty is a function of the stimulus probability. For example, if you know that it is raining outside and someone tells you that it is cloudy, your uncertainty about the cloud cover has not been reduced and no information has been conveyed because clouds are virtually always present when it is raining. In the case of a laboratory task with four equally likely stimulus events assigned to four responses, the probability of any one stimulus occurring on a trial is 1 in 4. For this case of equally likely stimulus alternatives, the information value of the stimuli (H_S) is given by the formula $H_S = \log_2(N)$, where N is the number of stimulus alternatives. This measurement is in bits, a dimensionless unit which gets its name from *bi*nary digi*ts*. More generally, the relation between stimulus probability and information value is

$$H_S = \sum_{i=1}^{N} -p_i \log_2 p_i \, ,$$

where H_S is the average amount of information conveyed by a stimulus from the set and p_i is the probability of occurrence of the ith stimulus. The value of the stimulus information for the four-choice task described above thus is two bits. The information contained in the response set (H_R) is defined analogously. It is sometimes useful to calculate the quantity of *information transmitted*, H_T, which is based on the stimulus information, the response information, and the joint information (H_{SR})—a measure of the consistency with which the responses are made to the stimuli. Specifically,

$$H_T = H_S + H_R - H_{SR} ,$$

where

$$H_{SR} = \sum_{i=1}^{N} \sum_{j=1}^{N} -p_{ij} \log_2 p_{ij} ,$$

with p_{ij} the probability of the *i*th stimulus paired with the jth response. Essentially, the amount of information transmitted reflects the extent to which the information available in the stimulus set is preserved in the response set.

In 1952, Hick published an influential article in which he applied information theory to the description of set-size effects. Hick noticed that data published by Merkel in 1885 (summarized in Woodworth, 1938, pp. 332-333) showed a regular, logarithmic relation between the number of stimulus-response alternatives and reaction time. In two additional experiments, he established that reaction time was a logarithmic function of the number of stimulus alternatives and suggested that it is the information extracted from the stimulus to select the response that determines reaction time. At about the same time, Hyman (1953) made the similar observation that information theory could be applied to choice-reaction tasks. In his experimental work, he found that reaction time could be expressed as a linear function of information transmitted. This function also held when the information value of the stimulus set was varied by altering the probability of a given stimulus or introducing sequential dependencies among stimuli.

The relation between reaction time and information has come to be known as the **Hick-Hyman law** and is written as

$$\mathrm{RT} = a + bH_T ,$$

where RT is reaction time, H_T is information transmitted as defined above, *a* is a constant reflecting base processing time, and *b* is a constant, the slope

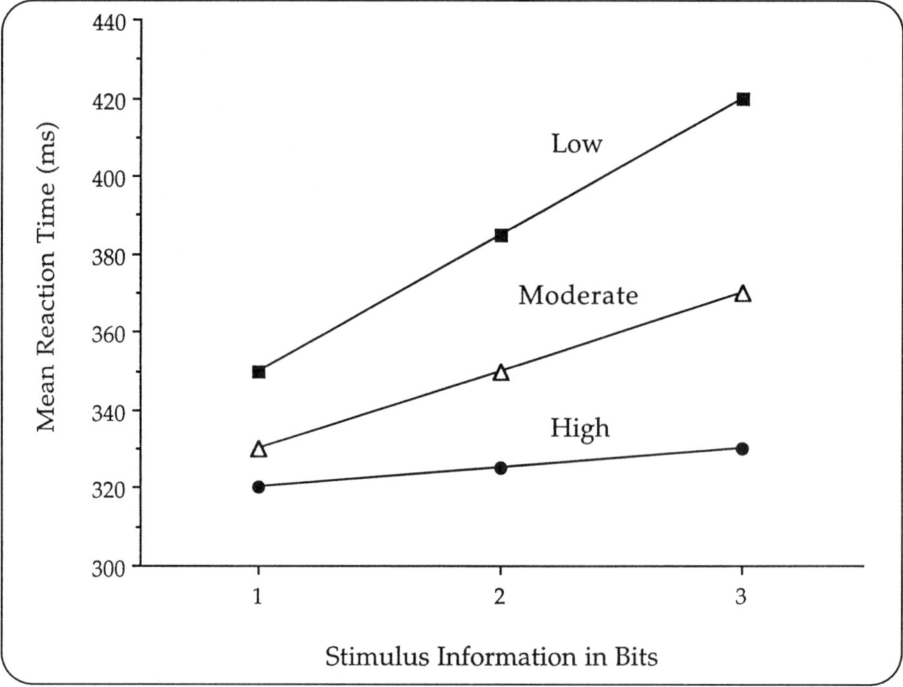

Figure 3.2. Changes in the relationship between stimulus information ($\log_2$ of the number of stimulus alternatives) and performance of a hypothetical reaction-time task at low, moderate, and high levels of practice.

of the linear function, which reflects the amount that reaction time increases as information increases. This lawful relation holds across a range of situations, with the value of b depending on such things as the specific stimulus and response sets and the amount of practice (see Figure 3.2).

The Hick-Hyman law describes the relation between uncertainty and reaction time, but it does not provide an explanation for this relation. However, Hick did outline a simple processing model consistent with the empirical observation that reaction time increases a constant amount with each doubling of the number of stimulus-response alternatives. In this model, the task is represented as a decision tree in which each branch is a binary decision. As an example, consider the case for which the stimulus set is a row of four lights and each light is assigned to a unique response. One way to characterize response selection is to suppose that when a stimulus is presented, an initial decision is made as to whether the stimulus is one of the two leftmost or two rightmost elements. Having made this choice between two alternatives (left vs. right side of the display), the person next decides which of the two possible stimuli occurred. Thus a four-alternative task requires two binary decisions. Hick's binary decision model is appealing both because it is simple and because the binary decision process fits well within the information theory framework. Despite its initial appeal, the model did not receive wide support from subsequent research. For example, when a precue that designates the locations either to the left or right of center is used, thus reducing the set of possible stimuli in a centered visual display of six stimulus locations by half, the time by which the precue must precede the display for a reaction time benefit to occur is much longer than the estimated time to make one binary decision (Leonard, 1958).

Practice and Set-Size Effects

Practice virtually eliminates set-size effects (see Figure 3.2). This phenomenon was demonstrated some time ago by Mowbray and Rhoades (1959), who had one individual practice two-choice and four-choice reactions to stimulus lights presented in two or four locations, respectively, for 1,500 trials and 3,000 trials, respectively. Thus the number of occurrences of the particular stimulus-response pairs was equated, but the total amount of practice for the four-choice task was twice that for the two-choice task. Although the measured reaction times were slower initially for the four-choice task than for the two-choice task, no difference between the tasks was apparent by the end of the experiment.

Seibel (1963) conducted an even more extensive investigation of the influence of practice on set-size effects. He and two other people performed a task in which there were 1,023 alternatives for an extended period of time. This great number of alternatives was obtained by assigning 10 lights directly to 10 different keys and using all possible combinations of the 10 lights as stimuli. For example, if the first, third, and fifth lights were illuminated, the corresponding keys should be pressed. Performance at this task continuously improved with practice, following a power function, and after more than 75,000 trials had been performed, reaction times were less than 25 ms slower in the 1,023 alternatives task than for a 31 alternatives task. It is remarkable that reaction times in a task with approximately 10 bits of stimulus information can become almost as fast as in a task with approximately 5 bits of stimulus information. The virtual disappearance of set-size effects, which are localized primarily at the response selection stage, is one of the most convincing pieces of evidence that practice has its influence in large part on response selection processes.

Precuing Effects

One natural question that emerges from the finding that reaction time is an increasing function of the number of alternatives is to what extent advance information can be used to reduce reaction time. For example, in a four-choice task with a row of lights as stimuli, advance information provided by a **precue stimulus** might indicate that only either the two leftmost or the two rightmost stimulus-response alternatives were possible on a given trial. This advance information essentially reduces the four-choice task to a two-choice task and, if used, should reduce reaction time accordingly. This is what Leonard (1958) found to be the case for the six-choice task he had used to evaluate Hick's binary decision model, if the precue preceded the stimulus by a sufficient amount of time.

Differential Precuing Benefits

The precues used by Leonard always cued either the left or right subset of stimulus-response alternatives. However, it is possible to cue any subset of these alternatives, and it might be expected that some precues would be better than others. For example, in a four-choice task, three types of precues can be used to cue pairs of stimulus-response alternatives (see Table 3.1 for examples of each type). Miller (1982) explored the relative benefits for these three types of precues in a task for which a row of four stimuli was assigned to a row of four response keys and the index and middle fingers of each hand were used for responding. On a given trial, a warning row designating the four locations was displayed. Then, 500 ms after the onset of the warning row, a precue row was displayed immediately below it. This row contained stimuli in two or four locations, depending on the trial type (see Table 3.1). After a variable amount of time, the target stimulus occurred in one of the locations indicated by the precue. Consistent with Leonard's (1958) findings, Miller (1982) found a benefit on performance when either the two leftmost or two rightmost locations were precued. This benefit increased as the precuing interval increased up to 500 ms. In contrast, little or no precuing benefit relative to the uncued condition was apparent when either the two inner or two outer locations or either pair of alternate locations was precued.

Table 3.1 Stimulus Displays for Each Precue Condition in the Spatial-Precuing Task When the Target Indicates the Leftmost Response

Condition and Stimulus	*Locations*			
	Left Outer	*Left Inner*	*Right Inner*	*Right Outer*
Uncued				
Warning	+	+	+	+
Precue	+	+	+	+
Target	+			
Left-right				
Warning	+	+	+	+
Precue	+	+		
Target	+			
Inner-outer				
Warning	+	+	+	+
Precue	+			+
Target	+			
Alternate				
Warning	+	+	+	+
Precue	+		+	
Target	+			

Motoric or Response Selection Basis?

Miller interpreted this pattern of differential precuing benefits as indicating that two responses could be prepared in advance only when they were on the same hand and that if the precue specified locations that corresponded to one finger from each hand no benefit could arise. Miller's explanation thus attributed the pattern of differential precuing benefits to motoric, response preparation processes rather than to more central response selection processes. An alternative account in terms of response selection processes is that the differential benefits reflect the time required to translate and use the information provided by the respective precues. In other words, it may be that the information conveyed by the precues associated with the left-right spatial distinction is more accessible to response selection processes than that conveyed by the other precue types.

To distinguish between the response preparation and response selection accounts, Reeve and Proctor (1984) used Miller's (1982) procedure but extended the precuing intervals up to a maximum of 3 s to allow additional

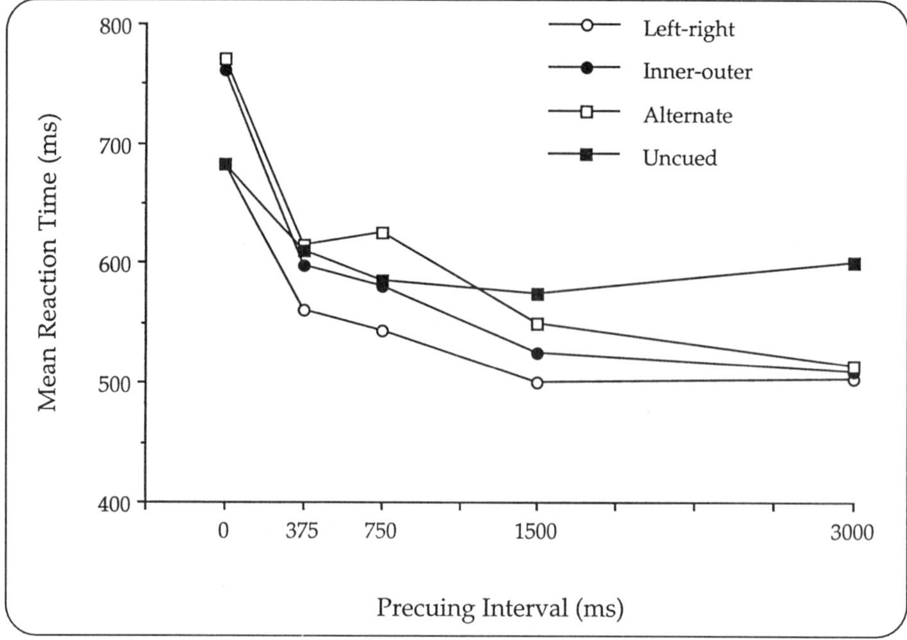

Figure 3.3. Mean reaction times for the respective precuing conditions as a function of precuing interval.
SOURCE: From Reeve and Proctor (1984).

time to process the precue information. As in Miller's experiment, only precues that designated the two left or two right locations benefited performance at short intervals. However, at longer intervals, benefits emerged for the other pairs of precued locations (see Figure 3.3). For precuing intervals of 3 s, the various types of precues showed benefits of approximately equal magnitudes. Thus all pairs of responses, including those for which each precued response is on a different hand, can be selected and prepared if sufficient time is allowed.

More direct evidence against a motoric account of the advantage for precuing the left or right locations was obtained in experiments by Reeve and Proctor (1984) and Proctor and Reeve (1986, 1988) in which different hand placements were used. In addition to the normal placement of the two hands adjacent to one another, an overlapped placement was used in which one hand was placed on top of the other so that the index and middle fingers from the two hands were alternated (i.e., the left-to-right ordering of fingers was right index, left middle, right middle, and left index). If responses on the same hand can be prepared more easily than those on different hands, as suggested by the response preparation account, it is the alternate location precues that should benefit performance the most with this overlapped placement. Contrary to this prediction, it was found that the left-right precues afforded the most benefit. Thus a pair of finger responses designated by a precue can be selected faster when based on the left-right spatial distinction of the display and response arrangements than when not so based, regardless of whether the fingers come from the same hand or different hands. This dependence of response selection efficiency on stimulus and response locations, which is found in many situations, is often attributed to **spatial coding** of the stimulus and response set features.

Practice and Precuing Benefits

The advantage for the left-right over the other precues in the four-choice task is eliminated with practice. In fact, Proctor and Reeve (1988) showed that fewer than 1,000 trials of practice were needed to equalize the benefits of the different precue types. Although precuing the two leftmost or two rightmost responses produced more benefit than precuing any other pair of responses in the first of three 310 trials sessions of their experiment, there was little difference among the various types of pairs in the third session. Thus, by the third session, translation occurred approximately as rapidly for the alternate and inner-outer location precues as for the left-right precues. As found for the learning of perceptual procedures (see Chapter 2), the changes that occurred with practice for the respective precue conditions were relatively durable in that they were shown in another study to be retained for at least one week (Proctor, Reeve, Weeks, Dornier, & Van Zandt, 1991). Thus, with only a relatively small amount of practice, the nature of the processes involved in selecting subsets of responses is altered in such a way that it is no longer dependent on the left-right spatial feature of the arrangements.

Stimulus-Response Compatibility Effects

Even when very simple tasks are performed, such as Leonard's (1958) task of pressing a key in response to a light in a certain location, reaction time and accuracy are almost always influenced by both the relation between the specific stimulus and response sets that are used and the way in which the members of the stimulus set are assigned to the responses.

When the accuracy and speed of performance in a choice-reaction task depend on these factors, **stimulus-response compatibility** effects are said to occur.

Set-Level and Element-Level Relations

As indicated above, there are two types of relations between stimuli and responses that affect performance (Kornblum, Hasbroucq, & Osman, 1990). First, some stimulus sets have a natural correspondence with certain response sets. For example, visually displayed digits and spoken digit names naturally correspond by virtue of our extended experience with the reading response to digits. This correspondence is called **set-level compatibility** and, when it is intact, leads to relatively fast response selection. Alluisi and Muller (1958) demonstrated this by having people respond to Arabic numerals or other symbolic visual codes with either vocal number-naming responses or keypress responses. For the numeral stimuli, the naming responses were considerably faster than the keypress responses. The advantage for naming over keypress responses was much less for the other stimulus sets, suggesting that it was the nature of the relation between the set of numerals and the set of number-naming responses that was important.

The second type of relation affecting reaction time and accuracy is at the element level, or the level of individual stimulus-response pairs within the two sets. Given that there is some degree of correspondence or similarity between the stimulus and response sets (i.e., there is set-level compatibility), an additional effect of the mapping of particular stimuli to particular responses is found (i.e., there is an **element-level compatibility** effect, such that some pairings of stimuli and responses will produce faster and more accurate responses than others). For example, if the task is to say a digit name in response to a visually presented digit, the reaction time to name the digit (e.g., "nine" in response to the digit 9) will be faster than the time to say an arbitrarily assigned digit name (e.g., "five" in response to the digit 9).

Stimulus-response compatibility can be manipulated either by selecting particular stimulus and response sets or by varying the assignments of individual stimuli to responses within the chosen sets. A wide range of stimulus and response sets have been studied, but compatibility effects have been investigated most extensively using stimulus and response sets for which spatial location is the distinguishing feature of the elements.

Fitts and Seeger (1953) established the existence of set-level compatibility effects with spatial stimulus and response sets, finding that responses were faster and more accurate when eight spatial location stimuli were arranged in a way that corresponded with the spatial layout of an eight-response panel than when they were not. Additionally, Fitts and Seeger found some evidence suggesting that this spatial compatibility effect persists with practice.

Fitts and Deininger (1954) went on to explore element-level compatibility effects. In their study, a circular response panel with eight buttons was used to respond to several stimulus sets, including a circular display of eight lights. Responding was much faster when each light location in the display was assigned to the button at the corresponding location on the response panel than when random pairings of lights to buttons were used. Many subsequent researchers have used simpler versions of the spatial compatibility task in which just two or four stimuli and responses are used because it is easier to isolate the critical factors influencing performance and thus to determine the nature of the underlying processing.

Coding of Stimuli and Responses

In perhaps the most basic version of the two-choice task, a stimulus can appear in either a right or left display location and a response is made by pressing a right response key with the right hand or a left response key with the left hand. The typical finding is that responding is faster when the left response is assigned to the left stimulus and the right response to the right stimulus than when the assignment is reversed. One possible explanation for this effect lies in the neuroanatomy of the perceptual-motor system. Namely, because a stimulus in the left visual field is transmitted to the right hemisphere, which in turn controls the left hand, and vice versa for a stimulus in the right visual field, responding could be facilitated for left-hand responses to left stimuli and right-hand responses to right stimuli. However, this account was ruled out by studies in which people performed with their hands crossed, so that the right hand operated the left key and the left hand the right key (e.g., Anzola, Bertoloni, Buchtel, & Rizzolatti, 1977). As with the spatial precuing effect described earlier, this compatibility effect was shown to be primarily a function of the relations between stimulus and response locations: Responses were still found to be faster when the left and right stimuli were assigned directly to the left and right response locations, relative to the reverse assignment, even though the responses to the stimuli were being made with the noncorresponding hands for this "compatible" assignment and with the corresponding hands for the "incompatible" assignment.

The occurrence of spatial compatibility effects, even when the left hand operates the right response key and the right hand operates the left response key, points to the often overriding importance of the spatial locations of the stimuli relative to the responses and implies that response selection is mediated by spatial representations (i.e., spatial coding). Further evidence that mediation between stimulus and response sets is independent from anatomical factors is that the two stimuli or two responses need not be located on opposite sides of the body midline for spatial compatibility effects to occur (Umiltà & Nicoletti, 1990). In other words, it is the relative locations of elements within the respective sets rather than their absolute locations that are crucial in most cases. Coding accounts of spatial compatibility effects propose that a stimulus code is compared to a response code and that translation is faster when the relative spatial codes correspond than when they do not (e.g., Wallace, 1971).

More generally, the **salient features coding principle** (Proctor & Reeve, 1985, 1991) states that the relative compatibilities of alternative assignments for any stimulus-response sets depend on the efficiency of translation between stimulus and response representations. Typically, the stimulus and response sets used in compatibility experiments are chosen to have salient structural features, thus allowing set-level compatibility effects to occur. When the mapping of stimuli to responses is such that the salient features of the stimulus set are in correspondence with those of the response set, response selection is facilitated relative to when the features of the two sets do not correspond. This is tantamount to saying that when there is a set-level match between any stimulus and response sets, spatial or nonspatial, element-level manipulations can produce compatibility effects (Hasbroucq, Guiard, & Ottomani, 1990; Kornblum et al., 1990).

The facilitative effect of structural correspondence has been illustrated in several studies. Again, some of the clearest demonstrations of the general phenomenon come from studies using relatively simple stimulus and response sets. In our earlier discussion of the spatial precuing task, we noted that the left-right distinction is a salient feature of a horizontally aligned response set. Miller (1982) and Proctor and Reeve (1985) showed that predictable compatibility effects occur with this response set even when the stimulus set is not spatial. Proctor and Reeve used stimuli composed of two dimensions—the letters *O* and *Z* in large and small sizes (i.e., *O, o, Z,* and *z*)—for which letter identity is a salient feature. A compatibility effect was obtained when these stimuli were assigned to the four response keys, both when the responses were made by the index and middle fingers of adjacently placed hands or by a single hand. The nature of this effect is that responses are faster for "*OozZ*-type" assignments in which the salient letter-identity feature of the stimulus set is mapped onto the salient left-right feature of the response set (e.g., a left-to-right assignment of *O, o, z,* and *Z*) than for "*OzoZ*-type" assignments in which it is not (e.g., a left-to-right assignment of *O, z, o,* and *Z*).

Just what will be salient in any given condition depends on both the stimulus and response sets and can be a function of prior experience or the current task context. For example, Proctor and Reeve (1985) found that the overlapped hand placement (described earlier), for which the index and middle fingers from the two hands are alternated, produced reaction times with the *OzoZ*-type of assignment that were as fast as with the *OozZ*-type assignment. This result can be interpreted in terms of the features that are made salient by the overlapped placement. When the hands are overlapped, the distinction between the pairs of alternate locations is made more salient because the fingers from one hand must first be placed on one pair of alternate locations and then the fingers from the other hand placed on the remaining two locations, thus providing a feature in addition to the left-right spatial feature by which the response set can be coded. That is, in this case, the salient letter-identity feature of both the *OozZ*-type and *OzoZ*-type stimulus assignments corresponds to a salient feature of the response set (left-right and alternate locations, respectively).

The relative salience of features also can be influenced by training. Proctor et al. (1991) gave practice in the spatial precuing task using the adjacent hand placement but presented only the subset of cues that signaled alternate locations in an attempt to make those pairs of locations more salient. After this training, the symbolic compatibility task, with either an *OozZ*-type or *OzoZ*-type assignment and with the hands placed adjacent to each other, was introduced. Even though the hands were placed in the adjacent position, the usual advantage for the *OozZ*-type assignment over the *OzoZ*-type assignment, for which letter identity coincides with the alternate response locations, was not eliminated. Because people who practiced with the complete set of precues showed the typical advantage for the *OozZ*-type assignment, it can be concluded that the practice with identifying and preparing responses to alternate locations contributed a new salient feature to the response set.

The Use of Rules in Coding

The fact that correspondence between the salient structural features of the stimulus and response sets is a factor in compatibility effects suggests that people rely on relationships between the features of the two sets. Several authors have proposed that when rules can be formulated to relate stimuli to responses, responding will be faster than otherwise. An early study illustrating just this point was conducted by Morin and Grant (1955), who varied the correlation between stimulus and response locations in the assignments of linear arrays of 10 stimulus locations to 10 response locations. Responses were fastest when there was a perfect positive correlation between stimulus and response locations (i.e., the response to each stimulus location was at the corresponding location in the response array) and slowest when stimuli were randomly assigned to responses such that there was little or no correlation between the stimulus locations and their assigned responses. A perfect negative correlation (i.e., the response to each stimulus location was at the same relative location on the opposite side of the response array) resulted in response times that were somewhat slower than those obtained with a perfect positive correlation but considerably faster than those obtained with either no correlation or an intermediate positive correlation. Thus, even though fewer of the stimuli were assigned to their spatial counterparts in the response set for the mappings with high negative correlations than in the mappings with little correlation, the presence of a consistent rule (i.e., "select the response opposite to the stimulus") allowed faster reaction times.

Rosenbloom and Newell (1987) developed a production system model of stimulus-response compatibility effects that captures the role that rules may play in selecting responses to stimuli. In their model, the task is described in terms of a hierarchy of goals and subgoals that must be met for responses to be executed. If the mapping for a spatial compatibility task is direct, there is only one rule: Press the corresponding key, and the only subgoal required is for the determination of the location of the stimulus light. If the mapping with a perfect negative correlation between stimuli and responses is used, an additional subgoal must be set to determine the location opposite to the stimulus location. Both of these cases are simpler than the case of a mixture of direct and indirect assignments because in the latter case one must first determine the appropriate mapping class for a particular stimulus. Thus the complexity of the task hierarchy is a function of the entire task environment, and performance is faster in those tasks for which the hierarchies have fewer branches to subgoals. The more branches leading to further subgoals, the less rulelike (and slower) is behavior.

The effects of rule complexity on performance can be illustrated with a task used by Duncan (1977) in which one of four keys was to be pressed in response to one of four stimulus lights. Three conditions were compared. The first, the *corresponding* condition, required that the key corresponding in location to the light be pressed. In the *opposite* condition, the key opposite in location to the stimulus light was to be pressed. In the *mixed* condition, either a corresponding or opposite key was pressed, depending on which stimulus appeared. Thus the mixed condition contained both corresponding and opposite trial types. Because of the need to compute the opposite key location, opposite trials were slower than corresponding ones. Because of the need to test stimulus position to determine which rule to use, the mixed condition had slower response times than the single-rule conditions. Moreover, these factors had additive effects on reaction time.

Sample algorithms reflecting the relative complexity of the three conditions in Duncan's (1977) study are shown in Figure 3.4. These algorithms demonstrate that a rule-based model can easily capture the primary findings of Duncan's study. However, it is important to note that the algorithms in Figure 3.4 are not the only possible ones for this task. Algorithm development, even when constrained by what is known about human information processing capabilities and guided by empirical results, is based to some extent on the researcher's assumptions and intuitions. In short, the algorithms usually represent just a reasoned guess about plausible underlying task structure. The algorithmic analysis gains credibility when it is shown, as Rosenbloom and Newell (1987) have, that performance in other tasks can be predicted from the algorithmic analysis of a similar task using the same estimates of the basic information processing (perceptual, cognitive, and motor) times.

Practice and Stimulus-Response Compatibility

Given that practice virtually eliminates set-size effects and the pattern of differential precuing benefits, it might be expected that stimulus-response compatibility effects would also be eliminated by practice. Yet compatibility effects seem surprisingly resistant to change. In their initial investigation of stimulus-response compatibility, Fitts and Seeger (1953) tested 5 people for 32 sessions each. In each session, 16 trials were performed with each of three variations of an eight-choice task, each of which

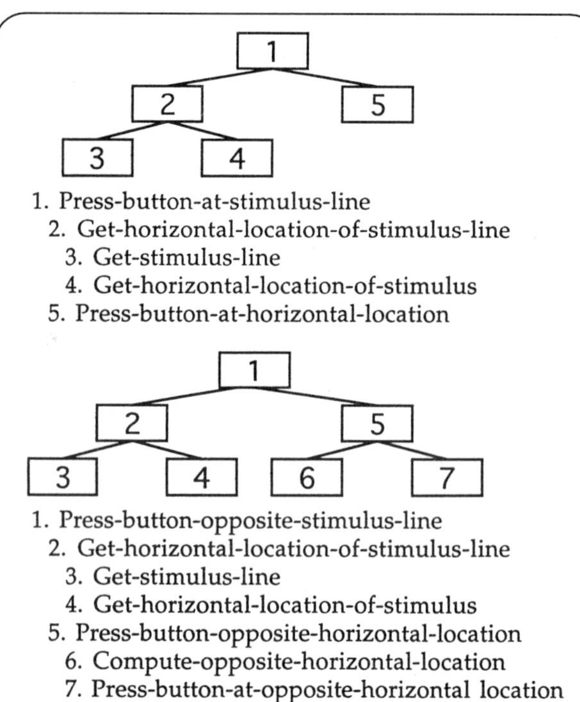

Figure 3.4. Sample algorithms reflecting the complexity of the three conditions, the corresponding, opposite, and mixed conditions, respectively, examined by Duncan (1977). "S" is "success" and "F" is "failure" to meet condition.
SOURCE: Adapted from Laird, Rosenbloom, and Newell (1986).

used different display configurations but the same response configuration. The difference in reaction time for the most compatible and least compatible situations decreased sharply from the first session to the second but only slightly thereafter. From approximately the 10th session onward, a 100-ms difference between conditions existed that showed no signs of abating.

Dutta and Proctor (1992) examined the influence of practice on compatibility effects in three tasks: the two-choice spatial task described previously, a two-choice spatial task in which stimuli that appeared above or below a fixation point (above-below stimuli) were assigned to left and

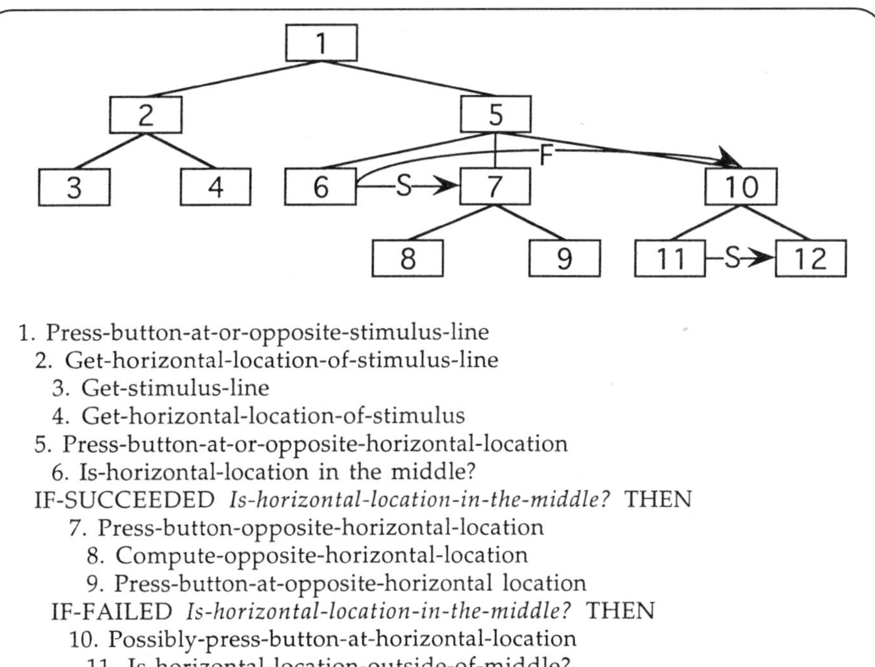

Figure 3.4. (continued)

right responses, and the four-choice task in which the two-dimensional symbolic stimulus set (*O, o, z, Z*) is assigned to four responses. To optimize the benefits of practice by maintaining consistent mappings, Dutta and Proctor had each individual practice in only a single condition rather than in each of several conditions, as in Fitts and Seeger's (1953) study. In the first session, typical compatibility effects were obtained, averaging 40 ms for the above-below stimuli assigned to left and right responses and 80 ms for the other two tasks. By the eighth session, after about 2,400 trials of practice, reaction times averaged about 40 ms faster for compatible assignments than for incompatible assignments for all three tasks, with no sign that the effects were diminishing further.

The finding that stimulus-response compatibility effects are not eliminated with practice suggests that there are limits on how efficient response selection processes can become. An initial incompatibility of assignment restricts the level of performance that can ultimately be attained. This persistence of compatibility effects might reflect information processing constraints that have evolved as a consequence of the spatial relations within the environment with which we interact. Alternatively, the persistence could be due to the fact that any task-specific procedures acquired from practice must be derived from the task representations on which initial performance is based. According to this interpretation, if the initial representations do not allow efficient translation, there are limits in the extent to which performance can improve.

Repetition Effects

Typically, when a stimulus in a choice-reaction task is repeated on consecutive trials, response time to the second presentation is faster than if a different stimulus is presented (Kornblum, 1973). Lesser benefits are also often obtained when the stimulus on a trial is the same as one that occurred two or three trials back (e.g., Rabbitt & Vyas, 1979). Like the other effects discussed in this chapter, such **repetition effects** are thought to arise primarily from influences on the processes of response selection. Response selection is implicated because the effect of repetition interacts with both set size (Kornblum, 1975) and stimulus-response compatibility (Bertelson, 1963; Kornblum, 1969), two variables affecting response selection. Specifically, when there is a repetition trial, set size and compatibility effects are reduced. According to the additive-factors logic (described in Chapter 1), if repetition had its effect on a stage other than response selection, such interactions would not be found.

The fact that the effects of stimulus-response compatibility and set size are reduced on repetition trials suggests that response selection is somehow facilitated on those trials, and researchers have been interested in determining the underlying reason for this facilitation in response selection. To evaluate this issue, it is important to know what aspect of a trial must be repeated for the repetition effect to occur. When each stimulus is assigned to a unique response, it is not possible to determine whether the repetition of the stimulus or the repetition of the response is the locus of the facilitation. This is because both the stimulus and response are repeated on a repetition trial and not repeated on a nonrepetition trial. However, by assigning more than one stimulus to each response, it is possible to repeat the response without repeating the stimulus. With this information reduction procedure, comparison can then be made between the trials with stimulus repetition and those with only a response repetition, to isolate the contribution of stimulus and response factors.

Pashler and Baylis (1991b) used the information reduction procedure in this way to evaluate the nature of repetition effects. In their experiments, letters, numerals, and nonalphanumeric characters were mapped to left, middle, and right keypress responses in either a categorizable or a noncategorizable manner. Categorizable mappings were those in which one and only one type of stimulus was assigned to each response, as in the study by Pashler and Baylis (1991a) described earlier in this chapter; for the noncategorizable mappings, one letter and one number were assigned to each of the responses. In most of Pashler and Baylis's (1991b) experiments, the repetition effect was substantially greater when the stimulus was repeated than when only the response was repeated. Based on this finding, Pashler and Baylis concluded that stimulus repetition enables the use of a transient pathway from a specific stimulus to its designated response. This pathway acts as a shortcut by which the normal response selection process is bypassed.

Several results are consistent with this "shortcut" interpretation. For example, the benefits of repetition are greater the larger the stimulus set size, regardless of whether each stimulus is assigned to a unique response or several stimuli are assigned to each response (Kornblum, 1973; Rabbitt & Vyas, 1979). In other words, the benefit of the response selection shortcut is greater for situations in which the normal response selection route should take longer. Repetition effects are also reduced in magnitude as people become practiced at the task. For example, Rabbitt and Vyas conducted three experiments in which people made left or right keypress responses to letter stimuli when either two, four, or eight letters were assigned to each response. Repetition effects were evident in the first block of 200 trials, with the magnitude being a positive function of the stimulus set size. The repetition effects decreased in magnitude across five additional blocks of 200 trials each, suggesting that the shortcut provided by repetition becomes less useful as the time for the normal response selection process to operate decreases.

However, there also is evidence to suggest that the benefit of response repetition does not always arise from bypassing the normal response selection processes. In the experiments of Pashler and Baylis (1991b) that used a categorizable mapping of stimuli to responses, there was some evidence for a repetition effect when the stimulus was not repeated but the response was (i.e., when the stimulus was from the same category as the preceding stimulus). Campbell and Proctor (1993) confirmed that a reliable response repetition effect of this type is obtained with categorizable mappings (e.g., only letters, numerals, or nonalphanumeric characters assigned to a given response) and that it is not obtained with noncategorizable mappings (e.g., one each of letters, digits, and nonalphanumeric characters assigned to each response). Campbell and Proctor conducted additional experiments using the categorizable mappings but with two sets of responses (three left-hand and three right-hand responses) assigned to each stimulus set. That is, a given stimulus could be responded to with either the left or the right hand. The hand to be used was designated by the location of the stimulus, which alternated between left, indicating that the left hand should be used to respond, and right, indicating that the right hand should be used, of center. When the responses in each of the response sets were assigned to the stimulus categories in such a way that the two possible responses for a given stimulus shared a common feature (either the relative spatial location of the response keys or the finger used to respond), an across-hands response repetition effect was obtained.

The results obtained by Campbell and Proctor (1993) showed that repetition effects are not tied exclusively to a specific stimulus and its corresponding response. Consistent with the view that response selection is based on representations derived from salient features of the stimulus and response sets, reaction times are facilitated on repetition trials whenever the stimulus and its assigned response share categorical features with those of the previous trial. Thus repetition effects seem to arise from at least two different aspects of information processing (see Figure 3.5). When a complete stimulus-response pair is repeated, the normal response selection processes are effectively bypassed. When there is not complete repetition of the stimulus-response pair but the mapping of stimuli to responses is categorical, the selection of a response category is facilitated by repetition of the stimulus category.

The relation between repetition and practice effects has been a subject of concern in several studies from the 1960s to the 1990s, but this relation is still far from understood. One of the goals of Pashler and Baylis's (1991a, 1991b) two studies was to evaluate whether the two effects have a common basis. Because their findings suggested that repetition effects were due to repetition of the specific stimulus, whereas practice effects were primarily a function of stimulus-response categories, with only a secondary influence of the specific stimuli responded to during practice, Pashler and Baylis concluded that there was likely little relation between the processes responsible for the respective effects. However, Campbell and Proctor's (1993) demonstration that categorical relations also play a role in the repetition effect reopens the possibility that repetition and practice effects

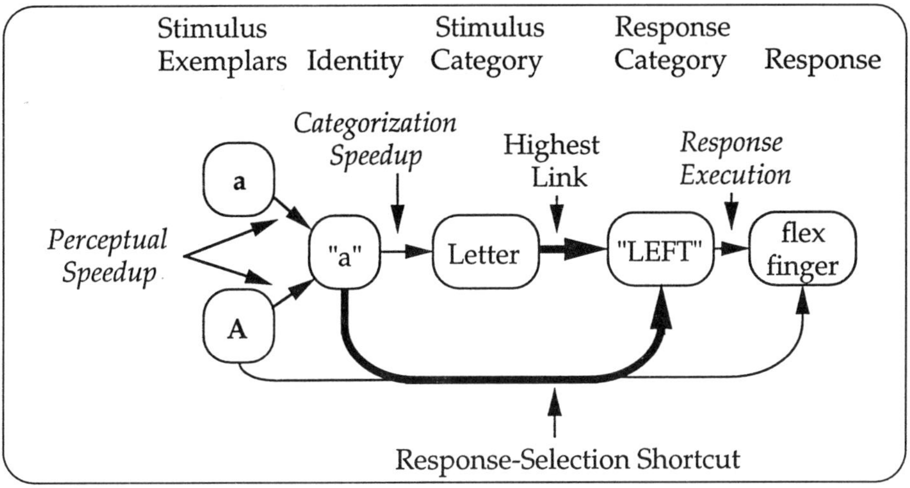

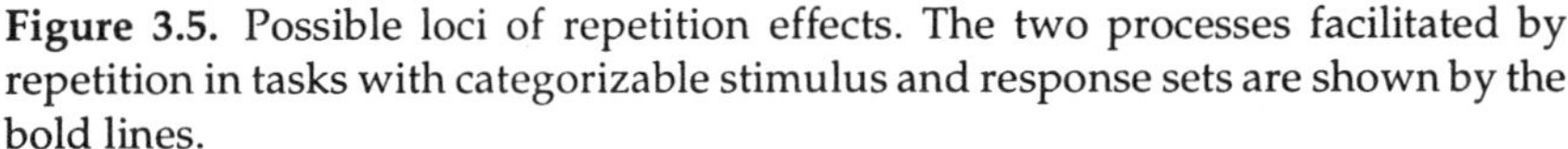

Figure 3.5. Possible loci of repetition effects. The two processes facilitated by repetition in tasks with categorizable stimulus and response sets are shown by the bold lines.

may be closely related. Perhaps the strongest evidence for a close link is that, although the major component of the repetition effect initially is that of specific stimulus repetition, with practice the repetition effect becomes largely a function of the category component (Rabbitt, 1968; Rabbitt & Vyas, 1979).

Characterizing Practice Effects

In the previous sections, we discussed how response selection plays a critical role in the initial performance of even very simple tasks. We also reviewed many studies showing practice to have profound effects on response selection processes, often reducing and sometimes eliminating initial differences in reaction times between conditions. Newell (1990) has argued that the realm of immediate behavior that is studied with choice-reaction tasks (i.e., behavior taking place within a time frame of less than 1 minute) is the appropriate one for understanding the basic architecture underlying human cognition. Thus the findings that we have reviewed in this chapter have implications that are fundamental to understanding the nature of human information processing. In the remainder of the chapter, we survey attempts to characterize the processes of change that act within the cognitive architecture as a task is practiced.

Qualitative or Quantitative Changes?

Given that response selection seems to be speeded significantly by practice, the question can be asked whether the changes are qualitative in nature or only quantitative. In other words, does practice allow the response selection stage to be effectively bypassed, as appears to be the case when a stimulus from the preceding trial is repeated and as suggested by the taxonomies that propose distinct automaticity as the final phase of skill acquisition (e.g., Fitts, 1964), or is translation just getting faster? Evidence for this latter view was obtained by Gopher, Karis, and Koenig (1985) in a study that examined the use of chord keyboards for typing. In a chord keyboard, letters are assigned to combinations of keys so that a separate key is not needed for each letter. With the keyboard used by Gopher et al., each hand could independently classify the entire alphabet through pressing combinations of five keys.

Two principles for coding the letters of the alphabet to each of the hands were used (see Figure 3.6). For the *spatial congruence* principle, the keys assigned to a given letter were in the same relative spatial locations for each hand. For example, if a letter was assigned to the two rightmost keys for the left hand, it was also assigned to the two rightmost keys for the right hand. For the *hand symmetry* principle, letters were assigned to keys so that the same fingers would be used across hands. For example, if a letter was assigned to the two rightmost keys for the left hand so that the thumb and index fingers were used, the letter would be assigned to the two leftmost keys for the right hand so that the thumb and index fingers would again be used. In a third, *combined* condition, the keyboards were placed vertically so that spatially corresponding keys were also pressed by the same fingers from each hand.

On each trial, either one or two letters were presented. A left-hand response was to be made to a letter in a left location and a right-hand response to a letter in the right location. Responses were fastest for the combined group, for which both spatial congruence and hand symmetry obtained, intermediate for the spatial congruence group, and slowest for the hand symmetry group. Most important, the relative ordering of the groups did not change with practice. In fact, the differences between the groups actually increased. Gopher et al. interpreted these results as indicating that different coding strategies were adopted early in training and

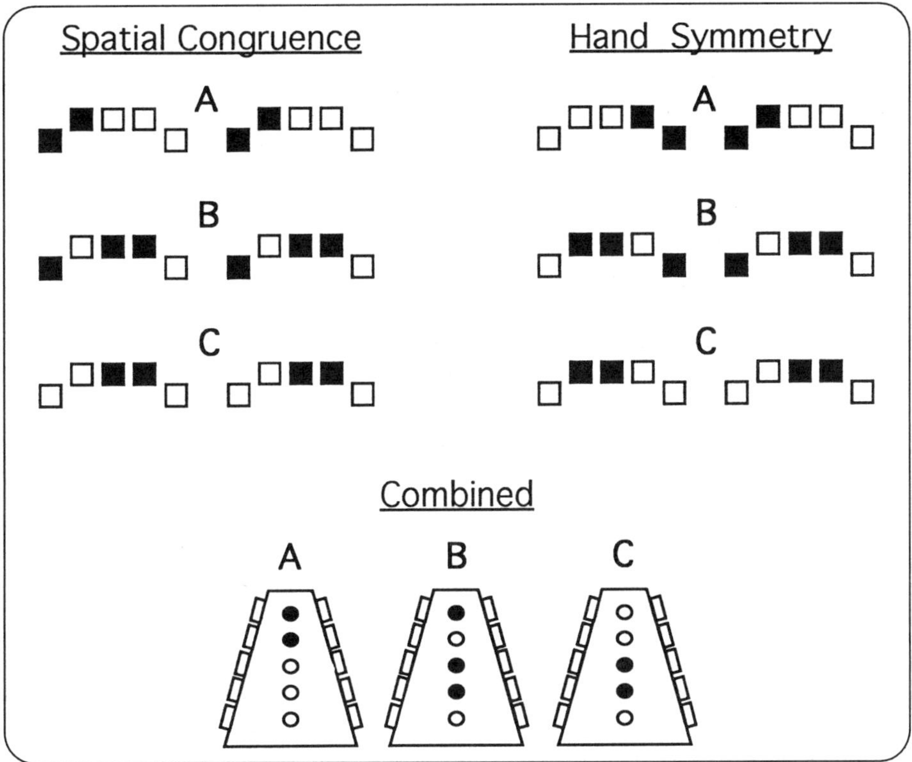

Figure 3.6. The spatial congruence, hand symmetry, and combined coding principles used by Gopher, Karis, and Koenig (1985).
SOURCE: Gopher et al. (1985). Reprinted by permission.

that these coding strategies continued to be used throughout the practice period.

Proctor and Dutta (1993) used the spatial two-choice task described earlier to test more directly whether the same translation procedures continue to be used throughout practice. After practicing for three sessions with either a spatially compatible or an incompatible mapping of stimuli to response keys using either an uncrossed or a crossed hand placement, a transfer session took place in which the hand placement, the mapping, both the hand placement and the mapping, or neither was changed. The results for the first session showed the standard spatial compatibility effect: Regardless of hand placement, responses were faster with the compatible mapping than with the incompatible mapping. Moreover, responses were slower with the crossed hand placement than with the uncrossed placement, reflecting the additional difficulty of determining the position in space of the finger that is to respond. Similar to the findings of Gopher et al. (1985) in their much more complex task, the ordering of the conditions remained the same throughout the three sessions of practice.

In the fourth session, when one fourth of the persons in each group were transferred to each of the mapping/placement conditions, positive transfer was evident for those groups in which the spatial mapping used for practice was maintained in the transfer session, even when the hand placement was changed. This and subsequent experiments demonstrated that the spatial relations between stimuli and responses are the most important for performance and that response selection seems to be based on spatial codes both early and late in practice. Pashler and Baylis's (1991a) finding, discussed near the beginning of the chapter, that virtually perfect transfer is obtained when the hand used to respond to categories of stimuli is switched—so long as the spatial mapping remains the same—underscores the importance of spatial relations even when stimuli are symbolic.

Changes in Speed/Accuracy Criterion Setting

Rabbitt (1989; Rabbitt & Vyas, 1970) has proposed that the speedup in responding as people become practiced is due at least in part to learning an optimal setting on the speed-accuracy trade-off function. Recall that speed and accuracy of responding trade off in many tasks, such that faster performance is possible with some sacrifice of accuracy—but only up to a point. Because of the S-shape of this function (see Figure 1.5), very large changes in accuracy lead to small changes in speed when performance is already quite fast and vice versa. This suggests that a point on the function exists at which it is no longer advisable to adjust accuracy to increase speed and vice versa.

According to Rabbitt, when a person begins to perform a novel choice-reaction task, the criterion that would allow fast, accurate responding (the **speed-error trade-off limit**) is not known. Thus the appropriate criterion must be determined as the task is practiced. This can be accomplished by responding progressively faster across trials until an error is made and then slowing down for the next trial. In terms of the speed-accuracy trade-off function, such changes correspond to progressively lowering the criterion for emitting a response and then abruptly raising it. By repeating this process iteratively, the speed-error trade-off limit is found. As the person learns to respond at this determined point, the variance of the reaction time distribution is reduced as is its skew (i.e., the number of extremely long reaction times is reduced). As a result of the skew being reduced, the mean reaction time is reduced as well. Thus, according to this account, the practice effect is due to learning when to select a response rather than to developing more efficient selection procedures.

If the sole benefit of practice is on the ability to locate the speed-error trade-off limit, the fastest correct responses after practice should not be any faster than the fastest correct responses early in practice. Alternatively, if processing becomes more efficient, so that the speed-error trade-off function is changed such that the limit is reduced, then the fastest correct responses late in practice should be faster than those earlier in practice. Rabbitt and Banerji (1989) evaluated these alternatives by giving people extended practice at a task that required pressing one of four keys to the stimuli *A*, *B*, *C*, and *D*. Although the primary changes were reductions in the skew and variance of the reaction time distributions, the data also indicated that the speed-error trade-off limit shifted. After practice, responses could be made faster without error than was possible early in practice. This suggests that processing became more efficient and that the benefit of practice involves more than just better tracking of the speed-error trade-off limit.

The Chunking Hypothesis

Newell and Rosenbloom (1981) developed the **chunking hypothesis** to account for power-law speedup in performance. According to this hypothesis, practice improves performance by means of the acquisition of knowledge about patterns in the task environment. Chunking is assumed to occur in a bottom-up manner. That is, smaller or simpler patterns are learned first, followed by increasingly larger patterns. It is assumed that chunks are learned at a constant rate from the relevant patterns of stimuli and responses in the task environment. Thus, because the probability of recurrence of a pattern decreases as the pattern size increases, the learning rate decreases as a function of the number of times that the task has been performed. Another assumption is that the time to process a chunk is nearly independent of its size. This means that as larger chunks replace collections of smaller chunks performance will be faster.

The chunking hypothesis has been implemented in a computer architecture, and simulations of several of the experiments discussed in this chapter have been performed. One of the experiments simulated is that of Seibel (1963) in which the 1,023-choice task was practiced extensively. To run a simulation of a task, it is first necessary to develop an algorithm for task performance. The algorithm used by Newell and Rosenbloom to

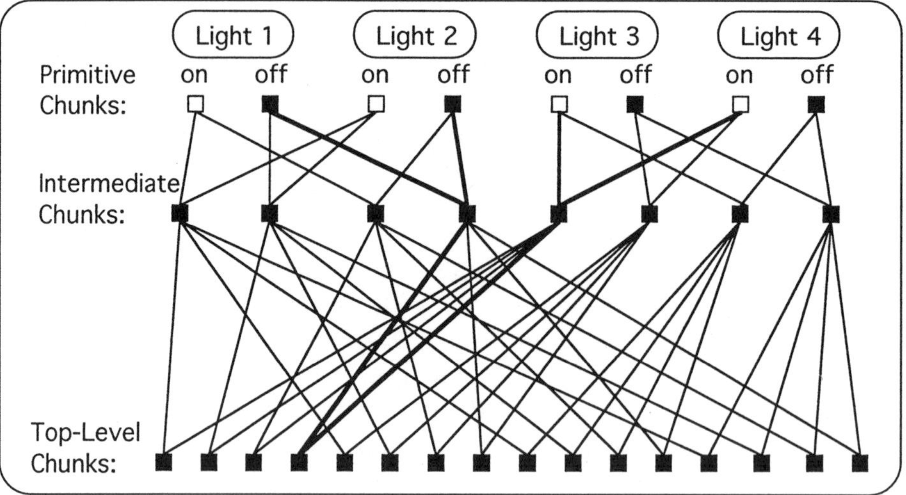

Figure 3.7. Perceptual chunks of increasing complexity in a four-light version of the Seibel (1963) task. The primitive chunks code each light as on or off. The intermediate chunks encode the state of pairs of lights, and the top-level chunks encode each possible on-off combination. The heavy lines in the figure indicate the chunks that encode the stimulus display: off off on on.

simulate the Seibel task assumed that the stimulus lights were processed in a left-to-right manner, as follows:

Focus a point to the left of the leftmost light.
While there is an *On*-light to the right of the focal point *Do*
- *Locate* the *On*-light.
- *Map* the light location into the location of the button under it.
- *Press* the button.
- *Focus* the right edge of the light.

As the task is practiced, perceptual "chunks" composed of increasingly complex patterns of lights are formed (see Figure 3.7). These chunks enable the processing of groups of lights rather than single lights, thus speeding processing.

Rosenbloom and Newell (1987) incorporated the chunking hypothesis into a model of stimulus-response compatibility. They first developed algorithms to capture the differences among the various conditions of a number of compatibility tasks. Simulations of these tasks were then performed, with the result that most aspects of the data were captured. Although the form of the practice curves was generally well characterized by the model, one prediction of the model is at odds with the data. The model predicts that any initial difference in performance times for tasks of different compatibility will be eliminated with sufficient practice. As discussed earlier, the evidence to date suggests that asymptotic levels of performance in choice-reaction tasks depend on the initial compatibility of the stimulus-response assignments.

▣ SUMMARY ▣

In this chapter, we have considered the effects of many variables on the performance of tasks for which response selection is the major component. Alertness was shown to affect the speed and accuracy of performance, such that when a warning signal is presented at an optimal interval before stimulus onset, responding is faster—but often at the cost of increased errors. Reaction time also is affected by the size of the set of possible stimulus-response alternatives, increasing as a logarithmic function of set size. The slope of this function decreases with practice, as the effect of set size becomes progressively smaller.

Response selection can be speeded by providing advance information that reduces the number of possible stimulus-response alternatives. The effectiveness of this advance information depends on the structure of the stimulus and response sets, as do stimulus-response compatibility effects. Response selection is faster when the assignment of stimuli to responses uses the structure inherent in the respective sets. Whereas practice appears to eliminate set-size effects, stimulus-response compatibility effects have been shown to persist. The effects of factors such as set size and stimulus-response compatibility are attenuated when the same stimulus or, in some cases, the same response is repeated from one trial to the next.

Most of the evidence presented in this chapter points to gradual changes in performance as a function of practice. There is little evidence that a major shift in strategy occurs in choice-reaction tasks of the type covered in the chapter. Relatively few attempts have been made to model the changes in response selection processes that occur with practice; those attempts that have been made predict gradual improvement with no plateaus or discontinuities.

Tasks and Methods

Problems of Movement Control

Perspectives on Motor Learning

Factors Influencing Motor Skill Acquisition

Summary

CHAPTER 4

Motor Skill

If you have ever been to a magic show, you have probably been amazed at the deftness by which you were fooled. Even though you felt sure that there must be some sleight of hand for the magician to produce ping-pong balls from a person's ears or the ace of hearts from an unmarked deck of cards, the smooth, integrated performance of the accomplished magician prevented you from detecting anything that would spoil the illusion of magic. The magician's tricks exemplify the integrated movements associated with perceptual-motor skill. As with other motor skills, the emphasis in magic is on the product of performance: a rapid series of movements that achieve an external goal (e.g., pull the rabbit from the hat or the bird from the air).

Another good example of a motor skill is bicycling. Riding a bicycle involves the motor system in the act of pedaling to generate power, the maintenance of balance, and steering. Any motor skill has other components, especially perceptual ones, and bicycling is no exception. Motor acts must be coordinated not only with one another but also with continually changing sensory input. Thus the cyclist must also perceive and respond to changes in the environment. Rapid adjustments in posture must be made in response to potholes and other variations in the road surface, and obstacles must be avoided. When riding a bicycle in a crowded place, such as a university campus, these adjustments require precise timing and anticipation to avoid collision with other vehicles or pedestrians. This example illustrates the major characteristics of motor skill: the linking of receptor and effector functions; precise timing of movements and anticipation of motor requirements and consequences; and graded variations in the amount, direction, and duration of responses.

Early studies of skilled behavior, such as Woodworth's (1899) experiments in which lines of specified lengths were to be drawn and Bryan and Harter's (1897) studies on the acquisition of telegraphic language, both of which were described in Chapter 1, focused primarily on the product of performance rather than changes in the underlying processes. These early studies fit well with Pear's (1927) characterization of skill as being concerned with the quantity and quality of motor output. Motor components of skill received even greater emphasis in Pear's (1948) later definition that "skill is the integration of well-adjusted muscular performances" (p. 92) and have continued to be emphasized by many researchers (e.g., Adams, 1987). Although skill has been conceived more broadly in more recent research, as it is in the present text, and emphasis has shifted to analysis of the processes that underlie skill acquisition and performance, consideration of motor requirements is important both historically and for a full understanding of skilled performance.

Tasks and Methods

The tasks used to study motor performance can be classified along several dimensions. One important dimension is the continuum between **discrete** and **continuous** movements. Discrete tasks have a recognizable beginning and end and require that a single action be performed on each trial. A grasping task, in which a person is to move from a starting location to grasp an object at another location, is an example of a discrete task. Continuous tasks are those with no recognizable beginning or end and action is ongoing from the arbitrary start of the trial to the arbitrary end. Steering a real or simulated car through an obstacle course is an example of a task that is continuous in nature. Intermediate to discrete and continuous tasks are serial or sequential tasks that require a series of discrete movements, such as a sequence of finger taps, to be executed within a given trial. Other dimensions that might be considered are the complexity and intricacy of the required movements and the predictability of the environment during performance of the task. As discussed in Chapter 1,

Table 4.1 Computation of Constant Error (CE), Variable Error (VE), Absolute Error (AE), and Root Mean Square Error (RMSE)

Trial	*Error (cm)*	*Squared Deviations About CE*	*Absolute Error*	*Squared Error*
1	−2	$(-3)^2$	2	$(-2)^2$
2	0	$(-1)^2$	0	$(0)^2$
3	1	$(0)^2$	1	$(1)^2$
4	4	$(3)^2$	4	$(4)^2$
5	2	$(1)^2$	2	$(2)^2$
Sum	5	20	9	25
	CE = 5/5 = 1.0	VE = $(20/5)^{.5}$ = 2.0	AE = 9/5 = 1.8	RMSE = $(25/5)^{.5}$ = 2.25

tasks vary along a continuum from those performed in completely predictable environments (closed skills) to those performed with complete uncertainty about future environmental conditions (open skills; Poulton, 1957).

The performance of simple, discrete tasks, such as moving a stylus to a target location, can be described with several measures. **Reaction time** to begin the movement can be recorded as can **movement time** to the target once the movement is begun. Error measures are based on the distance by which the target is missed and are of four major types. **Constant error,** illustrated in column 2 of Table 4.1, is measured by averaging the signed error distance for all trials; it can be regarded as a measure of bias. For example, if a person consistently overshoots the target distance, the constant error will be positive and the person is said to have a positive bias. **Variable error,** illustrated in column 3, is measured by finding the standard deviation of the error distances about a person's constant error; it reflects variability in performance. **Absolute error,** illustrated in column 4, is measured by averaging the absolute values of the error distances for all trials; it specifies overall error. Because absolute error combines bias and variability in a complex manner, a measure of total variability, or **root mean square error,** has come to be used more often; it is the square root of the average squared deviations of the individual errors. In sequential tasks, such as typing, an additional measure that is often used is the **interresponse interval,** which is the time that elapses between successive responses. Also, these data can be examined for sequential errors, such as transpositions.

The continuous task that has been studied most often is tracking, which was introduced in Chapter 1. In **pursuit tracking,** the task is to keep a controlled element (often a cursor) aligned with a displayed track (often a dot) whose movement is not under the operator's control. In **compensatory** tracking, which is typically more difficult than pursuit tracking, the display shows only the error between the controlled element and the track. For both pursuit and compensatory tracking, the relation between a control action and the resulting movement of the controlled element can be characterized in terms of the derivative of the movement. If the control setting directly determines the position of the element, then the relation is **zero-order.** For a **first-order** control, the positioning of the control determines the direction and velocity of the element, and for a **second-order** control, control movement determines the direction and acceleration of the element. In all cases, the measure of performance can be the time on target or the root mean square error distance (i.e., the square root of the mean deviation of the controlled element from the track) measured continuously across time.

Problems of Movement Control

The study of motor skill must begin with an understanding of the complex processes involved in controlling and coordinating movements. To guide investigations of these processes, motor control researchers have focused on three problems (Pew & Rosenbaum, 1988). The **degrees of freedom** problem regards how a particular means for achieving a movement goal is selected from many possible alternative means. The **serial order** problem concerns how sequences of movements are ordered and timed. The **perceptual-motor integration** problem deals with the direction and nature of the interrelations between perception and motor control. These problems, along with their implications for skill acquisition, are addressed in turn.

The Degrees of Freedom Problem

In the performance of any motor act, only one of many alternative means for achieving the desired outcome must be selected. Because of our anatomical structure, many ways exist for accomplishing virtually any movement objective. Even a simple action, like reaching to turn on a computer, can follow a number of different trajectories, constrained primarily by the possible movements of the joints involved. The constraints on a movement can thus be characterized by the degrees of freedom of the joints, with 1 degree of freedom associated with each dimension in which movement can occur. For example, to determine the degrees of freedom in the shoulder-hand system, we add up the degrees of freedom for all the joints involved. The elbow allows movement in one dimension and so has only a single degree of freedom. The elbow's associated joint, the radio-ulnar joint, contributes a second degree of freedom by allowing rotation about the axis of the forearm. The wrist permits movement in two dimensions, horizontal and vertical, and so has 2 degrees of freedom. The shoulder allows movement in three dimensions: The upper arm can move left or right, up or down, and about its own axis of rotation. All in all, the shoulder-hand system has 7 degrees of freedom. If movement is specified with respect to the motion of the individual joints (i.e., in joint space), then seven movement parameters would have to be specified for a hand movement.

In general, the greater the degrees of freedom, the greater the complexity of the problem that must be solved by the motor system. If a way could be found to minimize the degrees of freedom, then the movement problem would be simplified. One line of research has pursued the idea that the degrees of freedom problem is solved in part by planning movements at a more abstract level than joint space (Morasso, 1981). For example, it has been proposed that hand movements are planned with respect to the trajectory of the hand (i.e., in hand space). Because a trajectory can be specified in three coordinates, the planning of movements in hand space involves considerably fewer degrees of freedom than planning in joint space, thus simplifying the problem. That movements are planned in hand space is suggested by the finding that the preferred movement trajectory of a hand from one location to another is linear in hand space but corresponds to a more complex, nonlinear function in joint space (Morasso, 1981; see Figure 4.1). It seems reasonable to assume that the coordinate system giving the least complex function (in this case, hand space) is the one in which the movement is actually planned.

The degrees of freedom associated with a movement can also be reduced by restricting the movement of some of the joints, thereby forming rigid couplings between multiple degrees of freedom. Such "freezing" of degrees of freedom has been proposed to be characteristic of the early phases of skill acquisition (Bernstein, 1967), and some experimental evi-

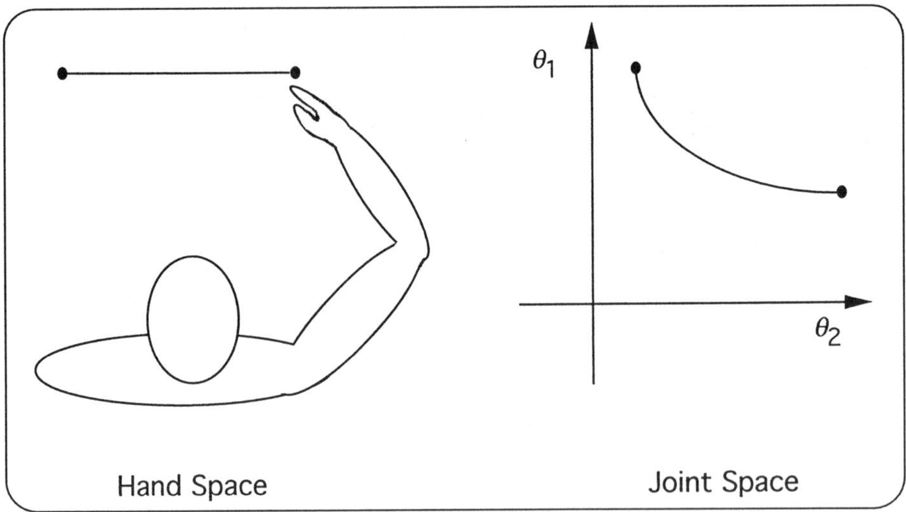

Figure 4.1. Preferred trajectory for moving a hand from one location to another. The trajectory is a straight line in hand space and nonlinear in joint space. θ_1 is the shoulder angle and θ_2 is the elbow angle.
SOURCE: Adapted from Pew and Rosenbaum (1988).

dence has supported this view. For example, Vereijken, van Emmerik, Whiting, and Newell (1992) measured the angular motions of the major joints of the upper body and legs as people practiced making slalomlike movements on a ski apparatus to investigate whether the allowed movements of the joints changed as skill was acquired. The foundation for their analysis was the fact that as a joint angle becomes more actively involved in the performance of a movement task, the variability around the mean angle of the joint will increase. Consistent with the idea that freezing of degrees of freedom occurs early in practice and that these degrees of freedom are freed up later in practice, the range of angles observed for the ankle, knee, and hip joints tended to increase across the early stages of practice and remained relatively constant after the participants had obtained some degree of skill. Changes in the coupling of the degrees of freedom were also observed, with the movements of the joints becoming increasingly independent with practice.

The Serial Order Problem

When tasks require sequences of discrete movements, some means is required to organize their execution. The serial ordering problem concerns how the timing and ordering of the movement elements in the sequences are controlled. One possibility is that the sensory feedback produced by one response acts to initiate the next response in the sequence. This type of account is called a **linear chain,** in that one movement acts as the stimulus for the next in the series. In a famous piece, Lashley (1951) discussed some limitations of this type of account (see Bruce, 1994, for an evaluation of the significance of this work). Most serious, the same motor elements enter into acts in many different orders and permutations. Because no single response element invariably follows another, Lashley proposed that some higher-order control elements must be involved to select the appropriate movement in any specific context.

An alternative to the linear chain account that is consistent with Lashley's (1951) proposal is **hierarchical control.** Evidence suggestive of hierarchical control has been obtained in studies using movement sequences that have some underlying structure. For example, Povel and Collard (1982) used a task in which the index, middle, ring, and little fingers of one hand were tapped in particular sequences. These fingers were designated by the numbers 1, 2, 3, and 4, respectively. Initially, a sequence of numbers, such as {1 2 1 2 2 3 2 3}, was shown on a computer screen, and the movement sequence indicated by the numbers was practiced until it could be performed without the visual prompt. Subsequently, when a signal was given, the sequence was to be tapped as fast as possible six times in succession.

The top part of Figure 4.2 shows a possible decision tree for the sequence described above. If a decision hierarchy such as this underlies performance, response latencies for the successive responses should be a function of the number of nodes that need to be traversed. In this example, the interresponse time between finger 1 and finger 2 should be fast because only one node needs to be traversed. The next movement of finger 1 will take more time because an additional node must be traversed. The longest interresponse time will be between the two middle responses in the sequence because all levels of the hierarchy must be traversed. The bottom part of Figure 4.2 shows the predicted pattern of response latencies for the sequence based on the number of transformations to be applied. Several of Povel and Collard's tapping sequences produced latency patterns consistent with such hypothesized hierarchical models.

The Perceptual-Motor Integration Problem

The perceptual-motor integration problem can be viewed from two sides: How does perception influence movement, and how does movement affect perception? Movement does not occur in a perceptual vacuum

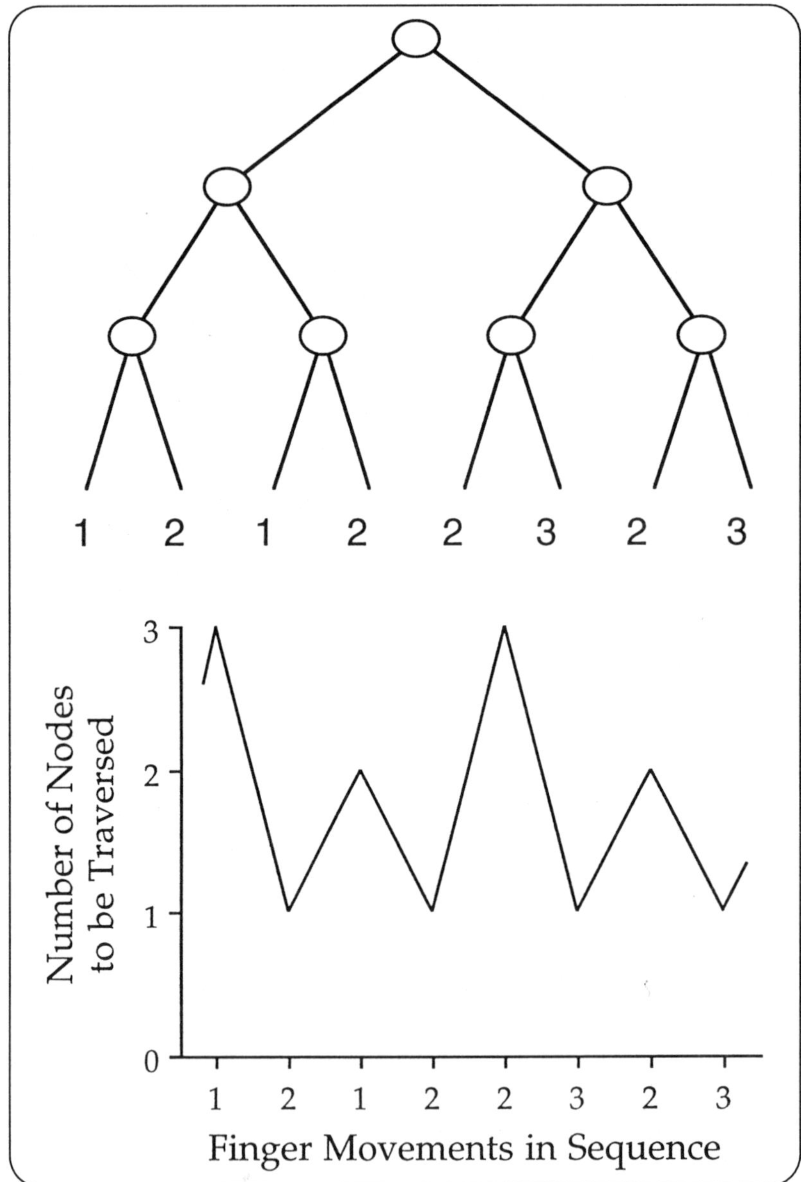

Figure 4.2. A hierarchical decision tree for the sequence {1 2 1 2 2 3 2 3} (top) and the predicted pattern of response latencies derived from the number of nodes to be traversed (bottom).
SOURCE: Adapted from Povel and Collard (1982).

but is dependent on perceptual information. Before a movement can be initiated, the relevant aspects of the environment must be perceived. The movement itself can produce additional perceptual information that must also be taken into account. The characteristics of the environment and the behavioral intentions of the actor together determine which movements will be appropriate. For example, if one's intent is to grasp an object, the trajectory that the movement takes will be a function of the position of the object to be grasped and the current position of the limb to be moved. Moreover, the movements of the fingers and hand also are determined by perceived properties of the object that is to be grasped, such as its size and estimated weight, well in advance of contact with the object (Jeannerod & Marteniuk, 1992). Perception comes into play at many points in the process of grasping as well as in the execution of other actions. Besides providing visual information, sensory input from receptors in the muscles, tendons, joints, and skin (i.e., proprioception) plays an important role in the guidance of action.

It is clear that perception guides movement, but there also is evidence to suggest that perception is itself influenced by the nature of the movements that the human motor system is capable of producing. For example, Viviani and Mounoud (1990) found that pursuit tracking of a target (i.e., moving a cursor to keep it in contact with a visually displayed target) in two-dimensional space was more accurate when the target motion complied with the constraints that characterize the movements of organisms than when it did not. Similarly, a point moving in two dimensions can produce illusions of velocity as a function of biological constraints. Viviani and Stucchi (1992) showed that when the velocity of a displayed point was varied according to the biological constraints that characterize drawing movements, the movement was perceived as having a uniform velocity even though the actual velocity of the point varied by more than 200%. Conversely, if the point followed the same path but at a constant velocity, it was perceived as moving at a nonuniform velocity. Results such as these suggest that intrinsic properties of the motor system influence perception, and they emphasize how richly interconnected the two systems must be.

Although everyone agrees that perception and action are mutually dependent, there has been considerable debate about the way in which they are linked (see, e.g., Meijer & Roth, 1988). Central to this debate is the issue of whether representations of perceptual and motor information are necessary to mediate between the two systems. Some researchers emphasize the use of high-level plans to mediate between intention and action. In this view, movements are presumed to be specified by action plans, relative to which the resulting sensory feedback is evaluated. Other researchers feel there is little need for central mediation and emphasize a direct relation between perception and action. Accounts of this latter type characterize movement control in terms of the dynamical properties of the motor system. Each of these perspectives is explored in some detail in the next section.

Perspectives on Motor Learning

Whereas motor control refers to the way that movements are executed, motor learning refers to the acquisition of motor skill. The alternative perspectives on motor control introduced in the previous paragraph provide contexts for the study of motor learning. Both the **motor programming** perspective, which places emphasis on central control of movements, and the **dynamical** perspective, with its stress on the role played by the mechanical properties of the body, are concerned with how the coordination and execution of motor acts are achieved and new motor skills acquired.

Motor Programming Perspective

The impetus behind the motor programming perspective was the discovery that several classes of actions can be controlled without sensory feedback. For example, Lashley (1951) noted that many rapid sequences of movement seem too fast for the feedback from one movement to serve as the stimulus for the next. Similarly, Schmidt (1975) concluded that unitary aimed movements can be made sufficiently fast so as to preclude the use of feedback. Finally, Taub and Berman (1968) showed that monkeys who have been deprived of proprioceptive feedback by deafferentation can still execute many actions, even when they are not receiving visual feedback about the positions of their limbs. Because sensory sources of feedback have been eliminated, the ability of the monkeys to execute specific actions must depend on more central mechanisms. All of these findings suggest that the link between perception and action is not inviolable and may at times be bypassed. If perception does not guide action, what does? Researchers adopting the motor programming perspective suggest that high-level plans, or **motor programs** (Keele, 1968), fulfill this role.

When the mode of control does not involve the use of sensory feedback in the execution of a movement, it is called **open loop.** When feedback is used and integrated into the plan of action, the mode of control is **closed loop.** (Do not confuse the distinction between open- and closed-loop control with the open/closed skill distinction discussed earlier. Open skills are performed with feedback, that is, they are closed loop, whereas closed skills may be performed without feedback.) The motor programming perspective stresses that movement can occur in an open-loop manner, but it does not deny that much of movement control is closed loop. Sensory feedback is presumed to play a role during the execution of slow movements as well as after a movement is completed. In the former case, deviations from the desired movement are detected and corrected on-line as the action is being executed. In the latter case, the sensory feedback obtained as a result of the movement is evaluated relative to feedback about the success of the action so as to modify the next action from that movement class.

Early motor programming accounts of movement control characterized motor programs as specifying the muscle commands for particular actions (Keele, 1968). However, the current view is that the programs are more general (Schmidt, 1988). These **generalized motor programs** extend to entire classes of movement. To execute a particular movement from the class represented by a generalized motor program, values of its parameters or variables must be specified. For example, to sign your name, you must specify the force and duration of the strokes as well as the muscle groups to be used. Still, whether signing a check or writing your name on a blackboard, the signature is recognizably your own even though different muscle groups are involved.

Schmidt's (1975) **schema theory,** which has been the most influential theory of motor learning and control in recent years, takes the motor programming perspective. According to schema theory, generalized motor programs of the type described above control action. As a class of movements is practiced, the performer learns the appropriate parameter values to supply to the program and the movements become faster and more accurate. Two schemas, a recall schema and a recognition schema, are involved in this process. The recall schema serves the function of specifying in advance the initial parameter values for generating the intended movement; fast, ballistic movements are entirely controlled by these parameter specifications. The recognition schema serves as a referent against which feedback regarding performance can be compared. For slow positioning movements, mismatches between the feedback resulting from performance of a task and that expected by the recognition schema lead to modifications of the movement as it is being executed. For both fast and slow movements, comparison of feedback to the recognition schema enables learning to occur through the development and modification of both the recall and recognition schemas.

According to schema theory, four types of information that contribute to the learning of schemas are stored when a movement is executed with a generalized motor program:

1. Environmental conditions prior to the movement
2. Parameter values assigned to the program
3. Knowledge of the correctness of the outcome
4. Sensory consequences of the movement

Because the learning and refinement of schemas depends on this information associated with particular instances, exposure to a range of conditions is necessary if accurate schemas are to be learned. Consequently, schema theory predicts that the schemas for a movement class will be learned better if a person performs a variety of movements within the class rather than just practicing one specific movement repeatedly. Also, because it is one of the four critical sources of information on which learning is based, knowledge of the outcome of the movements is deemed to be essential to efficient learning. We have much more to say about practice schedules and the role of knowledge of action outcomes later in the chapter.

Dynamical Approach

The dynamical approach is based on the idea that much if not all of the regularity found in skilled movements can be explained in terms of mechanical characteristics of the body. For example, a muscle and the bones to which it is attached can be viewed as a mass-spring system. In this system, the tension that develops at any given level of muscle activation is a function of the muscle's length (Fel'dman, 1966). It has been hypothesized that the nervous system produces movement of a limb at a single joint by gradually adjusting the relative intensities of neural signals to opposing muscles (Bizzi & Mussa-Ivaldi, 1989). This would act to specify a series of equilibrium positions at which the length-dependent forces of the muscles would be equal, which in turn would cause the limb to move through the positions solely as a result of its mechanical properties. Evidence for the mass-spring model has been obtained primarily from studies of single-joint movements, but in principle it is possible to account for many characteristics of more complex movements in terms of the dynamics of mass-spring systems. Such reliance on the mechanical properties would serve to reduce the computational demands of movement control.

In general, the dynamical approach puts less emphasis on central action plans than does the motor programming approach and more emphasis on synergies between muscles, joints, and the force producing mechanisms of the nervous system. These synergies, often called **coordinative structures,** have been defined as "temporarily and flexibly assembled functional organization[s] that [are] defined over a group of muscles and joints and that convert these components into task-specific coherent multiple-degree-of-freedom ensemble[s]" (Saltzman & Munhall, 1992, p. 50). The primary hypothesis of the dynamical approach is that the central nervous system achieves coordinated action by means of these coordinative structures assembled from abstract, functionally specific equations of motion, or dynamics.

The architecture of a dynamic action system can be represented by a set of equations that determines the range of movement forms that the system can exhibit. To execute a particular class of movement, an appropriate set of parameters must be assembled to constrain the architecture to produce the task-specific, multiple-degree-of-freedom ensemble that acts as a coordinative structure. The system architecture and parameter specifications establish the boundary conditions for performance, with moment to moment performance described in terms of the states of the system. That is, instead of relying on the construct of a motor program to explain the guidance of movement, control of a movement is described as occurring on-line in response to the immediate environmental conditions.

Following the intent to perform an action, **state dynamics** shape the spatiotemporal patterns of movement within the constraints of a particular coordinative structure. For example, Kelso and his colleagues (e.g., Zanone & Kelso, 1992) have used the term **intrinsic dynamics** to refer to these constraints, which reflect the preexisting capacities that a person brings to a new task, and the term **behavioral information** to refer to the movement pattern that is to be performed in the task. From the dynamical perspective, tasks for which the behavioral information is consistent with the intrinsic dynamics should be easy to perform, whereas tasks for which the behavioral information conflicts with the intrinsic dynamics should be difficult to perform.

These predictions have been verified in tasks requiring coordinated bimanual rhythmic movements. Kelso (1984) had people flex and extend homologous fingers on each hand (e.g., both index fingers) rhythmically at a common frequency. In addition to varying the specified frequency, the phase relation between the two fingers that the person was to try to maintain was varied (e.g., if the phase relation was 180°, one finger was fully flexed at the same time that the other was fully extended). At low movement frequencies, two patterns of coordination were found to be stable (i.e., the required phase relation could be maintained): in-phase (simultaneous flexion and extension of both fingers) and antiphase (flexion of one finger coinciding with extension of the other, and vice versa). For other target phase relations, the rhythms deviated toward being either in-phase or antiphase. However, at higher movement frequencies, only the in-phase pattern remained stable, and even for antiphase movements of high frequency, the pattern shifted to in-phase.

These results and many related findings can be explained by models in which the intrinsic dynamics are bistable (i.e., have two preferred or "attractor" phase relationships) below a critical movement frequency and monostable (i.e., have a single attractor phase relationship) above that frequency. Figure 4.3a visually depicts the potential [$-a \cos(\phi) - b \cos(2\phi)$, where ϕ is the relative phase] of the intrinsic dynamics as a function of phase relationship for the bistable regime. The attractors are indicated by the basins of the functions at 0° and 180°, with their relative stability reflected by the depths of the basins. Phase relations less than 90° will be attracted to 0°, whereas those greater than 90° will tend to be attracted to 180°. Figure 4.3b shows the resulting potentials when behavioral information for three different target phases (0°, 90°, and 180°) that the performer is to try to maintain is provided. The behavioral information interacts with the intrinsic dynamics such that certain behavioral states are easier to maintain accurately. The stability of the 0° and 180° relations is indicated by the fact that the minimum of the resulting potential for these phase relations is well defined and at the required phasing. The relative instability of the 90° relation is indicated by its wider, less articulated minimum.

Skill acquisition in the dynamical approach involves modification of the coordinative structures. This modification can occur through the actions of graph and parameter dynamics (Saltzman & Munhall, 1992). The **parameter dynamics** control the acquisition of the parameter values that are appropriate for the particular action classes. They operate on a longer time scale than do state dynamics and govern skill acquisition as well as other longer time scale aspects of performance. **Graph dynamics** operate on an even longer time scale than parameter dynamics and are the processes that cause changes in the architecture of a system. Saltzman and Munhall (1992) suggest that acquisition of skill such as that of using a new

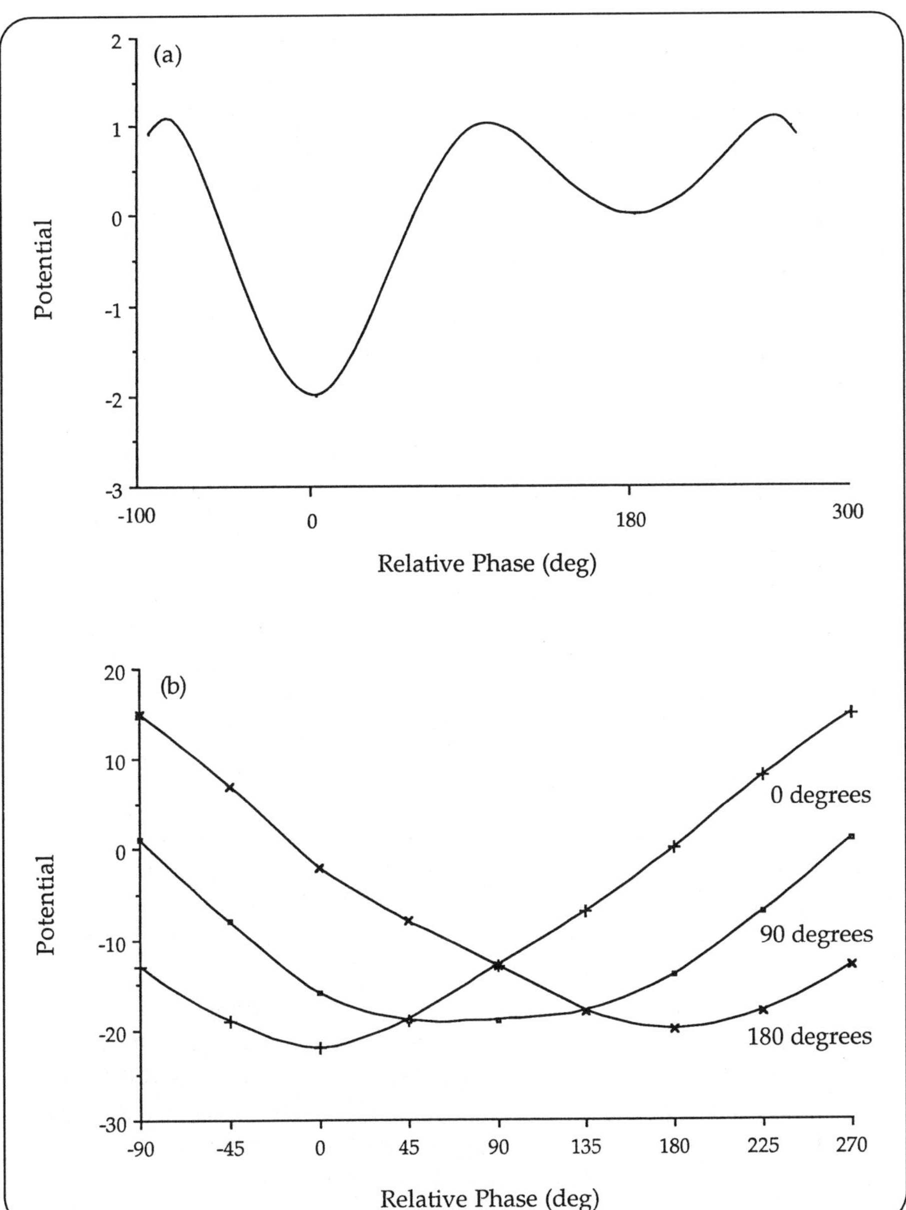

Figure 4.3. Depiction of the potential [V(rel. phase)] (a) of the intrinsic dynamics alone and (b) with behavioral information added for required phasings of 0° (+), 90° (box), and 180° (x).
SOURCE: Adapted from Zanone and Kelso (1992).

tool likely involves graph-dynamic processes that incorporate the state variables and parameters specifically associated with the tool. Graph dynamics are also thought to govern changes in parameterization that must occur due to the physical growth of a developing organism (e.g., growth of the vocal tract requires changes in the mappings between acoustic and articulatory coordinates and between muscle activation and the resulting articulatory motion).

In the terminology used by Kelso and his colleagues, the intrinsic dynamics of the action system serve as the general foundation of coordination on which learning of the specific control requirements for the task must be based. Zanone and Kelso (1992) provided evidence that the intrinsic dynamics can influence the nature of learning in the bimanual coordination task described above. They had people practice a specific phasing pattern at a relatively low movement frequency for 15 trials on each of 5 days. This pattern required the left finger to lag in phase by 90° behind the right finger. Note that this phase relation is intermediate to the in-phase (0°) and antiphase (180°) patterns that are stable attractors at low movement frequencies. With practice, the mean relative phasing progressively approached the required phasing of 90°, suggesting the development of a new attractor specific to this phase relation.

Even more convincing evidence for a new attractor was obtained by examining supplementary trials performed prior to each block of five practice trials. In these supplementary trials, the required relative phasing was progressively increased from 0° (in-phase) to 180° (antiphase) in 15° steps. Initial performance on these trials showed the standard finding of best performance when in-phase and antiphase movements were required, with other phasings being attracted toward these two extremes. However, by the end of the fifth session, performance was as good for the 90° phasing that had been practiced as for the in- and antiphase relations, and required phasings of 60° to 105° were attracted toward 90°. These data suggest that the initial bistable dynamics changed to a tristable dynamics, with 90° relative phasing as a new attractor. Moreover, when recall of the practiced phasing pattern of 90° was tested a week later, there was no deterioration in performance relative to the fifth practice session.

Results such as these are promising and suggest that the dynamical approach can provide considerable insight into motor skill acquisition, possibly even providing a basis for integrating the areas of motor learning and motor development. However, as recently noted by the editor of an issue of the *Journal of Motor Behavior* devoted to the dynamical approach to motor skill acquisition, much of what the approach offers in principle is at present still "a promissory note" (Newell, 1992). Consequently, most of the studies that we describe in the remainder of the chapter have been conducted from the motor programming perspective.

Factors Influencing Motor Skill Acquisition

Many factors influence the acquisition of motor skill, including motivation, fatigue, practice schedules, and feedback. It is particularly important to distinguish between factors that produce the relatively permanent changes in performance characteristic of learning and those that produce only temporary changes in performance. Because any changes in performance that are observed during the training period (i.e., the acquisition phase) could be a function of either temporary or more permanent changes, it is necessary to include retention tests, in which performance is tested at some later period of time, or transfer tests, in which performance under altered conditions is evaluated, to determine unambiguously if the variables of interest have an effect on learning (Salmoni, Schmidt, & Walter, 1984).

Of the many factors that can be considered in studies of motor learning, methods of feedback and practice schedules have received the most attention. As you will notice in the following sections, these variables have both temporary and more permanent influences on performance.

Feedback

As discussed previously, movement-related sensory information plays an integral role in both the learning and performance of motor skills. A performer continually receives information through the senses about such things as the positions of the limbs, the locations of objects in the environment, and body posture. Moreover, additional information may be available regarding success in attaining the desired goal. Several categories of movement-related sensory information can thus be distinguished (Winstein & Schmidt, 1989), as illustrated in Figure 4.4. Information available prior to the initiation of an action can influence the nature of the movement plans that are specified, but the information that is available during or after action is particularly important for the acquisition of skills. Typically, a distinction is made between the intrinsic feedback that is inherent in producing a response and the extrinsic feedback that can be provided to augment the intrinsic feedback.

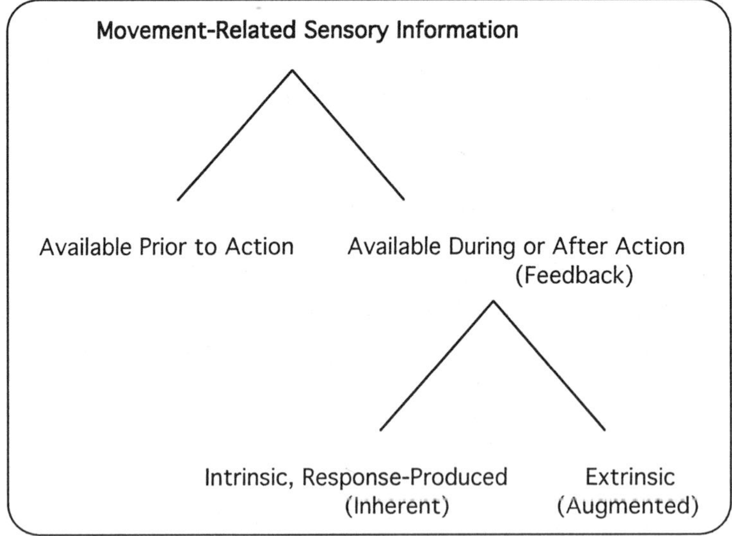

Figure 4.4. Categories of movement-related sensory feedback.
SOURCE: Adapted from Winstein and Schmidt (1989).

Intrinsic Feedback

There are several sources of intrinsic feedback: proprioception from mechanoreceptors in the muscles, joints, and skin that provide information about movement, pressure, and position; vision; and to a much lesser extent, audition. Additionally, the vestibular sense, which consists of receptors in the inner ear that respond to movement and changes in position of the head, is important for maintaining posture and balance.

One issue of concern for skill acquisition is whether the use of intrinsic feedback in motor control changes with practice. Most skill acquisition frameworks, such as Fitts's taxonomy as described in Chapter 1, presume that skilled performance is automatized and hence less reliant on feedback. This suggests that there should be a reduction in the use of sensory feedback with practice as motor performance becomes more fluent and open loop. Evidence consistent with this view was obtained by Pew (1966), who had people control the horizontal position of a cursor on a video display screen by alternately pressing two keys to keep the cursor in the center of the screen. A trial began with an experimenter-induced shift of the cursor to the right of center. If the left key was pressed, the cursor accelerated to the left and the leftward movement would continue without further acceleration after the key was released. Pressing the right key acted first to decelerate the leftward movement and then to produce acceleration in the rightward direction. Because the control keys always produced acceleration (i.e., control was second order), it was impossible to keep the cursor centered without alternately pressing the two keys.

Performance in this task was worse with higher acceleration constants, but absolute error decreased substantially across sessions for all of the acceleration values that were used. Most important, interresponse time was relatively long early in practice, suggesting a closed-loop mode of control in which visual feedback about the cursor movement was evaluated before the next response was made. In contrast, in the later sessions, individuals adopted a strategy of pressing the alternate response keys rhythmically, correcting the position of the cursor when necessary by occasionally pausing to make a discrete correction or by altering the relative durations for which the two keys were kept active.

Pew (1966) interpreted these changes in response patterns with practice as illustrating that the nature of control changes with the progression of skill, "beginning with strict closed-loop control and reaching levels of highly automatized action with occasional 'executive' monitoring" (p. 771). Kohl and Shea (1992) confirmed Pew's findings both in a task comparable to his and one in which the cursor had to track a moving target. They also tested some people who simply watched performers during 20 acquisition trials and then were tested along with the performers 24 hours later. Although the people who had only observed performance during the initial session showed more error in the subsequent session, their rates and rhythms of responding were similar to those of the actual practice group. This finding suggests that direct feedback from practice is not always necessary for open-loop control to develop. People with no actual practice, who received only indirect feedback from observation, could also select this mode of performance.

Although the individuals performing Pew's (1966) task appeared to adopt a strategy that can be characterized as more open loop in nature, it was not completely open loop. Feedback apparently was still used but primarily to monitor performance at a more global level than that of the individual keypresses (Pew, 1974). Several authors have suggested that in many tasks this change involves a decreased role for visual feedback and an increased role for proprioceptive feedback. In support of this view, Fleishman and Rich (1963) found that the type of ability that correlates with performance is different early in practice from late in practice. In particular, the correlation between performance of a two-hand coordination task and a measure of visual spatial ability decreased with practice, whereas the correlation between the performance measure and a kinesthetic sensitivity measure (difference thresholds for lifted weights) increased (see Chapter 10).

However, Proteau (1992) has marshaled considerable evidence to the effect that the role of visual feedback does not decrease with practice. Performance has been shown to be better with than without vision in many motor tasks performed by individuals with varying degrees of practice, particularly when the margin of permissible error is small. Moreover, when people practice with visual information available and are subsequently transferred to a condition in which this information is not available, performance typically suffers. For example, Proteau and Cournoyer (1990) examined performance on a manual aiming task in which a person practiced moving a stylus rapidly to a target for either 15 or 150 trials. Performance was compared under conditions of either full vision, vision of the hand-held stylus and the target, or vision of the target only. Initially, performance was much better with full vision than without. With practice, the performance of individuals who could see the stylus and target became better than that of those who could not see the stylus and approached the full-vision group in accuracy (see Figure 4.5). Thus these people improved in their ability to use the dynamic visual information about the position of the limb provided by the stylus. However, when visual information was eliminated in a transfer test given after 150 trials, both the full-vision and stylus-visible groups performed considerably poorer than the target-only group. This difference was not apparent when the transfer session was introduced after 15 trials, suggesting that the visual information had become more important for those who practiced longer.

Instead of sensory feedback becoming less important with practice, it appears that the sensorimotor basis for motor learning is specific to the conditions of practice. Not only does removal of visual feedback after practice with it disrupt performance but so does the addition of visual feedback about limb position when practice has been with visual information about target location alone (Elliott & Jaeger, 1988; Proteau, Marteniuk, & Levesque, 1992). Thus it appears that the central representation against which sensory feedback is evaluated when making a practiced movement loses its effectiveness in controlling movement when the sensorimotor context is altered.

Additional evidence for continued use of sensory information comes from the study of aimed movements. Recall that Woodworth's (1899; see Chapter 1) pioneering work on aimed movements distinguished two

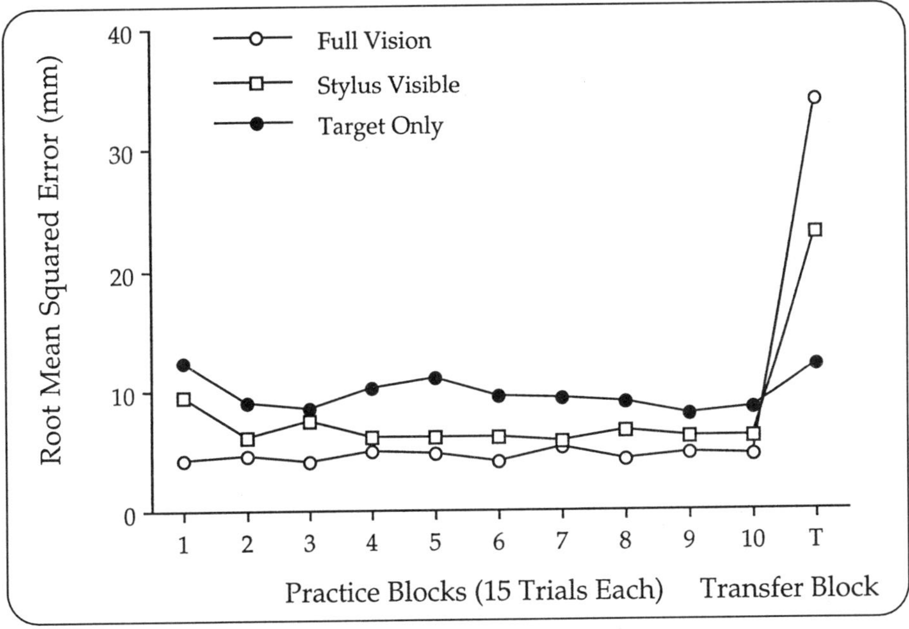

Figure 4.5. Practice and transfer (T) performance in Proteau and Cournoyer's (1990) experiment.

phases of movement control, a primary, ballistic submovement, called the initial impulse, and a secondary submovement, called current control, in which feedback information is used to make corrections to the movement. If movement control becomes less reliant on feedback as movements are practiced, the initial impulse phase should be the only one needed for control. However, if feedback is still used, albeit more effectively, as aimed movements are practiced, the primary benefit of practice should be a reduction in the amount of time required for executing the secondary submovement—not an elimination of this stage. Abrams and Pratt (1993) showed that movement time for rapid aimed arm movements decreased with practice (see Figure 4.6) and that this decrease in movement time was due entirely to faster secondary submovements. The time to make the initial submovement actually increased slightly! Moreover, there was no reduction in the percentage of trials on which secondary submovements were made, and additional measures of initial impulse performance showed little if any improvement. The continued reliance on current control and increased efficiency of this phase suggests that people become

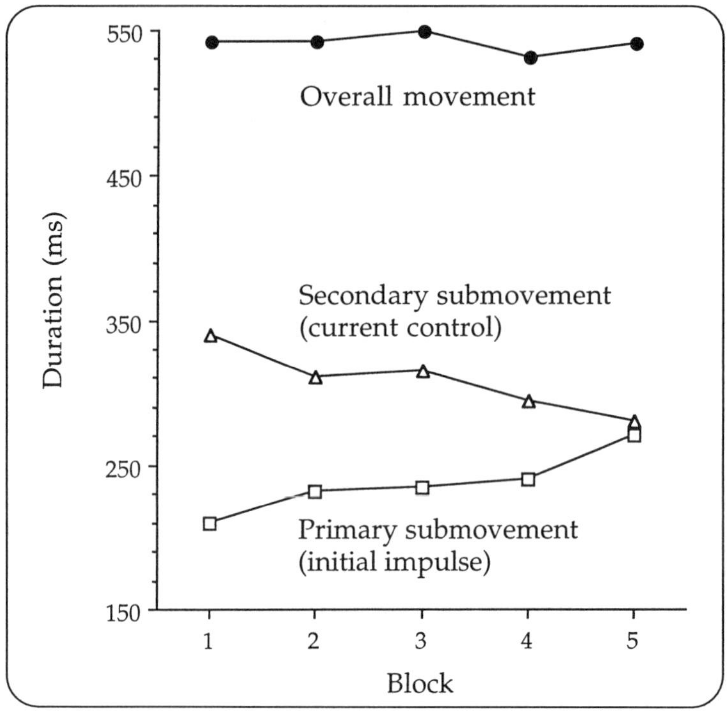

Figure 4.6. Mean durations of primary and secondary submovements, and the overall movement, as a function of practice block.
SOURCE: Based on Abrams and Pratt (1993).

more efficient in their use of sensory feedback as they become practiced but that it still plays a role in performance.

For a different class of movements, tracking tasks, the primary result of practice appears to be a shift to the use of higher-order control information. According to the **progression-regression hypothesis,** individuals rely more on the higher-order derivatives of movements as they become practiced but regress to lower orders of control when task demands become more stressful (Fitts, Bahrick, Noble, & Briggs, 1961). Evidence for progression to higher-order information has been obtained by several researchers. For example, Fuchs (1962) found that as performers practiced a second-order compensatory tracking task, the position of the stimulus (i.e., the first-order information) played a decreasing role in their control actions, whereas its acceleration (i.e., second-order information) became increasingly important.

The regression aspect of the progression-regression hypothesis also has received support. When a second task must be performed concurrently with a well-practiced first task, performance of the first task suffers in a predictable way. That is, as demonstrated by Fuchs (1962), people revert to a greater emphasis on lower-order information (e.g., stimulus position) and less reliance on higher-order information (e.g., the acceleration component). This regression to a lower order of control for the primary task not only occurs when the second task involves tracking but also has been observed with tasks involving visual detection (Garvey, 1960) and memory (Jagacinski & Hah, 1988).

Knowledge of Results

Although it is possible to learn at least some skills solely on the basis of intrinsic feedback, learning typically is much more efficient when extrinsic feedback is provided. Most often, this feedback is in the form of knowledge of results (KR), which is knowledge about the accuracy of performance that is provided after a response has been completed. Because KR benefits learning, it has generally been thought that the more KR provided, the better learning will be. The most influential theory of the past 20 years, Schmidt's (1975) schema theory, is among those that make this prediction.

However, Schmidt and his colleagues have established clearly that this prediction is incorrect. Winstein and Schmidt (1990) found that learning to perform a complex movement was at least as good when KR was provided at random 33% of the time as when it was provided on 100% of the learning trials. Moreover, when the proportion of KR trials was systematically decreased across practice, learning was enhanced relative to 100% KR conditions. Wulf and Schmidt (1989) showed similar results for learning a class of movements, each movement of which had the same relative timing structure but different absolute timing. That is, reduced KR also benefited learning of an entire action class governed by a single generalized motor program.

Another way in which KR can be provided is through a summary of performance provided at the end of a set of trials. Typically, the summary is in the form of a graph that plots a measure of error for each trial in the set. The fact that reducing the frequency of KR benefits learning suggests that summary KR may be more effective than KR provided for each individual trial. Lavery (1962) found support for this proposition in his examination of tasks for which a steel ball (which was out of sight of the performer) was to be driven a specified distance (e.g., 20 inches) by either pulling and releasing a plunger (as in pinball) or striking the end of a rod with a rubber hammer. A summary graph presented after each set of 20 trials that provided either qualitative KR (direction of error) or quantitative KR (direction and magnitude of error) for each trial in the set produced better long-term retention than did either type of KR provided immediately following each trial, although performance during acquisition was worse with the summary graph than with immediate KR. Schmidt, Young, Swinnen, and Shapiro (1989) confirmed this finding in a simple ballistic-timing task, finding that as the set of trials for which summary KR was provided increased from 5 to 10 to 15, acquisition performance decreased but retention increased.

Schmidt and his colleagues have proposed a **guidance** hypothesis to explain why 100% KR does not always produce better learning than a reduced percentage of KR trials or summary KR. According to this hypothesis, the information provided by KR guides the performer toward the performance goal. Immediate performance benefits from this guidance, but the performer may rely too heavily on this guidance if it is provided on every trial and thus be at a disadvantage when it is removed.

Although most data regarding KR are consistent with the implication of the guidance hypothesis that learning should be better when KR is not provided on every trial, the nature of the processing that underlies this learning is not clear. One possibility is that performance deteriorates during no-KR trials, making the errors more obvious and hence easier to correct when KR is finally provided (Schmidt et al., 1989). Evidence consistent with this possibility was obtained by Sparrow and Summers (1992), who found that the magnitude of error increased systematically across the sequence of no-KR trials that followed a KR trial. However, another possibility is that the inclusion of no-KR trials forces individuals to develop the internal representation necessary for detecting errors on their own. This latter interpretation suggests that the disadvantage for 100% KR schedules may be closely related to the disadvantage for blocked as opposed to varied practice schedules, which is discussed later. In both cases, it is possible to perform well during acquisition without having to engage in much of the elaborative processing of the type that produces learning.

Another issue regarding the timing of KR is when it should be given relative to the end of task performance. It has long been recognized that it takes time to process extrinsic feedback information (Salmoni et al., 1984); more recent work shows that time is also needed to process intrinsic feedback (Swinnen, Schmidt, Nicholson, & Shapiro, 1990). If KR is provided too soon after performance of a task, it can disrupt processing of intrinsic feedback, leading to a failure to develop the internal representation, or recognition schema, necessary for detection of error as a movement is being executed. Swinnen (1990) obtained direct evidence for the view that active information processing occurs in the interval between task completion and KR by interpolating a secondary, attention-demanding task, which required estimating the time taken by the experimenter to execute a movement, in the intervals before and after KR. This interpolated task interfered with learning, as evidenced by poorer performance on a no-KR retention test, and the interference was greater when the task was performed before the KR rather than after the KR. Swinnen suggested that the interpolated task likely required development of a recognition schema to serve as a referent for evaluating the experimenter's movements, and this requirement could have interfered specifically with the development of such a recognition schema for the performer's movement task.

Knowledge of Performance

Feedback provided at task completion works well for tasks that require single degree-of-freedom movements or scaling of a single general movement pattern (Newell, 1991). However, for the multiple degrees-of-freedom tasks that are more characteristic of behaviors in natural situations, KR is less effective. In these cases, knowledge of performance, with respect to the forces applied during performance (**kinetic** feedback) or the temporal and spatial properties of the movement that was executed (**kinematic** feedback), is needed to provide information not just about the outcome but also about the dynamics of the movement used to produce the outcome. Whereas KR provides no information about what aspects of the movement contributed to successful performance, knowledge of performance can provide such information and direct the performer's attention to those aspects that are critical to performance (Young & Schmidt, 1992).

English (1942) reported early anecdotal evidence for the efficacy of kinetic feedback. He described a study of the instruction of military recruits in rifle shooting that had been conducted in the 1920s. It was determined that a central factor in successful shooting was the "trigger squeeze," so a rifle was modified to provide feedback regarding trigger pressure by incorporating a fluid-filled tube into the stock. When the trigger was squeezed, a change in the level of the liquid occurred corresponding to the force of the squeeze. A recruit could thus receive direct

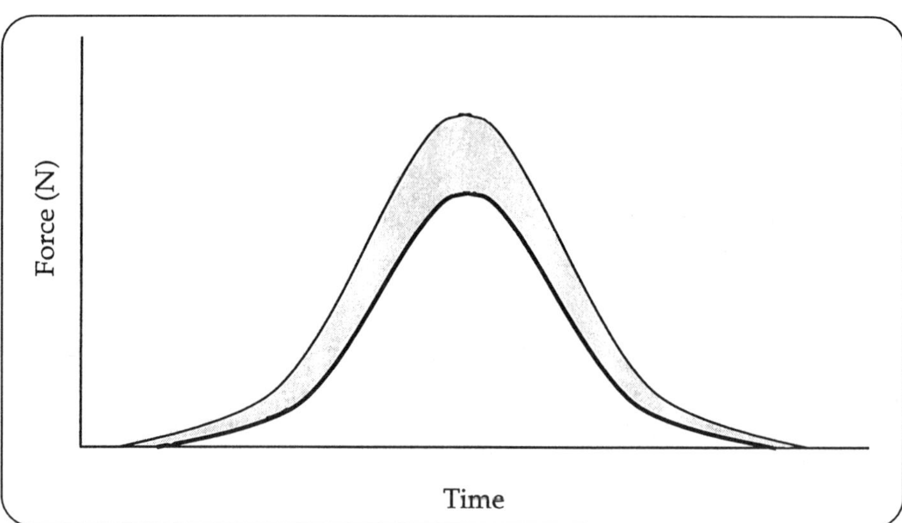

Figure 4.7. Knowledge of performance provided by Newell, Sparrow, and Quinn (1985). The sample force-time response curve (narrow line) is superimposed on the criterion force-time template (heavy line). The shaded area represents the absolute impulse error.

feedback about whether a proper squeeze had been applied. English characterized the results obtained when this form of feedback was used during training as excellent, noting that "men given up as hopeless by their officers and non-commissioned officers showed rapid improvement in a large percentage of cases" (p. 4).

English went on to stress that the success of the training was due to the recruit acquiring "a local kinesthetic insight into what he is required to do . . . [and that] sound instruction must first discover the particular kind and locus of the insight required for each sort of situation" (p. 5). These points have been emphasized more recently by Newell and his colleagues, who have advocated the use of performance feedback (e.g., Newell & Walter, 1981). In most cases, the task criterion specifies what information the feedback must provide in order to be effective. For example, the provision of a graph showing the force-time history for isometric task performance (i.e., the force exerted throughout a trial as a function of time; see Figure 4.7) benefits the production of a particular force-time relation but not that of a particular peak force (Newell, Sparrow, & Quinn, 1985). The feedback regarding force-time history is not beneficial in the

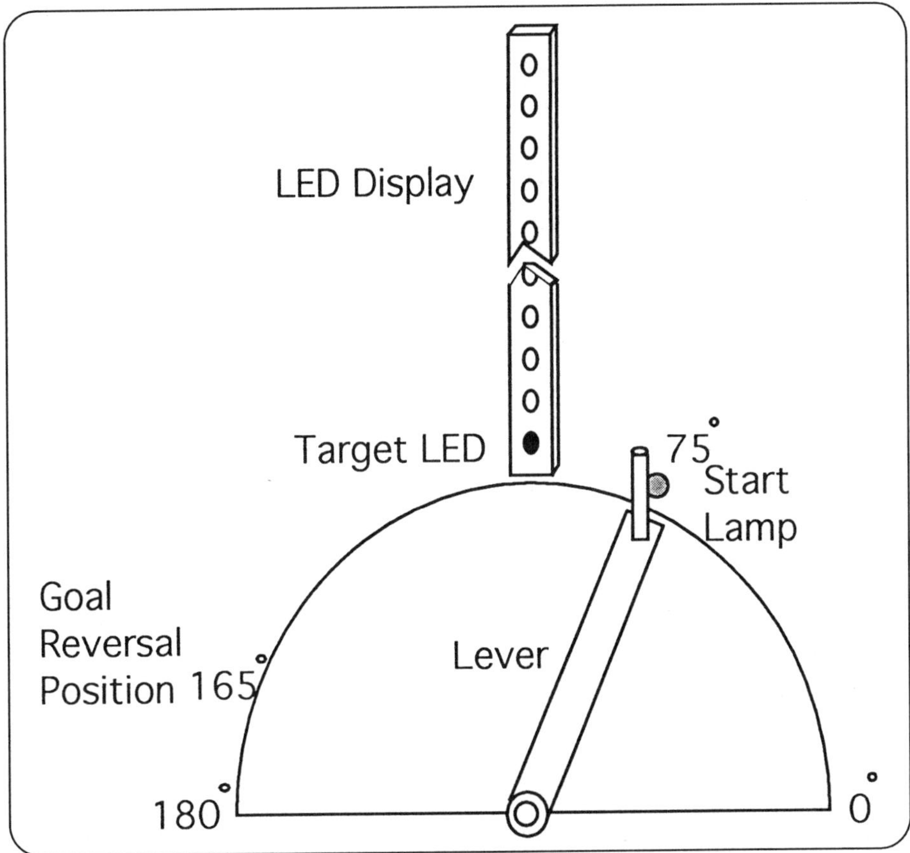

Figure 4.8. Schematic diagram of Schmidt and Young's (1991) apparatus. The performer grasps the handle of the lever at the 75° start position. When the light starts "moving" down the display, a backswing of the lever to the opposite side is performed, followed by a foreswing intended to arrive at the display simultaneous with the light reaching the bottom "target" location.

latter case because the time course of the forces exerted is not pertinent to the task criterion of producing a specified peak force.

In the preceding example, the kinetic pattern provided as feedback was also the task goal. Thus, for the force-time production task, the feedback could be characterized as KR. To demonstrate the greater effectiveness of performance feedback over KR, a task for which the kinematic pattern is not isomorphic with the goal is required. Schmidt and Young (1991) developed an apparatus for such a task, as shown in Figure 4.8. The task is much like hitting a baseball with a bat. The performer grasps a vertical handle at the far end of the lever, which is initially positioned at 75°. After a warning tone, the lights on the LED display column are lit sequentially to simulate downward movement of the target. The performer is to make a backswing to the left, passing through 90°, then to swing forward to "intercept" the moving light.

To determine what performance information might be useful, Schmidt and Young initially had people practice this coincident timing task with only KR and then take a no-KR retention test. They found that the best performers conducted the backswing and forward swing as distinct units and processed information about the positions of either the light, the limb, or both before initiating the forward swing. Other characteristics of the most effective movement pattern were reversal positions near 165°, onset of the forward swing approximately 940 ms after the first light movement, and low variabilities in these movement attributes.

Young and Schmidt (1992) used this information to design a system of feedback for the task. For blocks of five trials, individuals received either information about their reversal position relative to the goal reversal position of 165° or about the time of initiation of the forward swing relative to the goal initiation time of 940 ms. Although both positional and temporal feedback improved performance relative to a KR-only group during acquisition, only positional feedback led to significantly better performance on a subsequent no-feedback retention test. In a second experiment, Young and Schmidt showed that the benefit of performance feedback is influenced by the same scheduling factors that influence the benefit of KR. Specifically, when feedback about the location error was provided in a summary form after a block of trials, performance was better on later retention tests. The similar effects of scheduling on the two types of feedback suggest that they may both be used in a similar way.

Schedules of Practice

In addition to the type and schedule of feedback, the scheduling of the practice trials itself can have an influence on the acquisition of motor skill. The most studied practice variables are the spacing of the practice trials and whether variations of a task are practiced in a blocked (only trials of one type practiced together) or randomized (different movements practiced within a block of trials) manner.

Massed Versus Distributed Practice

The distribution of practice has a long history of research in the study of motor learning (Adams, 1987). Many studies show that massed practice results in considerably poorer performance during acquisition than does distributed practice, but the effects on learning are not so clear. Lee and Genovese (1988) conducted a meta-analysis of the literature to determine whether distributed practice produces better learning than massed practice. They argued that the absolute performance level in the transfer sessions is a relatively uncontaminated measure of learning and examined how this measure varied as a function of intertrial interval across studies. Their meta-analysis showed that massed practice does result in poorer learning than does distributed practice, although the effect is smaller on retention tests than during acquisition.

All of the studies in Lee and Genovese's (1988) meta-analysis used continuous tasks, with the exception of a study by Carron (1969) that used a discrete peg-turning task. In contrast to the inferiority of massed practice for both performance and learning in the other studies, Carron's study showed no difference between massed and distributed practice during acquisition and an advantage for massed practice when retention was measured. To determine whether different principles of distribution of practice operate for discrete and continuous tasks, Lee and Genovese (1989) directly compared learning of discrete versus continuous versions of the same task. The task they used required people to move a stylus between two metal plates at as close to 500 ms as possible. For the discrete version of the task, only a single movement between the two plates was made on each trial, whereas for the continuous version, a trial consisted of 20 consecutive movements between the two plates. For massed practice, a 500-ms interval intervened between trials, and for distributed practice, the interval was 25 s. The results of the experiment confirmed that massed practice was beneficial for learning the discrete version of the task but detrimental for learning the continuous version. Lee and Genovese suggested that the differences likely reflect the occurrence of different types of information processing during the intertrial interval for discrete versus continuous tasks.

Blocked Versus Random Practice

When different tasks or task variations must be learned, the tasks can be practiced either in blocks of one task at a time or with the tasks randomly intermixed. Blocked versus random practice has been shown to be a major factor influencing learning and performance, and its effect extends to nonmotor domains. Contemporary interest in this variable dates from a study conducted by Shea and Morgan (1979). During the acquisition phase of the study, three tasks were performed in which the right hand was used to knock down three of six barriers in a specific order. The three tasks were practiced one at a time in distinct blocks of trials or were randomly intermixed. The blocked-practice group performed the tasks considerably faster, on average, than the random-practice group during acquisition. However, when tested after a retention interval of 10 minutes or 10 days, the blocked-practice group performed much more slowly in the condition in which the trials were randomly intermixed, and the random-practice group was faster for both the blocked and random conditions. The random-practice group also showed broader transfer to new versions of the barrier-knockdown task.

This general pattern of results, that blocked presentation improves performance during acquisition but retards learning, has been replicated in a variety of situations, although it is not found for all tasks (Magill & Hall, 1990). Both the disadvantage for random practice during acquisition and its advantage for retention and transfer have been treated as due to the changes in context in blocked versus random practice, or **contextual interference.** Shea and Morgan's (1979) study was based on Battig's (1979) conceptualization of contextual interference as developed from his work on verbal learning. According to this view, contextual interference is greater when changes in the experimental context occur from trial to trial. Battig proposed that this interference results in more elaborate and distinctive processing and a decreased dependence on the specific context of practice, resulting in better learning and retention. Shea and Morgan adapted this account to motor learning, proposing that the advantage for random presentation in their study resulted from the use of multiple processing strategies.

Lee and Magill (1983) proposed as an alternative that random practice conditions are effective because information from previous executions of the task is forgotten and effort must be devoted to "reconstructing" the action plan. They found that a group who practiced three tasks according to a sequential schedule, in which the tasks were cycled through repetitively, produced learning comparable to that of the randomized schedule. According to the elaboration view, there should be less elaboration with the sequential schedule than with the random schedule—because the stimuli can be predicted—so the two schedules should not have produced equivalent learning. However, because a new action plan must be recalled on each trial for both random and sequential schedules, the reconstruction account predicts equivalent learning.

Additional evidence for the reconstruction view has come from tasks using a short-term retention paradigm in which a target movement is made twice during acquisition and, following a distractor task, must be subsequently recalled. In such tasks, retention is better when a difficult task intervenes between the two presentations of the target movement than when it does not (e.g., Weeks, Lee, & Elliott, 1987), suggesting that the repetition of the movement is more beneficial for retention when the plan used to produce the movement initially is no longer in working memory and, therefore, must be reconstructed. However, Shea and Wright (1991) have shown that forgetting alone is not sufficient to produce the better retention. They used a variation of the short-term retention paradigm in which the similarity between the target movement and the task intervening between the two presentations of it was varied. The similar and dissimilar intervening tasks caused the same amount of forgetting of the initial presentation, but only the interposition of the similar distractor task significantly improved subsequent retention. This outcome suggests that although reconstruction of the movement plan may be necessary to improve retention, it is not sufficient. Engaging in a reconstructive process that is merely repetitive, which likely occurs when the movement is well differentiated from the alternatives, is of little long-term value, whereas engaging in a reconstructive process that involves additional information, as likely occurs when the movement is similar to the alternatives, is beneficial.

SUMMARY

Extensive research on motor skill acquisition has been conducted since the early studies of the late 1800s. Three problems of concern in the study of motor control—the degrees of freedom, the serial order, and the perceptual-motor integration problems—have guided much of this research. Two approaches, the motor programming perspective and the dynamical perspective, have been applied to issues in motor control and learning. The former perspective emphasizes central plans for action, whereas the latter stresses the mechanical properties of the body.

The majority of studies conducted on motor learning over the past 20 years have been guided by the motor programming perspective. Virtually all of the studies on practice and feedback schedules have arisen from issues regarding the role and nature of motor programs. This research has resulted in a wealth of data regarding such things as how the role of intrinsic feedback changes during practice and how practice should be scheduled and extrinsic feedback administered for optimal learning to occur. Among the more salient findings are that control of movements continues to rely on intrinsic feedback after extensive practice, with this feedback processed more efficiently, and that the schedules of practice and extrinsic feedback that support good performance during acquisition often do not result in the best learning.

The motor program construct continues to provide the impetus for new investigations of motor learning. However, the construct, at least as it is usually formulated, has deficiencies. One major concern is that the utility of the motor program concept may be restricted primarily to classes of movement more typical of laboratory studies than of real life. A second concern is that researchers from the motor programming perspective may fail to consider sufficiently the dynamical properties of the motor system and the constraints on movement that they provide. These concerns have led to the rise of the dynamical perspective, which emphasizes the properties of the motor system in particular contexts. The dynamical perspective has already been shown to provide some fresh insights into the execution of coordinated movements and the acquisition of motor skill, and the interplay between the motor programming and dynamical approaches will likely lead to a more complete understanding of motor skill acquisition.

CHAPTER 5

Performance of Multiple Tasks

Most of our daily activities require that information from multiple sources be attended to and acted upon. We must deal with multiple sources of stimulation while driving, when trying to work in spite of distractions, or even during lunch with friends. Usually, only a fraction of the stimulation present in the immediate environment is relevant to our current task concerns. When only a subset of the possible information sources must be attended and all other sources should be ignored, we say that **focused** attention is required. When two or more sources of information are important and must be attended simultaneously, we say that **divided** attention is required. Most real-world tasks have both divided and focused attention components. For example, you may need to focus on what your friend is saying, filtering out all other voices and noises, but still devote attention to eating your lunch.

A prime example of a job with high attention demands is that of the air traffic controller (see, e.g., Sperandio, 1978). The controller has two primary objectives: to avoid crashing the aircraft currently under control and to move each aircraft through the airspace at a sufficient rate of progress. Numerous objectives of lesser importance are choosing the shortest flight paths, accommodating preferred descents of pilots, avoiding stormy zones, and so on. The controller must keep track of the flight path of each aircraft, preserve appropriate spacings between the aircraft, maintain communication with the pilots, and be on watch for emergency situations. At some times only a few airplanes may be involved, but at others the controller may have responsibility for 10 or more planes at once. The controller must coordinate the activities of the planes in a manner that will satisfy the objectives, which requires the division of attention between many sources of visual and auditory input, while carrying out vocal communications and maintaining considerable information in working memory.

All of the factors—perceptual, cognitive, and motor—that we have discussed so far still must be considered in multiple-task environments such as that of air traffic control. However, additional factors come into play when we take one task out of isolation and place it in the context of other tasks, and it is important to ask whether additional specialized skills develop as multiple tasks are performed. One such skill may be that of time-sharing. How does a skilled performer in a multiple-task environment efficiently allocate processing resources to component tasks at the appropriate times? We can also ask whether restructuring of component tasks will occur when two or more tasks are performed together, such that the multiple tasks are effectively treated as a single task. In general, it is important to consider task interactions that may arise, such as interference in making a manual response for one task from the execution of a similar response for another task, and whether any deleterious effects of such interactions can be overcome by practice or training.

Multiple-Task Paradigms

In the study of attentional limitations, researchers have devised several multiple-task paradigms. One widely used task is that of dichotic listening, in which auditory messages are presented independently to each ear. Often, the listener is required to attend selectively to one message while ignoring the other. Typically, such focused attention is enforced by requiring the observer to **shadow,** or repeat back, the message in one ear as it is heard. Alternatively, divided attention can be studied by requiring listeners to process information from both of the messages. Analogous types of tasks have been used for visual stimuli and for cross-modal stimulus presentations (i.e., stimuli from two or more perceptual modalities). As we discuss later in the chapter, results from these studies have been used to develop and evaluate models of attention.

A common way to measure the attentional demands of one task (designated the **primary task**) is to pair it with a second task (designated the **secondary task**) and examine concurrent performance of the two tasks (Kerr, 1973). Most often, the performer is instructed to emphasize the primary task, letting secondary task performance suffer if there is any conflict. Relative performance of the secondary task under various conditions is taken to reflect the processing resources required by the primary task under those conditions. In one version of this secondary task method, the **probe-task** procedure, the secondary task is intermittent, such that the stimulus for it is presented at different points in time during performance of the primary task (Posner & Boies, 1971). Reaction time to the probe stimulus is measured, with longer reaction times indicating higher attentional demands by the primary task. This procedure allows construction of a profile of the attentional demands of the primary task at various points in the processing sequence.

For example, the probe-task procedure was recently used to evaluate the demands on viewers' attention when viewing transitions between scenes in television programs (Geiger & Reeves, 1993). The time course of the attentional demands was evaluated for two types of transitions: *unrelated* cuts (i.e., discontinuous transitions between two different scenes) and *related* cuts (i.e., transitions within a single scene). Viewers were assigned the primary task of watching sequences containing related and unrelated cuts, with the intent of answering later questions about their content. As a secondary task, the viewers were to press a button whenever a probe tone was presented. For probe tones that occurred 33 ms after a cut, reaction times were slower following related than unrelated cuts. However, for probe tones that occurred 1 s after the cut, this relation was reversed: Reaction times were slower following unrelated than related cuts. Because both related and unrelated cuts interfered with probe detection to similar extents but at different times, these results suggest that the overall attentional demands for each type of cut do not differ much, but the time courses of processing do.

Although it is common to designate one task as primary and the other as secondary in dual-task situations, this designation is not necessary. Instructions can emphasize giving equal weighting to both tasks, or the relative weightings assigned to the respective tasks can be varied systematically. Just as we showed that bias to respond "yes" or "no" in signal detection tasks can be manipulated, it is possible to bias the relative emphasis given to one task over another, such as when attention is diverted from driving a car to carrying on a conversation with a passenger.

In most cases, any sudden change in driving conditions will cause an end to the conversation as attention is returned to the task of driving. The ability to trade off attention between two tasks is discussed later in the sections on resource allocation and time-sharing.

Attention and Workload

Everyone agrees that attention plays a major role in the acquisition and performance of most skills. Moreover, it is obvious to all of us that severe attentional limits exist and that it is often difficult to keep attention focused on just the pertinent information. Because attention is limited, attending to the wrong information (and hence failing to attend to relevant information) can result in poor learning or performance. For example, listening to a conversation that is occurring nearby instead of attending to a lecturer may result in an immediate embarrassment if you are called on to answer a question or a later one if the unattended material appears on an exam. In other cases, such as when operating heavy machinery, a momentary lapse of attention may have more severe consequences, including even injury or loss of life. To characterize and predict performance in all but the simplest situations, it is necessary to have an understanding of the properties of attention.

Attentional Models

Despite widespread agreement on the existence of attentional limitations, there is some disagreement regarding their explanation. Early models concerned with attentional limitations conceptualized attention as a bottleneck on processing at a particular processing stage. For example, Broadbent (1958) proposed an early selection **filter theory** of attention in which the bottleneck was assumed to be the processing stage involved in the identification of stimuli. According to filter theory, the capacity of this stage is presumed to be one item, and a selective filter operating on sensory features of stimulation allows the appropriate stimulus to enter the bottleneck (see Figure 5.1, top). This stimulus alone will be identified, and all others will be lost. Broadbent proposed this model in part because numerous studies had shown that when observers in a dichotic listening task were instructed to attend to an auditory message presented to one ear while ignoring the message presented to the other ear, they were not able to report anything about the content of the unattended message.

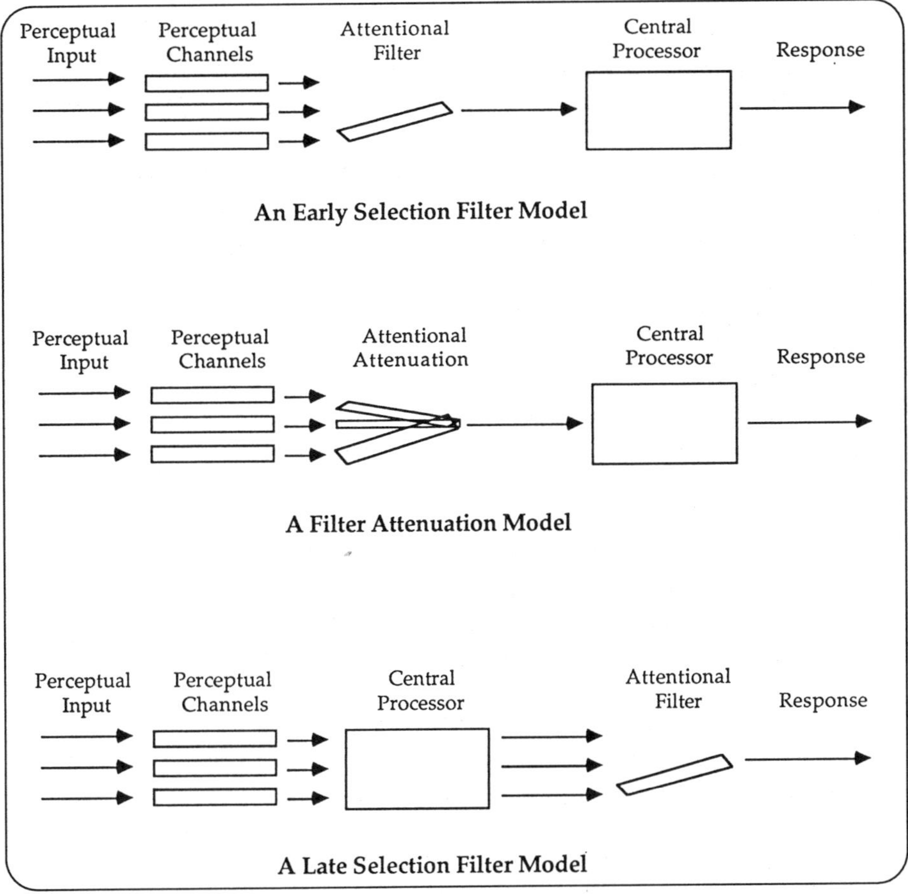

Figure 5.1. Filter models of attention.

Contrary to the predictions of Broadbent's (1958) model, subsequent studies showed that in at least some situations material that is not attended to is identified. The finding cited most often in this regard is that a person will usually be aware of their name being spoken in a message to which they were not attending (Moray, 1959). To use an example with which most people have had experience, at a party you may find your attention diverted from a conversation you are having by the sound of your name being pronounced in a nearby conversation. This indicates that the early selective filter, if it exists, is not "all or none." Treisman (1964) took this point into account in her modification of filter theory in which the filter only attenuates unattended messages rather than blocking them completely. In this **filter attenuation** model, most of an unattended message will not be identified (see Figure 5.1, middle). However, items that are unattended but that fit within the context of attended items or with other expectancies may be identified. For instance, Treisman found that people who were shadowing a prose passage presented to one ear while ignoring a second passage presented to the other ear would inadvertently continue shadowing the first passage for at least a few words when the passages were switched to the opposite ears. This demonstrated that the semantic content of a shadowed message can override a selective "filter" set to exclude information from one source.

The finding that unattended items that fit into the primary message context are identified suggested to some researchers that complete stimulus information may be received and identified, even when there is no memory for it. This observation led to the development of so-called **late selection** models of attention, for which any filtering of messages occurs relatively late in the processing sequence. For example, Deutsch and Deutsch (1963) and Norman (1968) proposed models in which all stimuli are identified by contacting their representations in memory, with only those items that are deemed to be pertinent receiving further processing. That is, in these models the bottleneck is in some processing stage after stimulus identification (see Figure 5.1, bottom). The primary difference between this late selection view and the early selection view is whether all or only some of the stimuli are identified. Both classes of models allow only some limited number of stimuli to be acted upon at a given time, regardless of how the stimuli are presented.

In part because it is difficult to determine whether all stimuli are identified, alternatives to bottleneck models have been proposed that treat attention as a limited resource available to all processing stages. **Unitary resource** models propose that there is a single, undifferentiated resource common to all task demands. For example, Kahneman (1973) proposed a unitary resource model in which the total amount of attention available was presumed to vary as a function of task difficulty, with allocation strategies becoming important when the demands exceeded the supply (see Figure 5.2). According to this model, if one task is performed concurrently with either of two other tasks that are of equal difficulty, the total attentional demands should be equivalent for the two dual-task situations and hence performance should be the same. However, numerous studies have shown that the ability to time-share two tasks depends not only on the difficulty of the tasks but also on their composition. Thus this predic-

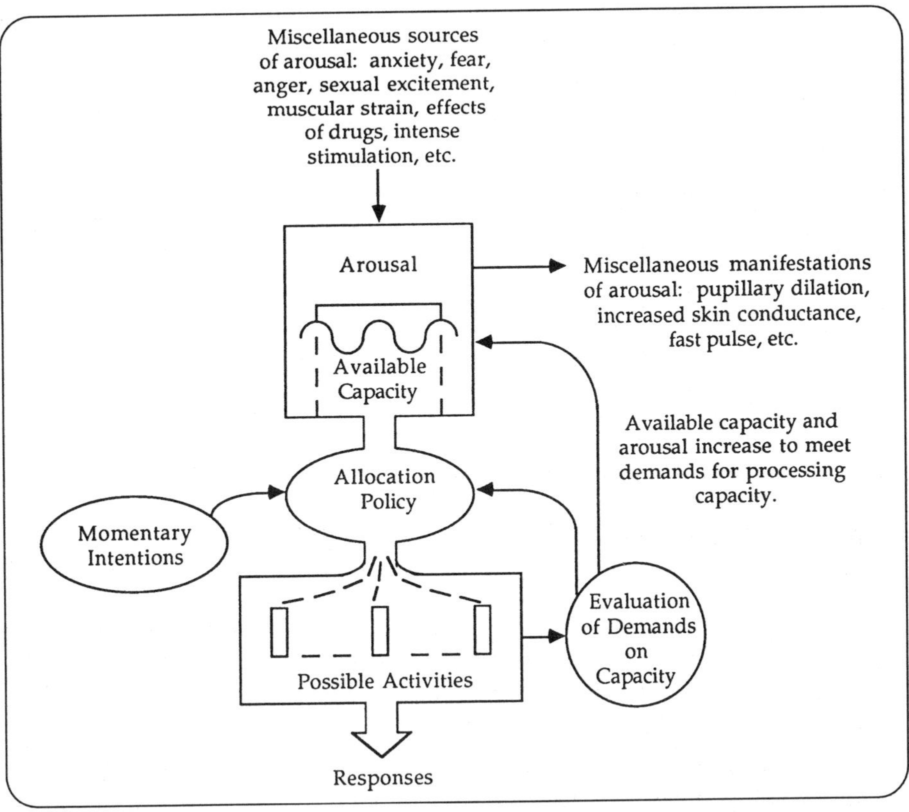

Figure 5.2. Kahneman's (1973) unitary resource model of attention.
SOURCE: Kahneman (1973, p. 18). Reprinted by permission of Prentice-Hall, Inc., © 1973.

tion of unitary resource models is incorrect. Kahneman maintained the unitary resource model in the face of such findings by allowing not only for interference due to attentional resource limitations but also for structural interference that occurs when tasks involve the same perceptual modality or response mechanism. Structural interference is invoked to explain such findings as that performance of two concurrent monitoring tasks tends to be worse when the stimuli for the tasks use the same perceptual modality (e.g., vision) rather than different modalities (e.g., vision for one and audition for the other; Treisman & Davies, 1973).

Other authors have proposed instead models that treat attention as a collection of specialized resources (Navon & Gopher, 1979; Norman & Bobrow, 1975). The degree of interference would then depend on the extent to which the same or different resources were required by two tasks.

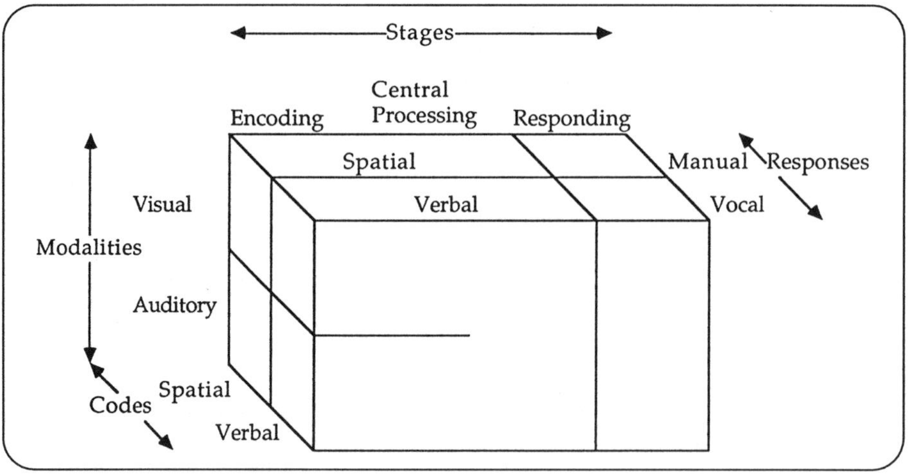

Figure 5.3. Wickens's (1984) multiple resources model of attention.

A popular **multiple-resource** model is that of Wickens (1984). In this model (see Figure 5.3), processing stages (encoding, central processing, and responding), codes of perceptual and central processing (spatial and verbal), and modalities of stimuli (auditory and visual) and responses (manual and vocal) all have their own share of attentional resources. The interference between two tasks performed concurrently will depend on the extent to which common resources are required. In general, the more similar the resource demands of the two tasks, the greater the interference because the share of attention allocated to the particular resources would be used up and additional resources cannot be borrowed from other modalities or stages. Although the multiple-resource view has been useful for evaluating and predicting performance in multiple-task environments, it has been criticized as being theoretically weak (Navon, 1984; Neumann, 1987). The major criticism is that it is impossible to know how many distinct pools of resources there are; whenever an unanticipated result is encountered, a new resource may be postulated to account for it. Consequently, some version of multiple-resource theory will be consistent with virtually any pattern of results, making the theory untestable.

Mental Workload

A concept closely related to that of attention and important to multiple-task performance is **mental workload,** which refers in a general way to the resource demands imposed on a performer. When task demands are too high, performance deteriorates and considerable stress is placed on the performer. Conversely, if the demands are too low, the performer may experience boredom and be easily distracted from the task, which also may result in a deterioration of performance (see Chapter 11 for a related discussion of the rôle of arousal in performance). In some environments, such as supervisory control of a system in which a person monitors computers that perform most of the required control actions, there may be extended periods of low demand punctuated by periods of high demand.

The ability of people to react to changes in task demands and to maintain performance under high demand conditions is a major concern, and a branch of engineering psychology has developed that is devoted to evaluating and predicting attentional demands in various task environments (Hancock & Meshkati, 1988). It should come as no surprise that secondary-task methods, which have been used extensively in the investigation of attention, are often used to measure mental workload. Multiple resource theories of attention have been useful in this regard because they provide a rationale for varying the nature of the secondary task so as to derive a complete profile of task demands. Unfortunately, from our viewpoint, relatively little concern has been given to the ability of performers to learn new skills under high-workload conditions.

Response Inhibition and Refractoriness

In some situations, we have trouble ignoring information that is defined as irrelevant to the task at hand and must work to prevent responses to this information, as, for example, when trying to read in the same room with a television that is turned on. In other situations, such as when a batter in baseball must first swing the bat to hit the ball and then start running to first base when the ball is hit, we need to make separate responses as quickly as possible to two or more sources of information presented in close succession, and problems arise here as well. Examining human performance in these situations helps us understand the way in which actions are coordinated in task environments that contain multiple stimuli.

Interference From Irrelevant Information

The research literature is replete with demonstrations of interference from information that is defined as irrelevant to the selection of the correct

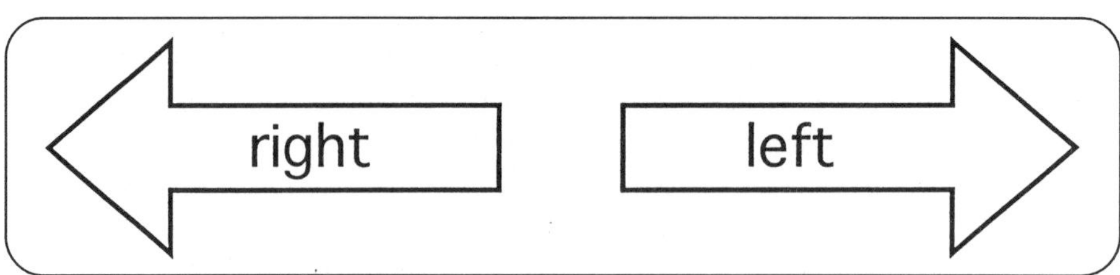

Figure 5.4. A spatial variation of the Stroop task for which the time to name the direction in which each arrow points is slowed by the superimposition of an incongruent location word.

response for a particular situation. Perhaps the most widely known interference effect is the Stroop effect (Stroop, 1935/1992), which was first demonstrated for color-naming responses to colored inks. The effect is that when people are asked to name patches of color they are much slower if the patches spell color words different from the ink colors than if the patches are neutral forms, such as rows of Xs. Similar interference effects have been demonstrated for spatial rather than color stimuli. For example, when the spatial location of a word must be named (e.g., "left" or "right" position) and the meaning of the word presented indicates a conflicting response (e.g., the word *left* presented on the right or the word *right* presented on the left), the naming response is slowed relative to congruent or neutral location-naming conditions. Figure 5.4 illustrates the stimuli for a variation of this latter task in which an incongruent location word interferes with naming the direction in which an arrow is pointing.

One of the more interesting properties of Stroop interference is that it is asymmetric (Virzi & Egeth, 1985). For example, although incongruent color words slow color naming, incongruent ink colors do not slow the reading of the color words. Similarly, although vocal responses to stimulus location are slowed by incongruent location words, vocal responses to the location words are not slowed significantly by incongruent physical locations. However, this asymmetry for the location stimuli is reversed when the responses are keypresses: Responses to the location words are interfered with by incongruent physical locations, whereas responses to the locations are not interfered with by incongruent location words. Such findings are generally consistent with a variation of the multiple-resources model in which verbal stimuli and vocal responses are processed in one system and spatial stimuli and keypress responses in another. Interference occurs when the response to the relevant stimulus attribute requires translation into the same system as the irrelevant stimulus attribute (e.g., when spatial location must be translated into the verbal-vocal system for a vocal response; Virzi & Egeth, 1985), thus producing two possible responses in that system.

The interference evident in the Stroop effect is thought to arise from competition between the response indicated by the irrelevant information and the response indicated by the relevant information (Dyer, 1973; MacLeod, 1991). A phenomenon called **negative priming** suggests that the incorrect response must be actively inhibited (i.e., blocked) for the correct response to be executed. In the color Stroop task, negative priming is said to occur when the response to name a color is slower if that color is the one indicated by an immediately preceding distractor word than if it is not (e.g., Dalrymple-Alford & Budayr, 1966; Neill, 1977). That is, the inhibition of the incorrect response on the previous trial persists such that selection of that response on the current trial is impeded.

A question of interest is whether the magnitude of Stroop interference is reduced through practice. The answer is "yes," although an effect of considerable magnitude remains (e.g., Dulaney & Rogers, 1994; Stroop, 1935/1992). It has been suggested that the reduction of the Stroop effect is due at least in part to the development of a "reading suppression response" (Dulaney & Rogers, 1994; Ellis & Dulaney, 1991). Suppression of reading is implicated by the finding that after several thousand trials of performing the Stroop color-naming task, color word naming takes longer (i.e., naming color words while ignoring the ink colors) than it did before the practice. An alternative explanation is that the naming of colors becomes automatized during practice and then must be inhibited when the color words are to be read. As would be expected if this were the case, color word reading is not slowed nearly as much after practice at the Stroop color-naming task when the words are printed in a neutral ink color rather than in incongruent ink colors (Dulaney & Rogers, 1994). Further research is needed to discriminate between these alternative explanations.

The Psychological Refractory Period

The common theme addressed by all models of attention and acknowledged in the study of mental workload is that there are limits on our ability to process information, and a major point of concern has been the identification of the precise loci of these limitations. One way that this concern has been investigated is by having people perform dual tasks in which two stimuli, each of which requires a response, are presented in

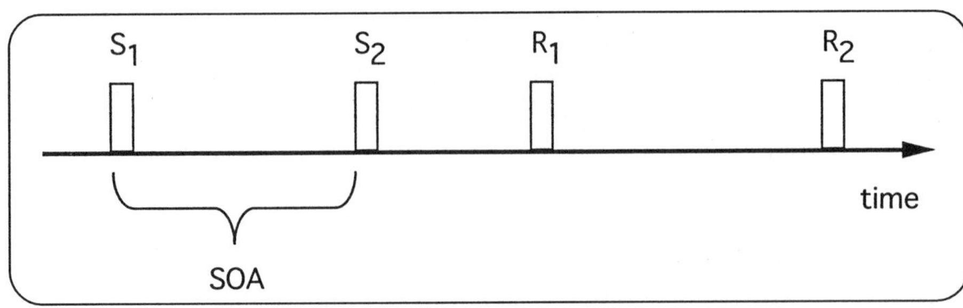

Figure 5.5. The psychological refractory period paradigm. S_1 and S_2 are the two stimulus occurrences, separated by the stimulus onset asynchrony (SOA). R_1 and R_2 denote the responses to S_1 and S_2, respectively.

rapid succession (see Figure 5.5). The most robust finding in this situation is that reaction time to the second stimulus is slowed relative to when that stimulus is presented alone, with this prolongation of reaction time being a decreasing function of the interval between the two stimuli. That is, at short stimulus onset asynchronies (SOAs; i.e., the interval between the onsets of the two stimuli) the relative delay in making the second response is greater than at long SOAs. This slowing of the response to the second stimulus is called the **psychological refractory period** (PRP) effect (Smith, 1967; Telford, 1931), by analogy to the refractory state in nerve fibers. Early theorists thought that there was a central refractoriness such that the first stimulus had a physiological inhibitory effect on the processing of the second. Although this explanation has long been discredited, the name has been retained.

The account of the slowing of the response to the second stimulus that has received the most attention is that there is some point in the information processing sequence at which only one stimulus at a time may be processed. Broadbent (1958) applied his filter theory of attention to the PRP effect and proposed that the bottleneck is perceptual, with perception operating on stimulus samples of approximately 0.33-s duration. If the second stimulus occurs immediately after the first, the sample cannot be sent until the 0.33-s sampling period has elapsed. The quantitative nature of Broadbent's theory has allowed precise predictions to be made—and falsified. Most notably, the delay in responding to the second stimulus should be a function only of its separation in time from the first stimulus. Thus manipulations of the time required for response selection to the first stimulus should not provide an additional influence on reaction time to the second stimulus. As we will discuss, this prediction does not hold.

The theory of the PRP effect that is currently most widely accepted attributes the effect to a bottleneck in the stage of response selection. Welford (1952) and Davis (1957) were the first to develop detailed accounts of this type, and much additional work has been based on their accounts. The core of the model is that the selection of two responses cannot occur in parallel. Consequently, selection of the second response cannot begin until selection of the first response is completed. During the time when the first response is being selected, information about the second stimulus can be accumulated, but it must be held in store until the response selection mechanism becomes available.

According to the simplest version of the response selection bottleneck theory, the function relating second stimulus reaction time to the interval between the onsets of the two stimuli should be linear with a slope of –1.0 (see Figure 5.6). This predicted linear relation is a result of the assumptions made about the bottleneck and can be written, for a delay less than or equal to the reaction time to the first stimulus, as follows:

$$RT_2 = RT_n + RT_1 - \text{delay},$$

where RT_1 is the reaction time to the first stimulus, RT_2 is the predicted reaction time to the second stimulus, RT_n is the normal reaction time to the second stimulus when presented alone, and delay is the time interval between the presentation of the two stimuli. Because reaction times to the second stimulus are often prolonged even when the delay exceeds the reaction time to the first stimulus, Welford suggested that additional time is devoted to attending to proprioceptive feedback from the first response.

Converging evidence that the PRP effect has its basis at least in part in response selection processes comes from several sources. The basic logic underlying one approach is that the locus of any processing bottleneck can be determined by the patterns of interaction or additivity resulting from the manipulation of stimulus and response factors. **Latent network theory** (Schweickert, 1983; Schweickert, Fisher, & Goldstein, 1992; Townsend & Ashby, 1983) can be applied to determine whether the processes affected by the manipulated factors are executed sequentially or concurrently. Latent network theory takes its name from the purpose of the analysis, which is to derive the processing network, called a **precedence network,** that underlies cognitive performance. The method by which a latent network analysis is carried out is to manipulate several factors and then to examine the interaction contrasts for these factors. An interaction contrast has the form: $T_{ij} - T_{1j} - T_{i1} + T_{11}$, where T_{ij} is the time taken to respond

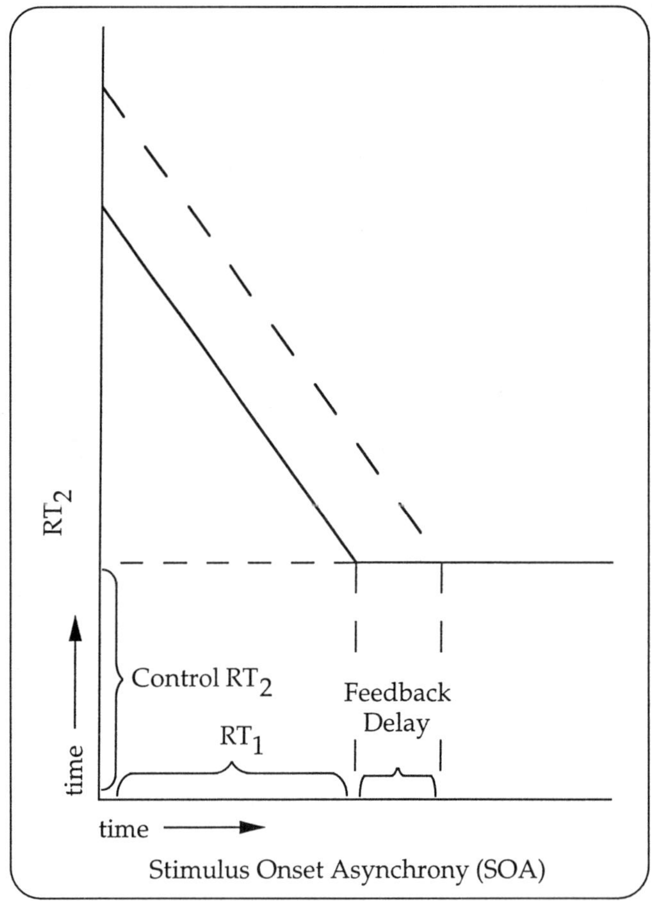

Figure 5.6. Functions predicted by response-selection bottleneck theory relating second stimulus reaction time (RT_2) to SOA, assuming that the processing of S_2 begins immediately upon the response to S_1 (solid line) or after a delay for processing feedback (dashed line).

at level *i* of one factor (e.g., stimulus-response compatibility) and level *j* of the other factor (e.g., the time between the two stimulus presentations) and the factor levels are numbered in order with respect to the length of the prolongation produced. The usual finding is that the interaction contrasts are monotonic with increases in the factor levels, all have the same sign, and are themselves monotonic. If the values of the interaction contrasts are positive or zero, the processes are sequential. If the interaction

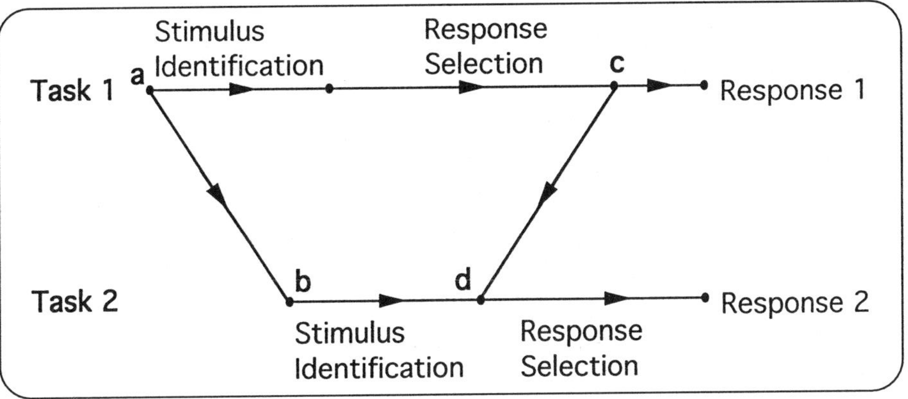

Figure 5.7. A possible network underlying the performance of the McCann and Johnston task. Processing beyond any point in the network cannot occur until all processes leading directly to that point have finished.

contrasts are negative, the processes are carried out concurrently or are in a special arrangement called a Wheatstone bridge, discussion of which is beyond the scope of this book.

If a processing bottleneck exists in response selection, such that only one response can be selected at a time, the precedence network shown in Figure 5.7 would apply. The processing of the stimulus for the first task starts at point *a*. After some interval, represented by the line from point *a* to point *b*, the processing of the stimulus for the second task begins. Processing beyond any point in the network cannot occur until all processes leading directly to that point have finished. Thus the selection of a response to the second stimulus, which would begin at point *d*, cannot proceed until the response to the first stimulus has been selected, which occurs at point *c*. The line from *c* to *d* illustrates the dependency of Task 2 response selection on the completion of response selection for the first task.

An important construct in latent network theory is **slack**, which can be defined roughly as the time during which task information is not being processed. Slack exists for Task 2 whenever the time to identify the stimulus and select the response for Task 1 exceeds the delay between the two stimuli and the time to identify the second stimulus. In this network, increasing the difficulty of identification for the second stimulus reduces the amount of slack. There will be no effect on Task 2 reaction time until the slack is used up. Thus we will not see additive effects of increasing the stimulus identification difficulty if the changes are sufficiently small. However, because there is no slack in the system after Task 2 response selection begins, additive effects will be observed if factors influencing Task 2 response selection difficulty are manipulated.

Pashler (1984) tested one prediction of the network: that increasing the difficulty of Task 2 stimulus identification would be underadditive with the effect of changing the SOA between the stimuli for the two tasks. That is, because stimulus identification for the second task can be carried out during the time in which the response to the first task is being selected, the effect of increasing discrimination time by making the stimuli more difficult to process is partially obscured. To test this prediction, Pashler used a visual search task and varied the contrast of the stimulus array. Some people practiced the task alone, whereas others practiced the task in conjunction with a primary task. Consistent with the network shown in Figure 5.7, there was less effect of the contrast manipulation when the search task was performed in the dual-task context than when performed alone. The negative interaction contrasts imply that stimulus processing for the two tasks can be carried out concurrently. Thus there is not much evidence for limits in perceptual capacity in these simple tasks.

McCann and Johnston (1992) obtained additional experimental evidence consistent with the network representation in Figure 5.7. They used the PRP paradigm with two tasks of varied stimulus-response compatibility to determine whether there is a bottleneck in processing at the response selection stage. McCann and Johnston prolonged the duration of the response selection stage by making the selection problem more difficult. They also manipulated the time at which response selection processes should be occupied by varying the time that elapsed between the presentation of the stimulus for the first task and that for the second. When they influenced the difficulty of Task 2 response selection by decreasing stimulus-response compatibility, additive effects of compatibility and delay in the onset of the second stimulus on Task 2 reaction time were found, consistent with a bottleneck located at response selection.

Despite the agreement of many results with the response selection bottleneck account, some findings are difficult to reconcile with it. For example, Karlin and Kestenbaum (1968) manipulated response selection difficulty for the second task by requiring either a simple or a two-choice reaction. Additive effects of selection difficulty with SOA similar to those found by McCann and Johnston (1992) would be expected if there were a response selection bottleneck, yet an interaction was obtained such that the difference in reaction times was much greater at long SOAs than at short ones. De Jong (1993) proposed that findings such as these indicate that there is also a response initiation bottleneck, located after the response selection bottleneck, that prevents two responses from being initiated in close succession. He obtained evidence for this response initiation bottleneck by using go/no-go reactions for the first task and showing that several manipulations of the second task, including that of simple versus choice reactions, showed interactions with SOA on **go** trials (for which two responses had to be initiated and hence the response initiation bottleneck should have been a factor) but additive effects on **no-go** trials (for which the bottleneck should not have been a factor because only one response had to be initiated). Thus, while studies of the PRP effect provide compelling evidence for a response selection bottleneck, the evidence suggests that there is also a response initiation bottleneck, at least when two manual responses are required.

Of concern for skilled performance is the question of whether the bottlenecks implied by the PRP effect can be eliminated or bypassed with practice. Gottsdanker and Stelmach (1971) sought to answer this question by giving extensive practice in a dual-task paradigm. Their major finding was that although the PRP effect was reduced to approximately 25 ms when extensive practice with one SOA was given, there was little transfer of this benefit to shorter or longer SOAs. In fact, reaction times were greater at the next longer intervals (200 and 400 ms) than they had been at the 100-ms interval used during practice. This finding is in contrast to the common finding that the PRP effect decreases monotonically as the interval between stimulus onsets increases and led Gottsdanker and Stelmach to conclude that the decrease in the PRP effect over the 87 days of practice was due to a strategy specific to coordinating responses at short intervals rather than to a more general improved ability to perform two tasks in rapid succession. Thus it appears that the bottlenecks in response selection and initiation cannot be bypassed even when the joint tasks are practiced extensively.

Resource Allocation

The previous section discussed decrements in response speed that occur when two tasks must be performed in rapid succession. More generally, we can ask how people are able to coordinate the performance of multiple tasks. The means of coordinating performance that has been most widely studied is based on the controlled allocation of attentional resources to one task or another. Here we discuss research concerned with graded allocation of resources across tasks as well as the switching of attention between tasks or information sources. Implicit in the resource allocation approach to studying multiple-task performance is the assumption that the way in which each of the multiple tasks is carried out is fundamentally unchanged. That is, the timing of component parts of the task may change, but the component parts themselves do not. This assumption is violated if tasks or information sources are actually recombined or integrated such that their separate identities are to some extent lost in pursuit of the goal of more efficient performance. We discuss some situations in which recombination is likely to occur in a later section.

Trade-Offs Between Tasks

Perhaps the simplest model of multiple-task performance is based on the unitary resource model discussed earlier (e.g., Kahneman, 1973), for which there is one undifferentiated pool of attentional capacity that can be allocated at will to the respective tasks. In this view, two tasks can be performed together without decrement so long as the total amount of attentional capacity required does not exceed the available supply. If the capacity is exceeded, at least one task will suffer. Under the assumption that attention is under the person's control, it can be removed from one task and devoted to the other in varying degrees. Performance of two tasks as a function of the attention devoted to each can be represented with the performance operating characteristic (POC) curve, which is used to depict the possible trade-offs between two tasks (see Figure 5.8; Norman & Bobrow, 1975).

In Figure 5.8, performance on Task A is represented on the vertical axis and performance on Task B on the horizontal axis. If we plot single-task performance for each task, the point representing the intersection of performance on the two tasks (point *P*) serves as a referent for the measurement of the efficiency of dual-task performance. The more successfully two tasks can be performed together, the closer plotted performance will be to point *P*. However, even if one task is strongly emphasized over the other (as in the probe-task procedure described earlier), performance is typically worse in the dual-task context than in the single-task context. This **cost of concurrence** may be due to such things as distraction by the secondary task (resulting in an inability to allocate sufficient attention to the primary task) and the need to coordinate the two tasks. A POC curve is obtained by biasing the performer to emphasize one task over the

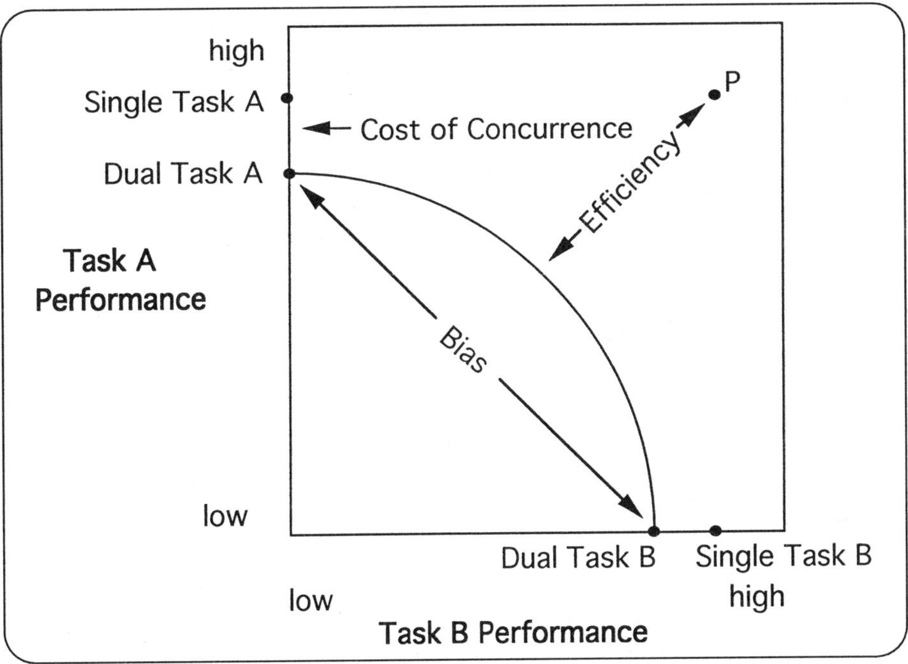

Figure 5.8. A performance operating characteristic.

other in different blocks of trials. This procedure can be used to yield several points, from which a curve is derived to reflect the degree to which resources can be traded off between the two tasks.

The validity of the POC analysis depends on the assumption that the resources required for the two tasks are interchangeable and allocable. Of course, it is also assumed that voluntary attentional control can be exercised to comply with the task emphasis manipulations (Gopher, 1993). The former assumption will only hold when the two tasks draw on the same resources. According to the unitary resource view, all tasks draw on some central capacity and hence will trade off whenever this capacity is exceeded. However, according to the multiple resources view, only tasks that draw on the same specialized resource will demonstrate the effects of bias illustrated in a hypothetical POC curve. Moreover, to the extent that different resources are used by the two tasks, overall time-sharing efficiency should be increased.

Tsang and Wickens (1988) obtained results consistent with the multiple-resource view when they combined a primary tracking task with secondary tasks that used either visual or verbal stimuli and manual or speech responses. In general, time-sharing performance with the tracking task was more efficient when the secondary task required speech responses rather than manual responses. By increasing the difficulty of the primary tracking task, Tsang and Wickens were also able to examine the ability of performers to grade their allocation of resources to the two tasks. Graded resource allocation was observed only when the secondary task had manual responses. Moreover, in the conditions with manual responses, this ability to allocate resources efficiently improved with practice. The fact that graded allocation was found only for manual responses suggests that a common resource is used in both the tracking and manual response tasks but not when tracking is combined with the verbal response task. When two tasks tap the same resources, as for tracking and manual response tasks, strategic control of task performance plays a greater role than when the tasks tap different resources.

Effects of Task Content on Time-Sharing Performance

If performance is only dependent on the overlap in processing resources required by two tasks, then performance of one task should be influenced by the difficulty of the other task but not by the specific semantic content of the information presented in the other task. However, the mere availability of needed resources for two tasks may not be sufficient to guarantee interference-free performance. As an illustration, it has been shown that the similarity of semantic content for tasks of equal difficulty affects performance. Navon and Miller (1987) showed this with two visual search tasks for which an item from a designated category was to be detected. The categories of the target items were different for the two tasks, but the distractor for one task could belong to the target category of the other task (see Figure 5.9a) or to a category similar to the other target category (see Figure 5.9b). For one task, words were displayed to the left or right of center; for the other task, words were displayed above or below center. Either one or two words for each task were shown on a given trial, and the semantic relatedness of the target for one task to the distractor for the other task was varied. For example, as shown in Figure 5-9, the horizontal arm of the display may have been searched for a city name and the vertical arm for a boy's name. In both examples shown in the figure, the correct responses in the dual-task condition would be that a city name is present but that a boy's name is not.

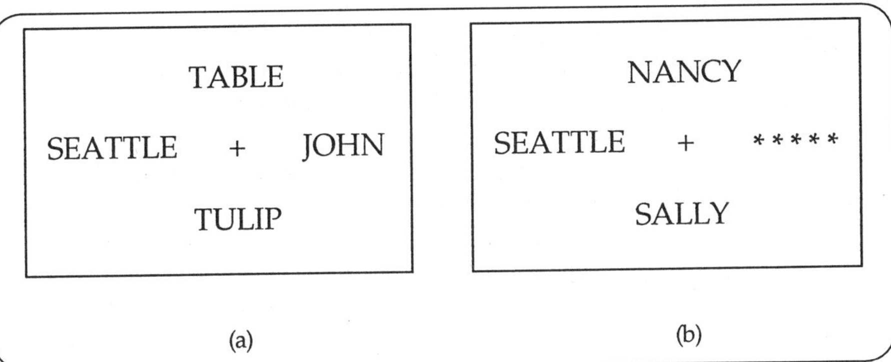

Figure 5.9. Possible stimulus displays in the Navon and Miller (1987, Experiment 1) task. The horizontal arm of each display is searched for a city name and the vertical arm for a boy's name. In (a) the presence of the boy's name John in the city channel may interfere with the correct response (target absent) to the boy channel task. In (b) the presence of distractors on the boy channel that are semantically related to boys' names may also interfere with the correct response.

As predicted by many theories, increasing the difficulties of the respective tasks by adding distractors caused reaction time to increase. The important finding was that when a word from the category for one task occurred as a distractor for the other, or when a distractor for one task was from a category similar to the other target category, the disruption was even greater. Hirst and Kalmar (1987) obtained analogous semantic similarity effects in a dichotic listening task. Thus cross talk between tasks is a function not just of resource availability but of task content. Navon and Miller (1987) proposed that **outcome conflict** was responsible for the observed interference. Outcome conflict occurs when a task produces outputs that inhibit or compete with the processing of the other task, as occurs in the Stroop task (Stroop, 1935/1992) discussed earlier. Thus output interference occurs relatively late in processing, after semantic information has been identified.

Time-Sharing Without Cost

Both resource views imply that if one of two tasks is automatic, such that it does not require any attentional resources, it should be possible to perform the two tasks simultaneously with little or no cost, even if they initially required a common resource. In agreement with this implication,

Allport, Antonis, and Reynolds (1972) found that skilled pianists showed almost no decrement in playing sight-read music (which should be highly automatized for them) when the requirement to shadow auditorily presented words was added.

In experimental studies, Schneider and Fisk (1982a) examined whether two visual search tasks could be carried out without a cost of concurrence when one of the tasks was automatized. The first visual search task had a consistent mapping of items (numbers and letters) to either the target or distractor sets; thus automatic responding would be expected to develop in this task (Shiffrin & Schneider, 1977; see Chapter 2). The second task used a varied mapping of items to the target and distractor sets so that, for example, digits may have been the target for one trial but distractors for the next, thus precluding the development of automaticity. Each task was practiced in isolation as well as in combination with the other. In the dual-task situation, only either a consistently mapped or variably mapped target occurred on any particular trial, and instructions emphasized attending to the varied-mapping task.

As is customarily found, single-task performance in the varied-mapping condition showed little improvement with practice, whereas single-task performance in the consistent-mapping condition did. Performance of the consistent-mapping task was worse initially in the dual-task condition than in the single-task condition, which demonstrates that automatized processes are not entirely "encapsulated" and immune to interference. However, with practice in the dual-task situation, performance of the consistent-mapping task improved to the level of the single task, as did that of the varied-mapping task. The relative improvement with the varied mapping in the dual-task context is apparently due to a freeing up of resources as the consistently mapped task becomes automatized. This hypothesis gains additional support from the results of subsequent experiments in which more emphasis was placed on the consistent-mapping task. In this case, performance of the varied-mapping task seriously deteriorated in the dual-task context.

Another example of dual-task performance without apparent cost is a study by Hirst, Spelke, Reaves, Caharack, and Neisser (1980) in which prose was read by itself or while copying auditorily presented words or sentences. Initially, reading was slower in the dual-task context than in the single-task context. However, after extensive practice of several weeks, all of the people who performed the task were able to read equally fast in the dual- and single-task contexts. Hirst et al. used two types of reading material: short stories and encyclopedia articles. To test the hypothesis that reading while taking dictation is a skill, they introduced one of the materials after the other, once the performance criterion had been met. Excellent transfer to the new material was apparent, suggesting that a general skill at reading while taking dictation had been acquired.

On the basis of results similar to these, Spelke, Hirst, and Neisser (1976) concluded,

> Although individual strategies may have their own limitations, there are no obvious, general limits to attentional skills. Studies of attention which use unpracticed subjects, and infer mechanisms and limitations from their performance, will inevitably underestimate human capacities. Indeed, people's ability to develop skills in specialized situations is so great that it may never be possible to define general limits on cognitive capacity. (p. 229)

As an illustration of this point, consider Underwood's (1974) comparison of the performance of a skilled shadower (the attention researcher, Neville Moray) to that of average performers on a dichotic listening task. In this task, which had originally led to the view of the human as a single-channel processor of limited capacity, Moray was able to detect 66.7% of digit targets embedded among letters in the nonshadowed message, compared to the detection rate of less than 10% that is typically found.

Time-Sharing Skill

The effects of practice on improving the efficiency of time-sharing have been documented in both graded resource allocation (Spitz, 1988) and attention switching (Allport & Styles, 1990) paradigms. The development of efficient time-sharing strategies appears to be dependent on the provision of augmented feedback regarding the effects of time-sharing on each of the shared tasks (e.g., Gopher, Brickner, & Navon, 1982). These results suggest that resource allocation ability develops over time to become more efficient: In other words, attention control can be thought of as a skill.

As with other skills, a question of interest is which practice schedules produce the most rapid and effective learning of attention control. Spitz (1988) examined this question in a study in which people performed a letter cancellation task using a chord keyboard concurrently with a continuous tracking task. Four groups received an equal amount of training with on-line feedback but under different schedules of priorities. For the *equal priority* group, all practice was with the two tasks given equal weighting (50% for each task); for the *extreme priorities* group, practice was also given under conditions in which either the tracking task or the letter cancellation task was strongly emphasized (90% priority for one task and 10% priority for the other); for the *wide range* group, practice involved not only the three priority conditions used for the extreme priorities group, but also conditions under which the priorities were less extreme; a final group, the *narrow range* group, received the same number of priority conditions as the wide range group but with the priorities varying over a narrower range. The wide range group improved more in the dual task and evidenced better control over resource allocation than did the other three groups. This benefit for receiving practice under a wide range of conditions, which is reminiscent of the advantage for variable practice (at least when the conditions are randomized) in motor learning (see Chapter 4), suggests that a better schema for the flexible allocation of resources was developed.

The view that attention control is a skill suggests that the ability to allocate attention, or time-sharing ability, may differ across individuals. Because most complex, real-world tasks require selective attending to different information sources, time-sharing ability might be a good predictor of success in many tasks. Gopher (1982) and his colleagues developed a time-sharing test of selective attention and validated it on several populations, including flight cadets in the Israeli Air Force and bus drivers. For the test, lists of words and digits were presented dichotically. Digits detected in the relevant ear were to be written down immediately, whereas digits occurring in the irrelevant ear were to be ignored as were any words. Each list was preceded by the presentation of a brief tone of high or low frequency to indicate whether the right or left ear was to be considered relevant for the first portion of the list. Sixteen letter-digit pairs of items were then presented, one item to each ear, with at most one digit in each pair. After these pairs, another brief tone designated the right or left ear as relevant for the remainder of the list. In this part of the list, zero, one, or two pairs of words, followed by three pairs of digits, were presented dichotically.

Three types of errors were recorded. In the first part of the list, the person being tested could omit a digit in the relevant ear or intrude a digit from the irrelevant ear. These types of errors were called *omissions* and *intrusions*, respectively. Either type of error could also occur in the second part of the list, but because omissions were almost always accompanied by intrusions and vice versa, Phase 2 errors were grouped for analysis as *selective attention* errors. In the validation studies, the number of second phase selective attention errors was the most diagnostic measure of future complex task performance. The number of selective attention errors correlated negatively with successful completion of flight school and positively with the accident rate of bus drivers. Because few errors of selective attention occurred when digit pairs were presented in isolation, without the requirement to switch attention from a previous task it seems that the ability to switch attention from one ear to the other when required from the first to the second phase is the important factor.

Integrating Across Information Sources

In the previous section, we emphasized the need to keep information from different sources separate. However, in some cases, good performance requires the integration of separate sources of information. Particularly when the task environment is complex and multiple subtasks must be performed, it is important to look for ways to simplify the environment. One way to simplify complex environments is to learn relations between different aspects of the environment such that information sources or task components are effectively recombined.

Multiple-Cue Probability Learning

It is useful to think about the many sources of information present at any one time in terms of the cue that each of the sources provides regarding either the state of the environment or the required action. Typically, the predictive power of the different cues will vary, and successful task performance will depend on learning the relation between each cue and the task criterion (Brunswick, 1955). **Multiple-cue probability learning** is an area of study concerned with how the structure and interrelatedness of task information affects a person's judgments (Cuqlock-Knopp, Wilkins, & Torgerson, 1991).

Brunswick's (1955) lens model provides a foundation for much of the multiple-cue probability learning research. The basic elements of the model are the true level of the criterion variable (i.e., the variable that the person is required to predict), the information sources or cues regarding the criterion, and the person's prediction of the criterion variable. In Figure 5.10, the cues are represented by X_i and are probabilistically related to the criterion Y_e. The correlation between a cue and the criterion, known as its validity, is denoted $r_{e,1}$. The prediction of the criterion is denoted Y_s, and

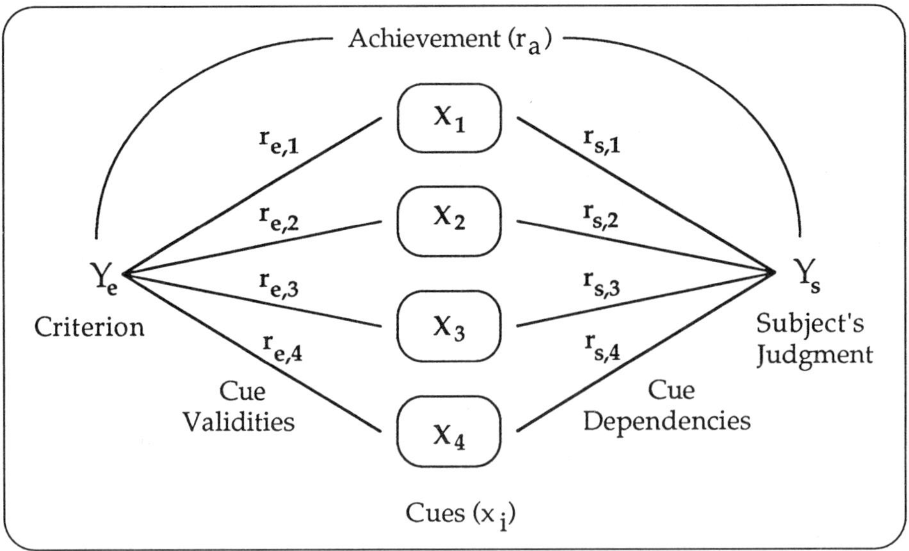

Figure 5.10. Brunswick's (1955) lens model for multiple cue-probability learning. See text for explanation.

the correlation between a cue and Y_s, denoted $r_{s,1}$, reflects the dependency of the final judgment on the cue. Two independent variables that can be manipulated are the nature of the cues and the cue validities. The goal of the researcher is to infer what cues people depend on and whether these dependencies are optimal for the task.

Several important findings have emerged from this research. The first is that, in general, cues that are positively correlated to the criterion are processed more efficiently than are negatively correlated cues. This is probably due to the fact that when a cue is positively correlated with the criterion, less transformation of the cue value is required to determine the value of the criterion. The intercorrelations between cues also influence performance. Performance improves when cues are positively intercorrelated but may deteriorate if negative correlations between cues are present. Another significant finding is that cues that are linearly related to the criterion are easier to use than nonlinear cues. This was illustrated by Sniezek and Naylor (1978), who found that performance was better with both positive and negative linear cues than with inverted U-shaped cue-criterion relations. In fact, when cue validities are low, people may assume that linear functions exist whether or not this is justified (Alm & Brehmer, 1982).

Learning to use cue information is facilitated when task predictability is high. Predictability may increase as more valid cues are introduced, but associated costs in the workload imposed by the requirement to process more information sources can lead to a decrease in performance. Adding low validity cues to the task environment may lead to performance decrements for this reason (Cuqlock-Knopp et al., 1991).

An example of a multiple-task environment in which many cues or values of variables are available is complex process control. In process control, an operator must monitor an assortment of system variables and perform corrections to the system, as indicated by the values of the variables. The learning of correlations between variables may be the most important factor in understanding and, hence, control of complex processes. Moray (1987) has suggested that operators reduce the processing load imposed in system control by using learned relationships between variables and correlations of cues with system performance. Most complex systems can be decomposed into a number of relatively independent subsystems. Learning the interrelationships of the variables and the system response to changes in these variables allows the operator to form mental models (i.e., working representations) of the relevant subsystems. The processing load is reduced when a simpler model can be used, which would be the case when correlations between cues can be used to identify simpler subsystems. Thus a major determinant of skill in system control will be the degree to which relationships among variables and between variables and system response have been learned. We will have more to say about this work in Chapter 9, where the training of system operators is discussed.

Separable, Integral, and Configural Dimensions

Most of the stimuli encountered in a task are multidimensional. For example, a visual stimulus has a size, shape, color, spatial location, and so forth. Particular dimensions can be characterized by the degree to which they facilitate or hinder the processing of other stimulus dimensions (Garner, 1974). The processing of multiple stimulus dimensions has most often been studied in classification tasks in which two stimulus dimensions are varied. So-called **separable** dimensions can be perceptually isolated and perceived as distinct attributes of stimuli. That is, they permit selective attention to either dimension, with no facilitatory or inhibitory effects. For example, observers who are asked to classify colored shapes according to their color can do so without being influenced by variation in the geometric forms that are presented (as long as the forms are not color words, as in the Stroop task!).

If stimuli are composed of **integral** dimensions, they are perceived as unitary wholes, and selective attention to either dimension is difficult. Thus, judgments that must be based on the property of an individual dimension are difficult, whereas judgments that can be based on the stimulus as a whole are relatively easy. For example, it is difficult to make judgments about the saturation (purity) of a color when its brightness also varies, but it is relatively easy to distinguish a bright, highly saturated stimulus from a dim stimulus of low saturation. It is also difficult to attend selectively to a specific dimension when the dimensions are **configural,** that is, when the dimensions interact so that the combination results in a new emergent feature that may dominate processing of the component dimensions. For example, pairs of parentheses are configural. It is easy to classify a single parenthesis as left pointing ")" or right pointing "(", but when a single parenthesis is presented with a second one, such as "((", "))", "()", or ")(", the task of classifying only the left or right parenthesis of the pair is very difficult. One implication of the research on separable, integral, and configural dimensions is that performance should be best when the dimensions used to display information are chosen to match task requirements of either keeping the sources of information separate or combining them.

Recently, performance has been studied with regard to the match between task requirements and displayed information. Barnett and Wickens (1988), for example, studied performance in a task in which participants were to integrate information about the state of the aircraft, weather conditions, and intent of the enemy to determine whether an imagined mission of a military aircraft should be continued or aborted. Each source of information had two attributes, reliability (the accuracy with which the displayed information reflected the true state of the world) and diagnosticity (the relevance of the information to evaluating the potential success or failure of the mission). The major manipulation was whether the reliability and diagnosticity of a cue were displayed as two separate bar graphs (the heights of two parallel bar graphs are separable; Figure 5.11, left) or as a rectangle where the height displayed the diagnosticity and the width the reliability (the height and width of a rectangle are relatively integral; Figure 5.11, right). Performance for this task, which required information integration, was better with the integral, rectangle display of cue worth than with the bar graph display. This study shows that the choice of integral or separable display formats has practical consequences.

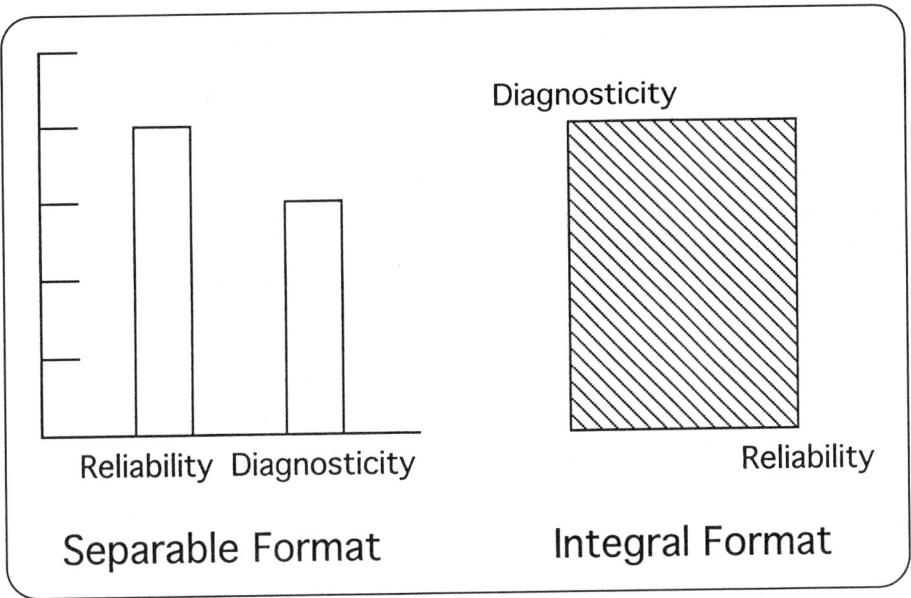

Figure 5.11. Separable (left) and integral (right) displays of two system attributes, the reliability and diagnosticity of information.

Wickens and his colleagues proposed the **proximity compatibility** principle to describe the relation of display features to task performance. This principle is that "to the extent that information sources must be integrated . . . , there will be a benefit to presenting those dimensions in an integrated (i.e., objectlike) format" (Wickens, 1992, p. 98). Whereas some implications of this principle have been supported by findings such as those of Barnett and Wickens (1988) described above, other predictions of the principle have not been confirmed. The most serious discrepancy is that the principle predicts a crossover interaction such that performance of integration tasks should be better with displays that have high proximity, whereas performance of focused attention tasks should be better with displays of low proximity. As yet, such a crossover interaction has rarely been found, and the more common outcome is that when high-proximity displays are used, performance is clearly improved for integrated tasks and somewhat improved for focused tasks (Bennett & Flach, 1992).

Components of Multiple-Task Performance: The Learning Strategies Project

Performance of complex skills involves perceptual, cognitive, and motor components, all of which must be efficiently coordinated. In previous chapters, we emphasized performance on single tasks with the goal of describing particular processing components. In the present chapter, we have considered more complex tasks, with particular emphasis on the coordinating role of attention. Because the research in the different domains has been conducted with a variety of distinct tasks and from diverse theoretical perspectives, it is difficult to compare across studies and to make predictions for tasks in which these components are combined. This difficulty prompted the initiation of the Learning Strategies Project (Donchin, Fabiani, & Sanders, 1989).

In the Learning Strategies Project, researchers from a variety of perspectives used the same computer-based task to investigate strategic factors influencing skill acquisition. The task was a video game called Space Fortress (Mané & Donchin, 1989). The object of the game is to shoot missiles at and destroy a "space fortress." The player controls a spaceship from which missiles are fired. While attempting to destroy the fortress, the player must protect his or her ship from damage. The positions of the spaceship and fortress, and other relevant information, are displayed on the video screen (see Figure 5.12). Sound effects are presented through headphones, and a joystick and trigger are manipulated to control the ship and fire missiles, respectively. To destroy the fortress, not only does the fortress have to be struck by a missile but shots must meet specific timing requirements. Throughout the game, the subject must monitor and avoid certain objects identified by letter codes of varying lengths. Finally, the player must monitor for the appearance of a "bonus symbol" and respond when it appears in order to score extra points or acquire more missiles.

Altogether 50 parameters can be varied to manipulate different aspects of game presentation. Visual monitoring and scanning difficulty can be varied by manipulating such things as stimulus discriminability and the amount of noise on the screen. Memory requirements can be varied by manipulating the length of the codes displayed on the screen and the complexity of the information presented for decision making. Motor demands can be manipulated by changing the order of control for the joystick response and spaceship flight characteristics. An array of 150 data variables is collected as the task is played. These variables describe such things

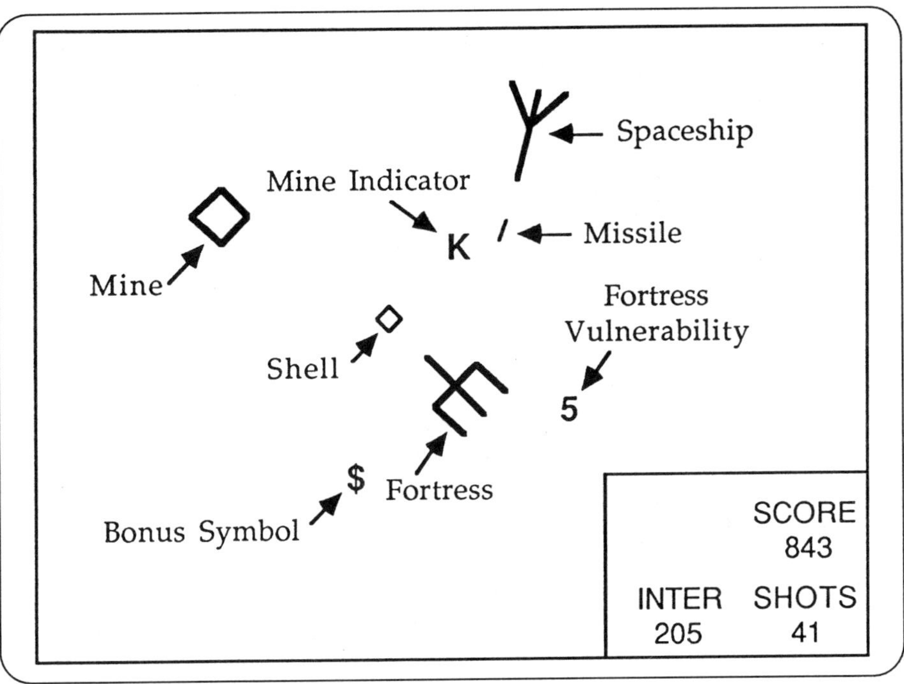

Figure 5.12. Visual display for the Space Fortress game.
SOURCE: Adapted from Mané and Donchin (1989).

as joystick movements, button presses, and movements of the game elements on the screen.

To provide a baseline for future comparisons, an initial group of 40 people played the Space Fortress game for 10 one-hour sessions (Foss, Fabiani, Mané, & Donchin, 1989). They were given instructions concerning the rules of the game at the start of practice and received no further instructions or extrinsic feedback other than their total score for the game. The participants in the experiment were divided into five ability groups based on their performance in a screening task that involved only aiming the ship and firing missiles at a target. Across sessions, all of the groups improved substantially (for example, the average total score was approximately –700 for the first session and 2,500 for the 10th session), and the difference between the five groups on the various performance measures was maintained, and for some measures, even increased. Different strategies of ship handling were identified, with players who scored higher on the initial screening task tending to adopt more sophisticated strategies.

The other studies in the project all manipulated factors expected to affect learning strategies, with the goal being to determine whether specific interventions could facilitate skill acquisition. Several of the studies examined issues in part-whole training, and we defer discussion of them until Chapter 9. In this chapter, we focus primarily on the studies that examined the primary information processing components described thus far.

Shapiro and Raymond (1989) concentrated on the perceptual component of the task by instituting procedures to train eye movements. In the Space Fortress game, eye movements are required to track relevant moving objects, to identify whether objects are friend or foe, and to update the information that must be held in memory. To perform efficiently, the number of eye movements should be minimized by eliminating movements to stimuli that are known to be invariant or irrelevant and by not fixating on stimuli that can be analyzed sufficiently from the peripheral visual field. Players were trained to use either efficient or inefficient eye movement strategies through drills that either encouraged or prevented the use of efficient strategies. The group taught efficient eye movement strategies performed better on the Space Fortress game than either the group who received training in inefficient eye movements or a control group who received no special drills. Thus it appears that eye movement strategies can be learned and, if they are appropriate, contribute to successful performance.

Logie et al. (1989) used the secondary-task methodology to identify the major aspects of Space Fortress game performance and to evaluate the role of working memory in the game. A range of secondary tasks was used, some of which required paced generation of responses, some of which imposed a verbal working memory load, and some of which imposed a visuo-spatial working memory load. These secondary tasks were imposed at different points in practice with the Space Fortress game. The various secondary tasks affected distinct aspects of game performance and had effects that varied as a function of the level of practice. The results suggested that two classes of skill are acquired, one of which involves response timing and accuracy and the other the monitoring of events and strategic control. Early in practice, performance was affected by working memory load, especially if the memory load was visuo-spatial in nature (e.g., to remember a sequence of movements through a 4 × 4 matrix). Later in practice, working memory load also had an effect, but it was approximately the same whether the load was verbal or visuo-spatial. Additionally, experienced players showed more interference from a concurrent, paced response task than did less experienced players, suggesting that strategies to control the timing of game responses developed with practice.

Finally, Newell, Carlton, Fisher, and Rutter (1989) focused on the motor component of the Space Fortress game. In a manner analogous to the training of eye movement strategies used by Shapiro and Raymond (1989), Newell et al. provided training on the response dynamics of the spaceship. Four subtasks performed prior to the beginning of the game required the players to control the ship's position and acceleration. When this training of the response dynamics was presented in the context of a specific control strategy (e.g., "circle the fortress"), subsequent performance on the Space Fortress game was facilitated in the initial session relative to a control group that did not receive the response dynamics training; this benefit was also evident throughout the remaining nine sessions. In other words, players who learned the response dynamics outside the context of the complete Space Fortress game were able to transfer this experience to the game.

Taken together, these three studies highlight the different components of skilled performance. Shapiro and Raymond (1989) showed that perceptual training influences performance, and, so, implicated a perceptual component of skill in playing Space Fortress. Logie et al. (1989) isolated some of the attentional requirements of the task and showed that skill in timing responses was important for successful performance. Newell et al. (1989) showed further that higher-level knowledge of motor requirements had a facilitative effect on performance. Although a complete understanding of how all these components combine to result in smooth, integrated performance may be beyond our grasp, this integrated effort highlights the many facets involved in skilled performance of complex tasks.

SUMMARY

Most investigations of multiple-task performance have been carried out with the intent of evaluating models of attention and the development of attentional skill, and many of the advances in the understanding of attention that have been made were based on the outcomes of these investigations. Although the research has identified many factors that influence performance in multiple-task contexts, it has not provided unequivocal support for any single model of attention. Debate continues in many areas of research regarding the adequacy of bottleneck and resource models of various types, as well as of other alternative views of attention.

Of most importance to skilled performance, whether or not a particular task can be performed well in a multiple-task context has been shown to depend on the nature of the additional tasks, the level of skill attained in each component task, and the relative amount of attention allocated to the respective tasks. Responding to a stimulus is slowed when irrelevant information activates a response that must be suppressed or when the stimulus immediately follows another to which a response is required. If performance for one of two tasks has been automatized, dual-task performance may show little loss in efficiency. Trade-offs between certain pairs of tasks that require attentional resources can be accomplished relatively effectively, and the ability to time-share is a skill that develops with practice in multiple-task contexts. Finally, correlations among multiple cues are learned in many situations, with performance enhanced as a consequence. As we will see in Chapter 9, these factors form the basis for formulating some of the basic questions regarding the training of the multiple tasks that make up complex skills.

Sequence Learning in Choice-Reaction Tasks

Learning Artificial Grammars

Implicit and Explicit Memory

Control of Complex Dynamic Systems

Learning to Operate Complex Devices

Summary

CHAPTER 6

Learning Through Experiences

When approaching a new task, we typically have some objectives for its performance in mind. For example, if the task is to press a particular key as quickly as possible in response to seeing a stimulus of a specific color, the objectives are to learn the color-to-key mappings, associate finger presses with the keys, and find the response criterion that allows quick responding with an acceptable level of error. In the process of meeting these task objectives, complex relationships that are incidental to the objectives may be learned as well. Performance will typically benefit from this incidental learning as long as the learned relations hold but may be disrupted when they are altered. For example, most people learn through repetition to dial their home telephone number or that of a close friend rapidly and effortlessly. Yet requiring that an additional digit (e.g., 9) be entered first to connect to an outside line may disrupt dialing of the phone number. This disruption can be attributed to the change of context instituted by the requirement to dial the extra digit. This change of context appears to interrupt the smooth, seemingly unconscious action of dialing a familiar number, even though the practiced number itself is unchanged.

The theme of this chapter is that the performance of a task often results in incidental learning that has its effect in and beyond the immediate learning environment. Many of the issues we discuss in this chapter have been touched on in earlier chapters. In Chapter 2, we introduced procedural learning, which was described as learning how to process stimuli. In our discussion of Kolers's work on reading inverted text, the point was made that although much of the observed improvement in performance could be attributed to learning procedural operations that are generally applicable to such text, some of the improvement was specific to the particular passages that were read. Thus two things were learned, one intentionally and the other unintentionally. The ability to read inverted text was acquired intentionally, whereas the benefit due to repeating particular passages of text was an incidental and unintended by-product of the learning process. We now explore learning without intention—and sometimes without awareness—and how it compares to intentional learning. We also cover in some detail system control and how the degree and type of learning that occurs seems to depend on the type of instructions or experiences that are given as well as the nature of the system to be controlled.

Sequence Learning in Choice-Reaction Tasks

You may recall from our discussion of the serial order problem in Chapter 4 that the proper sequencing of ordered stimuli and responses is an important part of many skills. For example, a skilled pianist must play the notes in a piece of music in the correct order, with proper timing and stress. Tasks such as comprehending speech and typing text also are serial in nature, and good performance depends on knowledge about the constraints on serial order inherent in particular tasks that restrict the set of possible events at any point in the sequence (Gentner, Larochelle, & Grudin, 1988; Miller & Isard, 1963). Because of its importance to human performance, the manner and extent to which sequential structure is learned has been the focus of much research.

Most recent investigations of sequence learning have been carried out using choice-reaction tasks in which a single stimulus is presented on each trial, and the task is to make an assigned response based on the identity of that stimulus. Typically, an experimental group is presented with stimuli that occur with some regularity, often in a predetermined repeating sequence, whereas a control group experiences the same stimuli but in random order. The most basic finding is a larger practice effect for repeated stimulus sequences as compared to stimuli presented in random

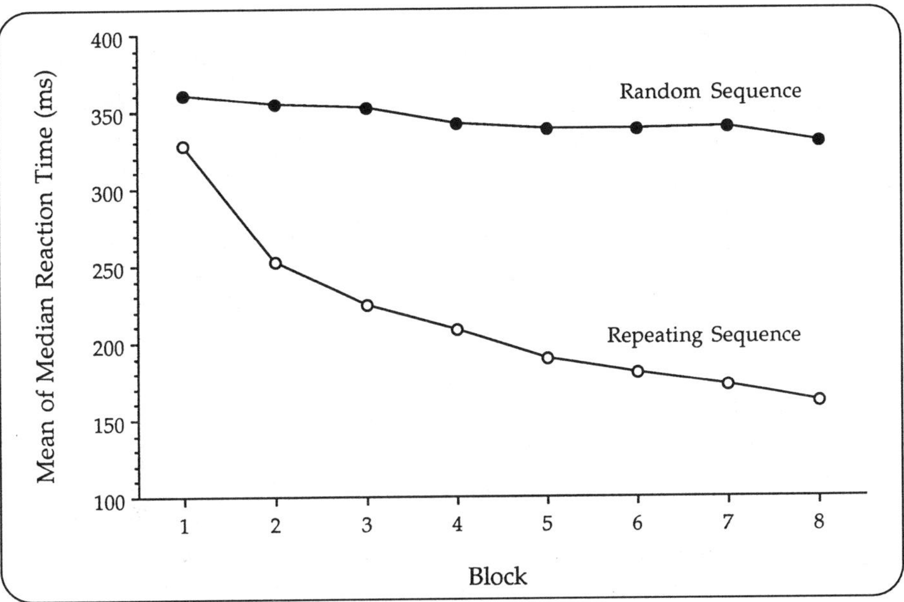

Figure 6.1. Mean of median reaction times in milliseconds for each block of 100 trials of repeating and random sequences in Nissen and Bullemer's (1987) Experiment 1.

order—even though performers are not told of the existence of the sequence or to try to use sequential constraints among stimuli. For example, Nissen and Bullemer (1987) had people perform 800 trials of a four-choice task in which the stimuli were asterisks in one of four, equally spaced, horizontal locations, and the responses were made by pressing response keys at corresponding spatial locations. In the *random* condition, stimuli occurred in the four locations (designated from left to right as *A, B, C, D*) in a random order. In the *repeating* condition, the locations of the stimuli followed the sequence *D-B-C-A-C-B-D-C-B-A,* which was repeated 80 times. As illustrated in Figure 6.1, performance in the random condition showed little improvement in reaction time with practice, whereas that in the repeating condition showed substantial improvement.

The Role of Awareness in Sequence Learning

Although the sequence learning exhibited in choice-reaction tasks appears to occur in the absence of instruction to look for or use sequential constraints, this does not necessarily mean that the performer is unaware of what has been learned. Whether learning can occur in the absence of awareness of the learned relations is a question that has been debated for many years. Attempts to answer the question typically try to determine whether knowledge that is evident in implicit measures of learning derived from task performance are also evident in explicit measures of learning obtained from tests of conscious recollection, such as recall or recognition of events or patterns of events that occurred previously.

Nissen and Bullemer (1987) evaluated the question of awareness by asking the people who received the repeating sequence whether they were aware of the sequence. All of them did indicate awareness of the repeating sequence. To evaluate better whether awareness of the sequence is a necessary requirement for obtaining the performance benefit of the repeated sequence, Nissen and Bullemer replicated their experiment with Korsakoff patients. Korsakoff patients, due to years of alcohol abuse and vitamin deficiency, suffer from amnesia, which prevents them from recognizing and recalling material to which they have been exposed. It is not surprising that the Korsakoff patients reported no awareness of the repeating pattern. However, their performance on the choice-reaction task indicated sequence learning comparable to that shown by nonamnesiacs, demonstrating that such learning can occur without awareness.

Other findings have suggested that awareness of the repeated sequence also may not be a prerequisite for the performance benefit in people with normal memory, even though awareness of the sequence typically develops with practice. Willingham, Nissen, and Bullemer (1989) showed that the number of persons who report awareness of a sequence increases as a function of the amount of practice given with the sequence. Willingham et al. evaluated the relationship between learning and awareness by asking the performers if they were aware of any sequence and then testing them on their ability to generate the sequence. For this generation task, the instructions were to press the key corresponding to the location in which the next stimulus should appear. The preceding stimulus was displayed until the correct prediction was made—even if this required several responses, at which point the next stimulus was shown. The instructions did not specify that there was a pattern to the sequence or that there was any relation to the previously performed choice-reaction task, although the pattern was the same for the two tasks.

Based on the reports regarding awareness of repetitions and on performance on the generation task, Willingham et al. distinguished three groups of people: those who had no, some, or full knowledge of the

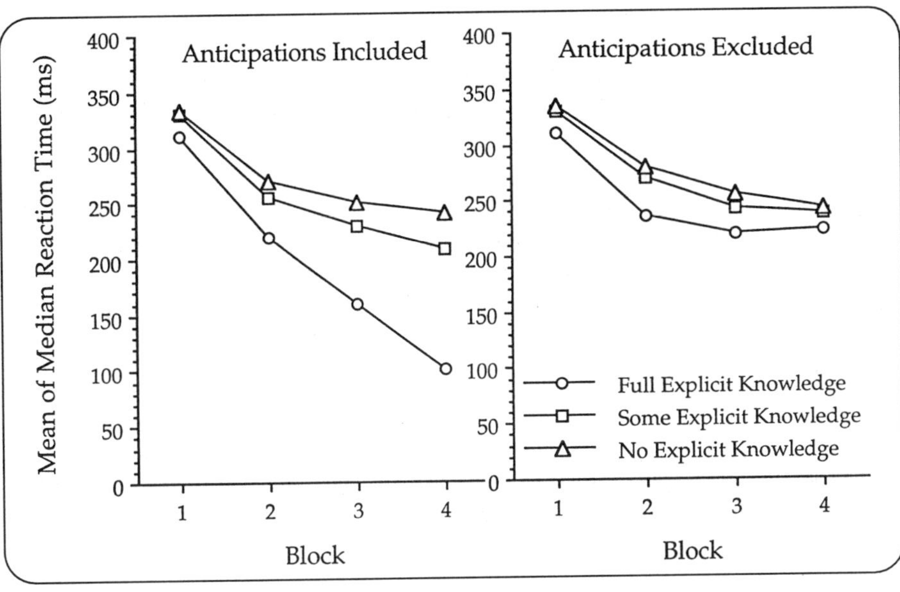

Figure 6.2. Mean of median reaction times in milliseconds for each block of 100 trials in Willingham, Nissen, and Bullemer's (1989) Experiment 1 including all responses (left panel) and excluding all anticipatory responses (reaction times < 100 ms; right panel).

sequence. All three groups showed substantial benefits of practice with the repeating sequence in the choice-reaction task, with the full-knowledge group showing a larger decrease in reaction times across blocks of practice than the groups who demonstrated less than full knowledge (see Figure 6.2, left). However, the additional benefit for the full-knowledge group seemed to be due entirely to anticipating the stimulus and initiating a response before its occurrence on some trials. When trials on which anticipations had occurred were removed from the data, the learning functions for the three groups were similar (see Figure 6.2, right), which suggests that the degree of sequence learning is independent of the degree of awareness of the repeating sequence.

Willingham et al. (1989) considered their generation task to be a relatively pure measure of performers' explicit, or clearly articulated, knowledge of the repeating sequence. However, the appropriateness of such generation tasks for assessing explicit knowledge has been questioned by Perruchet and Amorim (1992), because (a) the instructions used by Willingham et al. (1989) and other researchers did not explicitly require that the prior sequences be reproduced and (b) the procedure of requiring the performer to continue responding until the correct prediction was made would most likely obscure the sequential relations between the stimuli. Perruchet and Amorim (1992) thus modified the generation task by asking participants to generate without feedback a series of trials that looked like the series seen in the preceding phases. They also used an explicit recognition test in which four-trial sequences were judged according to whether they were parts of the series that had been seen previously. Even when administered after sufficiently few trials that performance differences between people who received random and repeating sequences were just beginning to emerge, both of the tests showed explicit knowledge for the repeating sequences that correlated highly with characteristics of the reaction time data. These results can be reconciled with the fact that amnesiacs show procedural learning in the absence of explicit knowledge (Nissen & Bullemer, 1987) by assuming that explicit awareness is not necessary for the learning to occur, but nonamnesiacs have at least some conscious access to the implicit knowledge reflected in performance improvements.

The Role of Attention in Sequence Learning

Although attention and awareness are often treated as synonymous, it is important to distinguish attending to the task itself from being aware of the information contained in the task. Thus, even though awareness does not seem to be necessary for sequence learning, it is possible that such learning may occur only when attentional resources are devoted to the task. Nissen and Bullemer (1987) obtained evidence to this effect from experiments in which, concurrent with the choice-reaction task, a distractor task was performed that involved counting the number of low-pitched tones within a series of high- and low-pitched tones. No evidence of sequence learning was apparent during a practice session in the dual-task situation or during a single-task transfer session with the same location sequence. The apparent inability to learn the sequence while performing an attention-demanding secondary task suggests that attention is necessary for sequence learning to occur.

Subsequent research has shown that learning of certain types of sequences can occur despite withdrawal of attention due to the demands imposed by concurrent tasks but that other types seem to require attention. In the sequence used by Nissen and Bullemer, the relation of any pair of stimuli was ambiguous in that one stimulus did not specify the other.

For example, *A* was followed by *C* in one case and by *D* in another, so it was impossible to know which stimulus would follow *A*. A. Cohen, Ivry, and Keele (1990) examined sequence learning for *ambiguous sequences* of this type as well as for *unique sequences* in which each stimulus uniquely specified the subsequent stimulus in the sequence (e.g., *A* always followed by *C*) and *hybrid sequences* that had both unique and ambiguous associations among successive elements. Choice-reaction performance showed no evidence that the ambiguous sequences were learned in a dual-task context but did show evidence that the unique sequences and, to a lesser extent, the hybrid sequences were learned under dual-task conditions.

A. Cohen et al. (1990) interpreted their data as suggesting that sequence learning typically involves two distinct processes. One process, which does not require attention, forms associations between adjacent items. The other process, which does require attention, builds so-called hierarchical codes. For example, in the sequence *D-B-C-A-C-B-D-C-B-A, D* is not always followed by *B*, nor is *B* always followed by *C*, and so forth. If we look at pairs of stimuli, we find that *D-B* is always followed by *C-A*, *C-A* is always followed by *C-B*, but *C-B* is not always followed by *D-C*. However, there are many ways to parse the sequence so that groups of stimuli do uniquely specify those stimuli that follow. A. Cohen et al. proposed that attention is required to parse the sequence appropriately. Thus, according to A. Cohen et al., only sequences with unique associations can be learned under attentional distraction because those sequences without unique associations must be learned using the hierarchical parsing mechanism for which attention is required.

Further evidence consistent with this distinction between automatic and attentional learning mechanisms has been obtained in experiments that examined training and transfer performance with hybrid sequences under conditions with and without attentional distraction (Curran & Keele, 1993). For example, when the initial performance is under single-task conditions, the amount of sequence learning is greater for performers who are aware of the sequence than for those who are not. However, for a dual-task transfer situation, there is no difference in the performance of the aware and unaware groups, with both groups continuing to perform better in the sequential than in the random condition. In terms of the distinction between learning and performance made earlier in the book, these results suggest that when attention is withdrawn due to a secondary task requirement, the component of learning associated with awareness can no longer be expressed in performance. Finally, when the initial training is in dual-task conditions, there is no improvement in the expres-

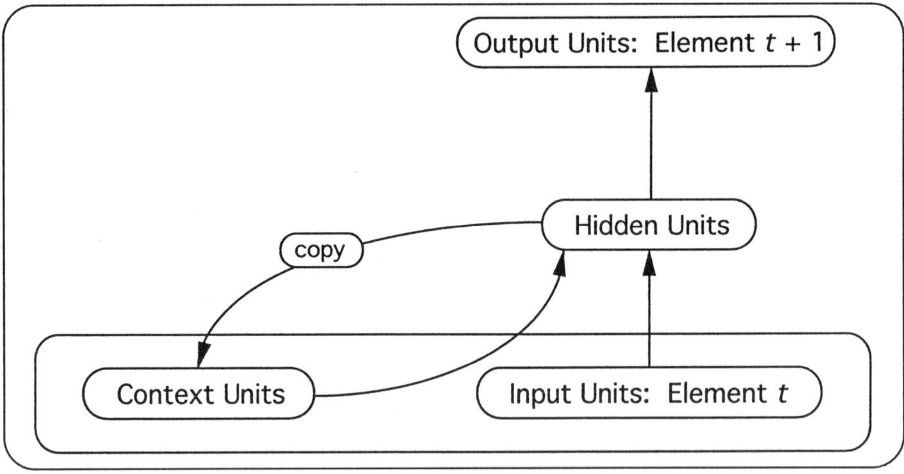

Figure 6.3. Schematic diagram of the simple recurrent network used to simulate sequence learning.

sion of sequential knowledge when the distracting task is removed during transfer. From these results, Curran and Keele (1993) concluded that the two types of sequence learning, automatic and attentional, occur in parallel but that the attentional form requires that attention be available both during learning and at the time when the task subsequently is being performed.

An alternative to the two-process model proposed by A. Cohen et al. (1990) is a single-process model in which temporal context extends to elements prior to the immediately preceding element in a sequence. Cleeremans and McClelland (1991) showed that as people learn sequences in choice-reaction tasks, they become increasingly sensitive to the preceding context, up to three elements back. Their data were fit well by a connectionist model with a back-propagation learning procedure that incorporates sensitivity to sequential structure. In this model, called a simple recurrent network (see Figure 6.3), a layer of hidden units (see Chapter 1) receives input not only from input units but also from context units. The pattern of activation from the hidden units for the stimulus presented at time $t - 1$ is fed back onto the context units (i.e., they take on that pattern of activation), which then affect the pattern of activation of the hidden units when the next stimulus is presented at time t. The role of the context units is thus to allow the immediately preceding activation pattern of the hidden unit layer to influence the subsequent pattern of activation. Initially, the context units provide an encoding of the previous stimulus in the sequence, and the pattern of activation for the hidden units is a function of both the input for the current stimulus and the context of the preceding stimulus. Because this pattern is fed back iteratively on the context units, the context units can come to encode the predictive features for at least the three preceding stimuli to which people were shown to be sensitive.

To accommodate short-term repetition effects of the type described in Chapter 3, Cleeremans and McClelland (1991) found it necessary to augment the simple recurrent network with short-term priming of particular responses and response pairings. Specifically, to account for facilitation in responding on trials for which the response was a repetition of the preceding one, rapidly decaying activations from the preceding trial were allowed to influence responding. To account for benefits in responding to a particular sequential pairing of responses (e.g., the response to event *D* is faster when it is preceded by the sequence *ADA*, for which the second occurrence of event *D* follows the same event as the first occurrence, than when it is preceded by the sequence *BDA*, for which it does not), an assumption was made that changes in the connection weights between units have two components: one that decays rapidly and one that does not. This augmented network model was able to reproduce the pattern of results obtained by A. Cohen et al. (1990), without postulating a distinction between automatic and attentional learning processes, simply by manipulating a single noise parameter. Thus the results obtained with unique and ambiguous sequences can be generated by a single associative representation, indicating that the data do not compel a distinction between associative and hierarchical sequence representations.

What Is Learned?

Sequence learning occurs when a series of stimuli and their associated responses occurs repeatedly, but what exactly is learned? Sequential dependencies might be learned that involve the perceived stimuli, the motor responses, or more central processes involved in response selection. A. Cohen et al. (1990) addressed the issue of whether specific motor responses are learned by having people first perform a three-location version of a sequential choice-reaction task with a repeating sequence, using the index, middle, and ring fingers of the right hand. After 1,000 trials of practice, the same sequence was presented but now the responses on all three keys were made with only the index finger. Virtually perfect transfer to the new response mode was apparent, indicating that the learning that had occurred was not specific to the particular muscle groups used in practice.

Willingham et al. (1989) obtained results that not only rule out specific effectors as the locus of sequence learning but also the locations in which the stimuli will occur, at least when stimulus location is not relevant to the task. In a 400-trial training phase, participants responded to the color of the stimulus and not to its location. For the *random* group, both the order of the color stimuli and the locations in which they appeared were random during training; for the *perceptual sequence* group, the sequence of the stimuli was random but the locations of the stimuli followed a 10-trial sequence; for the *response sequence* group, the stimuli followed a 10-trial sequence but the stimulus locations were random. After training, all of the groups were transferred to a task in which they responded to location rather than color. The same 10-trial sequence was used (corresponding to that of the stimulus locations for the perceptual sequence group and that of the response locations for the response sequence group).

Relative to the random group, the perceptual sequence group showed no evidence of sequence learning during the training phase and no advantage at transfer, suggesting that the difference between sequential and random conditions found in other situations may not be due to learning what location to attend to. The response sequence group showed sequence learning during practice, but this did not transfer to the standard location task. If the benefit of practice had been on the sequence of motor responses, positive transfer should have been observed for the response sequence group since the sequence of motor responses was the same in the training and transfer phases. Based on these findings, Willingham et al. concluded that both the relevant stimulus dimension and the responses are important for learning. In other words, they proposed that a series of condition-action rules that relate stimuli to responses is learned.

Although sequence learning in the Nissen and Bullemer (1987) procedure did not seem to involve the stimulus locations, such learning seems to occur in a more complex procedure, introduced by Lewicki, Czyzewska, and Hoffman (1987), where location is more important. In their task, a target digit (6) occurs in one of four quadrants of a display screen (see Figure 6.4, left panel), and a response is made by pressing one of four keys arrayed in a square to correspond to the quadrants. For the first six trials in a block, the target occurs alone in one of the quadrants. However, on the seventh trial, it is just one element in an array of 36 digits, with 9 per

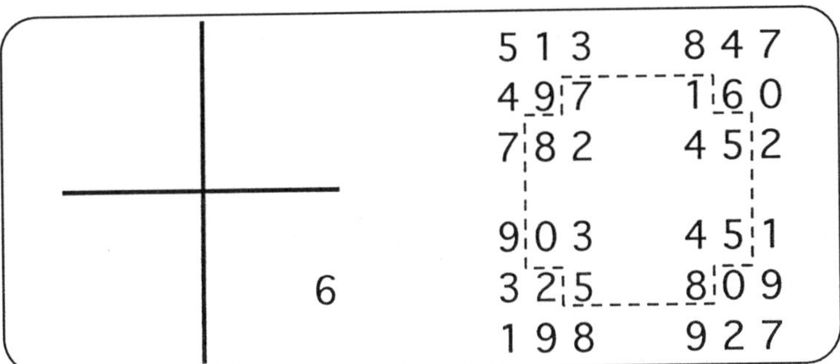

Figure 6.4. Arrays of the type used in Lewicki, Czyzewska, and Hoffman's (1987) experiment. The left panel shows an example of the arrays used on Trials 1-6 of each block; the right panel shows an array of the type used on the seventh trial. For arrays of this latter type, targets were never placed in positions inside the dotted line; the line did not appear in the display.

quadrant (see Figure 6.4, right panel). The location of the target in the more complex display of the seventh trial is determined by the sequence of the target location in Trials 1, 3, 4, and 6 of the simple trials. Despite the complexity of this relationship and the fact that performers do not show any awareness of its existence, something about the sequential structure is learned. Lewicki et al. demonstrated this by showing an increase in reaction time when, after thousands of trials of practice, the quadrant of the targets on the critical complex trials was changed.

Stadler (1989) evaluated whether the learning in this task was of the response sequence or perceptual locations by using transfer tests similar to those of the Willingham et al. (1989) study. On these tests, either the response apparatus and fingers used for responding were changed or the location of the target within the quadrant was changed but the response was the same (recall that Lewicki et al. changed the quadrant in which the stimulus occurred and hence the response as well). The results indicated little disruption from changing the way in which responses were enacted but considerable disruption from changing the target locations. This outcome suggests that the learning was primarily perceptual, depending perhaps on the eye movements that are made to locate the item.

In summary, it is apparent that people learn the sequential structure of trials in choice-reaction tasks even though this structure is not a stated part of the task objectives. This sequence learning can occur without conscious intent or awareness, but at least some of the knowledge that is acquired may be accessible to awareness. Although awareness may not be necessary for this learning to occur, being able to devote attentional resources to the task during learning and execution seems to be important, especially for ambiguous sequences. The evidence suggests that the sequence learning found in most standard choice-reaction tasks is of condition-action pairings that facilitate response selection, although perceptual learning may occur when locating a stimulus is crucial to task performance.

Learning Artificial Grammars

Performance improvements attributable to the presence of sequential dependencies have also been investigated extensively with artificial grammars (see Reber, 1989, for a review). Artificial grammars are sets of rules that are used to generate a large number of sequences. Sequences that are consistent with the rule sets are "grammatical"; sequences that cannot be generated with the rule set are not. For example, the grammar shown in Figure 6.5 generates grammatical strings by proceeding from left to right along any path from the initial state (S_1) to the end state (S_6 for the grammar shown in Figure 6.5). Because of recurrent nodes (i.e., nodes with arrows back to themselves), the grammar can generate an infinite number of strings, and it can be difficult to deduce the structure of the grammar just from looking at a sample of the strings that it can produce. For example, it is hard to find any regularities in the set of grammatical strings PVV, TXXVPXVV, TXS, and PTTTVPS. To make the set of possible strings finite, the maximum length of a string is usually constrained by the experimenter. Using such a subset of the grammatical strings, a typical experiment consists of an acquisition phase during which participants are exposed to exemplars generated from the grammar and a transfer phase in which classification of new strings as grammatical or ungrammatical is required.

The major question of interest is whether people learn the grammatical structure of the letter strings even when they are not informed that there is any structure to learn. Early experiments provided evidence suggesting that the constraints of the grammar are indeed learned. For example, Reber (1967) found that memorization of strings within the acquisition phase improved with practice for those people who were given grammatical strings, whereas performance of those who received strings

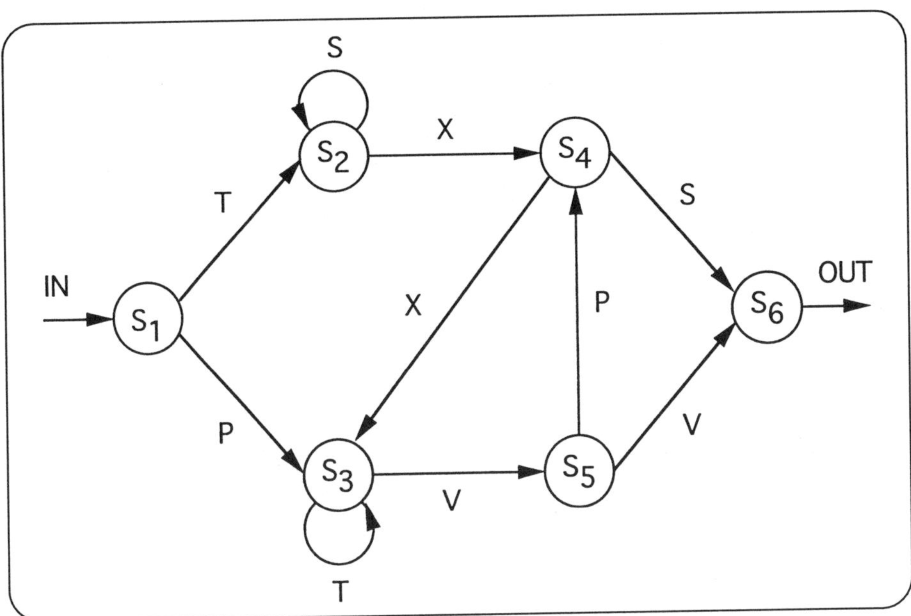

Figure 6.5. Schematic diagram of a finite-state grammar. (Stimuli are generated by following any path of arrows leading from the initial State 1 to the terminal State 6. The following are the five basic strings of the grammar with the loops or recursions in brackets: T[S]XS; T[S]XX[[T]VPX]VV; T[S]XX[[T]VPX]VPS; P[[T]VPX]VV; and P[[T]VPX]VPS.)
SOURCE: Adapted from Reber (1989).

that had no grammatical structure showed no improvement. In the transfer phase, the people who had memorized grammatical strings could also classify new strings as grammatical or ungrammatical with reasonable accuracy, although they were not able to state any rules verbally. Apparently, the underlying grammatical structure of the strings was learned despite the fact that the instructions did not explicitly state that there was any structure to be learned and the rules could not be verbalized even after successful memorization of the grammatical strings. Subsequent studies have shown that the grammar learning also transfers to new stimulus sets (Mathews et al., 1989; Reber, 1989), indicating that the structure of the grammar is being learned independent from the elements to which it is being applied.

What happens when the instructions for the memorization task state that there are regularities in the stimuli to be learned? In some cases, this information can actually impede learning. Reber (1976) instructed one group of people that there were regularities and encouraged them to look for the regularities. This group took longer to memorize the strings during the learning phase and performed less accurately at assessing whether novel strings were grammatical than did a group that was not told to look for regularities. Thus, in this study, the intent to learn evidently interfered with the learning that would normally occur simply as a consequence of memorizing the stimuli. The instructions to look for regularities in essence provide a secondary task to be performed in addition to the primary task of memorization. This suggests that the detrimental effect of intent to learn is closely related to the deleterious effect of unrelated secondary tasks on sequence learning in choice-reaction tasks and is due at least in part to attention being diverted from the memorization task .

Not all studies have found explicit instructions to interfere with learning, however, and some have even shown an advantage for them (e.g., Howard & Ballas, 1980). The key factor seems to be whether the stimuli are presented in such a manner that the underlying grammatical relations are made salient. Reber, Kassin, Lewis, and Cantor (1980) manipulated salience by presenting the strings to be memorized in a low-salience (Figure 6.6a) or high-salience (Figure 6.6b) format. The 21 strings were presented in lists of 3 to 5 strings. The high-salience format was such that the strings in a given list were the strings possible from traversing just one particular path of the finite state grammar. In this format, the strings within a list varied only in terms of the number of repetitions of recursive elements. For the low-salience format, the strings on a given list were selected randomly from the set of all permissible strings. Thus the high-salience format emphasized the relation between the strings, whereas the low-salience format did not. Explicit instructions to determine rules governing the structure of the strings facilitated learning when the relations were salient and, consequently, hypotheses about the rules were easy to generate and test. However, when the relations were not salient, the explicit instructions hindered learning.

Although general instructions to learn a grammar are not helpful when the relations between strings are nonsalient, specific information about the grammar can still be helpful. For example, when the diagram of a grammar is provided, along with instructions about how it can be used to generate strings of symbols, performance improvements are observed (Reber et al., 1980). An even greater benefit is observed when the grammar is provided earlier rather than later during practice, suggesting that the

PVV	TSSSXXVV	TSXXTVPS	PVPXTVPS	TSSXXVV
TSXS	PTVPXVV	TXXTVPS	TXXTTTVV	PVPVV
TSSXXVPS	TXXVPXVV	PTVPS	PTTTVPS	PTVPXTVV
PVPXVPS	PTTVV	TXS	TSSSXS	TXXTVPS
		TSXXTVV		

(a)

TSXS	TSSSXXVV	TSSXXVPS	PTTVV	PVPXVPS
TXS	TXXVPXVV	TSXXTVPS	PVV	PTVPS
TSSSXS	TXXTTVV	TXXTVPS	PTVPXVV	PVPXTVPS
	TSSXXVV	TXXVPS	PVPXVV	PTTTVPS
	TSXXTVV		PTVPXTVV	

(b)

Figure 6.6. Stimuli in the (a) low-salience and (b) high-salience formats used by Reber, Kassin, Lewis, and Cantor (1980).

model of the grammar can be used to guide learning. The benefit of the specific information in this case seems to derive from directing the learner's attention to the structural relations that characterize the stimulus set. In other words, it is another way of making the structural relations salient so that participants do not have to develop their own hypotheses about what the relations are.

To summarize, the grammar from which letter strings are composed is learned when the strings are memorized, even though the grammatical structure is incidental to the stated task objectives. Explicit instructions to look for regularities among the strings impairs learning unless the regularities are salient. This suggests that a passive mode of learning is more beneficial for learning subtle regularities within the environment. In other words, strategies explicitly devoted to trying to learn the relations tend to be beneficial only when substantial effort does not have to be invested in developing and evaluating hypotheses about the critical relations.

Implicit and Explicit Memory

In both the sequence learning and grammar learning studies, the knowledge of the sequence or grammar that is learned is implicit, in that it is acquired incidentally, it is tested without instructions to recollect specific prior instances, and the participants often cannot verbalize the sequential relationships even though their performance is affected by them. In contrast, the study of human memory historically has emphasized explicit measures, such as recall and recognition, in which the instructions are to recollect specific events or items that have occurred previously, usually during an earlier phase of the experiment. In recent years, however, there has been considerable interest in implicit memory tests in which the instructions are not to recollect specific instances but to perform some other task that draws only indirectly on memory for the specific episodes. Performance on that task is then evaluated with respect to the study conditions.

One task commonly used to assess implicit memory is **word fragment completion,** in which a few letters of a word are presented and the complete word is to be identified, and another is **perceptual identification,** in which very briefly exposed words are to be identified. Both of these tasks do not demand recall of previously presented words, yet the influence of prior presentations can be assessed by testing whether more fragments are completed or words identified for the previously seen words than for new words (i.e., whether **repetition priming** occurs).

There is most likely a close relationship between the implicit learning of sequential constraints and the findings of implicit memory studies. In fact, the primary way in which studies of implicit memory differ from those of implicit learning is that effects of individual stimuli, usually words presented once each, on performance of a later task are examined rather than effects of repeated presentations of patterns of stimuli in the current task (Seger, 1994). Because of this similarity, the research comparing performance on tests in which memory is expressed implicitly with that on explicit memory tests can provide insight into the mechanisms underlying implicit learning.

Dissociations of Implicit and Explicit Measures

Dissociations have often been obtained for the effects of variables on implicit and explicit memory tests. The most dramatic dissociation occurs between amnesiacs and people with normal memory. Amnesiacs perform much more poorly on the explicit measures of recall and recognition, but they show the same relative benefits of prior exposure to items as the normal population on implicit memory tests (Warrington & Weiskrantz, 1974). For example, Graf, Shimamura, and Squire (1985) found that when amnesiacs were given word stems as cues and told to complete each stem with the first word that came to mind, they showed the same degree of repetition priming as nonamnesiacs. However, when given the same word stems and told to use them as cues for recalling words that had been studied previously, the amnesiacs showed substantial impairment relative to normals.

Dissociations of other independent variables on explicit and implicit measures have also been demonstrated within the normal, nonamnesiac population (for reviews, see Roediger, 1990; Roediger & McDermott, 1993; Schacter, 1987). One such dissociation is found in the effects of changing surface features of the stimuli on implicit and explicit tests. For example, in the Graf et al. (1985) study described above, the study phase used either visually or auditorily presented words, and the test phase always used visual word fragments. Explicit recall of the words was unaffected by whether the words in the study condition were in the same or different modality as the word fragments. However, performance on the implicit completion task was worse when the modality of the studied words was different from that of the fragments. This dissociation between explicit recall and word fragment completion is sometimes taken as evidence that performance on the two types of tasks is mediated by different memory systems or processes and sometimes ascribed to the overlap of the characteristics of processing at study and at test.

As a means of exploring the distinction between implicit and explicit memory, researchers have taken phenomena that are well established for explicit memory and determined whether they also are apparent in implicit measures. One such phenomenon is the picture superiority effect, which is that recall is better if the to-be-remembered items are presented as pictures rather than as words. Weldon and Roediger (1987) tested to see whether pictures would lead to superior priming on an implicit word fragment completion test. They found that performance was much worse after seeing pictures than words. In contrast, if the stimuli for the implicit memory test are picture fragments, more priming is evident when the studied stimuli are pictures (Srinivas, 1993). Moreover, picture priming is specific to the exact contour that is studied, being reduced in magnitude when differences are introduced between study and test, which suggests that the degree of overlap between the specific perceptual processing performed at study and test is important. This specificity of priming effects is analogous to the previously discussed specificity of transfer for reading inverted text (Kolers, 1975b).

Another well-established phenomenon of explicit memory is that performance is influenced substantially by the type of orienting task (i.e., instructions given to process the stimuli) performed at the study phase. In many situations, orienting tasks that require processing of deep-level semantic features of stimuli result in better test performance than tasks that emphasize surface-level physical features. In one of the initial studies that generated interest in the implicit/explicit distinction, Jacoby and Dallas (1981) found the usual superiority of deep-level processing of the study items on an explicit recognition task but not on a subsequent test of implicit memory. Other studies have shown the type of orienting task to have a small effect on repetition priming rather than a complete absence of effect (Challis & Brodbeck, 1992), but nothing like the large effects that this variable has on explicit memory tests. This outcome again suggests that implicit and explicit memory tasks reflect different aspects of memory.

Attention is typically associated with conscious processing and, therefore, would seem to be a greater component of explicit memory than of implicit memory. To test this implication, Parkin, Reid, and Russo (1990) had people perform a tone monitoring task while carrying out a task in which they had to verify whether a target word in a sentence context made a meaningful sentence. When tested on the material the next day, recognition of the target words was considerably worse for the people who had judged the items in the dual-task context than for people who had only performed the primary task, but priming on a word fragment completion task was unaffected. Such a finding suggests that some memory expressed on implicit tests does not depend on the amount of attention devoted to the information during the study phase, whereas that expressed on explicit tests does.

Accounts of the Dissociations

Although research in human memory focused primarily on explicit tasks until the past decade, an underlying assumption was that performance on implicit tests is mediated by the same memory system as that involved in explicit tests. The dissociations demonstrated for explicit and implicit memory measures created problems for this assumption. Two approaches have been taken in accounting for the dissociations. One approach is to account for the effects in terms of distinct memory systems with different neural bases. Commonly, two systems—a declarative memory system that stores verbalizable knowledge and a procedural memory system that is responsible for learning and skilled behavior—are distinguished (Squire, 1987, 1992). Explicit tests are assumed to rely primarily on declarative memory, whereas implicit tests are assumed to rely primarily on procedural memory. The strongest support for the multiple-system view comes from the studies of amnesiacs.

Another view explains the dissociations in terms of the cognitive procedures that are involved in explicit versus implicit tests. This approach has been articulated by Roediger (1990) and his colleagues as the **transfer-appropriate processing** approach. An assumption of this approach is that performance on a memory test is an increasing function of the extent to which the cognitive operations performed at test overlap with those performed during study. It is assumed that the procedures for accessing information are different for explicit and implicit tests, so each type of test will benefit from different processing at study. In particular, most explicit tests are more semantic or conceptual in nature (i.e., **conceptually driven**), whereas most implicit tests are more sensitive to perceptual information (i.e., **data driven**).

Roediger (1990) suggested that evidence pertinent to distinguishing the cognitive procedures view from the memory systems view could be obtained by devising conceptually driven procedural tests and data-driven declarative tests and comparing performance on them to that on the more standard data-driven procedural and conceptually driven declarative tests. According to the cognitive procedures view, the two data-driven tests should produce similar results, as should the two conceptually driven tests, because of the similarity of the cognitive procedures involved; according to the memory systems view, the two declarative tests should produce similar results, as should the two procedural tests, as a function of the memory systems involved. Blaxton (1989) followed this approach, employing free recall as the conceptually driven declarative test and word fragment completion as the data-driven procedural test. The data-driven declarative test that she used involved answering general knowledge questions of the type found in the game Trivial Pursuit™. The conceptually driven procedural test was graphemic-cued recall, in which the cues were words that looked like and sounded like the corresponding words that had been studied but were not related to them in meaning. The important finding was that, as predicted by the cognitive procedures view, the two conceptually driven tests showed similar results, and these were different from those of the two data-driven tests, whose results were similar to each other. Although the issue is far from settled, this particular finding provides evidence against the view that distinct memory systems are involved in explicit and implicit memory tests.

Relation of Implicit Memory to Incidental Learning and Skill

The review of results obtained in implicit memory tests bears out the supposition that there is a close relation between implicit memory and incidental learning of sequential structure. The characteristics that they have in common include being preserved in amnesia, dissociable from explicit learning, disrupted in many cases by changes in surface stimulus characteristics, and more durable than explicit learning and memory (Berry & Dienes, 1991; Seger, 1994). Thus it seems that the processes responsible for the incidental learning of relatively complex sequential relationships among nonverbal stimuli are the same as those involved in repetition priming for verbal and pictorial stimuli.

More generally, you may have noted that implicit memory tests have certain similarities to the tasks used to study skill acquisition: A task is performed repeatedly, with performance on repeated stimuli compared to that on new items to distinguish general practice effects from benefits associated with specific stimuli. Empirical similarities also exist, such as the relatively limited transfer that occurs when some aspects of the situation are changed. These similarities were noted recently by Kirsner, Speelman, and Schofield (1993), who stated, "Indeed, the evidence that implicit memory and skill acquisition share procedures, data, and theory is so pervasive that consideration must now be given to the proposition that these two domains should be treated as one" (p. 120). Kirsner et al. went on to show that in implicit memory studies for which multiple repetitions of an item are allowed, the amount of repetition priming is a power function of the number of prior occurrences of the item as are both experimental and preexperimental practice effects. Their intriguing conclusion is that it may be possible to incorporate the findings regarding implicit memory into a more general model of skill acquisition, such as Anderson's (1993) ACT theory.

Control of Complex Dynamic Systems

The theme of the chapter so far has been the distinction between two types of learning or modes of remembering. Although several different types of processes, mechanisms, or systems were proposed to account for the different modes of learning and remembering, most of the proposed distinctions are between implicit and explicit processing. Another area in which the role of declarative knowledge in learning has been studied is the control of dynamic systems, such as operating a simulated city transportation system in which the amount charged for parking a car and the time interval between buses are manipulated to control city revenue (Broadbent, 1977); controlling a computer model of the British economy by adjusting rates of government expenditure, taxes, and limits on the money supply (Broadbent & Aston, 1978); managing a sugar production factory, with the goal of maintaining a specified level of sugar output (Berry & Broadbent, 1984); and interacting with a computer "person" with the instruction to shift and maintain the behavior of the person (Berry & Broadbent, 1984). Performance typically has been evaluated in two ways: Success in operating the system is measured by success in performing the control task, and declarative knowledge of the system dynamics is assessed by post-performance questionnaires.

In all of the studies cited above, performance at controlling the system improved with practice, but declarative knowledge as measured by the questionnaires was not correlated with performance improvement. Broadbent, Fitzgerald, and Broadbent (1986) and Berry and Broadbent (1984) further showed that providing information about the system improved the ability of people to answer questions about it, while having no impact on performance, and that system control performance and questionnaire scores still did not show positive correlations. The dissociation of the effect of instructions regarding system dynamics on system control and questionnaire performance, as well as the statistical independence of the two measures of learning, suggests that there are two alternative modes of learning relevant to the way the system operates.

This distinction between two modes of learning has been pursued in more recent studies by Berry and Broadbent (1988) and Hayes and Broadbent (1988). They have proposed that the two modes of learning can be characterized as **unselective** and **selective.** The unselective mode is thought to involve the passive aggregation of information pertinent to contingencies between all environmental variables; the unselective mode operates outside of awareness and hence will not support accurate verbalizable knowledge in many cases. The lack of awareness and nonverbal nature of this learning characterizes it as implicit. People may learn specific sequences of events and successful responses that were made to them, and then retrieve this information when faced with a particular situation (Stanley, Mathews, Buss, & Kotler-Cope, 1989). The selective mode involves actively attending to only a few variables and forming a representation of the relations among the variables that can be explicitly verbalized.

To study the characteristics of the selective mode of learning on performance, Berry and Broadbent (1988) instructed participants to search for the rules governing the behavior of a computer person while performing versions of the interaction task in which the response characteristics of the system were salient (this person was named Ellis) or nonsalient (the person named Denham). The search instructions facilitated performance in interacting with Ellis but interfered with performance in interacting with Denham. In other words, inducing the selective mode of learning had a positive effect on control performance when the task was based on a salient relationship but a detrimental effect when it was based on a nonsalient relationship. This finding, which suggests that the strategy of explicitly searching for rules is effective only when there is little difficulty in developing and testing hypotheses, is reminiscent of the effect of making aspects of artificial grammars salient. Recall that explicit instructions to search for regularities among letter strings hindered learning of the grammar from which the strings were composed when the grammatical structure was nonsalient but facilitated learning when the grammatical structure was made salient (Reber et al., 1980).

Berry and Broadbent (1988) showed that transfer is limited for system control tasks with nonsalient relationships, for which learning should involve the unselective mode. Their study used four system control tasks: two computer person interaction tasks (using the characters Denham or Fox, both of whom had nonsalient characteristics) and two transportation scheduling tasks (for a bus or train). After receiving practice with one of the four tasks (e.g., Denham), a second set of interactions was performed with either the same task (Denham again), a similar task (Fox), or a dissimilar task (the bus or train transportation task). Positive transfer was evident for people who switched to the similar task, with their performance being comparable to that of those who continued performing the same task; those who changed to the different task showed no transfer.

Two additional groups were tested with a similar or dissimilar task in the second session of performance and given an explicit hint about the similarity of the task to the task used in the first session. Not only did the hint provide no benefit for the group tested on the dissimilar task, but it eliminated the transfer shown on the similar task. Berry and Broadbent suggested that the negative impact of the hint might be due to its causing adoption of the selective mode of processing, which is less effective for these nonsalient systems, rather than the unselective mode used for the first set of trials.

Because the selective mode of learning is proposed to rely on attentional resources, it should be hindered by the requirement to perform a secondary attention-demanding task. In contrast, such a requirement should not hinder learning in the unselective mode because that mode is presumed not to require attention. Hayes and Broadbent (1988) confirmed these predictions using the computer person task with Ellis, for whom the relationships were salient and thus amenable to the selective mode of learning, and with Denham, for whom the relationships were nonsalient and hence should be learned in the unselective mode. During the first phase of the relevant experiment, practice was with one of the computer person tasks. For the next phase, a letter generation task was performed in which the participant was to say aloud a letter of the alphabet after each click of a metronome beating at a 2-s rate. As expected, the secondary letter generation task interfered with performance of the computer person task for those people interacting with Ellis (presumably using the selective mode) but not for those interacting with Denham (using the unselective mode).

A final question of interest is whether the properties important for system control can be learned through observation. Berry (1991) investigated the effectiveness of observational learning and demonstrated that whether it is successful depends on whether the underlying relationships between the variables of the control task are salient or nonsalient. After observing an experimenter performing either the sugar production task or the person interaction task for 30 trials, observers then performed the same task themselves for 30 trials. No evidence of learning from observing the experimenter was apparent for nonsalient versions of either task. However, observational learning was evidenced for the salient versions. Surprisingly, Berry also found that persons who made decisions about what actions to take during the first 30 trials of nonsalient task versions but did not enter the information into the computer (the experimenter did) or who had to enter the information but did not make the decisions did not perform well when subsequently required both to make the decisions and to enter the information for the second set of trials. These results suggest that decision making must be tied to action for learning to be maximal.

In sum, the research on system control suggests two distinct modes of learning similar to those implicated by the research on grammar learning. An unselective mode produces the best learning when the control relations are nonsalient, whereas a selective mode is best when the control relations are salient. Consistent with the view that implicit learning is a consequence of task performance, the unselective mode appears to require active performance of the control task and not just observation.

Learning to Operate Complex Devices

People are regularly confronted with new devices of some complexity that they need to learn to use. These include such things as videocassette recorders, word processing programs, and electronic games. Consequently, researchers have been concerned with establishing how such devices are learned, the role of instructional materials in facilitating such learning, and how to predict the relative complexity of alternative device designs. Because device learning usually takes place when there is an intent to learn, most studies have focused on what Broadbent and his colleagues call the explicit selective mode of learning, with particular emphasis on how mental models (i.e., users' representations of system components and relations between them; see Chapter 7) of devices are acquired and used.

In an early and influential treatment of this issue, Young (1981) analyzed the mental models that three designs of electronic calculators would suggest to users. He distinguished two kinds of mental representations as important: a model of the device's inner workings (which, in later work, is called a **device model**) and a **task-action mapping** that specifies the particular actions necessary to perform a given task. He showed that the more complex the device model and task-action mapping for a calculator, the greater the difficulty people had in using it. The distinction that Young made between the two types of device knowledge has continued to play a prominent role in more recent work on the ease with which devices can be learned and used.

Learning Without Instructions

Often, a person attempts to learn a device without the aid of instructions either because reading the instructions is perceived to be too time consuming or effortful or simply because the instructions accompanying the device have been lost. To what extent can people learn to use a

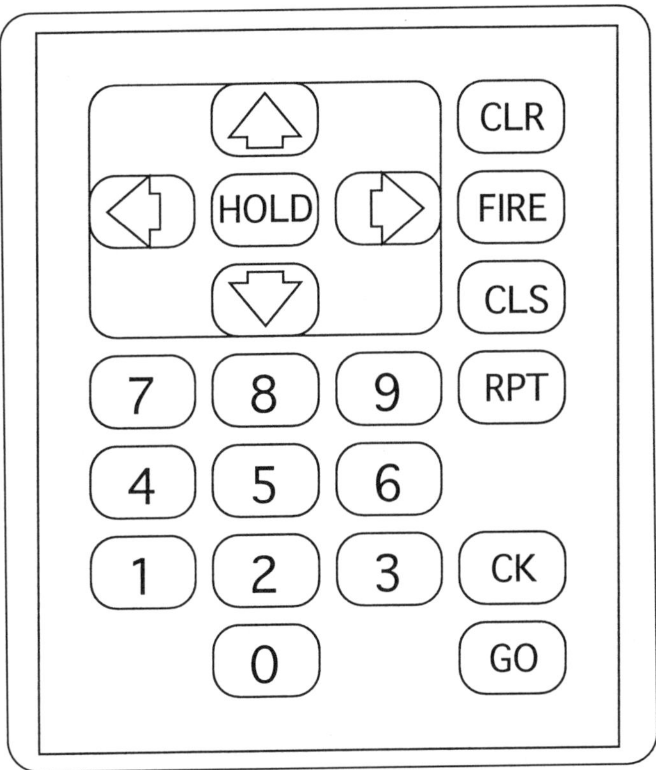

Figure 6.7. The keypad used to operate BigTrak™.
SOURCE: Adapted from Shrager and Klahr (1986).

moderately complex device under instructionless learning conditions? Shrager and Klahr (1986) answered this question in part by examining instructionless learning of a commercially available toy called BigTrak™. BigTrak is a self-powered six-wheel vehicle that is controlled by commands entered by the user via a keypad located on top of the vehicle (see Figure 6-7). Up to 16 instructions can be entered, each consisting of a function key command and a one- or two-digit number. When the GO key is then pressed, BigTrak executes the commands in sequence by moving around the floor in the specified manner. Feedback is provided in the form of a beep for each syntactically legal keystroke combination that is entered. In the experiment, Shrager and Klahr simply told people to learn as much as possible about BigTrak. The sequences of actions taken by the individuals in the experiment and concurrent protocols were recorded. Everyone learned to operate BigTrak effectively in the single 30-minute session. That is, all of the individuals were able to enter sequences of commands, without making syntactic errors, that would cause BigTrak to execute the intended actions.

Shrager and Klahr (1986) distinguished two phases of learning how to operate the BigTrak toy: **initial orientation** and **systematic investigation.** The initial orientation phase was the period until the first action from BigTrak was obtained. This period was typically brief (0.5 to 7.5 minutes) and was characterized by learners first pressing the GO or arrow keys by themselves to see if these keys directly initiated movement and then entering combinations of commands and numbers. The orientation phase ended when the GO key was pressed after a syntactically correct function had been entered, thus releasing the programmed action. Syntactic knowledge had been mastered by that point, as indicated by the fact that few syntactic errors occurred subsequently during the systematic investigation phase.

The behavior of learners during the systematic investigation phase was characterized by repetition of the following: A hypothesis about the nature of the device was generated, an experiment was conducted to test the hypothesis, and the results of the experiment were evaluated. Hypothesis testing of this nature is indicative of the explicit selective mode of processing. All learners were highly active, executing several hundred keypresses in the 30-minute session. The programs that were run were typically short, with 50% containing three or fewer commands. The majority of the hypotheses concerned task-action mapping knowledge about what a key does and device model knowledge of how programs are stored, modified, and executed. When an incorrect prediction was derived from the hypothesis, learners in many cases changed their device model to account for the disconfirming outcome. However, because these changes were often based on insufficient information, they sometimes led to further incorrect hypotheses, errors, and subsequent changes. When an outcome did not conform exactly to the prediction but was similar to it, the outcome often would be taken incorrectly as confirming the hypothesis.

Despite the fact that many incorrect hypotheses were considered, and some even seemingly confirmed, the high rate of interaction allowed the users to succeed in learning how to operate BigTrak. The device model was used primarily to support inferences—for example, to provide a causal explanation about an unexpected action of BigTrak—and to suggest the means for accomplishing goals internal to the system. Although a device model apparently was inferred and used to predict behavior of the

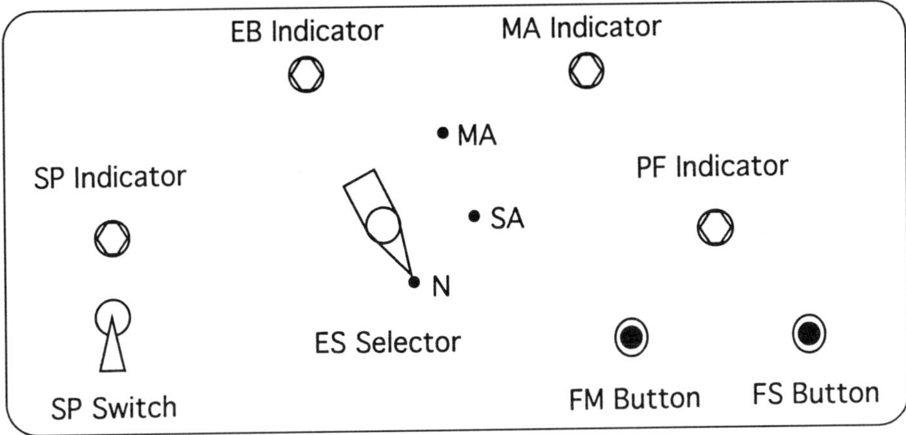

Figure 6.8. The control panel device used by Kieras and Bovair (1984).

system, in posttask interviews almost all of the explanations of BigTrak were in terms of rules of interaction, that is, the task-action mapping, and not the device model.

Learning With Instructions

Given that device learning in uninstructed situations seems to rely heavily on device models developed by the learners, the possibility exists that learning might be facilitated by instructions that provide an appropriate device model at the outset. Kieras and Bovair (1984) examined this possibility using the device shown in Figure 6.8, which is a control panel with a toggle switch, a three-position rotary switch, two push buttons, and four indicator lights. The task was to institute a series of procedures that would cause the indicator light labeled *PF* to flash. The *rote* group only learned the required procedures by rote. The *device model* group was provided knowledge about how the device worked in the form of a description based on the television show *Star Trek.* They were told that the device was the control panel for a "phaser bank" on the Starship Enterprise™ and that the flashing *PF* light indicated successful firing of the phaser bank. The internal components and processes of the system were explained in terms of the phaser bank.

During training, both groups learned two normal operating procedures that would cause the *PF* light to flash. They also learned two types of malfunction procedures, one for which an alternative procedure would cause the light to flash and one for indicating that an irrecoverable malfunction had occurred. After learning all of the procedures, retention tests were given immediately and one week later. The device model group showed superior performance on all measures: They required less time to learn the procedures, showed better immediate and delayed retention, and took less time to execute the procedures. Kieras and Bovair (1984) proposed that the benefit from the device model derived from its being used to infer how to operate the device. In a second experiment, the task was to infer the procedures rather than to learn them. Almost all members of the device model group inferred the correct procedures on their first attempt, whereas the rote group had to perform many actions before identifying the correct procedures. Moreover, verbal protocols showed that the device model group explained their actions entirely in terms of the model, whereas the rote group explained theirs in terms of superficial relations among indicators and controls. Thus a device model is helpful because it enables specific inferences about the operating procedures.

Payne (1988) has provided evidence that metaphorical instruction about a device, which does not support specific inferences about procedures, can also benefit learning. In his study, people learned a command language to perform a game of moving a pointer on the screen and to pick up and manipulate blocks in 3-D space. One version of the game was called Manipulation; for this game, the instructions described the objects and goals in an abstract manner. A second version was called Sea Mines; the instructions for it described the task in terms of the metaphor of an underwater robot rearranging sea mines. Although the device model provided by this metaphor would not support specific inferences about procedures, those persons who received the Sea Mines instructions evidenced better memory for available commands and distinctive patterns of command use that corresponded with the concept of a controlled robot. In other words, metaphorical instruction about the device apparently provided a mnemonic structure for learning the necessary command language and strategies.

The Yoked State Space Hypothesis

One problem hindering progress in understanding the role of device models is that there is little understanding or agreement about what a device model is. Payne, Squibb, and Howes (1990) have proposed a theoretical framework for the study of device models that they call the **yoked state space hypothesis.** This hypothesis is based on the problem space concept, which is described in detail in Chapter 7. According to this hypothesis, the user must construct and maintain at least two separate state spaces, a goal space of the possible states of the world that can be manipulated by the device and a device space that represents the possible states of the device. A semantic mapping must also be acquired that relates the entities in the device space to those in the goal space.

Payne et al. (1990) distinguished two modes for learning to operate a device. For one mode, the user develops an operational account based on a minimal device space for performing the requisite tasks that represents all of the states in the corresponding goal space. An operator in this minimal device space, such as the "copy string" operator for a text editor, will be effected by a sequence of more primitive actions (e.g., marking a string and specifying the copying operation). For the other, figurative, mode, the operators of the minimal device space are decomposed and elaborated with conceptual entities that provide meaning for the primitive actions from which the operators are composed. The main advantage of the figurative account is that it enables more efficient performance of certain tasks, such as copying the same string of text to two different places in the text, because the primitive actions are understood.

Payne et al. (1990) provided evidence for the yoked state space hypothesis by showing that the concept of a string of text, which is an element of the minimal device space for text editing, is a component of text editing competence. Also, Payne et al. found that users who adopted operational accounts for text editing used less efficient methods than users who adopted figurative accounts in which the minimal device space was elaborated with the concept of a buffer. Findings discussed previously can be interpreted in terms of the yoked state space hypothesis. For example, Kieras and Bovair's (1984) device model instructions were beneficial because they provided figurative accounts for individual switches, whereas Payne's (1988) robot metaphor was effective because it changed the goal space, which in turn changed the device model.

Cognitive Complexity and Transfer

To what extent can transfer from one device to another occur? Kieras and Polson (1985) developed a model for formally analyzing cognitive complexity to predict the time to learn to use a device and transfer of this learning to other devices. They distinguished two components of knowledge in operating a device: the user's task representation and the user's device representation. The user's task representation is described by the

GOMS model, developed by Card, Moran, and Newell (1983), which represents the user's understanding of the task in terms of goals, operators, methods, and selection rules (see Chapter 9). A distinction is made between device-dependent and device-independent knowledge. The user's device representation consists of four types of information: task-relevant information that is the counterpart to the user's task representation; knowledge about the physical layout of the device; knowledge about the relation between operations of controls and the device's behavior; and "how it works" knowledge, that is, the mental model of the internal workings of the device. The complexity of a device depends on three things:

1. Complexity of the user's task representation and its associated demands on information processing
2. Number of device-dependent functions that must be learned
3. Ease with which the device-model knowledge can be acquired.

Kieras and Polson (1985) formally represented these aspects of cognitive complexity in a production system framework. In such a framework, the number and complexity of the production rules needed to represent the knowledge are the primary indicators of the amount of knowledge that must be acquired by a person to use the device. It is assumed that practice reduces the number of the production rules by making them more compact, as in Anderson's (1983) ACT* model, rather than reducing the speed with which a rule can be executed. Also as in Anderson's work, transfer between devices is predicted by a variation of the identical elements theory. Each rule in the user's knowledge for a new device is compared with existing rules, with transfer occurring for rules that are identical or similar to previously learned rules.

Support for the cognitive complexity model was obtained by Kieras and Bovair (1986) using the "phaser bank" device described above. They had people learn the procedural tasks to operate the *PF* indicator light by rote and showed that the number of new production rules for a task predicted accurately the amount of training time that was required to learn it. Bovair, Kieras, and Polson (1990) similarly showed that training and execution times for five text editing methods were also predicted well from the cognitive complexity model. Payne et al. (1990) showed, in addition, that transfer from one word processing system to another is in part determined by the device model knowledge supported by the initial system. For example, efficient string deletion methods, which require treating adjacent words as a string, are learned more easily with the MacWrite™ system than with the IBM Personal Editor™ system. This is due to the fact that, in MacWrite, strings are marked by dragging a mouse that dynamically highlights the marked characters. People who first used MacWrite performed string deletions more efficiently when transferred to the IBM Personal Editor than did people who used the Personal Editor first. In short, specific methods of string deletion transfer between two word processing systems when the system used first facilitates grasping the concept.

SUMMARY

In addition to learning relations that are necessary to meet the objectives of tasks that we perform, we learn much that is incidental to the tasks. The research described in this chapter indicates that complex covariations in the environment can be detected and learned in the absence of intention to do so. Moreover, this learning can affect performance even when the learned relations cannot be described verbally. Although initial research suggested that much of what was learned incidentally was not open to conscious awareness, subsequent research using more sensitive tests has suggested that at least some knowledge acquired incidentally is available to conscious awareness.

A consistent finding across the several task domains reviewed in this chapter is that explicit learning strategies can be harmful to learning when the relations to be learned are not salient. In such situations, the hypotheses that the learner develops about the nature of the relationships among the variables are likely to be erroneous because they are based on inadequate information. Consequently, effort must be devoted to testing and revising the erroneous hypotheses rather than to the task that is being performed. Explicit learning can be facilitated by providing the learner with an appropriate mental model or by increasing the salience of the pertinent relations. Learning to operate a device depends on a mental model of the inner working of the device, called a device model, as well as on an understanding of how particular actions map onto operation of the device. The benefits of device models, as well as their complexity and transfer effects, can be explained well using concepts from the problem-solving literature, which we discuss in detail in the next chapter.

Measuring Problem-Solving Skill

Solving Well-Defined Problems

Solving Ill-Defined Problems

Acquisition of Problem-Solving Skill

Do General Principles Underlie Skill Acquisition Across Domains?

Summary

CHAPTER 7

Problem-Solving Skill

We are constantly confronted with problems of varying complexity in virtually every aspect of our lives. An interesting question is whether we get any better at solving the range of problems confronting us as we gain experience at solving them. Some problems, such as deciding on a major purchase or making a career choice, never seem to get any easier to solve. But others, such as determining which statistical analysis is appropriate for a given type of data or selecting an appropriate fishing lure to use for the prevailing conditions, clearly benefit from repeated problem-solving episodes. In this chapter, problems are classified by their degree of structure and theoretical accounts of problem solution are discussed. The nature of skill at solving problems in some rather restricted domains is also summarized; unfortunately, skill in solving many of the real-life problems that we encounter is not so readily described.

Researchers studying problem solving have tended to concentrate on problems for which there is a single correct solution, such as syllogisms and textbook physics problems. The early problem-solving research focused primarily on relatively simple puzzlelike tasks, or so-called **knowledge-lean** problems, that are well defined and can be solved on the basis of task instructions and general reasoning skills. Figure 7.1 shows a widely

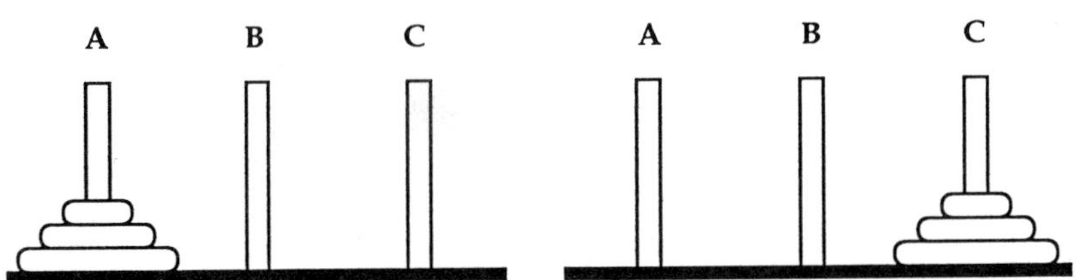

Task and Problem Statement
A board has three pegs, A, B, and C. On peg A are N disks (in the diagram, N = 3) graduated in size, with the largest disk on the bottom. The task is to move the stack of disks from the leftmost peg to the rightmost peg by moving one disk at a time and never placing a disk on top of a disk smaller than itself.

Problem Space
States:
All configurations of the N disks on the three pegs
Operators:
Move a disk by removing it from one peg and placing it on another peg
Recognize a configuration as an instance of a pattern

Problem
Initial State: The configuration shown at left in the diagram
Goal State: The configuration shown at right in the diagram
Path Constraint: No disk may be placed on a disk smaller than itself

Figure 7.1. The Tower of Hanoi problem.
SOURCE: Adapted from Newell (1980).

studied problem of this type called the Tower of Hanoi. The problem is to move the stack of disks from peg A to peg C by moving only one disk at a time and not placing a larger disk on a smaller one. Many tasks of this type have been used to evaluate how people go about structuring their problem-solving behavior.

However, as illustrated by the examples above, problem-solving behavior can be observed in a wider variety of situations than just puzzle solving. Most problems are not solved in relative isolation from prior knowledge, and not all problems have single correct answers. Often, uncertainty associated with the outcomes of specific actions further complicates the problem-solving task. Consequently, more recent research has concentrated on ill-defined, **knowledge-rich** problems that draw on the problem solver's knowledge about a specific domain, such as physics. In this chapter and the next, we consider a broad range of tasks that require problem solving, from doing puzzles to developing computer programming functions.

Measuring Problem-Solving Skill

Problem-solving performance can be evaluated using measures such as the percentage of correct solutions and the time to achieve a solution. However, these measures provide only global information about problem-solving episodes and tell us little about the processes used by the problem solver. Problems that require overt, observable manipulations, such as the movement of pieces on a gameboard, allow the researcher to follow more closely the steps being taken by the problem solver. Similarly, problems that have measurable intermediate outcomes or decision points allow for evaluation of the progress of the problem solver as well as determination of the relative difficulty of component parts of the problem.

Another way to evaluate problem-solving behavior is to look at the way in which practice with one set of problems influences success in solving other problems. In the course of problem solving, the problem solver gains experience that could alter the way that subsequent problems are approached. By measuring transfer to variations of the original task, the nature of any learning that has taken place can be evaluated. As with the use of transfer designs in other areas, positive transfer will occur to the extent that the processes learned can be applied appropriately to the new task. Perhaps even more interesting, problem solving is one of the few tasks in which evidence for negative transfer is observed. This was demonstrated dramatically by Luchins (1942), who showed that after people had used the same method to solve five problems involving manipulation of water jar capacities, they persisted in using this method for problems that could have been solved using a simpler, more direct method.

In addition to performance measures, verbal protocols are often collected during or after problem-solving episodes to obtain records of the knowledge used by the problem solver and the succession of mental states through which he or she passes in working on the problem. However, caution must be exercised in obtaining and interpreting protocols because the process of eliciting them may change the nature of the problem solving (see Chapter 1). Also, the protocols themselves may not accurately reflect all of the thought processes involved in the problem-solving episode. Even though protocols suffer these limitations, they continue to be collected and analyzed for the temporally dense evidence that they provide regarding intermediate states in problem solving.

Solving Well-Defined Problems

Most contemporary research on problem solving originates from the work of Newell and Simon (1972) on the General Problem Solver, a computer program that used general problem-solving procedures as well as knowledge of specific task environments to simulate human problem-solving behavior. Like others in the information processing tradition (see Chapter 1), Newell and Simon regarded the human problem solver as an information-processing system. They defined the information-processing system as a central processor that receives sensory information, operates on a memory composed of symbol structures, and produces actions. The conception of a central processor operating on symbolic structures is akin to the execution of an artificial intelligence program by a computer and reflects Newell and Simon's belief that in order to study human cognition one must have a good analysis of the task to be performed and of the possible problem-solving mechanisms for performing the task. Artificial intelligence research provided the requisite task analyses and a set of plausible mechanisms for executing a subset of tasks, including puzzle solving, theorem proving, and game playing. Highly developed programs that were able to perform these problem-solving tasks provided the necessary framework within which hypotheses regarding human problem solving could be tested.

The Problem Space Hypothesis

Central to Newell and Simon's (1972) view of problem solving is the **problem space.** Conceptually, the problem space consists of a description of possible problem states and operators for moving from one problem state to another. For example, in the game of chess the problem states are the various configurations of pieces on the game board and the operators are the legal moves for each piece. A sequence of operators that is applied to successive states, such as would be performed in the opening game, is called a **path.** Specific problems bring with them constraints on the paths that may be taken. In our example, constraints are placed on the ways in which each chess piece can be moved, and higher-order constraints, such as *protect the center*, may also be in place. A problem in a problem space thus may be defined in terms of an initial state, a goal state, and any path constraints. To solve the problem, a path must be found that moves from the initial state to the goal state while satisfying the path constraints. In the Tower of Hanoi problem illustrated in Figure 7.1, the states are the possible configurations of the disks on the pegs, with the initial state being the configuration with the stack on peg A and the goal state being the configuration with the stack on peg C. The path constraints are that only one disk can be moved at a time and that a larger disk cannot be placed on top of a smaller one. One operator is the action of moving a disk from one peg to another, and another is the recognition of the configuration of disks as an acceptable state.

According to Newell and Simon, the elements in the problem space that make up the various states are represented by symbols. Symbols and the relations between them form symbol structures. For example, a position in a chess game is a symbol structure that associates symbols for a square on the board with symbols for the piece that occupies it and the adjacent squares. Elementary information processes operate on symbols and symbol structures to transform one problem state into another.

The problem space hypothesis identifies two processes, **understanding** and **search,** as being crucial in problem solving (VanLehn, 1989). The understanding process produces the problem space from information that is provided about the problem and inferences that a problem solver derives from that information. Essentially, the problem space is a mental representation of the problem to be solved. For many problems, task instructions, background knowledge, and previous experience with the same or similar tasks can have a significant impact on this representation. Because the knowledge and experience that people bring to a problem-solving task vary, even the same task instructions may not result in all individuals adopting the same problem space. If the problem is misunderstood by an individual, its representation may be incorrect and solution difficulties will be likely to occur. The understanding process is of more concern for ill-defined problems than for well-defined problems, and will be discussed later in the chapter.

Although a suitable problem space is crucial to problem solving, it does not ensure that a correct solution will be found. That is, the problem space often is complex, with many possible paths to take, most of which will not lead to solution. The second process, that of search, involves finding an appropriate solution path within the problem space. The likelihood of successful solution is a function of the specific search strategies that are used.

Searching the Problem Space

If human information processing capacity were unlimited, it would be possible to consider simultaneously the entire set of problem states and relations between the problem states. However, processing capacity is limited such that only one problem space operator can be applied and only a limited number of states considered at a time (Newell, 1980). Consequently, strategies for searching the problem space are an important part of problem solving. To accomplish the problem solution requires a search through the problem space in which operators are applied and new states are considered. Search proceeds by selecting a state and then an operator; applying the operator to the present state, thereby producing a new state; and deciding whether to move into the new state and whether the goal state has been achieved. If the goal state has not been achieved, this general procedure is repeated. For all but the most trivial problems, successful search will depend on some strategy for evaluating progress toward the goal and selecting the next move within the problem space.

Methods for guiding problem solution that were initially developed by researchers in artificial intelligence are shown in Table 7.1. The use of these methods by human problem solvers has been documented in a variety of situations. The methods are independent of any specific problem domain and thus are applicable to many different problem types. However, by themselves they are not very powerful and hence are called **weak methods.** One of the most widely discussed strategies is **means-ends analysis,** which proceeds by attempting to select and apply operators that will reduce the difference between the current state and the goal state.

To illustrate the use of the means-ends search strategy, we use water jug problems of the type popularized by Luchins (1942) in which several jugs of various sizes and a fixed quantity of water are provided. The goal in a problem of this type is to distribute the water according to the experimenter's specifications. The jugs are not marked in any way; thus to keep track of how much water is in each jug, whenever water is moved from one jug to another either the recipient jug must be filled or the pouring jug emptied.

Atwood and Polson (1976) used water jug problems to evaluate a means-ends model of problem-solving performance. Each of the problems involved a large, medium, and small jug. Initially, the large jug was full,

Table 7.1 Methods for Guiding Problem Solution

Generate and test: Generate in any way possible a sequence of candidate steps, while testing each one to determine if it is the desired state

Heuristic search: Apply heuristics to guide the selection of operators and states, while remembering which states have been visited and which operators tried

Hill climbing: Apply operators to the current state and select the one that produces a new state that gives an improved evaluation of the objective function

Means-ends analysis: Compare the present state to the desired state and evaluate the difference and then select an operator to apply that leads to a new state that is closer to the goal state

Operator subgoaling: If no operator can be applied to the present state, create a subgoal to find a state in which an operator can be applied and then proceed using heuristic search or means-ends analysis

Planning: Simplify the present state by selecting a subset of information to process, solve the simplified problem, and then use what is remembered of the solution path to solve the complete problem

and the goal was to distribute the water equally between the large and medium jugs. For example, one of the problems used jugs of size 24, 21, and 3 units (the 24-21-3 problem), whereas another used jugs of size 8, 5, and 3 units (the 8-5-3 problem). The means-ends evaluation function, K, used by Atwood and Polson to evaluate progress toward the goal was based on adding together the absolute differences between the current contents of the large and medium jugs and their respective goal quantities. Thus the initial value assigned to the 24-21-3 problem was $K = |24 - 12| + |0 - 12| = 24$. The means-ends heuristic dictates that the action taken to change the current state leads to a reduction in the value of the evaluation function. For example, pouring from the large jug into the small jug yields the value $K = |21 - 12| + |0 - 12| = 21$. Because $K = 21$ is less than $K = 24$, this is an acceptable move according to the means-ends heuristic.

Each problem has two possible solution paths, as shown in Figure 7.2. The amounts in each jug are shown in parentheses for each state along the paths, and the value of the evaluation function K at each state is shown to the side. As can seen by observing the values of the evaluation function at each step of the respective solution paths, the solution of the 8-5-3 problem requires that moves be made that increase the value of K, whereas the

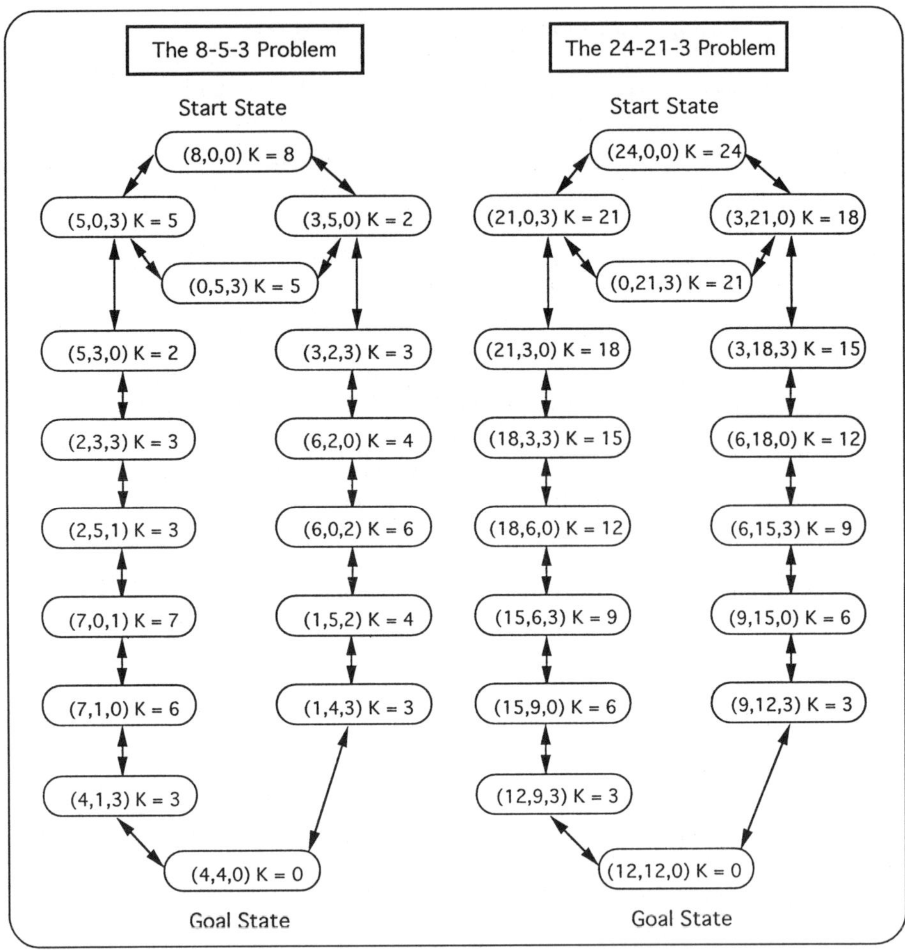

Figure 7.2. Solution paths for the (8, 5, 3) problem and the (24, 21, 3) problem.
SOURCE: Adapted from Atwood and Polson (1976).

solution of the 24-21-3 problem does not. If the means-ends heuristic is the one used by the problem solvers, then problems that require violating the heuristic for solution should be more difficult than those that do not. Consistent with this prediction, the 8-5-3 problem was indeed more difficult than the 24-21-3 problem, as measured by the number of steps taken to reach the solution.

Because the 8-5-3 problem is fairly complex, if the problem solver is asked to solve it repeatedly, he or she may try to identify intermediate states along the solution path that can then serve as subgoals for future attempts at problem solution. Many problems can be solved most efficiently by the creation of such subgoals. Although useful subgoals can sometimes be identified at the outset of problem solving, they may not be readily apparent. Anzai (1987) developed a theory called **learning by doing** that specifies how subgoals are identified and learned through experience at solving problems of a given type. For example, when using a weak method such as means-ends analysis, the problem solver may move from one state to another such that the difference between the current state and the goal state is greatly reduced. This state would now be identified as a "good" state, and in future problem solving a subgoal would be set to achieve this state. Experience with a variety of complex problems of a given type would thus lead to the acquisition of a hierarchy of subgoals for solving such problems.

Even though it is convenient to separate search strategies from problem understanding in the analysis of problem solving, an interactive relation exists between the two. The search process itself may uncover information that affects understanding of the problem and hence modifies the problem space. Such an interplay between search and understanding is particularly important when the problem to be solved is ill defined.

Solving Ill-Defined Problems

The problem space hypothesis has been successfully used to characterize the solution of well-defined, knowledge-lean problems. In such problems it is possible to specify unambiguously the initial state, the goal state, the permissible operators, and the path constraints. In the ill-defined problems more typically encountered in everyday life, uncertainty often exists regarding one or more of these components of the problem space. For these problems, steps must be taken to refine and elaborate the problem state representations and to seek information from memory or other sources to provide appropriate operators and necessary constraints. Furthermore, some problems require that processes of induction be invoked to create and modify knowledge structures.

Not only is additional information necessary to develop the initial problem space for ill-defined problems, but a restructuring of the problem space during the course of solving the problem may also be required. More recent formulations of the problem-solving process attempt to capture dynamic interactions with the external environment and the memory stores of the problem solver. Mental-model-based problem solving is one such formulation.

Mental Models

Mental models have been described as "transient, dynamic representations of particular unique situations" (Holland, Holyoak, Nisbett, & Thagard, 1986, p. 14). Although they are based on static prior knowledge, mental models are actively built on demand by integrating this knowledge in novel ways in response to a current goal. Like the interactions of the states and operators in a problem space, mental models can be described as rule systems. However, in addition to providing the condition-action rules that govern state transitions, mental models include rules for classifying environmental states or objects in different ways (e.g., if Sigmund Freud was a psychiatrist, then he also was a medical doctor, a human being, and a mammal) that allow the comparison of alternate categorizations of a problem.

Typically, mental models are described as dynamic representations that can be executed to simulate some aspects of the task environment. Thus the **transition function,** or set of rules governing changes in problem states, that is the core of the mental model must map on to the transition function that governs real-world transformations. The learning of a representation of the real-world transition function is therefore crucial to the development of a useful mental model. The representation need not be a duplication of the actual function but, rather, may be simplified such that nonessential details are omitted. In other words, the mental model does not have to be isomorphic with the aspect of the environment that it represents, but it must be homomorphic.

Holland et al. (1986) give an example of a rule-based mental model for predicting the behavior of fast-moving objects. The transition function that is the core of the model is the law that fast-moving objects slow down. This can be seen in Figure 7.3, which shows that objects identified as fast moving at time t are predicted to be slow moving at time $t + 1$. This model is a homomorphic representation of the behavior of objects in that the essential property of the objects is captured but their details are not.

Holland et al. (1986) suggest that most mental models are better described as quasi-homomorphs that include alternate transition functions. In a quasi-homomorph, there is a higher layer in the model with a transition function that captures most instances. Exceptions are handled by lower levels of the model with different transition functions. Lower-

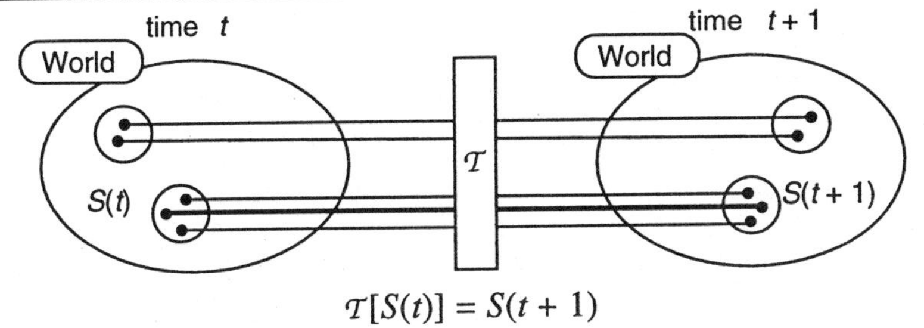

The transition function $\mathcal{T}$ includes the law that fast-moving objects slow down. $S(t)$ is a class of objects that is fast-moving and obeys the law "fast-moving" → "slow-moving." $S(t + 1)$ is the same class of objects, now slow-moving.

Figure 7.3. A homomorphic rule-based mental model for the behavior of fast-moving objects.
SOURCE: Adapted from Holland, Holyoak, Nisbett, and Thagard (1986).

level homomorphs are created when predictions based on the higher level fail. For example, the law illustrated by the homomorph in Figure 7.3 is violated by objects such as small, striped, fast-moving insects. When such an instance is encountered, a different transition function must be invoked that applies to self-propelled objects.

Learning by Analogy

As in other domains, the study of transfer from one situation to another has played a key role in understanding problem-solving skill. Perhaps the most important topic in transfer of problem-solving skill is the use of analogy to solve novel problems. When two problems have a similar underlying structure (i.e., share related problem spaces or mental models), the solution of one of the problems can sometimes guide the solution of the other. That is, a mental model that is applicable to a studied **source** problem may provide the necessary basis for a mental model that will help solve a related **target** problem. The potential value of an appropriate mental model is illustrated by the following example. If asked to predict the trajectory of a ball that is injected with some force into a coiled tube, many people predict that the ball will follow a curved trajectory even

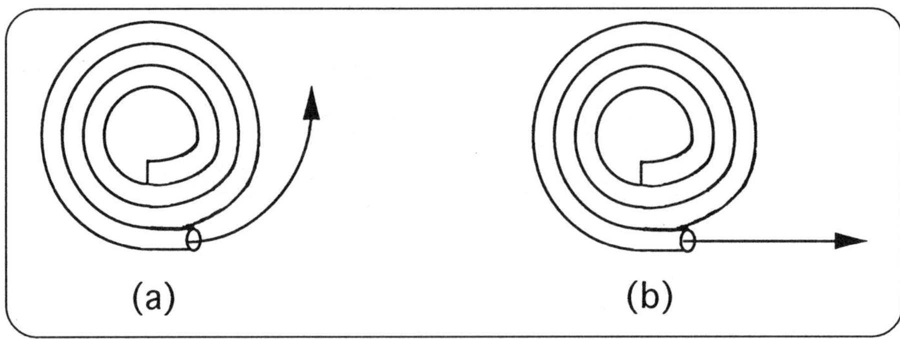

Figure 7.4. Typical, incorrect prediction (a) and correct prediction (b) of the trajectory of a ball leaving a curved track.

after leaving the tube (see Figure 7.4; Kaiser, McCloskey, & Proffitt, 1986). However, if the same question is asked regarding pressurized water traveling through a coiled hose, most people correctly predict that the trajectory of the water upon leaving the hose will be straight. If an individual is first presented with the hose problem and then asked to predict the trajectory in the ball problem, correct solution of the ball problem is more likely—provided that the similarity between the two problems is noted (Kaiser, Jonides, & Alexander, 1986).

The study of transfer from source to target problems has resulted in detailed descriptions of the process of solving problems by analogy. Holland et al. (1986) describe several steps in analogical problem solving. The first step is to construct mental representations of the source and target problems. Because the relation between the two problems may not be obvious, the next step is to detect similarities between the two and to select the source as a potentially relevant analog. The third step is the mapping of corresponding elements of the problems, that is, determining which elements play similar roles in the source and target problems. The final step is to adapt the mapping to generate rules that can be applied to the target problem to reach the parallel solution.

Merely presenting a similar problem does not ensure that transfer will occur. Several researchers have shown that instructions or hints must be given for analogies to be useful in solving subsequent problems. Gick and Holyoak (1980) came to this conclusion in studies in which the radiation problem (Duncker, 1945) was used to study possible transfer to other problems. In this problem, the task is to use a ray to destroy a tumor without destroying healthy tissue. To complicate matters, when the ray is of sufficient intensity to destroy the tumor, healthy tissue will also be destroyed. The solution, which is typically difficult to achieve, is to use many smaller rays, any one of which is not sufficiently strong to destroy healthy tissue, that converge at the site of the tumor. The cumulative effect of the rays at the tumor will be sufficient to destroy it, with the healthy tissue left intact at the other locations through which the rays pass.

Gick and Holyoak (1980) first presented people with a story about a general who was confronted with the problem of needing to capture a fortress at the center of a country. In the story, the general captured the fortress by dividing his troops into small groups that converged simultaneously on the fortress from multiple roads. This analogous problem had only a small effect on the solution rate for the radiation problem when no hint was given to use the analogy, but the solution rate increased greatly when such a hint was subsequently provided. The tendency to use the source problem as an analog only when a hint is provided emphasizes the importance of looking for similarities between the source and target problems.

One factor that likely restricts recognition of the underlying similarity between analogous problems is that many of their surface features will be different. For example, in the radiation problem above, surface features include a patient, a tumor, rays, and a doctor, whereas in the analogous military problem, the corresponding surface features are a country, a fortress, troops, and a general. There is little similarity between the surface features of these two problems, so it is not surprising that people have difficulty recognizing that the military problem is analogous to the radiation problem. Consistent with the hypothesis that differences in surface features impede recognition of analogies, studies have shown that when spontaneous recognition of an analog does occur it is likely to be based on the similarity of the superficial features (Ross, 1987).

In fact, similarity of superficial features between source and target problems may lead to transfer that hinders solution of the target problem. In addition to Luchins's (1942) demonstration of negative transfer between types of water jug problems, there are numerous demonstrations of **einstellung,** or set, effects in problem-solving tasks (e.g., McKelvie, 1985). Set effects reflect transfer of previously learned procedures on the basis of surface similarity to task variations for which the procedures are either inefficient or inappropriate. A phenomenon closely related to einstellung effects is that of **functional fixedness,** first reported by Maier (1930) and Duncker (1945). This phenomenon refers to the inability to use an object (e.g., a screwdriver) in a novel way (e.g., as a pendulum weight for a string) to solve a problem. Functional fixedness is a decreasing function of the time that has elapsed since the object was used in the conventional manner (Adamson & Taylor, 1954) and is negatively correlated with the ability to overcome set in water jug problems (Adamson & Taylor, 1954; McKelvie, 1984), suggesting that it also reflects inappropriate transfer of prior procedures to the novel task.

For analogs that have dissimilar surface features, spontaneous recognition should be more likely to occur if the problem solvers disregard the surface features and focus on the underlying similarities. Catrambone and Holyoak (1989) promoted spontaneous transfer by rewording target problems to emphasize their underlying similarity to source problems. Gick and Holyoak (1983) achieved similar levels of transfer by exposing problem solvers to two source problems and requiring that similarities between the two source problems be described. This procedure evidently made it possible for an abstract schema that was common to the solutions of the problems to be extracted from the details that were different. This schema could then be applied more readily to the analogous target problem. Schema extraction and identification of this nature is sometimes regarded as a fifth step in analogical problem solving.

An experimental investigation of the proposed steps in analogy use was conducted by Novick and Holyoak (1991) for mathematical word problems. In addition to measuring problem-solving performance as a function of the types of hints given experimentally, retrospective protocols were obtained in which problem solvers described similarities between source (determining how many plants a couple bought for their garden) and target (determining the number of students in a marching band) problems as well as between the manners in which they were solved. In one experiment, some people were given a specific hint regarding the mapping of elements in the source problem to the corresponding elements in the target problem. These hints were of two types, conceptual hints that pointed out the conceptual relations between the source and target problems (i.e., "the band members are like plants, the rows and columns of band members are like kinds of plants, and the number of band members per row or column is like the number of plants of each kind," p. 402) and mapping hints that provided information about which specific elements (in this case, numbers) mapped onto each other (i.e., "the 12, 8, and 3 in the band problem are like the 10, 4, and 5 in the garden problem," p. 402). The performance of the problem solvers who received conceptual or mapping hints was compared with that of those who were given either a general hint to use the source problem or no hint at all.

When the hint pointed out the conceptual relations between the source and target problems, performance was no better than with the general hint to use the source problem. This suggests that when solvers retrieve the source problem they automatically uncover the conceptual similarities and correspondences between the source and target problems. However, when the mapping hint—which provided specific information regarding which particular numbers in the two problems mapped onto each other—was given, performance was better than for the other hint conditions. Novick and Holyoak (1991) concluded that this additional benefit was found because the more specific mapping hint provided the necessary information for adaptation of the source solution procedure to the target problem. Adaptation is not simply an automatic consequence of successful mapping, however, because half of the people provided with the mapping hint still did not solve the band problem correctly.

Additional information about the representations used by the problem solvers in Novick and Holyoak's task was obtained by analyzing verbal protocols collected during the phase of the experiment in which similarities between the source problems were noted. The protocols were classified as indicating poor, intermediate, or good internal schemas on the basis of the number of necessary problem solution steps included. Novick and Holyoak found that the quality of the schemas was positively correlated with target problem performance, which suggests that schema extraction is a prerequisite for good transfer performance.

The findings of this study fit well with the five-step model of analogical transfer outlined by Holland et al. (1986). Furthermore, they suggest that adaptation of the solution of the source problem to the target problem is a major locus of transfer difficulty. Successful application of the source problem is not guaranteed even when the mapping of elements from that problem to the target problem is known by the problem solver.

Acquisition of Problem-Solving Skill

In previous chapters, we discussed the acquisition of perceptual, response selection, and motor skills. The problem-solving tasks described in this chapter differ from the tasks described in earlier chapters primarily in their complexity. This complexity is evident in two different ways. First, considerable demands are placed on the limited resources available to compare alternatives, retrieve and integrate information, and keep track of problem states. Second, because of these demands, efficient problem solution requires the use of appropriate strategies and selective access of relevant knowledge from past experience. Moreover, these demands dictate the conscious use of strategies to organize problem-solving behavior. The use and evaluation of the success of these strategies in turn requires self-monitoring, or **metacognitive,** skills.

Metacognitive Skill

One attribute of skilled problem solvers is that they are better able to monitor their own cognitive processing. These metacognitive skills apply to the selection of problem representations and search strategies, planning of the next move in executing a problem-solving strategy, monitoring of progress toward the goal state as the strategy is executed, and evaluation and, if necessary, revision of the strategy (Sternberg, 1988). Not only do good problem solvers monitor and evaluate the efficiency of their actions more than do poor problem solvers (Gick & Holyoak, 1980), they are also able to state rules that describe their actions. This raises the question of whether training problem solvers to verbalize condition-action rules will facilitate learning and transfer.

To address this question, Ahlum-Heath and Di Vesta (1986) evaluated performance on a six-disk Tower of Hanoi problem (refer to Figure 7.1) under different conditions of verbalization of performance rules and practice. The most important conditions for comparison were the ones in which two-, three-, four-, and five-disk problems, with or without the requirement to verbalize a condition-action rule prior to each move, were practiced prior to the six-disk problem. The verbalizations were of the form "*if* this disk is moved from peg x to peg y, *then* these conditions, effects, or subgoals will be achieved." When tested on the six-disk problem, people who had been required to verbalize rules during practice outperformed those who had not been required to do so.

The effectiveness of the verbalization requirement was likely a consequence of making the problem solver more aware of the task structure. By emphasizing consequences of actions, the verbalization requirement encouraged consideration and evaluation of the effectiveness of each particular move toward achievement of the goal. This, in turn, encouraged the development of the metacognitive skill needed to evaluate the validity of planned transformations of the problem states, thus allowing more efficient selection of actions. Also, as suggested by Anzai's (1987) theory of learning by doing, focusing on the effectiveness of actions on attaining the task goal should facilitate the identification of subgoals that can then be incorporated into the representation of the target problem. Thus verbalization of performance rules may influence both the representation of the problem and search of the problem space.

Phases of Skill Acquisition and the ACT Model*

A view of problem-solving skill that is consistent with the finding that transfer is greater when problem-solving strategies are verbalized and that captures analogical transfer is that of Anderson (1982). As discussed in Chapter 1, Anderson distinguished three phases in the acquisition of cognitive skills similar to those that Fitts (1964) proposed for perceptual-motor skills. Anderson recognized that the demands of problem formation and solution are primarily demands on working memory. Thus successful learning should involve restructuring the problem space in ways that reduce the load on working memory. Recall that the three stages of skill in Anderson's ACT* model (and its recent successor, ACT-R) are the declarative stage in which verbal mediation is required to maintain facts in working memory so that they may be used; a transition stage in which the process of knowledge compilation converts the declarative knowledge into productions (i.e., condition-action pairs); and the procedural stage in which these productions are refined and strengthened.

When a novel problem is encountered, general interpretive procedures, such as the use of analogy, are required to operate on the information contained in the problem. This requires that all pertinent information be kept active in working memory. Consequently, interpreting instructions and applying them to the problem conditions places considerable demands on working memory capacity. The function of the knowledge compilation process is to create efficient domain-specific productions that have as conditions the specific problem information and as actions the appropriate step to be taken based on that information. After knowledge compilation has occurred, information no longer has to be interpreted by general procedures but is directly recognized and linked to the appropriate action. Learning is therefore a process of building productions.

Two additional processes, **composition** and **proceduralization,** further reduce demands on working memory and increase problem-solving efficiency. Composition is a process of collapsing sequences of productions into single productions, thus reducing the number of productions required to perform a task. For example, dialing a telephone number might initially require a separate production for each digit to be executed. With enough practice at dialing the number, these productions might be combined into a single "macroproduction" for the whole telephone number. Composition is goal oriented, in that productions are linked that have a common goal setting. Moreover, because composition can occur only for productions held in working memory, the capacity of working memory is a limiting factor on the rate at which the number of productions can be reduced. The other process, proceduralization, binds the required declarative information to the specific productions being used for the task. Following proceduralization, this information no longer needs to be held in working memory to perform the task. For example, after practicing the missionaries and cannibals problem—in which the task is to move a group of missionaries and cannibals across a river using a small boat, without ever having the cannibals outnumber the missionaries on either bank—the problem solver typically knows how many of which type of person to move first. Finally, the production system is refined as the productions most appropriate to the task are strengthened relative to those that are not.

Anderson (1987) provided an example of the transition from declarative to procedural knowledge in which the problem-solving behavior of an individual who was learning to write functions in the programming language LISP was evaluated. After receiving some preliminary instruction in LISP, which included description of some of the basic functions of the language, the neophyte programmer was presented with the task of writing a function called FIRST that would return the first item of a list. FIRST has the same purpose as the system function CAR to which the participant had already been introduced. Thus the task was just an exercise in the syntax of function definition. To start the problem-solving process, five pages of text were provided that described how to define functions using the LISP function DEFUN. Included in the text were an abstract template showing the parts of the function definition and some sample definitions. This information provided the declarative knowledge needed for the task.

Anderson found that the only parts of the five pages of text referred to in solving the problem were the abstract template and some of the examples. He concluded that the weak method of analogy was used to find the solution, with the template and examples providing the source analog. A schematized description of the programmer's steps in solving the problem is shown in Figure 7.5. The problem-solving behavior of this individual consists of setting subgoals for mapping each of the major components of the template. For example, lines 4 through 7 all involve determining the meaning of "parameters" in the abstract template. Because the abstract information in the template was not readily understood, concrete examples were used to check inferences about the meaning of the information. Through this process of matching components and evaluating results, the correct code was eventually produced. Apparently, productions to match task variables with the proper LISP syntax were developed during the execution of this task because positive transfer to a new task of writing a function called SECOND to obtain the second item in the list was found. The protocol for this task is in lines 22 through 27 of Figure 7.5. Notice that the writing of this function was accomplished much faster than the writing of the initial function.

Anderson, Farrell, and Sauers (1984) simulated the schematic protocol shown in Figure 7.5 with a computer program based on ACT*. The simulation captured the major result in the data, which was that after creating the function FIRST the function SECOND was created much faster. The simulation started with two different types of productions: ones to carry out structural analogy and ones that use the necessary LISP functions. Through the process of composition in the course of producing the function FIRST, the simulation converted the domain-general productions into two domain-specific productions. The two productions, P1 and P2, acquired by the simulation were

P1: IF the goal is to write a function of one variable,
THEN write (DEFUN function (variable) and set as a subgoal to code the relation calculated by this function and then write).

P2: IF the goal is to code an argument and that argument corresponds to a variable of the function,
THEN write the variable name.

This example illustrates how the weak method of analogy can be used to solve a novel problem. Through the application of the method, the requisite problem states are generated so that the process of composition can create the appropriate productions.

Another test of the ACT* learning mechanisms was conducted by Elio (1986), who trained people to solve complex mental arithmetic problems requiring several steps. She asked the question of whether learning to (a) perform intermediate calculations or (b) organize and integrate intermediate results was more responsible for learning. A more specific issue investigated in Elio's study was whether common parts of two different procedures share a single representation or are represented separately in each of the two procedures (see Figure 7.6). To test hypotheses regarding whether different procedures shared common representations, Elio had

1. Subject reviews template for function definition.
2. Subject reads problem.
3. Subject writes '(DEFUN FIRST'.
4. Subject is confused by "parameters" in the definition template.
5. Subject reviews F-to-C and TEMP is the parameter.
6. Subject reviews the function EXCHANGE and notes PAIR is the parameter.
7. Subject decides LIST1 is the parameter for FIRST and writes (LIST1).
8. Subject looks at INCREASE.
9. Subject decides to use CAR.
10. Subject looks at EXCHANGE.
11. Subject writes (CAR (LIST1)).
12. Subject balances parentheses. The function is

    ```
    (DEFUN FIRST (LIST1)
        (CAR (LIST1))).
    ```
13. Subject tries (FIRST '(B R)).
14. Subject reads error message "Error: Eval: undefined function LIST1."
15. Subject tries inserting a quote to prevent LIST1 from being treated as a function. The new definition is

    ```
    (DEFUN FIRST (LIST1)
        (CAR 'LIST1))).
    ```
16. Subject tries (FIRST '(B R)) again and reads the answer LIST1.
17. Subject claims not to know what to do. Tutor intercedes with a top-level example. She types (SETQ LIST1 '(B R)) and asks subject to get the CAR of (B R) using LIST1.
18. Subject writes (CAR LIST1).
19. Subject notes the difference between what she just wrote and what she wrote in the function definition. Subject decides to replace the code in the function definition by what she has just written.
20. Subject decides she does not need a SETQ in the function definition. Subject's definition now is

    ```
    (DEFUN FIRST (LIST1)
        (CAR LIST1)).
    ```
21. Function FIRST works.

---

22. Subject reads specifications of function SECOND.
23. Subject writes (DEFUN SECOND (LIST1).
24. Subject decides CDR will take her to the second element and CAR will extract it.
25. Subject reviews a previous top-level example,

    ```
    (CAR (CDR '(A B C))).
    ```
26. Subject finishes function definition which is now

    ```
    (DEFUN SECOND (LIST1)
        (CAR (CDR LIST1))).
    ```
27. Subject tests out definition on an example and it works.

Figure 7.5. Schematic protocol for writing two LISP functions.
SOURCE: Adapted from Anderson, Farrell, and Sauers (1984).

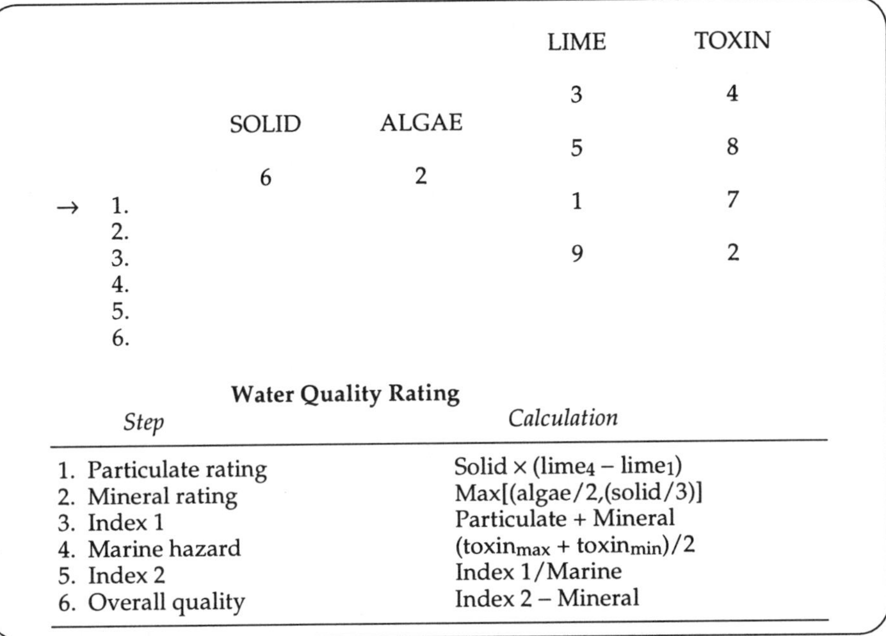

Water Quality Rating

Step	*Calculation*
1. Particulate rating	Solid × ($lime_4$ – $lime_1$)
2. Mineral rating	Max[(algae/2,(solid/3)]
3. Index 1	Particulate + Mineral
4. Marine hazard	($toxin_{max}$ + $toxin_{min}$)/2
5. Index 2	Index 1/Marine
6. Overall quality	Index 2 – Mineral

Figure 7.6. An example display screen (top) showing a solid count, an algae count, and four measures each of lime concentration and toxin rating for a sample of water and an example procedure (bottom) for rating water quality. The component steps are particulate rating, mineral rating, and marine hazard, and the integrative steps are Index 1, Index 2, and overall quality. The steps were executed in order, with the arrow on the screen pointing to the current step.
SOURCE: Adapted from Elio (1986).

people learn complex, multistep, mental arithmetic procedures that varied in their similarity to each other. In these procedures, intermediate results had to be calculated and integrated for problem solution, as shown in Figure 7.6. For example, when working on the water quality problem, the particulate rating and mineral rating must first be computed using the information displayed on the screen before Index 1 can be computed. The arithmetic procedures thus can be broken down into two parts: the calculation of the intermediate results by component steps, such as multiplying the solid count by the difference in two lime levels, and the integrative structure specifying how to combine these intermediate results to produce a final answer.

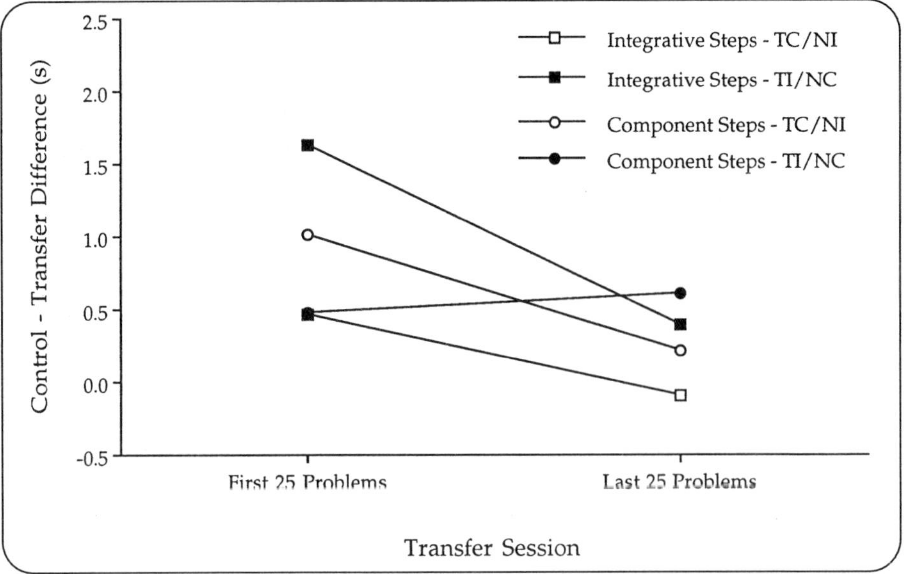

Figure 7.7. Positive (differences > 0) and negative (differences < 0) transfer resulting from prior practice of the same integrative structure or component steps encountered in the transfer problems. Differences between the control and transfer conditions are plotted as a function of the first versus the last 25 transfer problems. NOTE: T = transferred; N = new; I = integrative structure; C = component.

Evidence that the distinction between component steps and integrative structure was apparent to the problem solvers was found in the results of an experiment in which people practiced one procedure for 50 problems and then were transferred to 50 new problems that shared either the same component steps, the same integrative structure, or neither. Times to solve component and integrative parts of the problems were measured independently, and positive transfer was observed in the first 25 transfer problems when either the integrative structure or the component steps were the same as in practice (see Figure 7.7). The benefit of maintaining the same component steps disappeared in the last 25 transfer problems, although a small benefit for maintaining the same integrative structure remained.

In subsequent experiments, Elio (1986) had people solve 70 problems using two different procedures that shared either the same component steps or the same integrative structure. After training, in which people alternated between the two procedures, one of the procedures was changed to have either different component steps, a new integrative structure, or both. The task was then performed for 70 additional trials, 35 with the unchanged and 35 with the changed procedures.

The results from the training session were first evaluated to determine the magnitude of the practice effect. If the steps common to the two problem-solving procedures are represented separately from the procedures, such that the same representation can be used by each procedure, this shared representation would receive twice as much practice as would each of two independent representations. Thus there should be a greater practice effect for the shared steps when a procedure is practiced with another procedure having common steps relative to when it is practiced in isolation. This indeed was the case. Power-law functions were fit to the data and showed greater improvement for component steps in the two-procedure case relative to the single-procedure case only when the same component steps were used in both procedures. Additionally, there was some indication that only when the integrative structure was the same for both procedures was the amount of improvement increased relative to the single-procedure case. These results suggest that all the steps involved in each procedure were not composed into a single production. If they had been, each of the two procedures would have been distinct and no benefit of practicing one procedure on performance of the other should have been obtained.

The results for the transfer task showed that positive transfer to new procedures was obtained when either the same component steps or integrative structure was maintained. However, the degree of transfer observed for the component steps depended on the integrative structure used at transfer. When a new integrative structure was imposed, there did not seem to be much benefit of maintaining the same components. This suggests that the integrative structure provides a context for component steps, which in effect changes the "condition" in the condition-action pair that represents the component.

Power-Law Improvement

As is found for so many tasks, problem-solving performance improvements follow the power law of practice. That is, the most rapid improvement is seen early in practice, but performance continues to improve even after extensive practice. For example, Neves and Anderson (1981) had problem solvers provide justifications for geometrylike proofs developed from an artificial postulate set. As shown in Figure 7.8, performance improved across trials, with total time, total number of steps, and time per step all following power functions.

Various hypotheses have been offered for these changes in speed and accuracy with practice. Often, it is assumed that practice allows component procedures to come to be executed more rapidly and, possibly, even to become automatized (Anderson, 1982). Another way that practice has been proposed to benefit problem solving is by restructuring these procedural components through compilation or chunking (Newell & Rosenbloom, 1981). In either case, the demand placed on limited-capacity resources would diminish: When processing is automatic, it does not draw on working memory and hence imposes no processing load, whereas restructuring reduces working memory load by combining disparate components so that they can be processed as a unit. There is still considerable disagreement as to whether only one or both of these processes are responsible for improvement with practice.

The relative contributions of component processing speedup and restructuring have been investigated by Carlson and his colleagues. They have also investigated the ways in which working memory demands interact with task performance. Carlson, Sullivan, and Schneider (1989) had people learn the functions of seven types of logic gates. Each of these gates took one or two binary digits (0 or 1) as input and produced a binary digit as output (see Figure 7.9). Extensive practice was given at verifying the accuracy or predicting the output of each gate type. Performance on all of the gates improved with practice, with the judgment latencies following a power function (Anderson, 1989). Moreover, judgments were faster when the task was to predict rather than to verify output and when the gate type was positive (as for the BUFFER, AND, and OR gates) rather than negative (the INVERTER, NAND, and NOR gates). This ordering suggests that a sequence of operations is followed that includes classifying the logic gate, applying the integration rule to the input (for gates with more than one input), negating the obtained value (if required), and comparing the result to the displayed output value (for verification judgments). The differences in performance between tasks and gate types were maintained, although at reduced magnitudes, even after over 1,200 trials of practice with each gate.

At two points during practice, a memory load requirement was added to the task to test hypotheses regarding changes in the use of working memory at different levels of skill. On these trials, a three- or six-item memory load was presented before the logic gate for that trial. The load was presented by assigning digits to variables. In the *access* condition, the

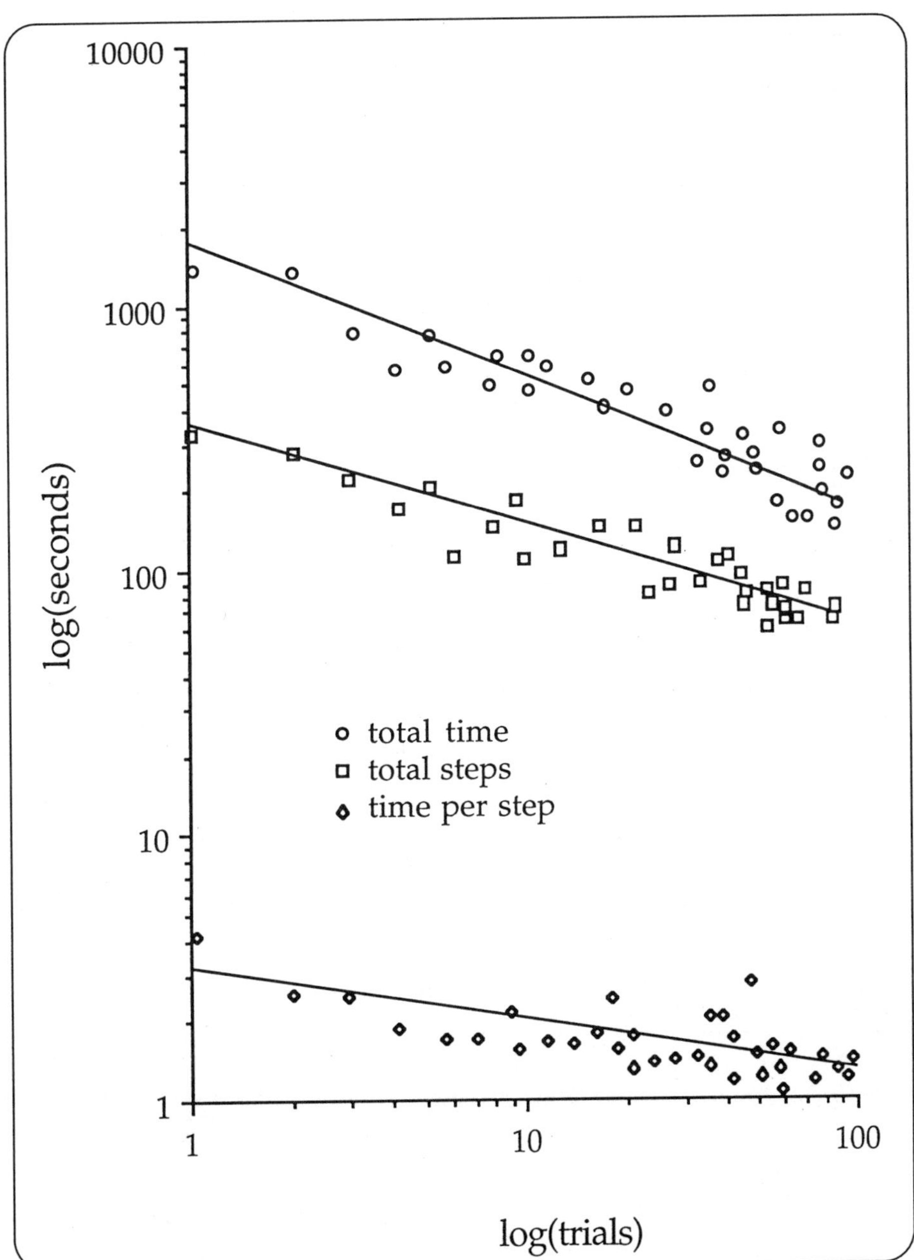

Figure 7.8. Total time, total steps, and time per step to generate proofs in a geometry-like proof system as a function of the number of proofs already done (trials) plotted on a log-log scale.
SOURCE: Based on Neves and Anderson (1981).

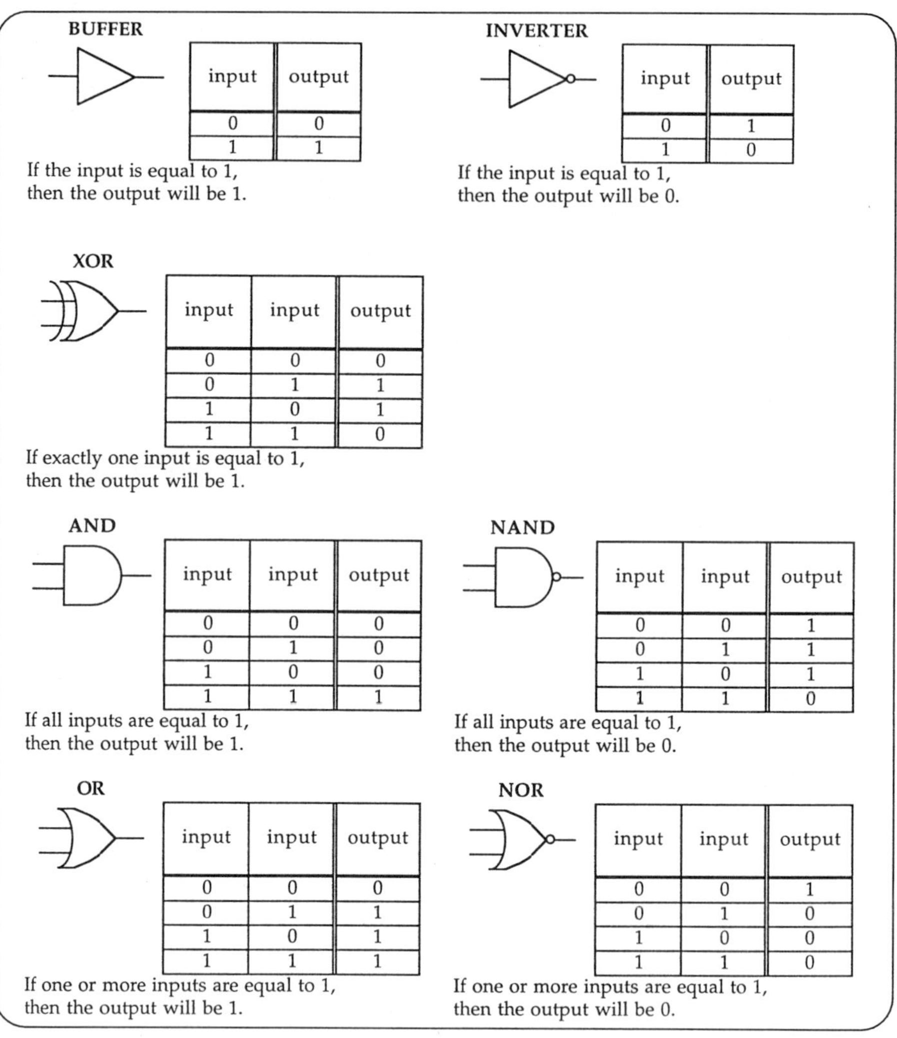

BUFFER

input	output
0	0
1	1

If the input is equal to 1, then the output will be 1.

INVERTER

input	output
0	1
1	0

If the input is equal to 1, then the output will be 0.

XOR

input	input	output
0	0	0
0	1	1
1	0	1
1	1	0

If exactly one input is equal to 1, then the output will be 1.

AND

input	input	output
0	0	0
0	1	0
1	0	0
1	1	1

If all inputs are equal to 1, then the output will be 1.

NAND

input	input	output
0	0	1
0	1	1
1	0	1
1	1	0

If all inputs are equal to 1, then the output will be 0.

OR

input	input	output
0	0	0
0	1	1
1	0	1
1	1	1

If one or more inputs are equal to 1, then the output will be 1.

NOR

input	input	output
0	0	1
0	1	0
1	0	0
1	1	0

If one or more inputs are equal to 1, then the output will be 0.

Figure 7.9. The seven types of logic gates used by Carlson, Sullivan, and Schneider (1989).

digits for the memory task were 0 and 1 (e.g., for a memory load of 3, the load might be $A = 1$, $B = 0$, and $C = 1$), and the gate judgment had as input the appropriate number of variable names (e.g., the AND gate might have as input A and C, and the problem solver should predict an output of 1). Thus in this condition the value of the variable had to be accessed from the memory load in order to make a judgment. In the *expect* condition, 0 and 1 were used as the memory load digits, but the logic gates also had as inputs either or both 0 and 1 rather than variables, so the memory load did not have to be accessed. Finally, in the *irrelevant* condition, the digits used for the memory load were 7 and 8; because these digits could not serve as input to the logic gates, there was no reason for them to be accessed during the logic gate judgment task.

Carlson et al. (1989) found a large cost of accessing items in the memory set. Responses were considerably slower for the access condition relative to the expect and irrelevant conditions, which did not differ, and memory set size had a large effect in the access condition but only a small effect in the other two conditions. This pattern of results indicates that merely holding a memory load does not place additional demand on the resources required for performance of the logic-gate task. However, the requirement to access the memory load as part of the judgment operation does require these resources. The fact that the same pattern of results was found for the imposition of a memory load both early and late in practice suggests that no major changes had occurred in the way that the judgment task was being performed.

Although Carlson et al. (1989) found no evidence for a qualitative change in the way that people solve problems as they become practiced, more complex problems with hierarchies and subgoals may show evidence of such a change. To examine this possibility, Carlson, Khoo, Yaure, and Schneider (1990) studied the acquisition of skill in troubleshooting electronic circuits composed of many logic gates (see Figure 7.10). Each circuit contained one faulty gate whose output remained fixed regardless of the input, and the troubleshooter's task was to identify this gate. The behaviors required to perform the task can be classified into three categories: applying problem-solving operators, using strategies for searching the problem space, and finding sequences of operators that will satisfy intermediate subgoals. The operators were individual steps that changed the problem state, such as requesting information about the present output of a gate and the correct output. Search strategies were made evident by recording the sequence in which information about particular gates was sought.

The number of moves required to solve the problem is a measure of the efficiency of the search strategies that are being used, and the time per move is a measure of the efficiency with which an operator is executed. Performance on both of these measures improved rapidly early in practice but showed little additional benefit from more extended practice. Thus learning apparently occurred at both the operator and search levels but

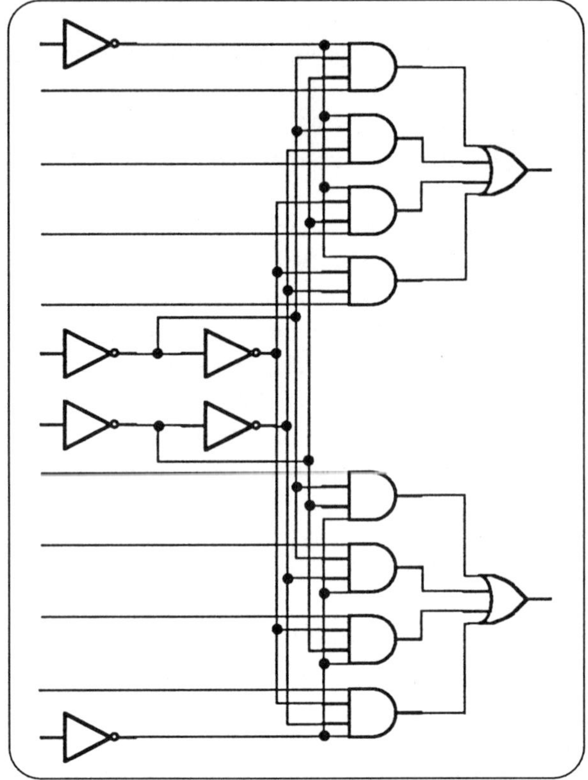

Figure 7.10. An electronic circuit (the data selector) of the type used by Carlson, Khoo, Yaure, and Schneider (1990).

only for the first 50 problems. Other aspects of the data indicated that additional changes in performance did occur, even though these changes were not reflected in overall time or number of moves. Namely, there was evidence that subgoals for determining the current state of individual gates were formed and were strengthened throughout the experiment. Finally, long-term retention tests given six months after the original sessions had been completed showed excellent retention at both the strategy and operator levels. Thus practice apparently can produce both restructuring of component steps, as suggested by Newell and Rosenbloom (1981), and speedup of component processes, as proposed by Anderson (1982).

Do General Principles Underlie Skill Acquisition Across Domains?

The question of whether skill acquisition in problem solving and other cognitive domains shares underlying mechanisms with the acquisition of perceptual and motor skills is an important one. If so, general theories of skill acquisition can be developed that will be applicable to all domains. An empirical approach to answering this question affirmatively is to identify phenomena that occur across domains. A theoretical approach is to apply with success a theory developed in one domain to performance in a different domain. We provide an example of each approach.

An example of a phenomenon that has been studied across domains is contextual interference, which we discussed for motor skill acquisition in Chapter 4 (for a more detailed review, see Magill & Hall, 1990). For motor skills, practice of different variations of a task in distinct blocks often produces better performance during acquisition than does randomized practice of the task variations but poorer performance on subsequent retention tests. The difference in retention indicates that learning is better with randomized practice schedules than with blocked schedules. This better learning is attributed to more elaborate processing that is brought about by the requirement to reconstruct action plans in working memory as the context changes from trial to trial under the randomized schedule (e.g., Shea & Wright, 1991).

Carlson and Yaure (1990) demonstrated that the contextual interference effect is also obtained when learning logic problems of the type used in Carlson et al.'s earlier studies. In their study, participants received practice with four types of logic gates (AND, OR, NAND, NOR) either in distinct blocks for each type or with the types randomly intermixed. The participants then were transferred to a condition in which they solved problems made up of sequences of these logic gates. Performance during practice was better with the blocked schedule than with the randomized schedule, but performance on the subsequent problems was better for those people who had practiced with the randomized schedule. This benefit of the randomized schedule persisted for 90-100 problems, the maximum number tested. On the basis of these data and a subsequent experiment, Carlson and Yaure suggested that there is a need to assemble the appropriate problem elements in working memory on each trial when conditions are randomized in practice. Because of this need, procedures for reinstating the conditions of the problem are developed and practiced.

When conditions are blocked, there is no need to assemble elements for each trial and procedures for accomplishing this are not developed. Thus not only is the contextual interference effect found in both motor learning and problem solving but the explanations provided for it also are similar.

An example of the theoretical approach to determining fundamental principles of skill acquisition can be found in the work of Newell and his colleagues, beginning with Newell and Simon's (1972) implementation of the problem space hypothesis to explain problem-solving behavior. Newell (1990) later developed *Soar*, an architecture for general cognition that uses the problem space to execute a wide range of cognitive behaviors. All behavior in this architecture is goal-oriented problem solving. That is, all tasks are represented as problem spaces. Long-term memory in *Soar* is implemented as a production system, to which access is gained through the conditions of the production rules that apply in a given context. The actions associated with the respective production rules produce the contents of memory. That is, if the description of the current problem state matches the conditions of a long-term memory production, that production will be executed and its action added to working memory. Knowledge search is thus guided by the productions that are executed and the information that they place in working memory. Learning in *Soar* is accomplished by chunking, a process that converts problem-solving episodes into long-term memories (i.e., productions).

Unlike many other production system architectures, *Soar* does not use a conflict resolution mechanism to select some subset of the possible productions for execution. Rather, all productions whose conditions are matched are executed and their contents activated in working memory. Included in each production is **preference information** that is evaluated by a decision procedure to determine what action should be taken next. If a decision regarding how to proceed cannot be made because the activated information is insufficient or conflicting, a subgoal is created that guides an attempt to resolve the impasse by searching for additional knowledge. The actions taken to satisfy the subgoal produce knowledge that is incorporated into a new production by the chunking mechanism so that the subgoal will already exist, ready for use, when the situation is encountered again.

Perhaps the most interesting aspect of *Soar* is that although its roots are in problem-solving processes, it has been applied to tasks as diverse as choice reactions (Laird, Rosenbloom, & Newell, 1986) and collision avoidance in driving (Aasman & Michon, 1992). In fact, Newell (1990) has proposed that *Soar* be considered a candidate unified theory applicable to all domains of human information processing. The same basic implementation of the problem space and subgoaling has been shown to be capable of capturing fundamental regularities of performance at different levels of behavior. For example, in the realm of immediate behavior, the chunking mechanism produces improvement that follows a power function, and in the problem-solving domain, *Soar* produces problem-solving episodes that closely resemble human problem-solving protocols. The success of *Soar* across such disparate domains suggests that general principles underlying skill acquisition can be found.

SUMMARY

Much of the research that we have discussed in this chapter has assumed that problem solving takes place in problem spaces. The problem space hypothesis is that the problem solver constructs a mental representation of the problem containing a goal state, a start state, and intervening states and then searches for a solution path from the start state to the goal state. The problem space hypothesis has been useful in part because it distinguishes representational and search issues, and it continues to be central to formulating problem-solving issues. More recently, the closely related concept of a mental model, which adds the notion of dynamic, mental simulation, has also been used successfully in addressing research issues.

Problem-solving performance improves with practice, as does performance at almost any task. This improvement seems to involve both speedup in the execution of component processes and restructuring of the procedures that are used. The benefits of practice are retained well, and transfer to related problems can be obtained when the conceptual similarity of the two tasks and the mapping of elements from one task to another are made apparent in some manner.

A recurrent theme in the chapter is the use of production system frameworks to model problem-solving performance. Two major production-system based theories, ACT* and *Soar,* were discussed in this context, and research studies evaluating assumptions of the theories were reviewed. ACT* and *Soar* differ in their assumptions about the structure of memory systems and the ways in which productions are selected to be applied, but they share the fundamental assertion that performance can be represented in condition-action rule systems. Although other modeling techniques, such as connectionist modeling, can, in principle, be applied to problem-solving behavior, thus far production system models seem better able to capture the regularities of complex cognitive performance.

Understanding Expert Knowledge

The Acquisition of Expert Performance

General Characteristics of Experts

Expertise in Three Specific Domains

Skilled Memory Theory

Summary

CHAPTER **8**

The Development of Expertise

In previous chapters we discussed extensive research regarding the substantial changes in performance that occur as people gain experience in a task or domain. Most of these findings have come from studies conducted in the laboratory over relatively limited periods of time. Due to the high degree of control that is possible in such studies, it has been possible to determine some of the specific changes that occur as skill is acquired. However, a large gulf exists between easily learned laboratory skills, such as responding quickly to a target letter in an array, and the skills exhibited by elite performers in the arts, sciences, and sports. The complex tasks required of these performers, as well as of experts in many other real life domains, must be practiced for months or even years for proficiency to develop. For example, it has been suggested that in the game of chess no one achieves the highest rating of Grandmaster with fewer than 9 to 10 years of intensive practice (Simon & Chase, 1973), and this 10-year rule appears to hold for a variety of other cognitive and physical skills as well (Ericsson, Krampe, & Tesch-Romer, 1993). To obtain a complete picture of skill, it thus is necessary to study how the knowledge and strategies possessed by experts are acquired and in what way they differ from those of novices.

The investigation of expertise typically proceeds in three steps (Ericsson & Smith, 1991). These steps can be clearly illustrated within the domain of chess, in which the earliest and most extensive research on expert/novice distinctions has been conducted (de Groot, 1946/1978; Simon & Chase, 1973; see Holding, 1985, for a review). Chess provides a convenient domain in which to study expertise because of the existence of detailed records of expert performance and an accurate scale that can be used to rank players according to their skill. The first step in the investigation of expertise is to identify the characteristics of superior performance in the domain of interest. This is often accomplished by developing laboratory tasks representative of the required skill and having both experts and novices perform the tasks under controlled conditions; in the study of chess expertise, tasks such as selecting the best next move to make for a particular game configuration have been used (de Groot, 1946/1978; Saariluoma, 1984).

The second step is to conduct a detailed analysis of the expert's performance in order to infer the nature of the cognitive processes involved. The cognitive processes of chess experts have been inferred by comparing their performance to that of novices on variations of the tasks that have been identified as capturing superior performance. Measurements that have been used include the time to select the best move, patterns of eye movements made while examining the board, and verbal protocols of the process of evaluating alternative moves. Research has shown that chess masters rapidly perceive a given game configuration as a whole, with the best move effortlessly retrieved as part of this process (de Groot, 1946/1978). This is in contrast to less expert players, who are not able to perceive game configurations holistically and must engage in deliberate, effortful evaluation processes to arrive at a decision.

The final step in investigating expertise is to develop an account of the expert's knowledge structures and processes. Such an account should provide insight into the nature of the expert's knowledge structures, as well as into the experiences and training that enable the development of expertise. Models of the knowledge structures and processes of chess experts have been developed based on the inferred characteristics of their expertise. The most widely cited model is that of Chase and Simon (1973), which is based on the concept of chunking (see Chapter 7). According to this model, experience with chess results in the ability to recognize increasingly larger groupings of game pieces (i.e., more complete problem states). This culminates in the chess master's ability to recognize chunks of sufficient size to allow the entire game configuration to be apprehended as a whole.

In the remainder of this chapter, we consider a range of methods for assessing the knowledge of experts in a variety of domains and characteristics of expert performance and its acquisition. The properties of expert performance are then illustrated for three specific skills that are primarily perceptual, cognitive, and motoric, respectively.

Understanding Expert Knowledge

Many techniques have been developed to analyze knowledge organization and problem-solving strategies. These techniques can be classified as **direct** or **indirect** on the basis of whether or not they rely on the elicitation of knowledge of which the expert is consciously aware (Olson & Biolsi, 1991). Direct techniques require that the expert report consciously accessed knowledge or relationships between items in his or her field. Typically, the reports are made in open or structured interviews, concurrent or retrospective verbal protocols, or classification tasks.

A commonly used direct technique is **hierarchical card sorting.** Investigators using card sorting assume that the expert's knowledge is stored in hierarchies and have the goal of revealing these hierarchies. First, the expert is given a stack of cards, each card of which contains a piece of domain knowledge. He or she then sorts the cards into categories. A knowledge hierarchy is determined by having the expert re-sort the categories into subcategories until no further meaningful subdivision is possible. If the initial sorting contained more than two categories, the expert may also be asked to re-sort the cards into a smaller number of superordinate categories. The card sorting task is subject to the same major limitation as protocol analysis, as discussed earlier: The requirement to express knowledge in the manner dictated by the experimenter may lead the expert to impose some ad hoc structure to the material that does not reflect the actual organization of the knowledge.

The direct methods in general have the potential limitation that they rely only on knowledge that is consciously accessible to the expert. However, one characteristic of the development of expertise in a domain is that much information processing becomes automatized and hence is not readily accessible to conscious awareness. Instead of asking experts to report their knowledge directly, indirect methods use some other task, such as making similarity judgments or recalling lists of domain items, to infer the structure of the expert's knowledge. A variety of analytic techniques have been developed to interpret the performance data thus ob-

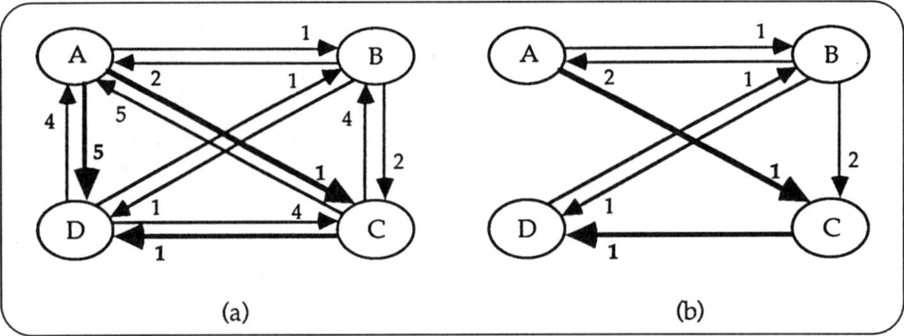

Figure 8.1. (a) A general weighted network and (b) the Pathfinder network derived from it. See text for explanation.

tained. Some of these techniques, including multidimensional scaling and hierarchical clustering, are general statistical methods. Other techniques, such as deriving **general weighted networks** from proximity data (e.g., similarity judgments), using the Pathfinder algorithm developed by Schvaneveldt and colleagues (Schvaneveldt, 1990), or **ordered trees** from recall data using the algorithm developed by Reitman and Reuter (1980), were developed specifically for knowledge elicitation purposes.

Of the indirect techniques used to infer knowledge structures, the Pathfinder algorithm demands the fewest assumptions. It will work whether items are organized hierarchically or not, when a given item belongs to more than one category and when the proximity relation between two items is not symmetric (e.g., *A* is judged to be more similar to *B* than is *B* to *A*). The first step in a Pathfinder analysis is to obtain proximity judgments for the data. These data can then be conceptualized as a complete network in which each pair of items is connected by a link and each link is assigned a weight equal to the proximity between the pair of linked items. The Pathfinder algorithm is applied to the complete network to reduce the number of links in the network in order to reveal relationships among items. The resulting Pathfinder network contains only those links between items that were of minimum weight in the original network. For example, the link between *A* and *D* might be assigned a proximity rating of 5 (with 1 being most proximal; see Figure 8.1) but the links between *A* and C and between C and *D* assigned values of 1. Because the direct path from *A* to *D* has a higher weight than the indirect path from *A* to C to *D*, the link from *A* to *D* will not be in the final Pathfinder network, whereas the links from *A* to *C* and from *C* to *D* will.

Pathfinder networks have been used to distinguish different types of experts from each other and from novices on the basis of their knowledge structures, as illustrated in a study by Gillan, Breedin, and Cooke (1992). They had two groups of experts in human-computer interface design—human factors experts and software development experts—and nonexperts sort human-computer interface concepts concerning user knowledge, display, control, interaction, and data manipulation. Proximity ratings among the concepts were derived from the categorical judgment data and then analyzed using the Pathfinder algorithm. Not only were the networks derived for experts much more organized than those derived for novices, but the networks for the two types of experts were also different. Whereas the network generated for the human factors specialists showed distinct subnetworks of related concepts (see Figure 8.2), the network for the software developers showed fewer, less interconnected subnetworks (see Figure 8.3).

Both similarities and differences exist between the two groups of experts in the organization of concepts pertaining to specific aspects of human-computer interface design. For example, the networks of both human factors and software design experts showed a link between *user interface management system* and *display manager*, indicating that both groups view the relationship between the software that manages the interface and the software for writing to the screen as close. However, for the human factors specialists, the user interface management system was also linked with *prototyping*, whereas for software developers, the user interface management system was linked to *application software*. This distinction may reflect that human factors specialists use prototyping to develop the user interface, whereas the software developers are concerned with the user interface only in relation to the use of application software and aspects of program management. In other words, not only is the overall structure of knowledge different for the two groups of experts but some of the specific links between concepts reflect the different concerns of their respective specializations.

The Acquisition of Expert Performance

The performance of virtually anyone will improve with practice, but not everyone will achieve the status of expert in their domain. What

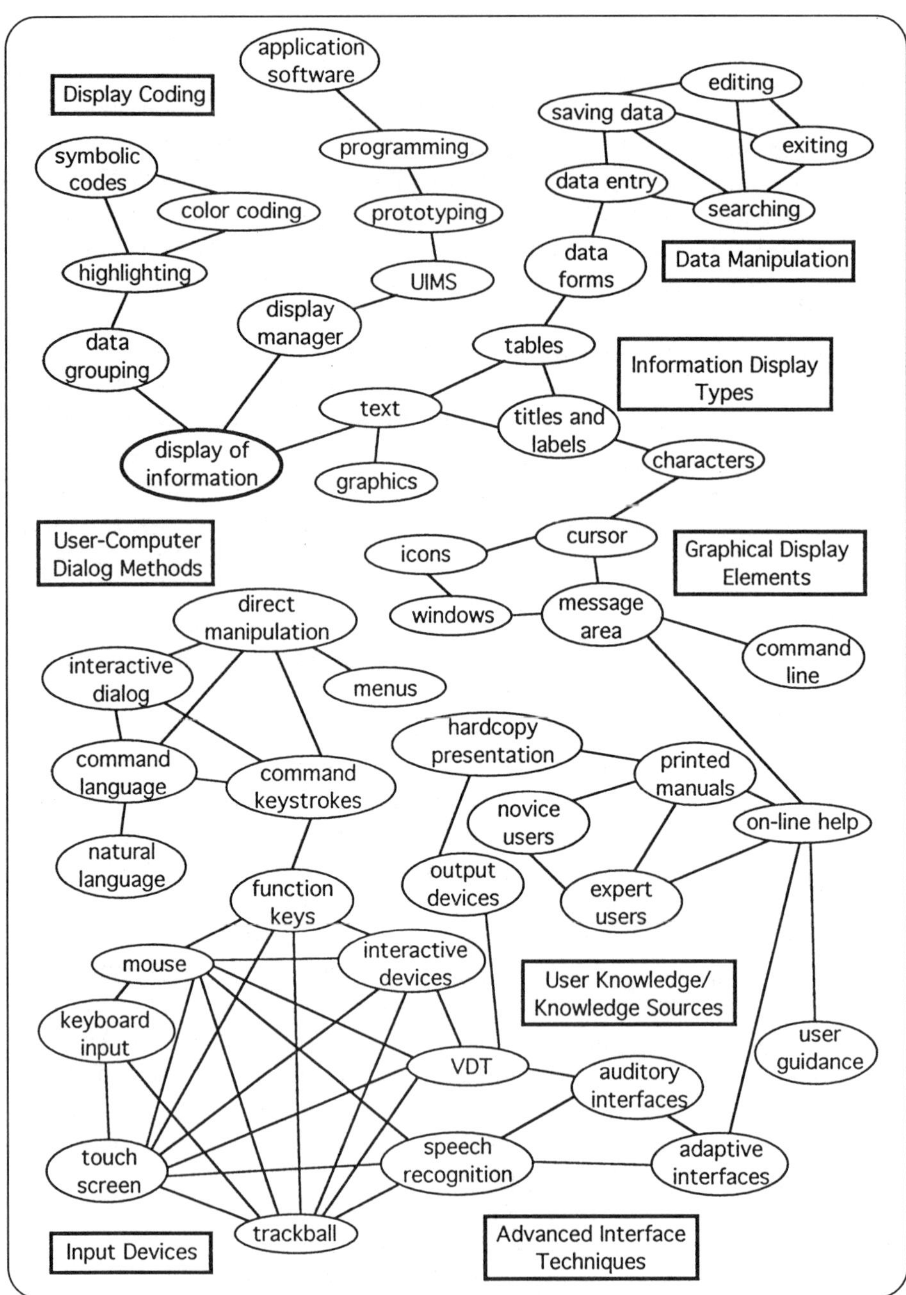

Figure 8.2. Pathfinder network of human-computer interaction concepts for human factors experts. Central nodes are indicated by bold lines.
SOURCE: Based on Gillan, Breedin, and Cooke (1992).

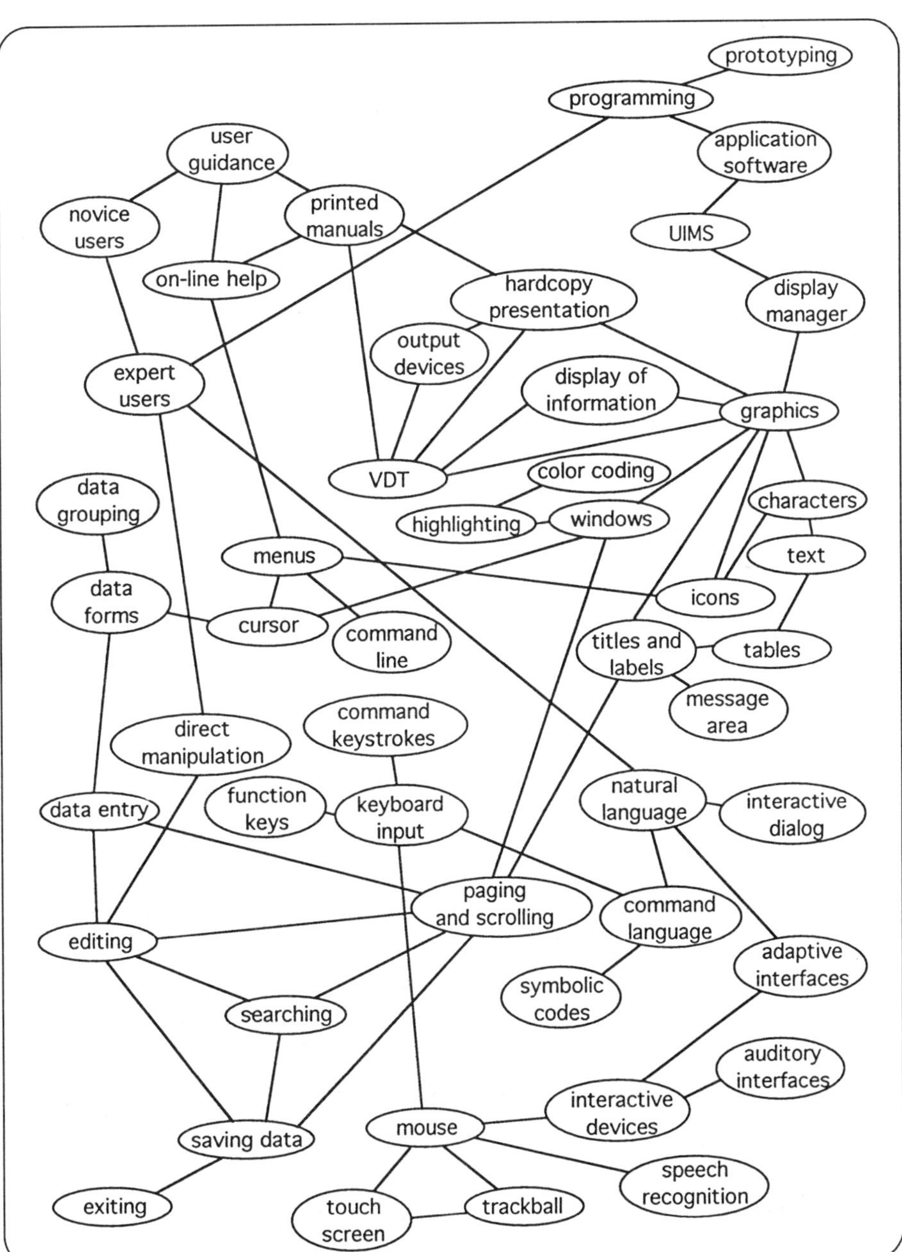

Figure 8.3. Pathfinder network of human-computer interaction concepts for software development experts.
SOURCE: Based on Gillan, Breedin, and Cooke (1992).

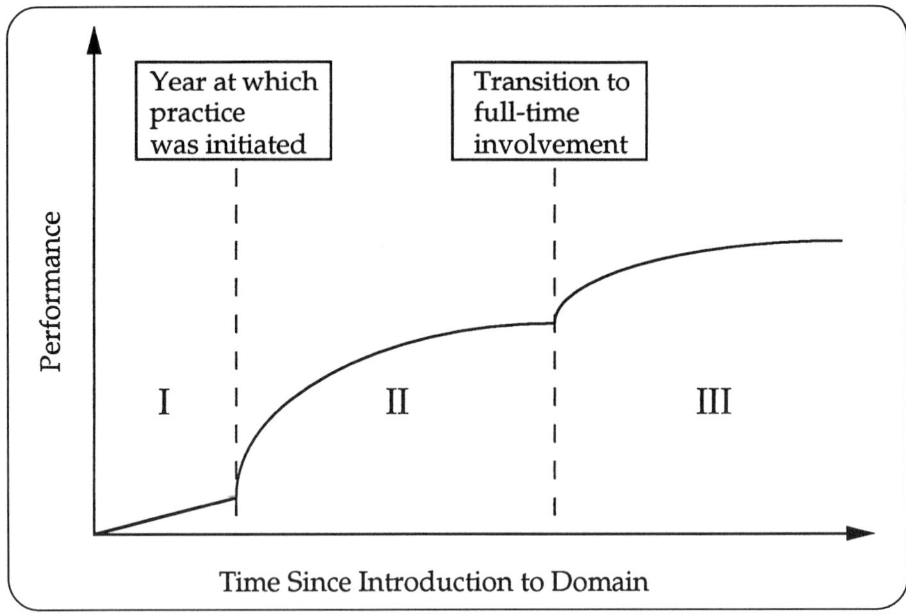

Figure 8.4. Three phases of development toward adult expertise.
SOURCE: Based on Bloom (1985).

qualities distinguish an expert? Does the expert have superior innate ability, or is expertise simply a result of extensive practice? Without question, differences in innate abilities play a role. However, most studies of experts have found that the special characteristics that define expertise in a particular domain do not transfer broadly outside that domain. To put it succinctly, expertise is specific to the particular domain. If some innate ability were the basis for this expertise, it should show up in other domains as well. That it does not suggests that the superiority of experts is primarily a result of practice (Ericsson et al., 1993).

Three distinct phases in the development of expertise have been identified (Bloom, 1985; Ericsson et al., 1993). As illustrated in Figure 8.4, the initial phase begins with an individual's introduction to the domain activities and is characterized by relatively slow progress. The first phase ends and the second begins when formalized instruction and deliberate practice—which involve activities specifically intended to improve the level of current performance—are undertaken. This phase continues for an extended period of time, ending when the individual decides to make a full-time commitment toward improving performance in the domain. The final phase that follows this commitment is characterized by even more intensive practice than during the second phase.

The theory of deliberate practice proposed by Ericsson et al. (1993) traces the development of expertise through these three stages. The primary assumption underlying the framework is that a person's level of performance is a monotonically increasing function of the amount of time that the person has engaged in **deliberate practice.** Deliberate practice is presumed by Ericsson et al. to be effortful and not intrinsically enjoyable. Hence the primary motivation for engaging in it is to improve performance. Many elite performers begin practicing at an early age, often with the encouragement of a parent who helps to maintain a regular practice schedule. The amount of deliberate practice in which the individual engages will tend to increase once a personal commitment to excel in the domain is made.

Ericsson et al. (1993) obtained support for this framework in a study of violinists. They examined violin students in a music academy who were classified into the categories of "the best violinists," "good violinists," and "music teachers," in order of decreasing skill. The category of skill in which a violinist fell was predictable from estimates of the total amount of deliberate practice in which the person had engaged during his or her life. Similar findings were obtained for pianists, leading Ericsson et al. to conclude, "Across many domains of expertise, a remarkably consistent pattern emerges: The best individuals start practice at earlier ages and maintain a higher level of daily practice" (p. 392).

Most of us have made the casual observation that certain individuals have better abilities than other individuals in specific domains. In fact, the perception that a young child is "gifted" is what usually leads parents to start the costly rounds of instruction and deliberate practice that are necessary for a person to become highly skilled. However, Ericsson et al. maintain that a "perceived" ability is not necessarily a true ability but that the perception of ability leads to deliberate practice, which then leads the person to perform better than his or her cohorts, thus reinforcing the perception that the individual is gifted. Although many skills researchers would not take as extreme a position as Ericsson et al. on the limited contribution of innate abilities to the acquisition of skill, virtually all would agree that extensive practice is necessary for skill to develop.

General Characteristics of Experts

Given that all skills are acquired through extensive training and practice, one might surmise that, although the specific skills of experts in different domains will differ, experts will exhibit certain general characteristics that distinguish their performance from that of novices. In fact, experts from a variety of domains display several common characteristics (Glaser & Chi, 1988). One of the most widely discussed is that experts can readily perceive complex, meaningful patterns within their domain. For example, as mentioned earlier, the ability to perceive complex patterns, as demonstrated by superior memory for briefly presented midgame configurations of pieces, is one of the most robust characteristics distinguishing chess masters from less accomplished players (de Groot, 1946/1978; Simon & Chase, 1973). This superior memory ability has been interpreted as indicating that the experts encode domain information into larger meaningful chunks. Novices are presumed to have to encode the configurations in more numerous, smaller chunks, thus overloading working memory, because they lack the knowledge base necessary to encode larger chunks. Consistent with this interpretation, the memory performance of chess experts falls to that of nonexperts when the configurations to be recalled are made up of randomly placed chess pieces. The excellent memory for chess positions demonstrated by chess masters illustrates another characteristic of experts, which is superior short-term and long-term retention for domain information. In the case of chess, experts have a large knowledge base of previous games into which new information can be integrated.

Because an expert has practiced extensively to acquire a particular skill, many of the basic components of the skill have become automatized. This frees up attentional resources for other aspects of the task, such as planning strategy. An example of this feature of skill can be found in a study of university-level ice hockey players conducted by Leavitt (1979). As a primary task, the players were required to skate as quickly as possible through a slalom course of pylons. Time to complete the slalom course was measured when the primary task was performed alone or along with one or both of two secondary tasks: stickhandling a puck and identifying geometric forms shown on a screen located at the end of the arena. The secondary tasks had little effect on the skating times of the skilled hockey players but substantially slowed those of novice players. It should be noted, however, that sizable interference is still obtained for experts when the primary and secondary tasks are more structurally similar—for example, dribbling a soccer ball while running a slalom course (Smith & Chamberlin, 1992) or performing a visuospatial secondary task while making judgments about visually displayed arrangements of chess pieces (Saariluoma, 1992)—and hence overlap to a greater degree in terms of the required processing resources.

The ability of experts to effortlessly recognize meaning in the information with which they are provided allows them to represent problems at a deeper, more principled level than can novices. As discussed above, problem representations can be inferred by having experts and novices classify problems by sorting them into groups. It has been shown, for example, that physics experts sort problems into categories according to fundamental principles, whereas novices sort the same problems according to the objects that are featured in the problems (Chi, Feltovich, & Glaser, 1981). Physics experts are also better able to generate solution plans before attempting to solve a problem (Priest & Lindsay, 1992). Because they are able to find appropriate problem representations and solution plans, experts spend a greater percentage of problem-solving time thinking about a problem before they begin to work on it than do novices. They may use this time to form a mental model of the situation that allows inferences to be drawn; or for ill-defined problems, constraints may be added to reduce the search space (Voss & Post, 1988). Associated with taking the time to gain conceptual understanding is a greater tendency to monitor one's progress toward the goal. Experts are more likely to recognize their own deficiencies or limitations and to evaluate their own performance.

All of these characteristics can be found in experts in a variety of domains. In the following section, expertise in three different domains is examined to illustrate particular manifestations of these general characteristics.

Expertise in Three Specific Domains

In our previous chapters, we found it convenient to discuss together skills with primarily perceptual, cognitive, or motor components. We follow this approach in the present section by choosing to cover in detail a predominantly perceptual task, diagnosing X-ray pictures; a cognitive task, computer programming; and a task with a significant motor component, transcription typing. All three of these domains are ones in which the characteristics of expertise have been investigated extensively.

Diagnosing X-Ray Pictures

Radiological diagnosis is a complex and difficult skill with a large perceptual component. It is not purely a perceptual skill because it also relies on formal knowledge of medicine and the integration of different sources of information, but the perceptual component is an important one. Because training is standardized for radiologists (after general training as medical doctors, radiologists spend several years in residency reading X-ray pictures to diagnose medical problems), it is relatively easy to find novices and experts in the domain and to estimate the nature and degree of their previous experience.

Early studies of radiological expertise emphasized the perceptual component of the skill by using tasks that involved detection of critical visual features in X-ray pictures. For example, Kundel and Nodine (1975) showed radiologists a series of 10 abnormal and 10 normal chest X-ray films for 200 ms each and, later, for an unlimited viewing time. In the brief exposure condition, approximately 70% of the radiologists' responses were correct (i.e., either an abnormality was correctly identified or the picture was correctly classified as normal). Although performance was quite good with the brief exposure, it was better when unlimited viewing was allowed. With unlimited viewing time, 97% of the abnormalities were correctly identified and 73% of the normal pictures were identified as such. Thus radiologists can often identify deviations from a normal X-ray picture in a single glance but perform more accurately when there is sufficient time to search the picture. These findings led Kundel and Nodine to propose that radiologists use a two-step process in which an initial global percept guides subsequent search for features.

Another finding from the early studies was that the nature of the search engaged in by a viewer of an X-ray picture depends on the viewer's level of expertise. Kundel and LaFollette (1972) recorded eye movements of untrained laypersons, medical students, radiology residents, and staff radiologists as they viewed normal and abnormal chest X-ray pictures. The radiologists scanned broad areas of the pictures, whereas the untrained people tended to restrict fixations to localized regions in the centers of the pictures. It seems that the global search pattern characteristic of the radiologist developed during medical school because the radiology residents and staff radiologists showed little difference in this regard. Thus Kundel and LaFollette concluded that the development of an appropriate search strategy depends more on the knowledge of anatomy and pathology that is learned in medical school than on the formal training given in residency programs.

The skill of diagnosing with X-ray pictures involves cognitive processes in addition to perceptual processes, so to assess skill in reading X-ray pictures adequately, tasks that involve both of these processes are required. Consequently, more recent studies have emphasized the cognitive evaluation component of skill in diagnosing X-ray pictures. Lesgold et al. (1988) developed a cognitive evaluation procedure in which concurrent verbal protocols are collected while radiologists examine X-ray films and then the radiologists' oral diagnoses of the problem are videotaped. Because diagnoses collected with this procedure were found to differ widely across radiologists, Lesgold et al. required the radiologists to substantiate their oral diagnoses by drawing the outlines of the relevant anatomy and areas of concern on an overlay of the X-ray picture. In a second phase of the experiments, the radiologists were instructed to draw the outlines of the features in the region of the X-ray picture known by the experimenters to be critical to the diagnosis. Following this, the radiologists rendered diagnoses again.

There were three main parts to the analysis of the data collected with this procedure: analysis of the verbal protocols that preceded the initial diagnosis, evaluation of the drawings done on the X-rays, and comparison of the first and second diagnoses. The performance of three groups—first- and second-year residents, third- and fourth-year residents, and staff radiologists with more than 10 years of experience—was evaluated. For the purpose of comparison, the protocols from the three groups were analyzed into *findings,* or statements of observed properties of the film, and *relationships,* or reasoning paths connecting findings (see Figure 8.5).

The performance of staff radiologists differed significantly from that of both groups of residents on all measures. Staff radiologists identified more findings, more causes of abnormalities, and more effects (outcomes of abnormal events) than did the residents. Perhaps most important, experts exhibited longer chains of reasoning—their findings were clustered and interconnected (see Figure 8-5). The staff radiologists appeared to do more inferential reasoning and developed more coherent models of the patient than did the two groups of residents, who did not differ on any of the measures. The protocols of all the residents were relatively fragmented and seemed to focus mainly on superficial features.

The differences between the staff and resident radiologists evidenced in the protocols were substantiated by differences in their drawings. Staff radiologists were able to make subtler distinctions in the X-ray films. Lesgold at al. (1988) reached the conclusion, similar to that drawn by Kundel and Nodine (1975), that experts' perceptions were apparently

Findings

(A)	Decreased Volume: Right Lung
(B)	Right Thoracotomy
(C)	Left-to-Right Shift of Trachea
(D)	Left-to-Right Shift of Heart
(E)	Left-to-Right Shift of Mediastinum
(F)	Right Minor Fissure Very Horizontal
(G)	Compensatory Emphysema
(H)	Increased Vasculature in Left Hilum
(I)	Age: Young
(J)	Heart at Upper Limits of Normal Size
(K)	Mediastinum is Wide
(L)	Prior Surgery
(M)	Heart Rotated

Reasoning Paths

Decreased Volume: Right Lung → Right Thoracotomy
Left-to-Right Shift of Trachea → Decreased Volume: Right Lung
Left-to-Right Shift of Trachea → Right Thoracotomy
Left-to-Right Shift of Trachea → Prior Surgery
Left-to-Right Shift of Heart → Decreased Volume: Right Lung
Left-to-Right Shift of Heart → Prior Surgery
Left-to-Right Shift of Mediastinum → Decreased Volume: Right Lung
Left-to-Right Shift of Mediastinum → Right Thoracotomy
Left-to-Right Shift of Mediastinum → Prior Surgery
Right Minor Fissure Very Horizontal → Compensatory Emphysema
Mediastinum is Wide → Heart Rotated → Prior Surgery
Mediastinum is Wide → Heart Rotated → Right Thoracotomy

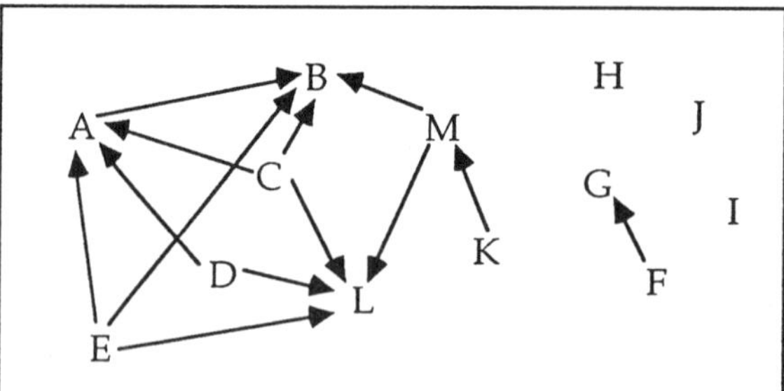

Figure 8.5. An analyzed protocol from a Lesgold et al. (1988) experiment listing all findings (A through M) and reasoning paths, and illustrating the relations between the findings (in the rectangle at the bottom). Findings with one or more reasoning links between them form a reasoning *chain*. A *cluster* is a set of findings with a path from each set member to every other set member, ignoring direction. A *cause* is the origin of a reasoning link and an *effect* is the termination.

guided by schemas of patient anatomy and disease history that were tuned to the specific cases being evaluated. The experts were also better able to decouple the features in the film from their mental models of the patient's anatomy when that was required due to ambiguities in the film. In short, they used their schemas of patients' anatomy and medical history, along with their knowledge of how the films were made, to guide perception. The novice radiologists were much more literal in their perceptions and were unable to make finer distinctions.

Lesgold et al. (1988) characterized the behavior of the expert radiologist as consisting of building a mental representation of the patient and refining a schema for interpreting the X-ray picture. The major difference between expert and less expert radiologists is the manner in which schemas are invoked and refined. Schemas are triggered quickly by the expert, who works efficiently to reach a stage where an appropriate general schema is in control. The expert performs tests on the schema to confirm that it is the appropriate one and modifies it as required to accommodate new data. Less expert radiologists may fail either to invoke a schema completely, to test the schema appropriately, or to complete the diagnosis process. The diagnosis process is incomplete if the radiologist fails to take into account additional information or to abandon her or his own earlier conclusions in favor of new data.

A final point of interest from Lesgold et al. (1988) is the apparent nonmonotonicity of the development of skill. First- and second-year residents were more accurate in their diagnoses than were the third- and fourth-year residents. In particular, they were better able to reverse their diagnoses when new evidence suggested that they should do so. Lesgold et al. explained this nonmonotonic skill development in terms of a two-process model of expertise in X-ray picture diagnosis. The first process, which develops early in training, is perceptual in nature and involves learning to identify and associate surface features and diseases. This associative process is eventually replaced by a deeper recognition-triggered reasoning ability. In the time during which the deeper reasoning ability is emerging, it is thought to compete with the perceptually based associative ability that is already in place. As a consequence of this competition, performance may get worse.

In summary, the acquisition of expertise in diagnosing X-ray pictures apparently consists of developing global search strategies, which are acquired relatively early in training, and schemas of increasing refinement, which develop with more extended experience through processes of generalization and discrimination. At some points in the development of expertise, the more shallow responding associated with special cases may prove more accurate than the developing deeper reasoning processes.

Computer Programming

Computer programming is a more purely cognitive skill than is reading and interpreting X-ray pictures. In a programming project, the programmer must understand the objectives of the program to be developed and translate them into a syntactically and logically correct computer program. An expert programmer will typically have many years experience writing programs to meet a variety of objectives and will know several programming languages. Expert programmers describe their progression as they developed expertise as being one in which qualitative changes in their abilities occurred (Campbell, Brown, & Di Bello, 1992). They report that whereas they initially relied on a cookbook approach, they later developed an intuitive understanding of how to approach programming problems. Research on programming expertise has revealed some of the changes in processing associated with the acquisition of programming skill.

As is characteristic of experts in general, programming experts are able to remember more from a brief exposure to a program than are novices, primarily because they organize the information into larger chunks. Just as chess masters show superior memory for game pieces only when game configurations and not randomly positioned pieces are shown, programmers generally show superior memory only for normal programs and not ones for which the order of the lines has been scrambled (Barfield, 1986; McKeithen, Reitman, Reuter, & Hirtle, 1981; Schneiderman, 1976). In a slightly different paradigm, Adelson (1981) presented lines one at a time for 20 s each from three programs written in the programming language PPL. Following the presentation of 16 lines, the participants recalled as many of the lines as they could. Experts recalled more lines than novices and in a qualitatively different manner. Experts recalled the lines in larger chunks than did novices, as measured by treating lines recalled within 10 s of each other as a chunk. They also tended to recall together the lines that belonged to each one of the three programs, whereas the novices did not.

McKeithen et al. (1981) conducted a similar study in which novices and experts studied 21 reserved words from the ALGOL W programming language until a criterion of recalling them all twice in a row was met. After this criterion was reached, the list was free-recalled 25 more times.

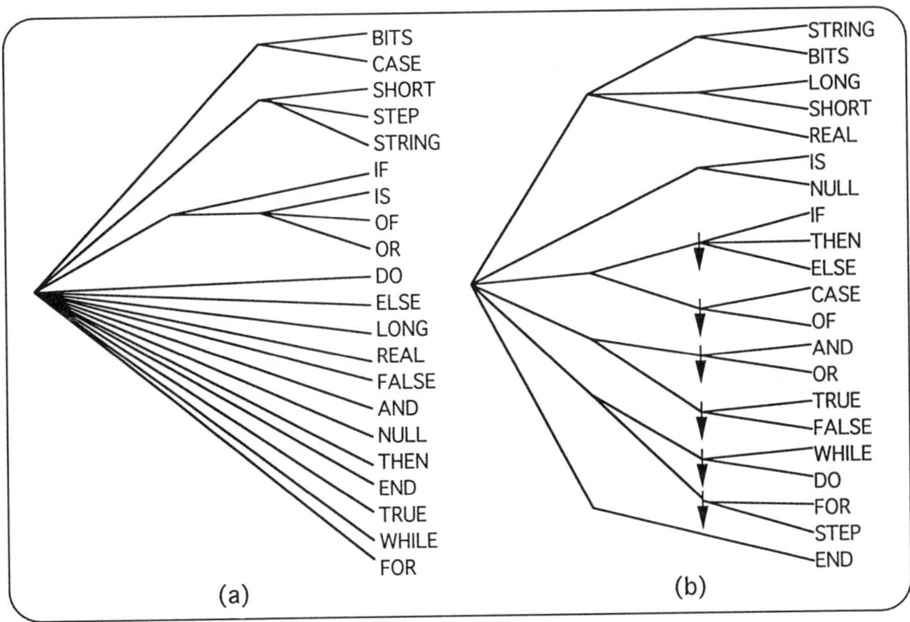

Figure 8.6. Ordered trees for recall of ALGOL W words derived from recall orders of (a) a novice and (b) an expert programmer.
SOURCE: Adapted from McKeithen, Reitman, Reuter, and Hirtle (1981).

The ordered tree algorithm developed by Reitman and Reuter (1980) was then used to identify chunks in the recall orders by searching for items that were always recalled contiguously. The algorithm produced ordered trees that captured the chunk structure of the list representations. By examining the recall orders, it was possible to determine whether the output order for items within an identified chunk was always the same (a unidirectional chunk) or one order and its reverse (a bidirectional chunk). Experts produced a greater number of chunks than did novices, and these chunks appeared to be based on different organizing principles. As illustrated in Figure 8.6a, novices tended to organize their recall by common language principles or orthography. For example, all the words that start with *S* were recalled together as were most of the two-letter words. In contrast, the experts organized their recall by the ALGOL W-specific meaning of the words. For example, the chunks *if-then-else* and *while-do,* shown in the tree in Figure 8.6b, are programming statements that are commonly used.

Table 8.1 Rules of Programming Discourse

1. Variable names should reflect function.
2. Code that will not be used should not be included.
3. A variable that is initialized via an assignment statement should be updated via an assignment statement.
4. Code should not do double duty in a nonobvious way.
5. An IF statement should be used when a statement body is guaranteed to be executed only once, and a WHILE statement used when a statement body may need to be executed repeatedly.

SOURCE: Based on Soloway and Ehrlich (1984).

The results of the study by McKeithen et al. (1981) emphasize that experts organize their knowledge by the meaning of the programming statements. How specific to a particular programming language is this knowledge organization? Petre (1991) has suggested that programmers approach tasks in an abstract, goal-dependent way that is independent of a particular programming language. Soloway, Adelson, and Ehrlich (1988) characterize the programmer's abstract knowledge as consisting of programming plans and rules of programming discourse. **Programming plans** are the stereotypic action sequences used in nearly all programs, such as looping through a sequence of instructions. The **rules of programming discourse** (see Table 8.1) govern the composition of programming plans to create the program needed to solve the task at hand. This way of conceptualizing the programmer's knowledge is similar to the theoretical approach to text comprehension in which schemas are said to guide comprehension (e.g., Bower, Black, & Turner, 1979).

If experts differ from novices in having programming plans and rules of programming discourse, then violations of this knowledge structure should interfere with the performance of experts but have little influence on the performance of novices. To test this hypothesis, Soloway and Ehrlich (1984) evaluated expert and novice programmers' comprehension of programs that differed only in whether or not a rule of programming discourse was violated. The experimental design required the participant to complete a blank line in each of eight programs, four of which violated a discourse rule and four of which did not. All of the programs were executable; that is, the violations were only against convention and were not incorrect ways of performing the task. The most important finding was that experts performed better than novices only when the programs were consistent with the rules of programming discourse. Moreover, when an incorrect answer to a program that violated discourse rules was given, it tended to be an answer that would have been correct if discourse rules had been followed.

The conclusion that experts possess programming plans and rules of discourse received further support in a separate experiment in which Soloway and Ehrlich (1984) tested verbatim recall of the two types of programs used in the previous experiment. As would be expected if programming plans and rules of discourse guided comprehension, the programs that were consistent with these plans and rules were recalled more completely by the experts than were the programs that violated them.

The picture that emerges of the expert programmer is consistent with the characteristics of the expert mentioned at the outset of the chapter. The knowledge structures of the skilled programmer lead to better and qualitatively different performance on memory tests, and program comprehension is guided in part by an abstract understanding of program structure.

Transcription Typing

The skills of diagnosing X-ray pictures and computer programming are largely independent of motor processes. However, many skills involve a significant motor component, and skill has traditionally been defined in terms of fluent motor performance. Expertise in most motor skills is difficult to study because of the complexity of performance and the associated difficulty of analyzing it in meaningful units. These problems can be circumvented to some extent in the study of transcription typing. Realistic typing tasks can be carried out in the laboratory, and typing performance can be analyzed in terms of its component parts. Measures such as the latency to execute responses and the types of errors made can provide precise information about the nature of skilled typing. Moreover, because many people type, large populations of typists at various levels of skill are readily available.

In addition to having a significant motor component, transcription typing also involves perceptual and cognitive processes. The typist must first perceptually encode a chunk of text that is to be typed. This chunk must be decomposed into discrete characters that are then translated into movement specifications. The perceptual and cognitive aspects cannot be eliminated, but their contributions can be dissociated from those of the motor processes involved in the execution of the finger movements. It is also possible to examine the precise coordination of the perceptual, cognitive, and motor processes necessary for skilled typing.

Empirical Regularities

From the systematic study of typing, a number of regularities have emerged. Salthouse (1986) enumerated 29 such regularities (see Figure 8.7) that involve primarily (a) the way in which text is perceived and comprehended while typing, (b) the manner in which the characters to be typed are held in memory, (c) the nature of response selection and execution, and (d) the characteristics of skill and expertise. With regard to the way in which the nature of the text to be read interacts with typing, typing is faster if the text is composed of words rather than random letters, but no additional speed is gained when the words are organized into meaningful text. As might be expected from the absence of additional gain for meaningful text over random words, comprehension of text, as measured by subsequent retention tests, is usually poor. Evidence that the text about to be typed is held in memory comes from studies that show severe reduction in speed of typing when looking ahead is limited by controlling the amount of text that can be previewed at a given moment.

Most of the errors that occur in typing fall into four categories. A **substitution error** occurs when an incorrect character is inserted in place of the correct character. Some substitution errors, such as striking the key adjacent to the one intended, can be attributed to errors in execution. However, most seem to be response selection errors for which an incorrect response is selected, but then the selected response is executed "correctly." When a substitution error is made, it is more likely that the correct letter will be replaced with one of higher frequency than with one of lower frequency (Grudin, 1983). For example, substituting the more frequently occurring letter *D* for the less frequently occurring letter *K* occurs approximately twice as often as substituting *K* for *D*. An **intrusion error** is one in which an extra letter is typed. These errors seem to occur primarily in response execution as a consequence of imprecisely positioning the finger on the correct key to be typed so that the adjacent key is pressed as well.

Another error in response execution is the **omission error,** in which a character is left out. In many cases, the interval between the keystroke preceding the omission and that following it is roughly twice the normal interval for successive strokes, suggesting that the omission was due to

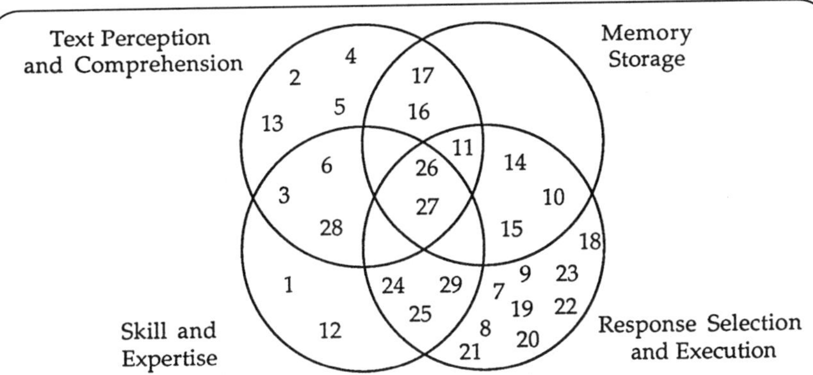

1. Faster than choice-reaction time
2. Slower than reading
3 Skill/comprehension independence
4. Word-order independence
5. Slower with random letter order
6. Slower with restricted preview
7. Faster alternate-hand keystrokes
8. Faster frequent letter pairs
9. Word-length independence on interkey interval
10. Word initiation effect (first keystroke 20% slower)
11. Specific preceding letter context counts
12. Dual-task independence for highly skilled typists
13. Copy span size: 13.2 characters
14. Stopping span size: 1-2 keystrokes
15. Eye-hand span size (moderate typists): 3-8 characters
16. Eye-hand span size less as meaning decreases
17. Replacement span size: ≈ 3 characters
18. 40-70% process-detectable errors detected
19. Substitution errors mostly adjacent-key errors
20. Intrusion errors mostly short interkey intervals
21. Omission errors followed by long intervals
22. Transposition errors mostly cross-hand errors
23. 2-finger digraphs improve faster than 1-finger digraphs
24. Tapping faster with typing skill
25. Decrease of variability with skill
26. Increase of eye-hand span with skill
27. Increase of replacement span with skill
28. Moderate increase of copy span with skill
29. Increase of stopping span with typing speed

Figure 8.7. The Salthouse 29 and a Venn diagram showing the processes and performance characteristics to which they relate. The numbers in the diagram correspond to the numbered regularities.
SOURCE: Adapted from Salthouse (1986).

insufficient force in typing the omitted letter. A **transposition error** involves reversing the order of two adjacent characters. Such errors primarily occur when the successive keystrokes involve fingers from different hands, which has led some researchers to suggest that transposition errors arise when advance preparation of a keypress inadvertently leads to it being executed out of sequence. The reason why this is more likely to occur across hands rather than for two fingers on the same hand is that it is easier to prepare the second of two finger movements in advance when it is not made by the same hand as the first of the movements.

Regularities in the performance of typists as they become skilled include greater speed, reduced variability, and more efficient procedures for preparing and holding items to be typed. Expert typists can type at speeds of up to 200 words per minute, and even average typists are fast enough that the intervals between successive keystrokes are less than the reaction time in a two-choice-reaction task. For example, Salthouse (1984) found that the median interstroke interval for a group of average typists during normal typing was 177 ms. These same individuals showed a mean reaction time of 560 ms when performing a choice task in which the left or right index finger was to be pressed in response to the stimulus *L* or *R*, respectively, presented in lowercase or uppercase. Measured rates of repetitive tapping, using either the same finger or alternating between hands, are greater for skilled than for unskilled typists, suggesting that at least part of experts' skill resides in motoric processes.

Besides looking at the speed of typing, we can look at the variability of the intervals between strokes. Interkeystroke variability refers to variations in intervals between different keystrokes and across different contexts, whereas intrakeystroke variability refers to variations in intervals across different instances of the same keystroke in the same context. Both types of variability are negatively correlated with skill, such that as skill increases, variability decreases (Salthouse, 1984).

Another change that occurs with skill is in the efficiency with which letter digraphs typed with two different fingers on the same hand (e.g., *st*) or two fingers on different hands (e.g., *pr*) are executed. Response latencies for both of these types of digraphs show relatively greater improvement with increasing skill than do digraphs typed with the same finger on the same hand (e.g., *tr*). This finding indicates that skilled typists learn to overlap the execution of successive keystroke movements performed by different fingers. More generally, the faster tapping rates, decreases in variability, and differential speedup in typing digraphs indicate that a major part of skilled typing is the precise, highly coordinated control of the keypress movements. Additionally, the decreases in variability indicate improved synchronization of all of the component processes involved in transcription typing.

Because the speed at which keypress responses can be selected and executed improves as skill at typing is acquired, there is a need for the information on which these processes operate to be available at correspondingly increasing rates. The availability of information for response execution can be measured in part by the **eye-hand span,** which is the number of letters of forthcoming text that must be available to the typist if performance is to be optimal. The size of preview at which performance ceases to improve further is larger with increased skill. However, the maximum size of the eye-hand span is just seven characters, presumably because this is the maximum number that can be held in working memory at any one time. Other span measures also indicate that the skilled typist operates with larger chunks of information than does the less skilled typist. The **replacement span** is how far in advance of the current keystroke the typist commits to a particular character (Salthouse & Saults, 1987). It is found by changing the test display to replace critical target letters at varying distances from the letter currently being typed and determining whether the target letter or its replacement is typed. Experts show a larger replacement span than nonexperts, indicating greater preparation for forthcoming keystrokes. As a result of this greater preparation, the **stopping span,** which is the number of keystrokes executed after a signal to stop, is also larger for expert typists.

A Model of Typing

Rumelhart and Norman (1982) developed the model of skilled typing that is shown in Figure 8.8. The model has four components: **Perceptual processes** act on the text input to produce identified words as output; the **parser** takes these words as input and outputs activations of single characters as well as the words; the activations sent from the perceptual processes and parser invoke **keypress schemas** that specify the target positions on the keyboard; and the **response system** informs the keypress system about the current locations of the fingers and executes the movements specified by the schemas.

Rumelhart and Norman's model is based on an activation-triggered schema formalism. Each target-position schema has an activation value that is a function of the amount of activation and inhibition that it has received. This activation value is determined not only by the perceptual

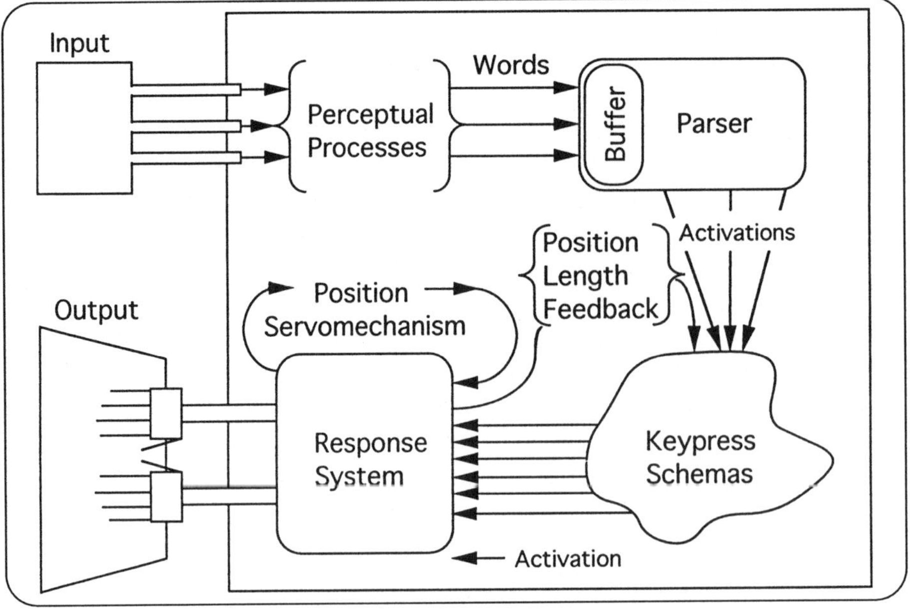

Figure 8.8. The Rumelhart and Norman model of transcription typing.
SOURCE: Adapted from Rumelhart and Norman (1982).

processes and parser but also by interactions among the schemas; each schema inhibits those that follow it in the to-be-typed sequence. When a schema is the one most highly activated and the current position of the specified finger is within some criterion distance of its target position, then the triggering conditions are satisfied and the actual keystroke is launched, with the force of the keystroke being proportional to the activation of the schema. After the launching of the keystroke, the associated keypress schema deactivates, thus releasing its inhibition on succeeding keypress schemas.

One of the central assumptions of the model is that schemas are types and not tokens. If the schemas were tokens, each particular instantiation of a letter would have its own schema. For example, the word *week* would have two schemas for the letter *e* if schemas were tokens. Instead, only one schema is presumed to exist for each letter of the alphabet. That is, a schema is a type. So, in this model the word *week* uses only three letter schemas, one of which has to be repeated. This is accomplished in the model by a doubling schema that causes the letter schema it is associated with not to deactivate itself after the launching of the keystroke for the initial occurrence of the letter. The need to explain errors involving double letters, such as typing *wekk* for week, was the main reason for using type rather than token schemas. Errors of this kind suggest that there is a special schema that signals the existence of double letters and that sometimes this schema is associated with the wrong letter.

The Rumelhart and Norman (1982) model, which emphasizes response selection and execution processes, provides a good fit to many of the findings regarding the performance of skilled typists. Among the findings that it accounts for are the major digraph effects described above. However, although it generates the correct ordering for digraph speed (two hand faster than two finger, which is faster than one finger), it does not generate large differences within the digraph classes. In Rumelhart and Norman's model, the amount of inhibition is the same regardless of the context, so any differences in latencies within a digraph class are a function of the physical constraints on finger movements.

This points to a deficiency in the model because, as noted by Gentner et al. (1988), typists show a wider range of interstroke intervals within all classes than those generated by the model, especially for two-finger digraphs. Gentner et al. established that the differences within a digraph class depend on the frequency of occurrence of the digraphs in language by showing that the differences were a function of frequency for both Dutch and English typists typing in Dutch and English, respectively. These performance differences seem to arise from the coordination of finger movements. For example, Grudin and Larochelle (1982) videotaped skilled typists and found that they had unique coordinated finger and hand movements for high-frequency, within-hand letter sequences. Thus, although digraph frequency is a language phenomenon, it appears to be manifested in the motoric processes.

Although, as illustrated in Figure 8.7, most of the phenomena in skilled typing have their basis in response selection and execution processes, some phenomena, such as word frequency effects and syllable boundary effects, appear to have their basis in perceptual processes, memory processes, or both. Because response selection and execution can occur faster for the two-hand digraphs than for the two-finger digraphs, any slowing of perceptual-memory processes should have a greater effect for the two-hand digraphs. Gentner et al. (1988) found such to be the case for word frequency and syllable boundary effects but not for the effect of digraph frequency, suggesting that the word and syllable effects are based in processes that precede response selection and execution.

Skilled Memory Theory

One of the most prominent characteristics of expertise is improved memory for information within the domain of expertise. Consequently, considerable effort has been devoted to determining the characteristics of skilled memory. As already noted from studies comparing experts to novices, the expert can encode domain-specific information more rapidly and efficiently than the novice but does not show a more general ability to do so for information that is outside the specific domain of expertise. Chase and Ericsson (1982) investigated the acquisition of efficient encoding and retrieval strategies and developed a descriptive theory of skilled memory. In their landmark study, two people practiced a digit span task for two years. The basic procedure involved listening to a sequence of digits spoken at a rate of 1 per second and then recalling the digits in the same order. If all digits were recalled correctly, the length of the next list was increased by a digit, and if they were not all recalled correctly, the length was decreased by a digit.

The original participant, SF, had a memory span of 7 digits for the lists presented during the first 4 hours of the experiment. This span is typical of untrained individuals. SF's digit span remained under 10 digits throughout the first 4 days of practice then and then on the fifth day suddenly increased to more than 10 digits. This increase could be attributed to the development by SF of a new mnemonic strategy. SF was a long-distance runner, and he used his knowledge of running times as a mnemonic aid. For example, he might encode the sequence 4003911 as 4 minutes, 39 and 11/100 s, and remember it as a good time for a mile. From the fifth day of the experiment onward, he expanded this scheme of encoding digit groups in terms of running times and also added other categories, such as years and ages, for digit groups that could not be encoded as running times. His performance continued to improve across 2 years of practice, reaching 82 digits by the time the experiment was terminated.

A second participant, DD, who was also a runner, was trained to use the system developed by SF. DD's performance also improved continually across 2 years of practice, reaching a high value of 68 digits. Interestingly, DD did not show a benefit initially relative to SF, even though the mnemonic system was provided to him, nor did he attain the same final level of performance as SF, perhaps because SF had developed the mnemonic system on his own.

Chase and Ericsson's (1982) investigations of memory span expertise identified three characteristics of skilled memory additional to those described earlier. First, they attributed the ability of SF and DD to remember so many digits to the development of a rich system of retrieval cues that enabled rapid access to the stored information. Second, although the digit span task often is thought of as an indicator of working memory capacity, Chase and Ericsson concluded that the superior performance of SF and DD was possible because long-term memory was used as well. Several findings, such as the fact that requiring recitation of the alphabet between list presentation and recall (which should disrupt working memory) only interfered with recall of the last few digits, suggest that these experts encoded a durable representation in long-term memory. Finally, after 2 years of training, memory span was still increasing for both SF and DD, leading Chase and Ericsson to conclude that the speed and efficiency of encoding continue to improve as the expert practices.

The Chase and Ericsson (1982) study examined memory skill for a task with no intrinsic meaning. That is, the material by itself provided no cues or context for remembering. Thus the participants in that study had to bring additional knowledge to bear to structure the information. In contrast to the knowledge-lean material used by Chase and Ericsson, most of the material that must be remembered in real life has much more inherent meaning and structure. We might wonder if skilled memory for more structured material also requires an external mnemonic scheme.

Ericsson and Polson (1988) explored the generality of the skilled memory theory developed in the context of the digit span task by seeing whether the same characteristics held for naturalistic exceptional memory. The participant in Ericsson and Polson's study was JC, a waiter who could remember up to 20 dinner orders without using pencil and paper. Several experiments were conducted to analyze JC's skill and to determine whether it conformed to skilled memory theory.

A procedure was devised for JC to attempt to capture the elements of the task performed at work while providing some experimental control. In this task, three, five, or eight pictures of people were laid out to simulate customers at a table. After examining the pictures, JC requested the order of one person, which was read to him by an experimenter. When JC indicated that he was ready to hear the next order, the experimenter read the order for the next person in sequence clockwise. At any point in this progression, JC could ask to review the items in the current customer order or any of the preceding orders. Each order consisted of four items, one of seven beef entrees, one of five cooking temperatures for the meat, one of five salad dressings, and one of three starches.

After all of the customer orders had been presented and any additional reviews completed, JC was instructed to recall the items in any sequence. Concurrent protocols were tape recorded as JC performed the task, and retrospective protocols were collected in interviews afterward. The data thus collected were analyzed so that a model of JC's skilled memory could be inferred.

The major results of the experiment were as follows. Rather than encoding each customer order as a unit, JC encoded the items from up to four orders in groups. JC's memory structure could be characterized as a matrix, with one dimension being the category of the menu item and the other being the customer order associated with the person who made it. Several mnemonic strategies were used to associate and remember the items within groups of orders. For example, the temperatures of the meat were remembered pictorially, with the degree to which the meat was cooked coded as the ordinate of a graph and each order arranged on the abscissa. In contrast, salad dressings were remembered by coding only their first letters. Thus the sequence thousand island, bleu cheese, thousand island, and oil and vinegar was coded as T-B-T-O.

Each time that a new order was presented, JC had to recall the previously encoded items and integrate them with the new items. Thus he had to choose the category of item that he wished to encode and to rehearse the new item along with the previously encoded ones in that category before choosing the next category. The need to rehearse the items within a category simultaneously is most likely responsible for the grouping of the items into blocks of four. By encoding the orders in terms of the categories of the items, JC was able to use the category labels as retrieval cues for the individual items.

Does JC's skill at remembering fit the framework of skilled memory theory? For the most part, it does. First, JC encoded the presented information efficiently and with the use of patterns. Existing semantic knowledge was brought to bear by JC in such ways as coding whether or not the starch selected was the starch usually served with a particular entree and encoding cooking temperatures in terms of an ordinal scale. JC encoded items within chunks of four to five items, presumably reflecting the limits of working memory. Second, JC encoded items with their category labels and used these labels for later retrieval. Additional support for this last statement comes from an experiment in which JC was required to remember nonfood items. When the items to be remembered formed categories, as the menu items had, his memory was much superior to when they did

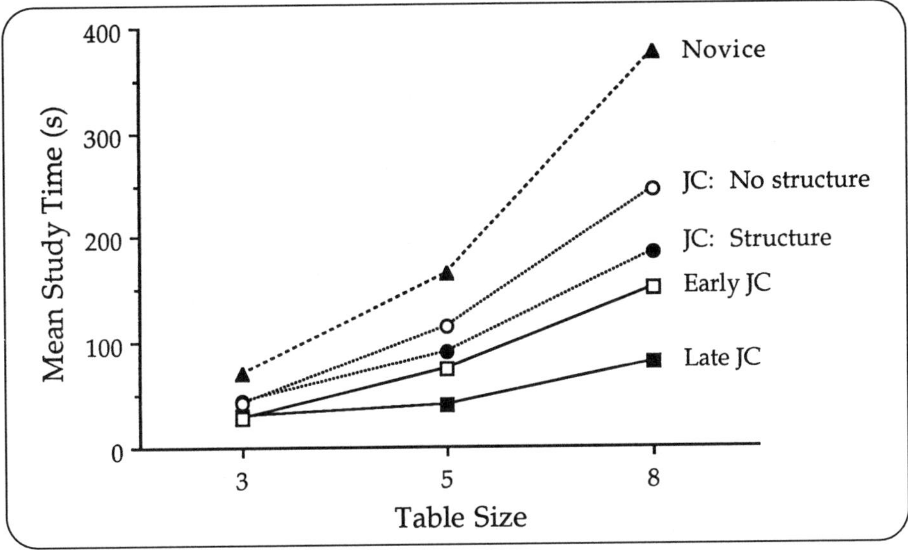

Figure 8.9. Mean study time as a function of "table size" for a novice and for JC (both early and late in practice) on the dinner-order task, and for JC for lists of words from non-dinner categories that were either categorically structured in a similar manner to the dinner lists or unstructured.
SOURCE: Adapted from Ericsson and Polson (1988).

not (see Figure 8.9). Third, JC used long-term memory to encode and retrieve the information, as indicated by the fact that he could recall many of the orders that he had taken at work earlier in the day. Fourth, the speed of encoding certainly was improved as a function of practice, even though JC was already highly practiced at remembering dinner orders.

One finding contradicts skilled memory theory. The theory asserts that the acquired memory skill is specific to the type of stimuli practiced and should not transfer to other types of stimuli. This statement is based on many studies of expertise in other domains and in the finding of Chase and Ericsson (1982) that the skill of remembering digits did not transfer to remembering consonants. The most likely reason for the unexpected generalizability of JC's memory skill is that the encoding schemes that he developed are relatively independent of the specific content of dinner orders and so can be applied to material of similar structure. For example, the graphic representation of cooking temperatures can be used for any category with an ordinal structure, such as units of time or length.

SUMMARY

The nature of experts' knowledge and the ways in which this knowledge is acquired and brought to bear on specific problems within domains of expertise have been the subject of considerable research over the past two decades. Expertise typically is acquired through many years of intensive, deliberate practice in a particular domain, with 10 years typically given as the minimum time for expert levels of performance to be achieved. The knowledge and strategies that an expert uses in performance of a task can be evaluated and compared to those of novices through numerous direct and indirect techniques developed for that purpose.

Although some characteristics of expertise are specific to particular domains, many characteristics are found for experts in a range of domains. The expert develops (a) knowledge structures that enable her or him to encode information in large meaningful chunks, (b) strategies that enable efficient coordination of the various components of task performance, and (c) metacognitive abilities that allow evaluation of progress. Typically, procedures used by the expert are restricted to the particular domain of expertise and cannot be applied to other knowledge bases.

Task Analysis

Training Component Tasks

Adaptive Training

Simulators

Summary

CHAPTER 9

Training

In ergonomics, the study of human abilities with respect to human-machine interactions, it is a truism that "good training cannot overcome bad design." Many of us have experienced situations in which it was difficult to remember how to perform a required action or have held a job in which it was difficult to acquire the necessary skills. It may seem that problems in design or procedure, when recognized, should be eliminated so that long and difficult training periods are not required. Certainly, this is the preferred course of action when design alterations are feasible. However, changes in materials or procedures may be sufficiently costly or skills so complex that there is no choice but to develop training procedures to prepare individuals to meet task demands. In this chapter, we review research on the training of skills and examine issues regarding how to construct successful training programs.

The need to develop effective training methods is one necessary consequence of the increased automation of many tasks that has occurred in recent years. Automation has done much to relieve physical demands on people and to increase the efficiency of operations. However, this efficiency and relief from many manual tasks is often accompanied by a change in task demands from those associated with control of the system to those pertaining to monitoring of the system status as well as by increased cognitive demands (Kantowitz & Sorkin, 1987). Appropriate training (or retraining) thus is necessary to enable operators to control automated systems safely and to take full advantage of their capabilities. This relatively obvious need is sometimes overlooked by system designers, with occasionally disastrous consequences, as illustrated by the following example.

One system that has been highly automated in recent years is the aircraft cockpit. Concerns have been raised as to whether the introduction of automation to the cockpit might increase rather than decrease mental workload as well as lower the proficiency of pilots when they are forced to take over and fly the aircraft manually (Dyck, Abbott, & Wise, 1993). One notable instance of the dire consequences of increasing automation without taking precautions to provide appropriate training occurred at a French airshow in 1988 (Casey, 1993). The incident involved the then new Airbus A320, which features a highly automated "flight protection" system that receives pilot commands as inputs, then checks the commands against current flight parameters (e.g., speed and pitch of aircraft) before sending the commands to the wings, engines, or other aircraft components. The flight plan called for by the airshow included some maneuvers that were outside those allowed for by the flight protection system. Therefore, it was necessary for the pilot to disengage some of the system functions prior to making the flight.

While performing the called-for low-altitude pass over the airshow grandstand, the Airbus A320 stalled and crashed into the nearby trees, killing many of the people on board. Investigators of the crash determined that it was not due to any mechanical failure but was largely due to the overconfidence of the pilot flying the aircraft. The pilot's overconfidence in the plane's abilities was apparently due to the nature of the training he had received. Training on the plane had been conducted with the automated systems fully engaged, and although the maneuvers carried out by the pilot for the airshow should have been safe, nothing in the training prepared the pilot for the actual differences between assisted and unassisted flight. A second Airbus A320 crash in 1990 was also attributed in large part to crew overconfidence. Subsequently, a special meeting was convened to discuss ways to counteract this "overconfidence syndrome," and new training procedures were implemented.

Because training is time consuming and costly, the most important concern is how to optimize the procedures to produce the maximal benefits for the least cost. Issues involved in optimization of training include how best to develop acceptable levels of performance, adequate retention of task-related knowledge and skills, and the flexibility and adaptability required for the range of situations that may be encountered in the job or task. Over the years, many methods of training have been developed and tested—with mixed results. The major conclusion to be drawn from this research is that successful training programs depend on an accurate and complete understanding of the task to be learned. For this reason, we begin the chapter with a review of the methods of task analysis.

Task Analysis

According to Lintern (1989), a first principle in developing operational training environments is to "know your task" (p. 304), which requires that a task analysis be performed. **Task analysis** can be defined as "a formal methodology, derived from systems analysis, which describes and analyzes the performance demands made on the human elements of a system" (Drury, Paramore, Van Cott, Grey, & Corlett, 1987, p. 371). Some method of task analysis, whether explicit or implicit, is embedded in every training program (Gopher & Kimchi, 1989). But to minimize ambiguity and inconsistency in training, the role of task analysis must be made overt, systematic, and objective. As illustrated in this section, many methods of analysis have been proposed, but there is little agreement on the best way to proceed.

The first step in performing a task analysis is to describe and analyze the human-machine system. After this has been done, the system requirements involving the human element need to be identified. For the final step, the specific tasks to be performed by humans should be analyzed, interpreted, evaluated, and transformed to reflect knowledge and theory regarding human characteristics. Several approaches to enhancing human performance and optimizing training procedures through task analysis can be taken. We defer discussion of one approach, that of identifying individual difference factors and selecting individuals on the basis of these characteristics, until Chapter 10. In the present chapter, we consider approaches that concentrate on common, normative performance capabilities.

For any task, it is important to understand the components of the task, interactions among the components, and the processing demands imposed by task requirements. These three aspects of tasks provide the basis for three approaches to task analysis. The need to understand task components is reflected in task analysis procedures based on task characteristics, including the information necessary to perform a task, the feedback provided at the completion of a component, and the amount of time to be spent on each component. Interactions among components are captured by analyses that focus on the function of the system and the movement of control within it. Major concerns in such analyses are the sequential dependencies among task components and the degree to which different operations can be carried out in parallel. Finally, the need to understand the processing demands imposed by task components has led to the development of task analysis methods that emphasize the perceptual, attentional, and cognitive capabilities of the operator. Because each of these approaches emphasizes different aspects of the task demands, all three must be followed to gain a full understanding of task training requirements.

Task Analysis Based on Task Components

An example of an approach based on the nature of task components is that of McCormick (1979). McCormick's approach is important because he took the position that jobs can be described best in terms of the human behaviors involved—rather than by listing technological activities. His approach is based on the structure and order inherent in human work and the so-called dimensions of that structure. McCormick identified many such dimensions and outlined the underlying performance requirements in terms of the human attributes necessary for success on each job dimension. Thus, although the analysis is begun with the identification of observable task elements, these elements are classified in terms of human behaviors that cut across particular tasks.

McCormick developed one of the most widely used job analysis questionnaires available, the Position Analysis Questionnaire (PAQ). The PAQ is a structured questionnaire that is used to analyze jobs according to 187 job elements. Although most of the elements mention materials to be manipulated or aspects of the environment, they are intended to characterize or imply the human behaviors involved in different aspects of the jobs. The PAQ has six job element divisions, which are outlined in Table 9.1. Each job element is rated according to its extent of use, its importance to the job, the amount of time it requires, and its applicability—or the element is given a special code.

The PAQ has been extensively documented, especially with respect to the human attributes associated with job elements. By specifying the relative contribution of human attributes to job elements, and the relative

Table 9.1 Organization of the Position Analysis Questionnaire (PAQ) and Some Representative Examples and Dimensions

Information input: Where and how the user gets the information he or she uses in performing the job

Example:	Use of written materials
Dimensions:	Perceptual interpretation
	Environmental awareness

Mental processes: The reasoning, decision-making, planning, and information processing activities involved in job performance

Example:	Level of reasoning in problem solving
Dimensions:	Decision making
	Information processing

Work output: Physical activities performed by the operator and with what tools or devices

Example:	Use of keyboard and mouse
Dimensions:	Manual/control activities
	General body activity

Interpersonal relationships: Nature and extent of relations with other people while performing the job

Example:	Contact with customers
Dimensions:	Job-related communications
	General personal contact

Job context: Physical and social contexts of the job

Example:	Low temperatures
Dimensions:	Personally demanding situations
	Potentially hazardous job situations

Other job characteristics: Additional relevant activities, conditions, or characteristics

Example:	Required work pace
Dimensions:	Special versus business clothing
	Continuity of workload

weightings of these elements to job performance, the contribution of specific human attributes to the job can be determined. Such a determination of relevant attributes has obvious benefit for selection purposes, but it is somewhat doubtful whether the PAQ is useful for determining training requirements (Patrick, 1992). One problem is that the job ratings determined using the PAQ apply to all tasks performed within a job element and, therefore, may not provide sufficient detail for the development of training protocols. Moreover, the dimensions identified from PAQ ratings (see Table 9.1), using principal components analysis (a statistical technique for reducing large amounts of data into primary components), are for the most part very general, and it is not obvious how one would train individuals to develop the necessary skills. For example, identifying a job as requiring "decision making" is helpful if the goal is to rate the difficulty of the job but only serves to identify a need for further analysis of the decision-making task if the goal is to train for that component.

Task Analysis Based on Interactions Within the System

Task analysis with an emphasis on interactions within a system has its basis in the pioneering work of Frederick W. Taylor and extensions by Frank and Lillian Gilbreth in the late 1800s and early 1900s. Taylor's method was called **time study** and had as its goal the description, analysis, and improvement of the efficiency of workers. The basic idea was to identify the elementary movements made by people performing a skilled job, to determine the best method for making each elementary movement by observing and timing skilled workers, and to combine the times for the elementary movements to estimate the total time required to do the work. Interestingly, Taylor characterized time study as making possible the "transfer of skill from management to men" (Subcommittee on Administration of the ASME, 1912, p. 1199).

The Gilbreths' method, called **motion study,** placed greater emphasis on precise analysis of the motions involved in performing work and on improving the work methods by replacing longer motions with shorter, less fatiguing ones. One technique used by the Gilbreths for determining inefficiencies in a worker's motions was to take a time-exposure photograph of the worker, with lights attached to his or her limbs, performing a task. You might note that the work of Taylor and the Gilbreths presaged two topics already discussed: Crossman's (1959) model of skill development as the elimination of inefficient methods (see Chapter 1) and the study of expert behavior to learn more about skill acquisition (see Chapter 8).

Time and motion techniques are still used today to identify problems in the design of work environments and manufacturing processes (see Drury et al., 1987). The early techniques of Taylor and the Gilbreths recognized the importance of the interactions of humans with machines and concentrated on identifying elements of the process that could be changed to improve the efficiency of operations. More recent approaches have focused on the dynamic interplay of people and products to improve both the efficiency of operations and the satisfaction of the human operators and users.

One such approach is **functional analysis,** or process analysis, which is a family of techniques that can be used to characterize complex systems so that training programs may be developed (Laughery & Laughery, 1987). Functional analysis is concerned with both static (e.g., the arrangement of equipment) and dynamic (e.g., the movement of people or materials) aspects of systems. Functional analysis is most often used either during the design process or when changes in existing systems are desired. Techniques exist to determine the logical flow of events, the allocation of functions to machines and people, and the coordination of events across time and space. Once task demands have been identified in terms of the interdependencies of people, products, and machines, additional analyses (e.g., in terms of information processing demands) can be carried out.

Task Analysis Based on Human Capabilities

Analyses focused on human capabilities have taken several different forms. One approach, illustrated by the Frederiksen and White (1989) study described below, is to concentrate on the knowledge base of the expert and to attempt to understand the task by decomposing the principles, rules, and goals contained in this knowledge. Other approaches have been to decompose tasks in terms of automatic and controlled subprocesses or in terms of the degree to which the allocation of attention can affect performance (e.g., Gopher, Weil, & Siegel, 1989; see also the discussion of Ackerman's work in Chapter 10). More generally, tasks can be analyzed in terms of the processing mechanisms involved in performance and the load on each mechanism.

The GOMS (Goals, Operators, Methods, and Selection rules) methodology (Card et al., 1983), introduced briefly in Chapter 6, has provided a tool kit for researchers wishing to take a processing mechanism approach to task analysis. The goal of task analysis as developed by Card et al. (1983) is to determine the constraints on behavior that are due to the nature and features of the task environment. The first step in performing a GOMS analysis is to identify the **goals** to be attained by performing the task. Once the relevant goals and subgoals have been identified, **methods** of achieving these goals are specified. For example, if the goal is to edit a manuscript, one subgoal is to check for misspellings and a possible method is to use the spell-checker included with a word processor. In general, methods are procedures for accomplishing goals and are a primary means by which knowledge of tasks is stored. **Selection rules** may be required to select one of several possible methods for meeting a goal. The detailed specification of the task is in the listing of the **operators**—perceptual, cognitive, or motor—that are executed to effect changes in the state of the person performing the task or of the task environment. Operators can range from specific motor commands, such as "depress the *L* key on the computer keyboard," to more abstract cognitive acts, such as "verify that the highlighted word is spelled correctly."

The GOMS methodology allows determination of real-time processing demands and processing times. Because of the degree of detail and the specific time calculations that can be achieved, this method can be used to calculate training times and devise training documentation to guide the selection of the most efficient methods of performing tasks (Olson & Olson, 1990). Most applications of GOMS methodology have been in the prediction of performance (e.g., John & Newell, 1990) or the development of displays and human-machine interfaces (e.g., Kieras, 1988), and considerable success in developing working models for specific design concerns has been realized. However, as Gopher and Kimchi (1989) warn, aspects of task analysis that are relevant to training may differ from those that are relevant to other concerns, such as the display of information. Thus further research in applying GOMS methodology and other cognitive analysis techniques within the context and concerns of the training problem is warranted.

A Task Analysis-Based Training Program

Frederiksen and White (1989) proposed that, for the purpose of developing a training program for a complex task, the high-level goal structure of the task should guide the analysis. After specifying the primary goals of the task, different strategies for obtaining each goal can be evaluated with respect to optimality. Finally, the optimal strategies can be analyzed to determine the skills and knowledge required for their implementation. Frederiksen and White also proposed that the perspective from which a task analysis is carried out should depend on the objective of the analysis. One objective of training might be to ensure the generalizability of the acquired skills. For this objective, the task analysis should emphasize the manner in which principles or general knowledge enter into task performance. Frederiksen and White pursued both of these proposals in their analysis and development of training strategies for the Space Fortress game, which was introduced in Chapter 5.

The first step taken by Frederiksen and White (1989) was to determine the skill and knowledge components of expert task performance. In what they referred to as **principled task decomposition,** the inherent structure of the Space Fortress game, its human information processing demands, and the characteristics of expert performance were described. Frederiksen and White's second step was to analyze the hierarchical relations among the skill and knowledge components of the task that allow the progression of a novice performer to the level of an expert. This stage of the analysis consisted of identifying prerequisite skills and knowledge and the stages of learning at which they become important. The final step taken by Frederiksen and White was to use the task decomposition to construct training activities for individual components and their integration, and to evaluate the efficacy of these activities.

Frederiksen and White (1989) compared training in which individual task components were practiced in isolation (i.e., componential training) to practice on the task in its entirety (whole-game practice), using performance in the Space Fortress game or a variation of it as the criterion task. To assess the generality of any obtained knowledge, they also administered a physics quiz before and after each experiment to test whether the knowledge obtained by the two different groups depended on the training received. In one experiment, 15 training games (consisting of ship control, missile firing, and ship aiming components) were practiced by the experimental, componential-training group, while the control, whole-game practice group practiced the criterion task (a modified version of Space Fortress with no mines or resource information) for an equivalent amount of time. After five days of practice, both groups played eight blocks of the modified Space Fortress game.

As can be seen in Figure 9.1, during the first block of transfer to the criterion game the experimental group performed worse than the control group who had been practicing the whole task all along. However, by the third block of play, the experimental group had surpassed the control group, and by the end of the eighth block, their scores were more than 25% above those of the control group. The interaction of training group and practice on the transfer game was significant and reflects a faster learning rate during the transfer session for the experimental group. Additionally, players in the experimental group did better on the physics posttest than did the control players, suggesting that the training games were successful in teaching some generalizable knowledge.

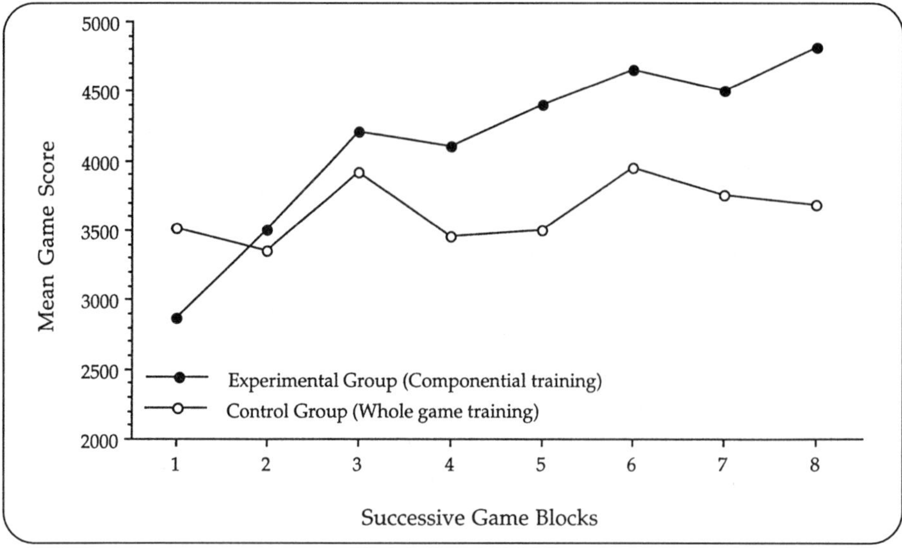

Figure 9.1. Performance of the control (whole game training) and experimental (componential training) groups across the eight game blocks of the transfer session.
SOURCE: Adapted from Frederiksen and White (1989).

In a second similar experiment, Frederiksen and White (1989) used 28 training games to emphasize all components of the Space Fortress game—ship handling, aiming and firing at the fortress and mines, and allocating available resources to maximize game score. The complete Space Fortress game was used as the criterion task in this experiment. Once again, the experimental group showed greater improvement in the physics quiz scores than did the control group, as well as better performance in the transfer session. To assess further the transferability of the skills and knowledge of the control and experimental groups, two additional game variations were introduced after the Experiment 2 transfer session had been completed. In one variation, processing load was increased beyond that of the standard Space Fortress game by introducing more mines and greater memory loads. The experimental group performed better at this task than did the control group, but the size of the decrement as compared to the regular game was the same for both groups. Thus, although the experimental group continued to perform better than the control group, they showed no greater resistance to disruption. The second task variation required control of a different trajectory for the ship from that previously practiced. The experimental group showed more transfer on this task than did the control group, which suggests that the use of training games to emphasize ship control resulted in better acquisition of generic ship control skills.

In summary, Frederiksen and White (1989) demonstrated that training based on task decomposition offered significant benefits over practice on the whole task. The specific benefits of the componential training program were the facilitation of learning of specific concepts and heuristics by practice with constrained tasks, the development of more generic forms of knowledge representation, and enhanced generalizability of skill due to the inclusion of many transfer conditions as part of the training regimen.

Training Component Tasks

The Frederiksen and White (1989) study described above exemplifies the component task or **part-task** approach to training. In general, part-task training involves practice on some subset of task components as a prelude to the practice or performance of the whole task. For this reason, part-task training is sometimes called part-whole training. Early research tended to suggest that whole-task training was preferable to part-task training (Adams, 1960). However, later research has shown that for difficult tasks and tasks with independent components, part-task training can lead to improved learning efficiency and reduced training costs (Holding, 1965; Wightman & Lintern, 1985). The critical question in part-task training is "How well will training on components transfer to whole-task performance?" Unfortunately, there is no universal answer to this question, but the application of task analysis to the specific task of concern can lead to predictions regarding the probability of transfer.

Methods of Part-Task Training

Wightman and Lintern (1985) outlined three methods of task decomposition for part-task training and evaluated their effectiveness for the training of complex tracking tasks, such as landing an aircraft on an aircraft carrier or performing air traffic control. The first method, **segmentation,** involves partitioning a whole task into components along spatial or temporal dimensions. For example, if a task contains subtasks with specific starting and ending points, it may be segmented into a series of

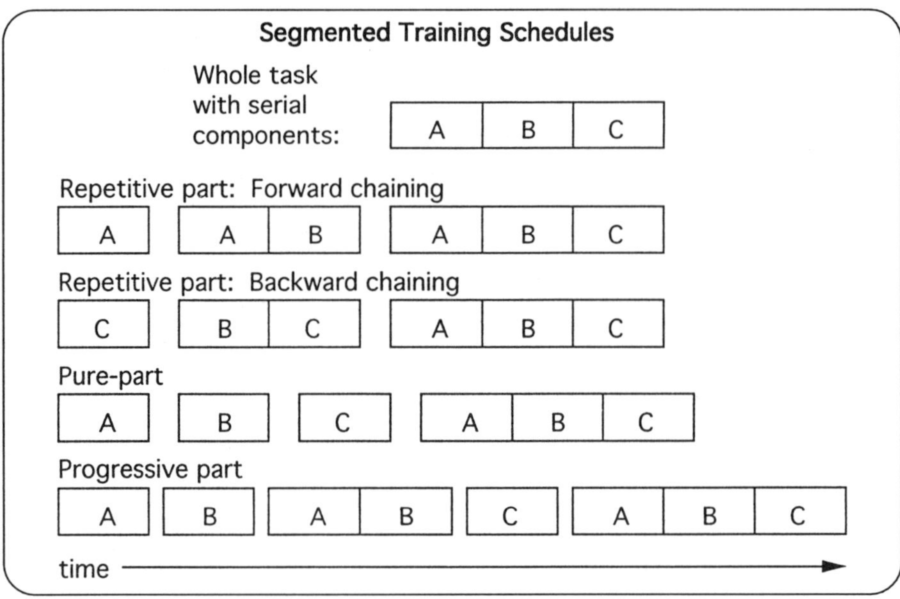

Figure 9.2. Segmented training schedules for a task with three serial components.

these subtasks (see Figure 9.2). A popular method of segmentation-based training is **backward chaining,** in which the last component of a task is practiced first and earlier components are introduced later in training.

The benefit of backward chaining over whole-task training that is sometimes observed may depend on the role of knowledge of results (KR) in learning (Wightman & Lintern, 1985). In a complex task with a specific end point, such as bombing a target, early stages of performance are far removed from the feedback that results from completion of the task. Thus the earlier parts of the task may be harder to learn. In backward chaining, the part of the task most proximal to the end-of-task feedback is learned first. Wightman and Lintern (1985) suggest that, as a result of training, the perceived competency in performing this final task component can act as KR for the preceding component, thus facilitating learning of earlier components of the task. It should be noted, however, that Ash and Holding (1990) found that **forward chaining,** in which the order for adding task components is first to last, was more effective for learning selected keyboarding skills. Forward chaining may sometimes be superior to backward chaining because in this method task component-completion feedback is always proximal to the component task being introduced.

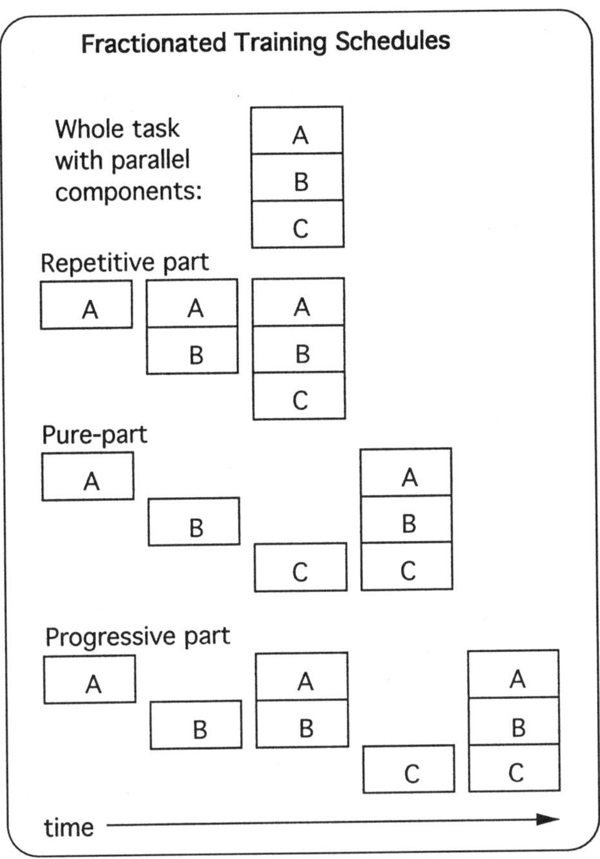

Figure 9.3. Fractionated training schedules for a task with three parallel components.

Unlike segmentation, the method of **fractionation** breaks into components aspects of a whole task that normally are performed concurrently (see Figure 9.3). For example, it may be desirable to practice the perceptual requirements of a task while temporarily ignoring the motor requirements. Several schedules of integration of task components are possible when fractionation is used (Holding, 1965; Wightman & Lintern, 1985). In **repetitive part** training, one part is practiced in isolation and then additional parts are added sequentially. In **pure part** training, each component is practiced in isolation before the parts are combined. **Progressive part** training is essentially a combination of the other two schedules, in that each part is practiced in isolation before being added one at a time to the task.

For fractionation to work, component task difficulties and subtask interactions that result in time-sharing demands must be well understood. If the most difficult part of a task consists of coordinating two or more components that are relatively easy to perform in isolation, practicing the components alone may result in very little (or even negative) whole-task transfer. In general, fractionation is best applied only when there is relatively little need for time-sharing between subtasks. Also, this technique appears to be of little use unless the fractionated components are themselves difficult to perform.

Fractionation and task recombination closely resemble the situation in which practice is with a single task and transfer is dual task. Schneider and Detweiler (1988) presented a model (the connectionist/control architecture; see Chapter 2) for capturing the interactions between subtasks and derived several predictions for training from it. First, they concluded that there is usually little transfer from single-task to dual-task performance and suggested that this is due to the need to develop procedures for coordinating different tasks. More specifically, the dual-task context requires the use of attention to coordinate information transmission and processing from the different input sources to the required responses. For example, it may be necessary to switch attention from the visual to the auditory modality and to keep the information obtained from these two sources separate for further processing. Because the mental workload (see Chapter 5) imposed in the dual-task (or whole-task) context is almost always higher than in the single- or part-task context, Schneider and Detweiler suggest that part-task training programs would do well to train component tasks under conditions of high workload. Unfortunately, an experimental confirmation of this suggestion has not been carried out.

The third technique outlined by Wightman and Lintern (1985), **simplification,** is often used in practice. For example, many of us learned how to ride a bicycle using training wheels to simplify the task of staying upright. Simplification has also been shown to be beneficial for the task of learning to use a word processor. Carroll and Carrithers (1984) modified a commercial word processor to create a "training wheels" interface that prevented many of the errors commonly made by new users. For example, new users sometimes try out inappropriate, exotic menu choices that lead them to get lost in advanced menus. When such choices are made with the training wheels interface, the function is not engaged. Instead, the message that the selected function is "not available on the Training System" is displayed. People who used the training wheels interface learned the word processor substantially faster than people using the complete system, and their performance on a comprehension posttest was better, too. Catrambone and Carroll (1987) demonstrated that the skills acquired with the training wheels interface transferred to the full-function system. Individuals who were trained with the training wheels interface learned and used advance editing functions on a subsequent transfer task better than individuals trained on the complete system. One major advantage of the simplified interface is that its users spend more time performing criterion tasks and less time recovering from errors. In other words, learning by discovery with the complete system is relatively inefficient because many of the options that are tried out are inappropriate, with the result that much of the individual's efforts are devoted to correcting mistakes rather than to learning the basic functions.

In complex manual control tasks of the type reviewed by Wightman and Lintern (1985), simplification also usually produces positive transfer. However, unlike the case of learning a word processor, there is little evidence for a benefit of practice with a simplified manual control task over whole-task training. The consequences of simplifying tasks during training will be discussed further in the section on adaptive training, below.

Hierarchical Versus Integrated Part-Task Training

The previous section outlined three methods of part-task training: segmentation, fractionation, and simplification. In this section, a study by Fabiani et al. (1989) is described that takes a slightly different approach. Fabiani et al. used the Space Fortress game described earlier to compare a fractionation method based on principled task decomposition, as in the Frederiksen and White (1989) study discussed previously, to a variant of part-task training in which the whole task was practiced but with different components emphasized at different points in the training period (see Gopher et al., 1989). Thus a more traditional part-task training program, called the **hierarchical** approach, was compared with specialized practice on the whole task (the **integrative** approach). In the highly interactive Space Fortress game, training using the whole task might be expected to result in better learning because time-sharing skills would still be practiced.

For the integrated group, 6 hours of whole-task training were combined with special instructions and feedback about two aspects of game

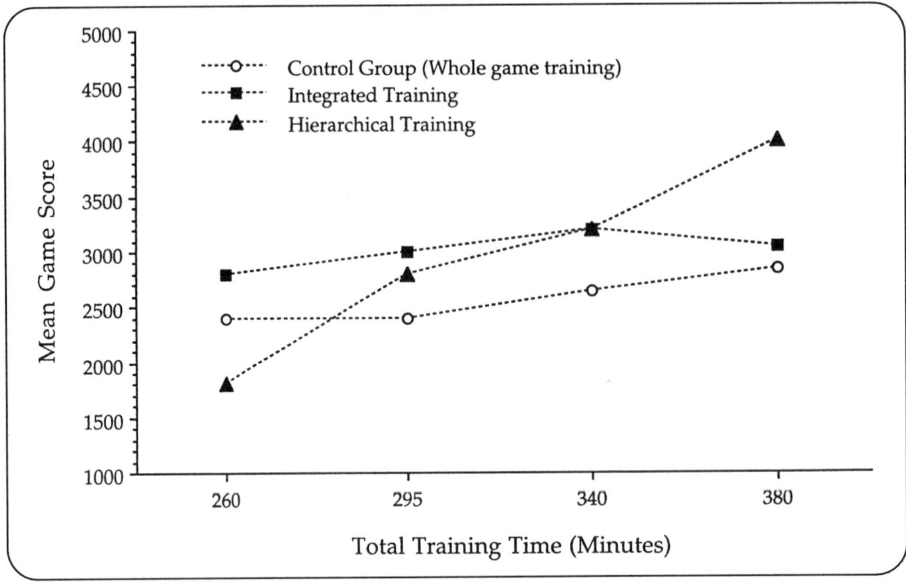

Figure 9.4. Performance of the control (whole game practice), hierarchical (componential), and integrated (whole game training with emphasis manipulation) training groups across the transfer session.
SOURCE: Adapted from Fabiani et al. (1989).

performance: ship control and the identification and destruction of mines. During the time in which this special feedback was given, players were instructed to maximize their score on just the components of the game for which feedback was provided rather than the total game score. The hierarchical group practiced 27 of the subtasks used by Frederiksen and White (1989) and received a limited amount of whole-task practice. The total training time equaled that of the integrated group. Finally, a control group practiced the whole task with standard instructions for an equivalent amount of time. Following the training period, all three groups practiced the Space Fortress game for 3 hours and then practiced the game in conjunction with various secondary tasks (see Logie et al., 1989) for an additional 5 hours.

The performance of the three groups during the 2 hours of Space Fortress play following training is shown in Figure 9.4. Although the hierarchical training group in Fabiani et al.'s (1989) study started out at a lower level of game performance than the other two groups (which is not surprising since the hierarchical group had practiced the game for only 15 minutes), they showed a faster rate of learning than the other groups and eventually surpassed them. Performance of the integrated training group had already surpassed that of the control group before the criterion trials were administered, and they maintained higher scores throughout the whole-task game period. These results demonstrate the advantage that may be gained from the performance of a detailed task analysis and the subsequent development of a specialized training program. In this case, as in Frederiksen and White's (1989) study, the identification and training of specific task components led to the best transfer performance—despite the fact that time-sharing between components is necessary for performing the whole task.

Although the hierarchical training group showed better performance than the integrated training group on the Space Fortress task when performed alone, their performance was disrupted relatively more when one of eight different secondary tasks was introduced. The pattern of disruption due to the type of secondary task was the same for all groups, but the integrated group showed the smallest percentage of disruption (approximately 12%) and the hierarchical group the largest (approximately 65%), with the control group being intermediate (approximately 34%). Thus it appears that the whole-task training with emphasis on certain game components, received by the integrated group, results in a superior ability to maintain the acquired level of performance while executing secondary tasks. However, in terms of absolute performance levels, the scores of the hierarchical group on the Space Fortress task still were approximately equal to those of the integrated group in most secondary task conditions, suggesting that little is gained by integrating practice on the component parts within the context of the larger task.

Developing Automaticity in Some Task Components

We have noted that the coordination of multiple processing demands can be the most difficult aspect of complex task performance. It stands to reason that processing demands might become more tolerable if some of the component tasks were automatized, thus freeing up processing resources for other subtasks. A common example of the benefit of automatic processing is that of driving a car and carrying on a conversation, mentioned in Chapter 5. For experienced drivers, many of the components of vehicle control have become automatized; hence it is possible to carry on quite a complex conversation while performing them. Of course, if an unusual driving situation suddenly emerges, the results of this time-sharing could be disastrous.

In Chapter 5, we discussed a study by Schneider and Fisk (1982a) that tested for the possible benefits of developing automaticity in a component task. In their experiments, people practiced a consistent-mapping visual task in which they searched for semantically related words (i.e., category exemplars). After asymptotic performance had been achieved, new category exemplars were introduced in either the same single-task context or in the context of a dual task (in which a varied-mapping digit search task was performed simultaneously). Under both conditions, excellent transfer to new exemplars was obtained. The good transfer seen under the dual-task condition suggests that once a process has been automatized it may still be performed without cost in a new performance environment. Results such as these led Schneider (1985) to propose the guideline that "training should develop automatic component skills to perform consistent task components and develop strategies to allocate limited controlled processing resources to inconsistent or poorly developed task components" (p. 297).

Schneider and his colleagues (Schneider, Vidulich, & Yeh, 1982) developed, and took initial steps toward validating, a training program for air traffic controllers that was based on the desirability of developing automatic task components. Table 9.2 lists the 10 rules followed by Schneider et al. in developing the training program. The training program itself consisted of 10 training stages made up of a mixture of part-training and transfer conditions. Such specialized skills as estimating the distance between aircraft and identifying the starts of turns were taught in discrete stages, and performance on the component tasks was measured under high workload conditions in which a secondary task was also to be performed. The initial results of the program suggested that perceptual learning of the type required for air traffic control can be accelerated when component skills are learned in a consistent environment.

Another extension of the consistent-mapping visual search paradigm was carried out by Myers and Fisk (1987), who sought to determine whether the benefits of a consistent mapping found in visual search tasks would extend to a task more like one encountered in the workplace. The task they used was similar to one performed by telecommunications workers and consisted of identifying specific conjunctions of letters in an array of letters. As in the earlier visual search work, memory-set size was manipulated by varying the number of patterns for which the participants

Table 9.2 Guidelines for Developing Automatic Skill Components

1. Present information to promote consistent processing by the operator
2. Design tasks to allow many trials of critical skills
3. Do not overload working memory and minimize memory decay
4. Vary those aspects of the task that vary in the actual situation
5. Minimize passive observation and maximize active participation
6. Maintain high motivation
7. Present information in a context that illustrates the criterion task without information overload
8. Train under mild speed stress
9. Train operators to use strategies that minimize workload
10. Test operators under high-workload conditions to assess competence and facilitate automatic process development

were to search, and display size also was varied. For the consistent-mapping condition, a given combination of letters could only occur as a target, whereas in the varied-mapping condition, a letter combination designated as a target on one trial could appear as part of the distractor array on a different trial.

The basic results of the Myers and Fisk study were similar to those obtained for other visual search tasks. That is, performance improved when the mapping was consistent: By the end of approximately 10 hours of training, performance was equally rapid regardless of memory-set and display size and was approximately the same for target-present and target-absent trials. When the target-response mapping was varied, a persistent effect of display and memory-set size was found, and target-absent trials took longer than target-present trials. However, those trained in the varied-mapping condition did show some improvement in performance, and this improvement was greater than that usually obtained for varied-mapping tasks. Why was this improvement obtained? The answer to this question is in the basic principles of training according to the automatic and controlled processing framework. That is, "a critical purpose of training . . . is to enable the trainee to identify task consistencies and to provide for multiple correct executions of those consistent task components" (Myers & Fisk, 1987, p. 257). Even in the varied-mapping condition of the task used by Myers and Fisk, there were consistent components (e.g., letter configurations to be searched for were repeated and hence could be learned).

In their second experiment, Myers and Fisk (1987) removed one of the sources of consistency in the task, the assignment of particular keypress responses to given letter configurations. In the absence of this consistent component, performance of the varied-mapping condition was greatly disrupted whereas performance in the consistent-mapping condition suffered very little. The authors suggest that, after practice in the consistent-mapping condition, performance becomes automatic and relatively independent of attentional demands. Thus attention should be available to cope with the new response assignments in the consistent-mapping condition but not in the varied-mapping condition. This finding parallels the finding of Schneider and Fisk (1982a) that performance of a consistently practiced task is relatively insensitive to the imposition of increased attentional demands.

Adaptive Training

The goal of adaptive training is to match the demands of the training environment with the skill level of the trainee. Adaptive training programs resemble the simplification method of part-task training, with the degree of task simplification modulated by the trainee's current level of performance. Thus an adaptive training program is an individualized training schedule. It also is a closed-loop training system, in that feedback (the level of the trainee's performance) affects the training system.

Figure 9.5 illustrates the basic elements of an adaptive training program for a generic control task. The **adaptive circuit** is an algorithm that takes some measure of the trainee's performance as input and produces a change in the difficulty of the training task as output. In tracking or system control tasks, perceptual difficulty may be manipulated by changing the forcing function that drives the object to be tracked, response difficulty may be modified by changing the system response dynamics, or the feedback display can be manipulated.

The idea of a training system adapted to individual differences sounds promising—after all, individuals and their learning rates differ in many respects. However, the research results regarding the usefulness of adaptive training regimes have been equivocal, at best. Several early studies thought to provide evidence for the superiority of adaptive training over whole-task training were shown by Lintern and Gopher (1978) to

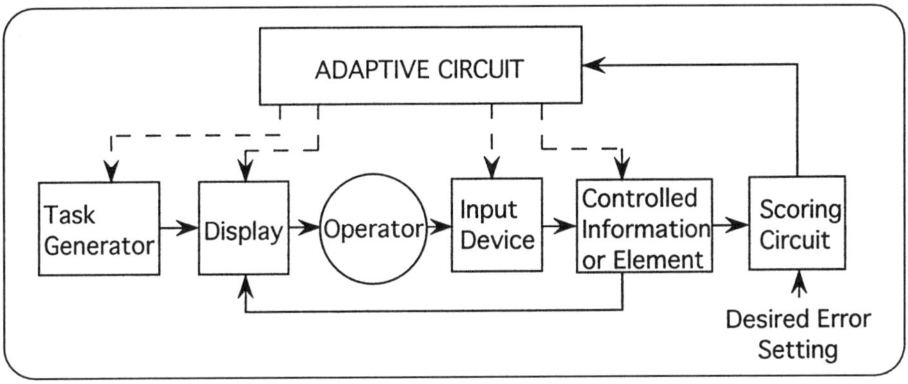

Figure 9.5. The basic elements of an adaptive training system.

be uninterpretable due to design flaws. The studies that have shown some benefit for adaptive training have been those that have a relatively large cognitive component, rather than being simply perceptual-motor tasks. For example, Gaines's (1967) study compared adaptive and full-task training programs using a tracking task and found an adaptive training advantage. However, the task was performed with keypresses whose control action was alternated, such that the task induced a greater cognitive load than is usual in tracking tasks.

The only other widely cited study to show an advantage for adaptive training used the Space Fortress game, which, as has already been pointed out, is quite complex. Mané, Adams, and Donchin (1989) used a transfer design to demonstrate that adaptive training can result in better learning than does whole-task practice. However, they also showed that the degree of transfer depends on the nature or degree of the adaptation. For the adaptive training conditions, the Space Fortress game was modified by slowing the speed of the hostile elements (the mines). The mines could be slowed to either one half or one fourth of the criterion speed for each of the two adaptive training groups, respectively. Only the group that practiced with the higher minimum mine speed showed enhanced transfer to the criterion task. Apparently, the additional slowing of the mines changed the task to such an extent that positive transfer was limited.

The usefulness of adaptive training regimes depends in part on whether more transfer occurs from harder tasks to easier ones or, as is the case when training is adaptive, from easier tasks to harder ones. As with most questions in training, there is no definitive answer to this one.

Holding (1965) noted that when tasks are of unequal difficulty, transfer between them is asymmetrical. He noted that, in general, more transfer is obtained in the difficult-to-easy direction than in the easy-to-difficult direction. However, the evidence is mixed on the direction of greatest transfer, with tasks having relatively small motor components, such as tasks that emphasize perceptual discrimination, often showing better transfer in going from an easy to a more difficult task. The main principle seems to be to note the degree and manner in which simplification changes the task. If an adaptive program teaches parts of tasks that are relatively independent of other task components, benefits similar to those seen in part-task training can occur. As is the case with other part-whole methods, if the adaptation is so great as to distort the nature of the skill that is acquired, little transfer can be expected.

Simulators

One way to circumvent the potential costs and dangers of training for the operation of complex systems, such as aircraft or power plants, is to use simulators for initial training. The goal of simulation is to represent a real situation in enough detail so that good transfer to the actual system is obtained while omitting those aspects of the situation that contribute to cost without providing corresponding benefits (Flexman & Stark, 1987). The usual approach to designing simulators has been to include as much detail as possible. However, it has been demonstrated that not all details provide training benefits. Moreover, the success of part-training programs suggests that some selection of certain aspects of the situation to emphasize over others may be beneficial.

Transfer From Simulator to Operational Setting

An illustration of the need to determine what is important to include in a simulator is found in a study by Lintern, Sheppard, Parker, Yates, and Nolan (1989) that evaluated issues of fidelity (correspondence of the simulator to the system being simulated) for the visual displays used in flight simulators. Lintern et al. manipulated the level of scene detail ("day" vs. "dusk" views of bombing targets), field of view (degrees of visual field shown), and degree of practice to evaluate the training value of each for the task of air-to-ground attack. A segmented training technique was used, in which pilots first practiced a straight approach to the target for 25% of the trials, then a curved path approach for 50% of the trials, and finally, a continuous path from bomb delivery to the next approach for the last 25% of the trials. Following 24, 48, or 72 twelve-trial blocks with one of the combinations of scene detail and field of view, the pilots performed transfer flights in jet trainers at Navy bombing ranges. Lintern et al. found that neither the degree of scene detail nor the field of view during training had a significant impact on transfer performance. Thus they were able to conclude that the cost of building simulators could be cut by eliminating this unnecessary information. All groups trained in the simulator performed better than those pilots who had received no simulator training, but there was no difference in transfer performance for those who practiced for 24, 48, or 72 blocks. That is, 24 blocks of practice was sufficient for maximum transfer. It should be noted that performance in the simulator did significantly improve for those people who practiced for the two longer periods. This additional improvement, however, did not transfer to the real situation.

The discrepancy between the relative performance of the training-level groups in the simulator versus in transfer in the Lintern et al. (1989) study illustrates the important point that to evaluate simulator training benefits, transfer to the situation being simulated must be measured. Assessing only simulator performance may provide a misleading indication of the efficiency of the training. Lintern et al. showed that additional gains due to practice in a simulator may not translate to gains in performance of the transfer task. Similarly, those simulators that lead to the best training performance may not lead to the best performance in the actual system.

The importance of measuring transfer to actual situations and of the need to understand the criterion task is illustrated in the following example. Caro (1979) reviewed the research regarding the use of motion cues in flight simulators with the goal of resolving the observed discrepancy between the effect of motion cues in the simulator versus in the actual task environment. The discrepancy was that motion cues improved performance in the simulator (e.g., Perry & Naish, 1964), but simulator training with motion cues did not result in positive transfer to actual flight (e.g., Jacobs & Roscoe, 1975).

The resolution of the discrepancy between training and transfer performance by Caro (1979) was based on an analysis of the types of motion cues used in the previous studies and their importance in the criterion task. Two types of motion cues are available to the pilot: **disturbance** cues, which arise from a source outside of the pilot and actions made by him or her, such as turbulence or equipment failure; and **maneuver** cues, which result from pilot control actions, such as changes in altitude and direction, and generally are redundant with visual cues or instrument readings. Because disturbance cues occur without the intention of the pilot and are essentially unpredictable, they provide information additional to that from other sources. Maneuver cues, on the other hand, can be anticipated and hence are less informative. As you may already have guessed, studies that failed to find a benefit of providing motion cues during training on subsequent performance almost exclusively used maneuver motion cues in the simulator. In those studies where simulator performance improved when motion cues were provided, the cues tended to be of the disturbance type.

However, if an aircraft is inherently unstable and difficult to fly (most aircraft are fairly stable and relatively easy to fly), training with maneuver motion cues may enhance subsequent flight performance and thus should be considered for inclusion in flight simulators. Deciding whether or not to include motion cues in a flight simulator is not a trivial question. The importance of providing adequate training for flight cannot be overestimated, but it must be recognized that if no real benefit is gained from providing certain cues, there is no need to spend literally millions of dollars incorporating them into simulator systems.

Cue-Response Relations and Functional Equivalence

The preceding paragraphs emphasize the major theme of this chapter, that to provide adequate training environments one must first understand the nature of the task. We touched on the issue of fidelity, or correspondence of the system being simulated to the actual system, and have reviewed research that indicates that only certain aspects of systems need be captured in the simulator. What is needed now is a theory for determining what aspects of a system should be simulated. One step toward such a theory was taken by Cormier (1987), who suggested an emphasis on **cue-response relations.** According to Cormier, the key concern is whether or not certain stimulus cues provide information necessary for the determination of responses. In the aircraft motion example described above, maneuver motion cues generally do not provide response information, whereas disturbance motion cues may do so. If the specific cues that control responding can be identified, simulators need include only these cues. However, if all the cues that control responding cannot be identified, it is necessary to rely on greater physical fidelity.

An interesting example of cue-controlled responding comes from the study of medical suturing performance. Salvendy and Pilitsis (1980) investigated the use of simulators to teach medical students how to suture. Training using an electromechanical device that capitalized on the auditory and visual information conveyed by punctured simulated tissue was compared to a purely visual training method (watching trained surgeons and inexperienced medical students perform the task), a combination of visual and electromechanical training, and standard classroom lectures. The groups receiving training with the electromechanical device showed better transfer performance than either the visual training or lecture groups. There was no difference between the lecture and visual training groups and no additional benefit for visual training combined with electromechanical training relative to electromechanical training alone. This suggests that the essential cue-response information in this task is provided by actually performing the suturing technique and that such high-fidelity simulation training is warranted.

Although a high-fidelity training device that is in many respects equivalent to the criterion task environment is warranted to train suturing, this is not always the case. Spears (1983) introduced the concept of **functional equivalence** to characterize the features of the criterion task environment that must be included in the training device for transfer to occur. Functional equivalence is based on response generalization, that is, the generalization of learned responses to new response conditions. Baudhuin (1987) used this concept to outline the conditions to be met for transfer of training. First, meaning must be ascribed to the stimuli used in the training situation that takes into account the goals of performance. Second, the trainee must associate appropriate responses with the stimulus context. Finally, generalization must occur from the training to the criterion task environment. If inappropriate conditions are present in the simulation, negative transfer to the actual task environment may occur. The risk of inappropriate generalization cautions against the inclusion of cues that can lead to inappropriate cue-response relations and poor transfer (Flexman & Stark, 1987). For example, if the trainee hears the click of a switch operated by an experimenter whenever a cue condition is introduced (e.g., a switch is operated to induce an equipment failure in a control training task), he or she may develop response procedures that depend on the auditory information conveyed by the switch, which, of course, would not transfer to the real situation.

The concept of functional equivalence takes into account that certain relations between aspects of the simulated environment and the real-world environment are more important than others, but it does not specify which identities are important. Lintern (1991) has proposed that sensitivity to perceptual invariants—properties of events that remain unchanged as other properties are changed (e.g., during aircraft landings, the ratio of the projected runway length to the projected breadth of the distal end of the runway is constant; Mertens, 1981)—is increased during perceptual-motor learning and that this sensitivity forms the basis for transfer. Thus, according to him, a simulator should support detection and discrimination of the critical perceptual features, patterns, and dimensions of difference. An implication of this view is that not only should it be possible to eliminate nonessential details from simulators with little impact on transfer to the criterion task, but that reduced environments that facilitate learning of the perceptual invariants may actually lead to better transfer than more realistic training environments. For example, Lintern, Roscoe, and Sivier (1990) found that, in a flight stimulator, transfer to crosswind landings was better if no crosswind had been used during training. Presumably, this is because it was easier for the trainee to learn the perceptual invariants related to system control when the extraneous changes due to crosswinds were not present. Regardless of whether Lintern's specific account is correct, it is clear that a simulated environment needs to capture only the relations that are crucial to the criterion task.

STEAMER

Although functional equivalence may be defined primarily in terms of perceptual invariants for psychomotor tasks, such as flying an aircraft, such a definition is difficult to extend to control tasks with larger cognitive components. An application of the broader concept of functional equivalence to the development of a simulator is exemplified by the simulator known as STEAMER (Hollan, Hutchins, & Weitzman, 1984; Williams, Hollan, & Stevens, 1981), which was developed to teach reasoning and problem-solving skills associated with steam plant operation and maintenance. Rather than relying on high physical fidelity, STEAMER's designers developed a graphical simulation to be run on a computer that conveys the conceptual components of the plant. This simulation allows controls to be manipulated and displays read by either trainees or teachers. The possibly unique aspect of STEAMER is that it allows the trainee to view abstracted representations of the plant such as those that are used by experts to reason about the system. STEAMER can present simplified versions of subsystems that are easier to understand than higher-fidelity depictions and also allows the trainee to "look inside" the system to see such things as rate of flow and other internal characteristics more directly.

STEAMER embodies the instructional philosophy that physical principles should be taught in the context in which they will be applied to the operation and maintenance of the system (Halff, Hollan, & Hutchins, 1986). The flexibility of the system and the power of the trainer to control the manner in which information is displayed makes it a good candidate system for teaching novices to reason like experts. Moreover, a system like STEAMER would seem to be a good candidate for teaching cognitive strategies for system control. In Chapter 5 we briefly mentioned that Moray (1987) outlined a theory regarding how individuals simplify complex systems in order to perform control operations. Central to Moray's conception of system control was that people learn interrelationships among variables and use these learned interrelations to form simplified mental models of the system under control. Forming a simplified mental model reduces the cognitive load on the system controller, thus enabling better performance under normal operating conditions. However, problems may arise when the system malfunctions or in some way exceeds tolerance levels. In this case, the controller may have to switch from using a simplified mental model to a model that captures the variables and interactions of concern. As pointed out by Moray, the need to switch mental models or system representations may severely limit the performance of controllers. For this reason, a promising area for future research is the use of a simulator like STEAMER to teach strategies for moving between system representations as situational demands change.

SUMMARY

The development of an effective training program begins with a task analysis that specifies the task components, their interactions, and the processing demands imposed on the individuals. Regardless of which of several alternative approaches to task analysis are employed, training programs based on a careful and thorough analysis of the task will be more successful than ones that are not. Numerous studies indicate that part-task training programs can be more effective than an equivalent amount of time spent practicing a task in its entirety. One reason for the benefit of part-task training is that it allows automaticity to develop for those task components that remain consistent across conditions. As a consequence, when the whole task is performed, the performer can devote more attention to those aspects of the task that cannot be automatized. Despite the effectiveness of part-task training in many situations, the usefulness of training programs that adapt to individual differences in the skill level of the trainee has not been clearly demonstrated.

When training is conducted on simulators, several additional concerns become important. Most significant for the justification of simulator training is that the skills learned in the simulator must transfer to the operational setting. High-fidelity simulation, which typically is very costly, is not always needed for substantial transfer to occur. A task analysis that isolates the conceptual components of the task and determines which perceptual information is relevant to system control can aid in achieving the necessary degree of fidelity. In simulation training, as in other training programs, functional equivalence between the practice conditions and the criterion task needs to be maintained for successful transfer to the operational system.

Tests and Measurement

Intelligence and Aptitudes

Task Analysis Based on Individual Difference Variables

Dynamic Accounts of Abilities and Skill

Problems of Interpretation in Understanding the Relation Between Abilities and Skill Levels

Individual Differences in Reading Skill

Skill and Aging

Summary

CHAPTER 10

Individual Differences

Previous chapters alluded to individual difference variables that determine to some extent the acquisition of skill. For example, the view that expertise depends on innate characteristics was briefly explored, and a training method that takes individual skill levels into account, adaptive training, was discussed. In both of these cases, it was concluded that the role of individual differences was relatively minor. You might recall that the evidence pertaining to the effectiveness of adaptive training is mixed. Similarly, accounts of expertise in terms of practice and experience have received more support and attention than accounts based on innate differences—to the extent that statements such as "experts are trained, not born" (Schneider, 1989, p. 10) are not uncommon.

What, then, is the place of individual difference research in the study of skill acquisition? Perhaps most notably, individual differences have been the focus of a great deal of research on the selection of personnel for training. Especially in the military, there is considerable interest in the selection of individuals for appropriate jobs and specializations. Those of you familiar with the history of psychology in the United States, in particular, will know what a large impact psychological testing for training-selection purposes has had on the field. Studying individual difference variables may also lead to a better understanding of specific skills and of skill in general. The determination of those individual characteristics that enable someone to become skilled at a task points to factors important for performance of that task.

In this chapter, we provide a general introduction to the study of individual differences and discuss some of the frameworks that have been offered to account for the relation between skill and individual difference variables. Particular emphasis is given to theories that address the interaction between stages of skill acquisition and cognitive and perceptual-motor abilities. As an example of the interplay between the study of skill and the determination of individual differences, we take a look at the research on reading skill. Finally, we consider a specific individual difference variable, aging, and its impact on skill acquisition and performance.

Tests and Measurement

Francis Galton (1869, 1883) was one of the first researchers to pursue the notion that, through testing, one could discover the innate "intellectual capacity" of individuals. In his search for the characteristics that made some humans more fit for survival than others, Galton used performance on simple sensory and motor tests and various physiological indices as measures of mental ability. (Galton was both a relative of Darwin and influenced by his work. The title of his book on the subject of ability testing, *Hereditary Genius,* belies this fact.) James McKeen Cattell (1890) extended the research begun by Galton in his own testing of the "fundamental sensory discrimination abilities" underlying differences in intellectual ability.

It could be argued that a more profitable approach to measuring intellectual ability would be to focus on cognitive tasks that involve comprehension, reasoning, and judgment, rather than on perceptual-motor tasks. Alfred Binet, who, as most of us are aware, is largely responsible for the development of the field of intelligence testing, took such an approach. Binet selected verbal and practical tasks that were performed successfully by more older than younger children and by more "bright" than "dim" children of the same chronological age. These tasks were presumed to reflect the cognitive abilities pertinent to educational settings. Along with Theodore Simon, Binet developed the first numerical scale for intelligence, the Binet-Simon scale, based on overall performance on a variety of such tasks. Binet's (Binet & Henri, 1896) "worksamples of life performance" (Cronbach, 1970/1990, p. 199) correlated with success in school and provided the basis for theories of general intelligence and ability.

The relative success of Binet's testing movement influenced Spearman's (1904, 1927) development of **two-factor theory,** which states that performance on any mental test is attributable to a general ability factor, *g*, and some ability (or abilities) specific to the test. Spearman's theoretical analysis complemented Binet's work and provided justification for the Binet-Simon scale, in which the measure of general intelligence is based on overall performance of a variety of mental tasks. In terms of two-factor theory, the contribution of specific abilities to the overall performance measure would be minimal because a range of distinct specific abilities are involved across the different tasks. Hence overall performance would reflect primarily general ability, as Binet and Simon assumed. Two-factor theory and the conception of general intelligence have had a lasting influence on testing and individual differences research, although the conception of general intelligence has been, and continues to be, hotly debated (for an amusing yet comprehensive analysis of this debate, see Gould, 1981).

For the most part, however, two-factor theory has been replaced by different "many-factor" theories. Thurstone (1935) laid the foundations for ability taxonomies based on many factors with his use of **common factor analysis.** Spearman had used factor analysis to identify *g*. The particular method used by Spearman was to find the so-called first principal component of the matrix of correlations between tests. Essentially, *g* represents the overall correlation between tests and should represent the common variance reflecting one underlying factor. Thurstone criticized Spearman's method and instead argued for a method by which multiple sources of variance underlying the matrix of aptitude test correlations could be identified. The technique of factor analysis, research programs based on the technique, and associated problems in interpreting this research are discussed in more detail later in the chapter.

This summary of some of the early research in the field of ability testing is both brief and incomplete. The major point we would like to make is that intelligence and ability tests have been developed and studied because of the need to classify people and as part of the search for general psychological theories of human intelligence. Ability tests have been useful for highlighting subgroups of strengths and weaknesses of individuals and for matching the characteristics of an applicant with the demands of a job. They have also been used to evaluate the contribution of specific abilities to more complex performance, as described below.

Intelligence and Aptitudes

Aptitude can be defined generally as "any characteristic of trainees that determines their ability to profit from instruction" (Cronbach & Snow, 1977). General intelligence, spatial ability, quantitative skill, possession of specific background information, and psychomotor ability all have been treated as aptitudes. According to Ackerman and Kyllonen (1991), there are three important questions to ask: How do we define an aptitude? How are aptitudes related to each other? What are the relationships between aptitudes and success in skill development?

Cognitive Correlates Approach

A common method for determining the nature of aptitudes is the so-called **cognitive correlates** approach (Fleishman & Quaintance, 1984). This technique is used to determine the interrelationships among aptitudes, abilities, and task performance. The general procedure is to compare similarities and differences between high- and low-ability individuals on a variety of tasks. For example, Hunt (1978) first divided people into groups of high and low verbal ability based on their performance in verbal aptitude tests and then tested these groups on basic cognitive tasks such as choice-reaction time. After testing, he determined which of the basic tasks correlated most highly with the global verbal ability measure. Among other things, he noted that the time to decode (i.e., to recognize) highly overlearned information (e.g., the letter *A*) was correlated with verbal ability, whereas the time to retrieve facts presented recently in the experimental context was not. On the basis of these findings, he concluded that people with high verbal ability can decode verbal stimuli faster than can people of low verbal ability.

The goal of research such as Hunt's (1978) is to obtain a better understanding of the general ability of interest, but critics of this approach (e.g., Carroll, 1989) have argued that it is of little use because the aspect of the general test with which the experimental tasks are correlated cannot be determined. For example, a correlation between performance in a choice-reaction task and a test of verbal ability could reflect only the fact that tests of verbal ability are speeded. Thus the correlation may reveal nothing concerning the ability of interest, but only something about the testing situation.

Despite this general concern, the cognitive correlates approach has been successful in adding to our knowledge of many skills. The prerequisite for success in using the approach seems to be a good understanding of the fundamental tasks that are used. A promising avenue of research using the cognitive correlates approach is illustrated by the work of Haier et al. (1988). Using the technique of Positron Emission Tomography, whereby the brain's glucose use (and hence its activity) can be measured during performance of relatively brief tasks, Haier et al. have found that relatively intelligent individuals (as measured by general intelligence tests) metabolize less glucose while solving problems. This finding suggests that efficient processing at a physiological level is correlated with intelligence. It should be noted that this does not imply that more efficient processing is the cause of intelligence differences; more intelligent individuals may develop more efficient processing.

Cognitive Components Approach

An alternative approach to understanding individual differences in information processing capabilities is to analyze a task in terms of its processing stages, and then to estimate an individual's performance at each of these stages. Measures of stage performance are then correlated with measures of overall task success so as to determine the relative contribution of each stage to success in the task. This approach, sometimes called the **cognitive components** approach (Ackerman & Kyllonen, 1991), was developed by Robert Sternberg (1979) as **componential metatheory and analysis.** To use the cognitive components method, the investigator must have a good understanding of the processing stages involved in performance of a task and a procedure that allows performance at each stage to be estimated.

Sternberg's (1979) theory of mental abilities satisfies the first objective by distinguishing four levels of abilities (see Figure 10.1). **Composite tasks** are the complete tasks for which abilities are studied. If a particular type of problem (e.g., analogies) is to be used as a composite task for measuring mental abilities, it must yield reliable performance, have construct validity, and have been shown empirically to be a valid indicator of the mental abilities that it is presumed to reflect. Composite tasks can be decomposed into **subtasks** and subtasks into **information processing components** that are employed to perform the task. The use of these components in tasks and subtasks is controlled by **metacomponents** that regulate the processes of planning, monitoring progress, and deciding on alternative courses of action. The components and metacomponents are the main parts of the theory, because they represent the basic abilities of the performers of the task.

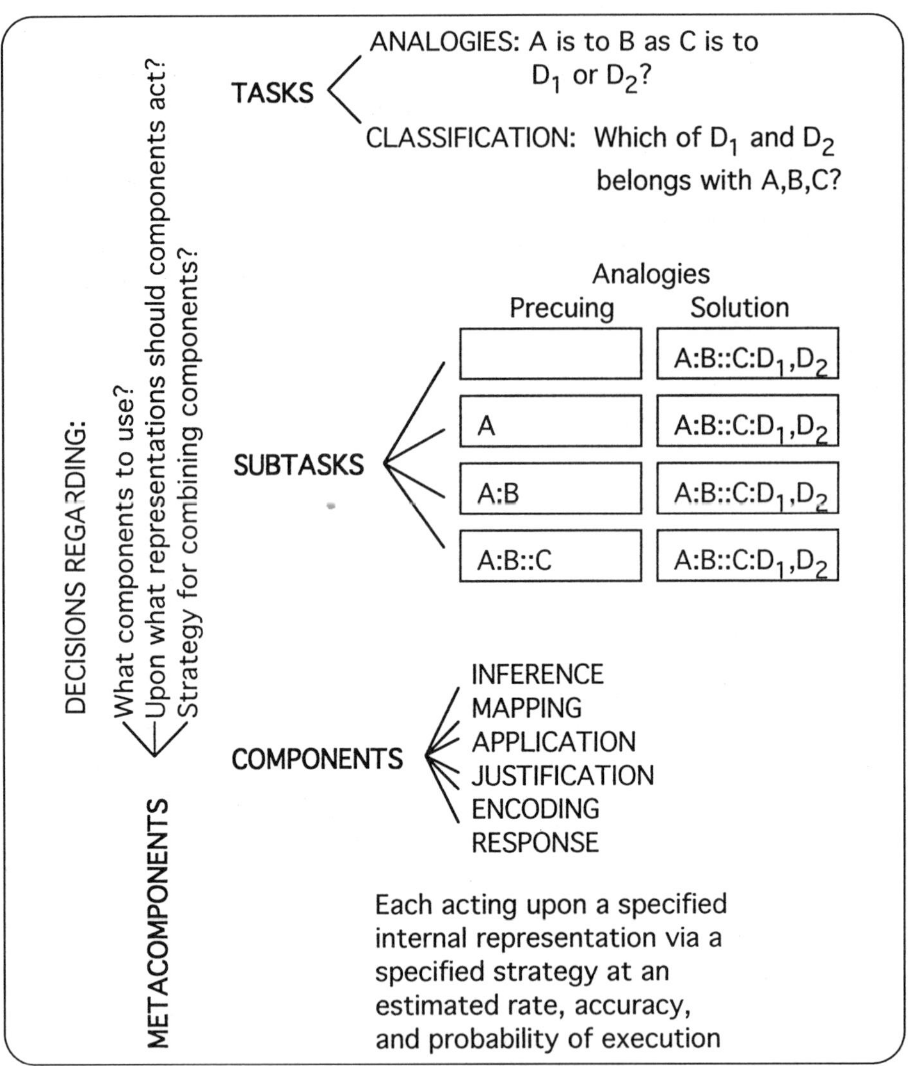

Figure 10.1. Sternberg's conception of intelligence, showing some possible tasks, subtasks, components, and metacomponents. The variety of subtasks shown illustrates Sternberg's precuing procedure.
SOURCE: Adapted from Sternberg (1979).

To satisfy the second objective, Sternberg (1977) used a precuing procedure that allowed the performance of each processing component to be isolated. In the precuing procedure, a portion of the to-be-solved problem is displayed until the problem solver presses a key, thus providing a measure of the time spent performing the processing components associated with the precued information. After a brief delay, the complete problem is presented until a response is made, thus providing a measure of the time to perform the remaining processing components. Performance on problems presented in this manner is contrasted with performance on problems presented all at once. By varying the proportion of the problem that is precued in a manner consistent with the analysis of the composite task into subtasks and processing components, it is possible to estimate the duration and properties of each component.

Sternberg (1977) applied the cognitive components approach to a variety of composite tasks, including analogy and classification problems of the form shown in Figure 10.1. We use his work on analogies to illustrate the approach. The analogies examined by Sternberg were of the form $A{:}B{::}C{:}D_1,D_2$, where A, B, C, and D_i are terms, ":" means "is to" and "::" means "as," and D_1 or D_2 is to be chosen as the answer. A specific analogy of this type is BASKETBALL: MICHAEL JORDAN :: ICE HOCKEY : (a) WAYNE GRETZKY, (b) EMILIO ESTEVEZ. Sternberg identified six processing components that pertain to the terms in an analogy problem, the four major components of which are **encoding,** in which attributes of each term in the problem are identified; **inference,** in which the rule relating A to B is discovered; **mapping,** in which a rule that maps the domain of the source analog onto the target is determined; and **application,** in which a plausible answer D' is generated and evaluated against the alternatives D_1 and D_2. Sternberg was able to isolate these components by examining performance on subtasks in which 0, 1, 2, or 3 of the terms were precued, as in Figure 10.1.

Sternberg (1979) evaluated alternative information-processing models in which the same component processes were performed serially, but that differed in the sequence in which the four major components were performed and the manner in which they needed to be executed (i.e., exhaustively, such that all attributes pertinent to the component are processed by it, or with self-termination, such that only as many attributes as needed for successful completion of the component are processed). Support was found for a model in which the encoding and inference components processed information in an exhaustive manner, but the mapping and application components processed information in a self-terminating manner. By far the largest percentage of time was spent encoding the terms of the analogy problem (54% of the total time for verbal analogy problems), with approximately equal percentages of time devoted to inference, mapping, and application (10% for each).

General reasoning ability, as measured by a standardized test, correlated with several aspects of subtask and component performance. The correlation between time to process the information in the precue and reasoning ability was a decreasing function of the number of terms that were cued. In contrast, the correlation of reasoning ability with time to process the uncued information was an increasing function of the number of cued terms. The results for both of these subtasks are somewhat surprising in that the correlation with reasoning ability decreased as the number of attribute comparisons in the subtasks increased (which would seem to impose greater reasoning demands). Analysis of the component processes provided some clarification of this finding, as reasoning ability was most highly correlated with the speed of the preparation and response components: Individuals with high reasoning ability tended to perform these information processing components faster than individuals with low reasoning ability. Reasoning ability was also found to be correlated with the relative time spent in encoding, with people of high reasoning ability spending relatively more time encoding the terms than people of low reasoning ability. Sternberg (1979) interpreted this finding as indicating that better reasoners adopt a strategy of obtaining good encodings before engaging in the attribute comparison processes, much as experts in a domain develop better representations of a problem before proceeding toward solution (see Chapter 8). From this example of solving analogies, it should be apparent that the cognitive components approach provides a more detailed analysis of abilities than does the cognitive correlates approach. Although empirical validation of Sternberg's componential theory is still under way, the theory has played a major role in guiding research.

Aptitude-Treatment Interactions

Individuals bring with them to any training task characteristics that determine their ability to benefit from instruction, and extensive research has been conducted on how these aptitudes interact with learning environments (Cronbach & Snow, 1977). Aptitudes can be divided into three categories: cognitive (intellectual), conative (volitional), and affective (personality) (Ackerman & Kyllonen, 1991). Although most of the research pertinent to skill acquisition has concerned cognitive variables, significant relations between performance and conative and affective aptitudes also have been found.

Whenever two or more treatments have differential impact on individuals varying on some trait, an **aptitude-treatment interaction** is said

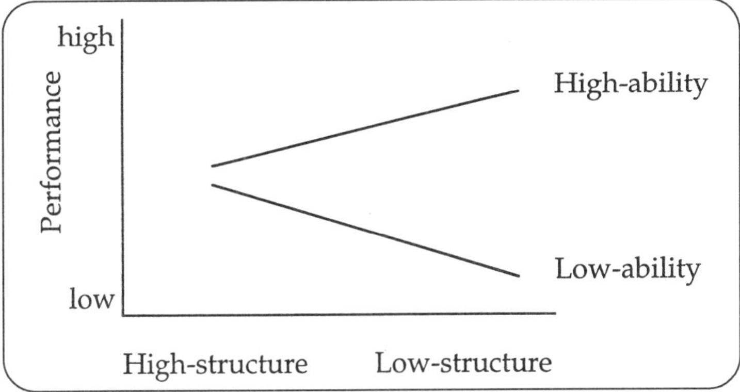

Figure 10.2. The form of the aptitude treatment interaction between ability level and learning environment structure.

to exist. Two aptitude-treatment interactions relevant to skill acquisition have received considerable attention. The first of these, the influence of high versus low structure in learning environments on learning in high- versus low-ability learners, concerns general cognitive aptitude. Figure 10.2 shows the nature of this interaction. High-ability learners tend to perform better in learning environments with low structure (e.g., independent readings, discovery learning) rather than high structure (e.g., lecture, drill, and practice), whereas for low-ability learners, the opposite is true. High versus low structure also interacts with the conative/affective aptitude of achievement motivation. Those individuals who seek achievement independently, with a low level of anxiety, perform best in low-structure environments, whereas individuals who are oriented toward achievement via conformance (i.e., having high levels of anxiety) perform better in high-structure environments.

Another aptitude-treatment interaction involves high versus low cognitive ability and part-training strategies (see Chapter 9). Recall that in part-training individual task components are first introduced in isolation, before the whole task is trained. Low-ability individuals may receive more benefit from such a strategy because, in essence, they have more to learn. Foss et al. (1989) performed an analysis of performance of the Space Fortress game (which we are sure you recall from previous chapters) that indicated that low-ability individuals are deficient in basic skills and employ less effective strategies. Part-training should be useful in remediating basic skills so that a better foundation for skill acquisition will be in place. As was emphasized in Chapter 9, the success of such remediation will depend on a thorough task analysis so that necessary skills are defined.

Task Analysis Based on Individual Difference Variables

Although some researchers have argued that human abilities are not a good basis for determining job requirements or training procedures because of problems of identification and definition of these abilities (see Patrick, 1992), a number of researchers have persisted in developing taxonomies of abilities to be used for just these purposes. A pioneer in the development of ability taxonomies was R. M. Gagné, whose book, *The Conditions of Learning and Theory of Instruction,* has been through four editions (1965, 1970, 1977, & 1985). Gagné, who has been explicitly concerned with the problem of training, has argued for the concept of varieties of learning and the determination of the conditions that promote them. An attractive aspect of Gagné's formulation is its emphasis on the process of learning, in which existing knowledge, skills, habits, and actions are modified. The five categories of learning capabilities, outlined in Table 10.1, are intellectual skill, cognitive strategy, verbal information, attitude, and motor skill. The third column of Table 10.1 gives the conditions necessary for each capability to develop. Gagné emphasized that each capability defines its own set of learning objectives and that conditions for learning will depend on the type of skill to be developed. However, empirical validation of the proposed categories of learning is lacking.

Another important abilities researcher is E. A. Fleishman, whose **ability requirements** approach, along with most other taxonomies of human performance, is described by Fleishman and Quaintance (1984). Fleishman's work in identifying human abilities has depended on extensive factor-analytic studies. As mentioned previously, factor analysis is a family of techniques for identifying the number and nature of factors present in a collection of data. Landy (1985) describes factor analysis as a two-step process: First, the number of factors in a data set is identified; this is called the **factor solution.** Second, the factor solution is analyzed using an operation called **factor rotation** to uncover the psychological sense it represents.

To perform a factor analysis, a matrix is prepared that contains all possible correlations between the variables to be analyzed. For example,

Table 10.1 Gagné's Categories of Learned Capabilities

Capability	*Description*	*Conditions*	*Example*
Intellectual skill	Learning and elaboration of discriminations, concepts, and rules	Not improved by practice or context but by learning of prerequisite skills	Predicting behavior of an individual based on classification of its type
Cognitive strategy	Internal skills that govern behavior when attempting to learn new material or in thinking and reasoning	Refined by practice in learning, remembering, defining, and solving problems	Using analogy to solve a novel problem
Verbal information	Learning facts, principles, generalizations, and bodies of knowledge	Acquired via the presentation of material within an organized, meaningful context	Stating Fitts's three stages of skill acquisition
Attitude	Preference to engage in a specified activity	Not learned by practice or modified by context but may be modified by observing a role model	Deciding to become a psychology major
Motor skills	Performing organized motor acts	Learned with practice over long periods of time	Playing tennis

SOURCE: Adapted from Gagné and Briggs (1974).

Table 10.2 Hypothetical Factor Loading Table

Variable	Factor 1	Factor 2	Factor 3
1	.80	.03	.24
2	.35	.71	.06
3	.21	−.72	.19
4	.06	.05	.19
5	.64	.43	.27
6	.17	.01	.41
7	−.80	.02	.13
8	.21	.14	.56
9	.02	.07	.07
10	.06	.44	−.54
Percentage variance accounted for	22	15	7

NOTE: Three hypothetical factors resulting from an analysis of 10 variables. Consider Factor 1: Variable 1 has a strong positive loading on this factor, whereas Variable 7 has a strong negative loading. The sign of the loading reflects the direction of the relationship between the variables and the factor. Factor 1 accounts for 22% of the variance in responses to the measures. Variables with the strongest loadings are underlined.

if 20 different measures were taken (e.g., tests of arithmetic reasoning, word knowledge, paragraph comprehension, mechanical reasoning, numerical operations, etc.), 190 correlation coefficients between variables would be computed. It is obvious that interpreting the joint effects of 20 different variables will be difficult, if not impossible. Using a series of mathematical operations, the information contained in the matrix of intercorrelations is reduced to a smaller number of dimensions, or factors, which are then interpreted in psychological terms (e.g., general ability, verbal ability, mathematical ability, and perceptual speed). The result of this factor solution and rotation is called a factor loading table (see Table 10.2). The factor loading table shows the correlations between the original variables and the factors identified in the factor solution. The correlations are called loadings because they indicate how much of each particular variable is represented in each of the factors. A high correlation indicates that the variable is central to understanding or interpreting the factor. The variables can be positively or negatively correlated with the factors, and the sign of the correlation indicates whether the relationship between the factor and the variable is positive or negative. Finally, the variability in the measures of the original variables that is accounted for can be computed for each of the identified factors. By comparing these "percentage of the variance accounted for" values, one can determine which of the identified factors has the greatest importance for task performance or construct identification.

Fleishman's basic procedure has been to give extensive training on a factorially complex task and to administer a battery of tests for reference. Measures taken at different levels of learning on the criterion task and scores from the battery of reference tests are then intercorrelated, and the resulting matrix is factor analyzed. The results of the factor analysis are taken to represent the percentage of variance accounted for by each factor as a function of stage of practice on the criterion task. As a direct outcome of his research program, Fleishman and his colleagues have identified numerous psychomotor and physical proficiency factors that underlie the performance of tasks (see Table 10.3). Fleishman (1978) described his work in classifying elements of human behavior as

> laboratory research in which tasks are specifically designed or selected to test certain hypotheses about the organization of abilities in a certain range of tasks. The experimental battery of tasks is administered to several hundred subjects, and the correlation patterns examined. Subsequent studies tend to introduce task variations aimed at sharpening or limiting our ability factor definitions. (p. 1009)

A usual (but not universal) finding is that the number of factors with significant loadings decreases from early to late in practice, and the nature of the factors also changes. In tasks with significant motor components, the shift seen with training is from early factor loadings on perceptual abilities to later loadings on motor abilities (see Chapter 4). For example, Fleishman and Hempel (1954) used four-choice reaction as a criterion task and a test battery that included both printed and motor tests. Two cognitive and perceptual factors, Spatial Relations and Verbal, accounted for most of the variance early in training. After an appreciable amount of training, two motor factors, Reaction Time and Rate of Movement, accounted for a large amount of the variance, with some additional loading on Spatial Relations.

Dynamic Accounts of Abilities and Skill

Ackerman's Modified Radex Model

Ackerman (1988) developed a theory of the determinants of individual differences in performance based on the three-phase account of skill

Table 10.3 Psychomotor and Physical Proficiency Factors Resulting From Fleishman's Factor Analytic Studies

Factor	*Description*	*Example*
	Psychomotor	
Control precision	Fine, highly controlled muscular movements performed to adjust the position of a control mechanism	Steer aircraft via joystick movements
Multilimb coordination	Coordinate the movements of a number of limbs simultaneously	Operate a back hoe
Response orientation	Rapid recognition of the direction of a visual stimulus and the initiation of an appropriate response	Flip switch in response to onset of light
Reaction time	Speed of reaction to simple stimulus (does not include choice between alternatives)	Press key when tone is heard
Speed of arm movement	Speed of gross, discrete arm movement with minimal regard to accuracy	Rapidly move series of controls
Rate control	Time continuous, anticipatory motor adjustments to reflect changes in track stimulus	Keep a cursor on a moving track
Manual dexterity	Skillful manipulation of large objects under conditions of speed-stress	Use hand tools to assemble engine
Finger dexterity	Skillful, controlled finger movements	Fit nuts on bolts
Arm-hand steadiness	Precise arm-hand positioning in which strength and speed requirements are minimized	Perform retinal surgery
Wrist-finger speed	Rapid pendular (back and forth) or rotary wrist movements with little demand for accuracy	Tapping test
Aiming	Accurate, restricted hand movements requiring precise eye-hand coordination	Using correction fluid to alter a document

Table 10.3 (continued)

Factor	*Description*	*Example*
	Physical proficiency	
Extent flexibility	Extend or stretch body	Twist to touch target on wall
Dynamic flexibility	Speed and flexibility of rapid trunk or limb movements	Perform sequence of precise large muscle movements
Explosive strength	Mobilization of energy for burst of effort	Perform long jump
Static strength	Exert maximum strength against fairly immovable objects	Lift heavy object
Dynamic strength	Exert muscular force repeatedly or continuously	Scale a wall
Trunk strength	Dynamic strength particular to trunk muscles	Perform sit-ups
Gross body coordination	Perform simultaneous movements involving the entire body	Perform the Tango
Gross body equilibrium	Maintain or regain body balance	Walk a balance beam
Stamina	Exert sustained physical effort involving the cardiovascular system	Run a mile as quickly as possible

SOURCE: Adapted from Fleishman and Quaintance (1984).

acquisition (e.g., Fitts & Posner, 1967; see Chapter 1) and a radex model of individual differences in ability that illustrates the relation between task complexity and human abilities (Marshalek, Lohman, & Snow, 1983; see Figure 10.3). The theory describes the relation of ability classes to phases of skill acquisition and can be used to predict the association between individual differences in ability and individual differences in performance across levels of skill.

The radex model of cognitive/intellectual abilities synthesizes much of the previous work on the structure of human abilities. Marshalek et al.

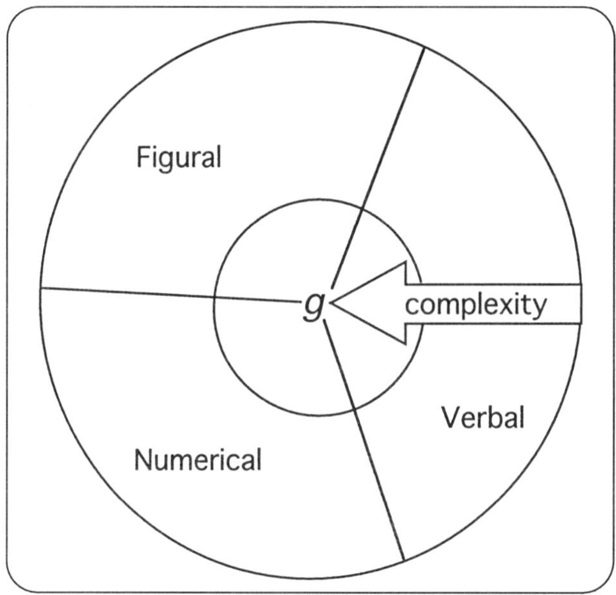

Figure 10.3. The radex model of Marshalek, Lohman, and Snow (1983). The dependency of performance on general intelligence increases as a positive function of complexity.

(1983) originally proposed the radex model of intelligence to capture the relation between task complexity and cognitive abilities. As shown in Figure 10.3, central to the model is general intellectual ability, *g*, which has been estimated to capture 20% to 40% of the variance in human ability. Abilities are then decomposed into Figural, Numerical, and Verbal factors. Each of these factors can be decomposed into component abilities. For example, the Verbal ability factor might include Vocabulary, Reading Comprehension, and Associational Fluency among other lower-ability nodes. The arrow shows that as the complexity of the task or material being tested increases, so does the covariation of performance with tests of general intellectual ability. As complexity decreases, measures have more in common with one of the groups of more specific abilities.

Ackerman (1988) extended the radex model by adding a third dimension (in addition to complexity and type of ability), speed of processing. This model, shown in Figure 10.4, is better able to distinguish between tasks requiring speeded versus unspeeded information processing. Be-

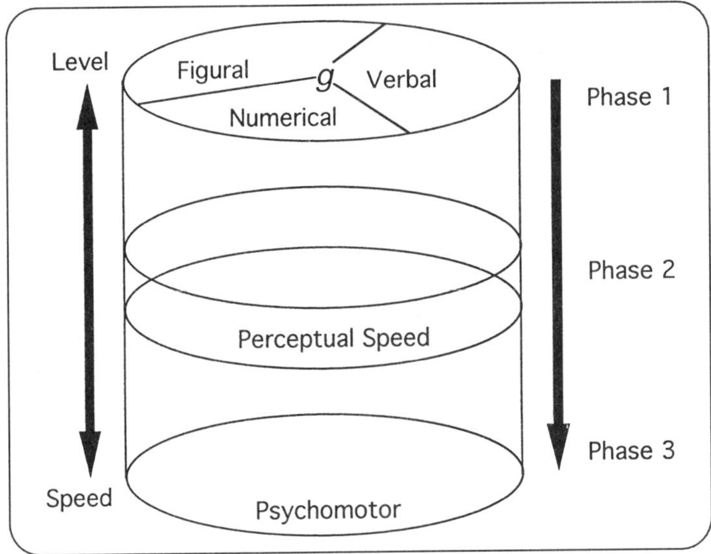

Figure 10.4. Ackerman's modified radex model of abilities and skill. As skill and hence speed increases, there is decreasing reliance on general abilities and increasing importance of psychomotor ability.
SOURCE: Ackerman (1988).

cause the transition from unskilled to skilled performance is largely characterized by increased speed of processing, Ackerman's version of the radex model can be used to locate abilities important to performance across phases of skill acquisition.

In the initial declarative phase of skill acquisition, substantial demands are made on cognitive abilities such as memory, reasoning, and knowledge retrieval. Because initial performance often depends on background knowledge and general spatial, verbal, and numeric abilities, general and broad content abilities should be predictive of individual differences in the declarative phase of skill acquisition. Figure 10.4 shows that the declarative phase of skill acquisition is associated with the general abilities shown at the top of the cylinder.

Performance in the associative phase of skill acquisition, wherein learners develop streamlined productions or rules for performance, depends more on task-specific associations and less on general declarative knowledge. As speed and efficiency of performance develop, the learner becomes less dependent on conscious mediation and the dependency of performance on general abilities is reduced. Moving down the cylinder in Figure 10.4, along the speed dimension, we see that Phase 2 performance is predicted to rely more heavily on perceptual speed ability than does initial performance.

In the autonomous phase of skill acquisition, procedures have become automatized and performance is fluent and relatively free of attentional demands. Declarative knowledge is now relatively unimportant and not consciously accessed. As can be seen in Figure 10.4, in this phase psychomotor ability becomes a more important determinant of performance.

Figure 10.5 provides a different graphical summary of the roles of general ability, perceptual speed, and psychomotor ability in the performance of a perceptual-motor task. The three functions illustrate the dynamic nature of the determinants of individual differences in skilled performance. An examination of the functions reveals that the question "What are the most important determinants of performance?" will depend on the stage of skill development that is considered. Thus a person high in general ability but low in psychomotor ability might initially perform better than a person with a different ability profile. For example, learning to use a new electrical gadget, such as an electronic planner with handwriting recognition capability, might initially depend more on the ability to understand the device's function and the instructions for its use. After the instructions have been mastered, the ability to enter information efficiently will become increasingly important. A person with hopeless handwriting, for example, might quickly figure out how to use the new planner but be unable to develop proficiency because of this psychomotor limitation.

Ackerman (1992) investigated the ability determinants of individual differences with both traditional ability testing and skill acquisition measures using a complex air traffic control simulator, with the finding that individual differences across different levels of skill were predictable from the battery of ability measures. In the complex task used in this study, general ability was a substantial predictor of performance across skill levels. Interactions in ability and performance were observed that were consistent with the principles of skill acquisition and cognitive ability determinants outlined in Ackerman's earlier work, in that correlations between perceptual speed ability and skill were observed even at high practice levels. However, the correlations for general ability and skill increased over time, perhaps because the amount of novel information that had to be processed throughout task performance was substantial.

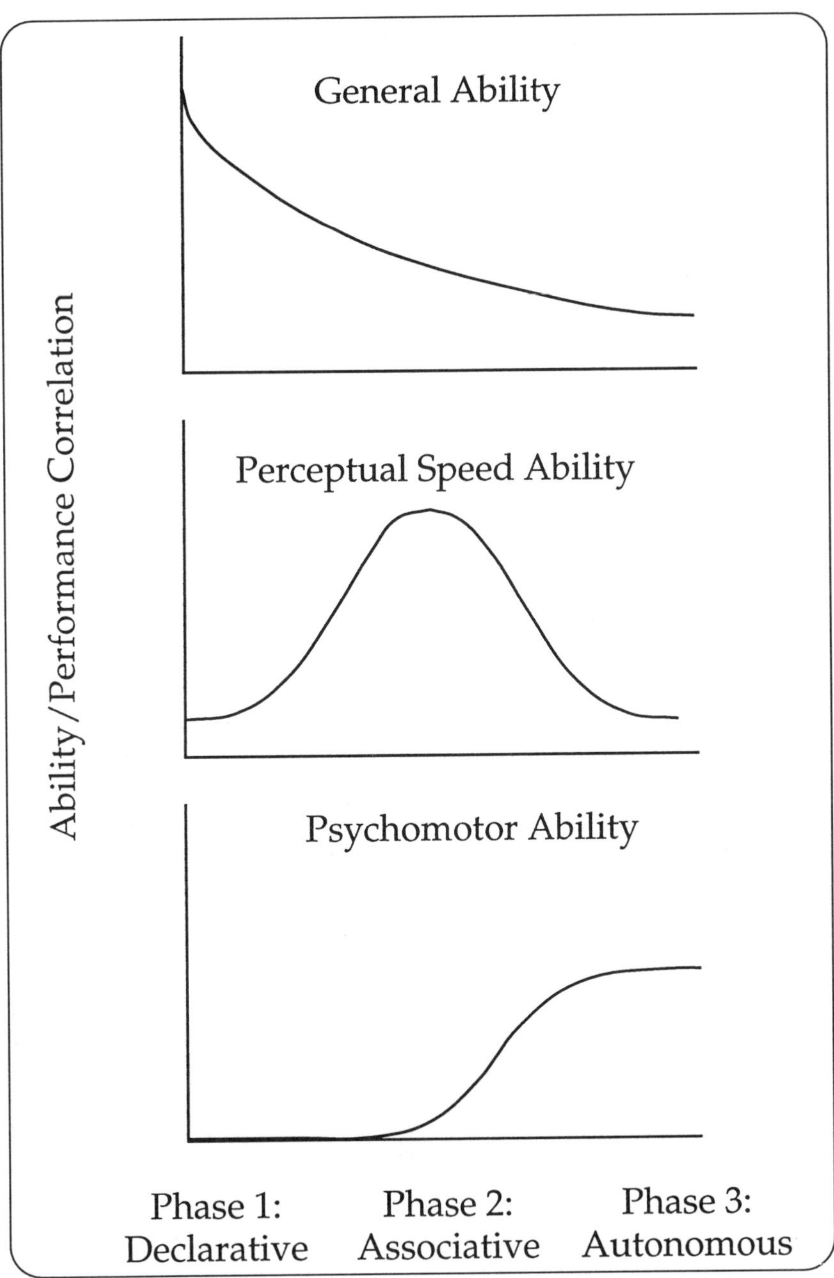

Figure 10.5. Ackerman's proposed functions underlying skilled performance.

Norman and Shallice's Levels of Action Control

An alternative account of skill acquisition is Norman and Shallice's (1985) **levels of action control.** This account describes the development of skill, given a consistent mapping of task components to responses, as a shift in the level of control exercised by the performer as a function of practice. Generally, Norman and Shallice explain the shift in performance from early to late in practice in terms of the development of appropriate schemas for action control. Early in practice, performance depends on attentional control to coordinate many different **component** schemas for the execution of component tasks. In the associative phase of practice, so-called **source** schemas are developed that coordinate the selection and control of the component schemas. In the autonomous phase, source schemas themselves are triggered in a reflexive manner.

It follows from Norman and Shallice's account that performance on component tasks should be a better predictor of performance early in practice than later, before the component schemas have been organized (and, in a sense, subsumed) by the source schemas. Additionally, the nature of attentional demands changes as a function of practice. Early in practice, control is more qualitative in nature and serves the function of selecting appropriate strategies. In the associative phase, attentional control is required to coordinate the selection and execution of the source schemas. Thus, in this intermediate phase of skill development, the ability to allocate attention should be predictive of performance.

Comparing Norman and Shallice's and Ackerman's Theories

Matthews, Jones, and Chamberlain (1992) compared the predictive ability of Norman and Shallice's (1985) theory of individual differences and skill with that of Ackerman's (1988) modified radex model. Recall that Ackerman's model posits decreased reliance on general intelligence, a transient role for content abilities, and final correlation of ability with perceptual-motor skill. This proposed progression depends on the performer's ability to proceduralize task components. Thus, if general ability is reflected in the rate and degree of proceduralization, the performance of low-ability individuals should be predicted better by general and content ability tests, whereas the performance of individuals with high ability should be predicted better by their perceptual speed and psychomotor performance.

Matthews et al. (1992) were pragmatic in their choice of a criterion task. With the support of the British Post Office, they applied these theories of learning and individual differences to the problem of predicting mail coding skill. In the British Postal Service, mail coding-desk operators code letters for subsequent automatic sorting. Using memorized codes and coding rules, the operator enters codes via a keyboard as letters pass in front of him or her. Not only are excellent keyboarding skills required, but the operator must also be proficient in a number of decision making and executive tasks, including determining whether a given letter should be passed to the machine at all. Operators typically receive 25 hours of training, so that by the end of training their performance should have developed beyond the declarative stage. However, the high memory demands and number of codes to be recognized likely preclude autonomous responding from developing. Therefore, after training it can be assumed that performance is at the associative phase.

To test the applicability of Ackerman's (1988) and Norman and Shallice's (1985) theories to the problem of performance prediction, Matthews et al. (1992) compared the performance of untrained persons recruited from the community with that of operator trainees already recruited by the post office. To examine the relation of component abilities and skill, four component measures thought to measure perceptual speed, ranging from letter matching to five-choice serial reaction, were administered. Digit span, which is strongly related to general intelligence, also was tested, as was a measure of psychomotor ability, tapping speed. To examine the influence of attentional control ability, two personality variables, introversion/extroversion and energetic arousal, were measured. Both of these personality variables correlate well with a range of tasks and so are thought to measure general attentional control. For example, extroverts perform better than introverts in a range of information processing tasks, particularly when high demands are placed on the individual. As will be discussed in the following chapter, a relatively high degree of baseline arousal is associated with good performance of tasks of medium difficulty, like the one investigated here. That arousal is directly associated with resource availability is suggested by the finding that, in general, greater effects of arousal are seen in more demanding dual-task situations than when single-task performance is examined (e.g., Matthews & Margetts, 1991).

Based on Ackerman's (1988) account, Matthews et al. (1992) predicted that low-ability individuals, being slow in proceduralization, should show a larger correlation with digit span than with the other measures because their performance should be at the cognitive phase where general intelligence largely determines performance. High-ability individuals should proceduralize task knowledge more quickly and show higher correlations with the perceptual components. From Norman and Shallice's theory, Matthews et al. inferred that low-ability individuals' performance would depend more on component abilities—and should correlate more highly with these abilities—than should high-ability subjects' performance. Because the high-ability individuals should develop source schemas that require attentional control, the personality variables representing control ability should be more highly correlated with performance for these persons.

The interpretation of Matthews et al.'s (1992) results rests partly on the assumption that the selection procedures used by the British Post Office resulted in a higher-ability group than did the selection procedure used by Matthews et al. (i.e., newspaper advertisements for participants in an introductory keyboarding skills course, with pay). Many possible confounds, including age of individuals in the two groups, sex of the individuals, and differences in the training procedures must qualify any interpretation. However, initial (pretraining) testing showed that the Post Office sample was higher in ability on most of the measures and could be assumed to represent a different ability sample from the experimenter-selected group. To generalize their findings further, Matthews et al. also compared low- and high-ability subsamples within the experimenter-selected group.

Correlations computed between mail sorting skill and the various component measures showed that both cognitive and personality measures were associated with posttraining mail sorting performance, and that the correlations depended on the ability sample. For the Post Office sample, the only consistent predictor was the degree of extroversion: Extroverts within this sample were faster at coding mail and also tended to be more accurate. Extroversion was not a good predictor of performance for the general sample. Rather, the cognitive measures were better predictors of performance for this group. High speed and accuracy of mail coding were associated with better performance on both of the speeded component measures and digit recall. Luckily for the British Post Office, performance on the mail-coding selection test was a good predictor of performance for both groups—but the cognitive and personality predictors were even better predictors of performance. Comparisons between low- and high-ability individuals within the general sample showed a similar pattern: Extroversion was a better predictor of performance for the high-ability group, and the cognitive measures were more predictive for the low-ability group.

The interaction between ability group and predictive variables is consistent with Norman and Shallice's (1985) theory if variability in skill is associated with variability in executing component schemas for low-ability individuals and with variability in executing source schemas in high-ability individuals. It is more difficult to reconcile Ackerman's (1988) model with these results. Perceptual speed and general ability did not seem to trade off as good predictors of ability as a function of the skill level of the individuals. Matthews et al. (1992) suggested that the reason why Ackerman's model fails to account for these data but has performed well in other cases (e.g., Ackerman, 1988) is that previous research used "ability factors as predictors rather than discrete elementary cognitive tasks whose variation would reflect task-specific procedures or schemas as well as abilities" (p. 416). In other words, in complex tasks with many subcomponents, such as mail coding, measures of elementary component processes and executive control of performance may account for variance in performance additional to that predicted by psychometric ability measures.

Problems of Interpretation in Understanding the Relation Between Abilities and Skill Levels

The modified radex model of abilities and skills developed by Ackerman (1988, 1992) predicts that the dependencies between specific abilities and performance will vary as a function of the skill level of the performer. This model is the latest in a long history of the study of the nature of the relation between abilities and performance. As illustrated by the Matthews et al. (1992) study, the generality of models of this type is questionable. The major problem in validating such models and determining the relation between abilities and skill has been the difficulty of measuring both changes in skill and the association of abilities with performance. For example, Woodrow's (1946) conclusion that there is little shared variance between measures of general intellectual ability and measures of individual differences in learning is suspect because most of the research leading to this conclusion was based on the use of gain scores (i.e., the difference between initial and final performance scores) to measure learning. As Cronbach and Snow (1977) have pointed out, gain scores can be unreliable because the reliability of gain scores is a function of the reliabilities of the two scores from which they are derived. That is, gain scores have two sources of unreliability, and low correlations between tests and gain scores could be attributable to this unreliability.

Problems also exist with the other major technique used to determine the relation between skill acquisition and abilities—factor analysis. We have seen how factor analysis might be used to examine individual differences and skill acquisition; now let us consider problems with the approach. First of all, factor analysis cannot properly be used to explain dependencies of performance on abilities. The goal of the approach, as described earlier, is to predict performance differences from ability measures. That is, we want measurements of some ability, x, to predict performance on some task, y. However, factor analysis is a technique in which all variables are treated alike, that is, in a nondirectional manner. As Thurstone (1947) stated, "Whenever the investigator pivots his attention on one of the given variables which is central in importance and which is to be predicted by a set of independent variables, he is not talking about a factor problem" (p. 59). Furthermore, each factor is determined by both the measures of criterion task performance and the reference battery scores. Because the factors are partly derived from the criterion task performance, it is difficult to justify their use in predicting performance.

Evidence that these criticisms of factor analysis in the context of identifying relations between abilities and performance should be given credence comes from a study by Adams (1953). This study challenged Fleishman's generalization that the number of factors with significant loadings decreases from early to late in practice and shifts from verbal-cognitive to perceptual-motor loadings. Adams used Fleishman's procedure of administering both practice on a criterion task and a reference battery of tests. But, rather than employing factor analysis, Adams used the reference test scores as predictors in a regression equation. In multiple regression, the question that can be asked is "Do the independent variables (reference battery scores) predict the dependent variable (criterion task performance)?" As the criterion task, Adams used a test called the Complex Coordination Test. The reference battery he used contained 32 printed tests, 13 fine motor control tests (such as sticking pins in holes), and 6 more complex motor tests. Practice was given on the complex motor tests so that performance both early and late in practice could be compared with criterion task performance. The scores on the printed and motor tests and the performance on the complex motor tasks both early and late in practice were used as independent variables in a regression equation to predict both initial and final criterion task performance.

The percentage of the variance in the criterion task performance accounted for by the printed tests, simple motor tests, and early performance on the complex motor tests was less for final than for initial criterion task performance. This finding is consistent with earlier work showing decreasing correlations of reference test scores with criterion task performance as a function of practice. However, an examination of the contribution of each type of test to the prediction of criterion task performance revealed that the predictive ability of the printed tests was equal for initial and final criterion task performance. For both verbal and motor tests, some regression weights (a regression weight is an index of the ability to predict criterion performance from a specific predictor task value) increased, some stayed the same, and some decreased. That is, individual differences in complex motor performance as a function of practice could not be predicted on the basis of an orderly transition from reliance on verbal-cognitive to perceptual-motor ability. Moreover, when performance late in practice on the complex motor reference tasks was used in the regression equation, more of the variance in final criterion task performance than in initial criterion task performance was accounted for. This last finding lends optimism to the problem of predicting final performance on a criterion task, since it shows that increasing skill does not result in highly specific ability but can be predicted from the performance of a related skill.

To summarize, interpretations of abilities and their use in predicting performance across levels of skill are fraught with problems. Reanalyses of data using alternative statistical techniques, such as Ackerman's (1987) reanalysis of several studies conducted by Fleishman and his colleagues, may show quite different patterns of results and lead to a different set of conclusions. For example, although Fleishman and Quaintance (1984) concluded that task-specific factors are increasingly important determinants of performance with increasing practice, Ackerman's (1987) reanalysis of the data showed that, in some cases, task-specific abilities play a decreasing role in performance as skill increases.

It is encouraging to find evidence that general abilities can predict later performance and that skill is not entirely specific to particular task components. However, a complete evaluation of specific models intended to characterize the relation between ability and skill, such as Ackerman's (1988) extended radex model, will depend on the development of better conceptions of abilities. Adams (1987) suggested that an approach whereby abilities are viewed as dynamic and developing (rather than static and not open to modification) may be more successful in describing determinants of individual differences in learning. From this perspective, measures of abilities should be taken at different levels of skill on predictor tasks as well as at different levels of skill on the criterion task to allow for the effects of practice on specific abilities. This conception of abilities as open to change brings into question the traditional distinction between abilities as enduring general traits limited in number and skill as the level of proficiency in a particular task. To quote Adams (1987), "Greater scientific advances may come from determining the fundamental nature of abilities than from assuming that abilities are existential entities that await discovery with a diligent application of factor analysis" (p. 57).

Individual Differences in Reading Skill

Perhaps because it is a skill fundamental to learning and education, reading ability has been extensively studied. Reading tasks, such as word naming and lexical decision (i.e., determining whether a letter string forms a word) are linked to more general tests of verbal ability, which is in itself correlated with a wide range of tasks. The study of individual differences in reading skill can lead to a better understanding of the components of verbal skill and the interrelationships among them (e.g., Butler, Jared, & Hains, 1984). Moreover, comparisons of readers from different skill levels can help identify the subskills necessary for efficient processing of verbal material.

Two subskills in which researchers have been interested are the abilities to use orthographic (word shape) and phonological (sound) information. Typically, the writing systems used to represent spoken language (i.e., the orthographies) closely match the phonological structure of the encoded words. This characteristic of written language can make it difficult to sort out the contribution of each type of information to the skill of reading. Thus, although some theories of reading state that the reader may access the meaning of a word directly on the basis of the recognition of a word shape or pattern of features without "sounding the word out" (e.g., Coltheart, 1978), other theories state that word recognition is based on a phonological code derived from the reader's knowledge of the correspondence between spelling and pronunciation (e.g., McCusker, Hillinger, & Bias, 1981).

Evidence for both direct access and phonologically mediated access has been found, and models that allow the passage of both visual and phonological information have been proposed (e.g., Carr & Pollatsek,

1985). One finding in favor of a dominant role for a phonological route is that people are more likely to classify a word falsely as a member of a designated category when the word is a homophone of a target category member (e.g., classify *break* as a car part) than when the word has spelling similar to a target (e.g., classify *brave* as a car part) (Van Orden, 1987). If orthography were more important, the word most similar in spelling to the target word should more often be misclassified as a target. Jared and Seidenberg (1991) challenged this evidence of a stronger role for phonological information by showing that the effect was obtained only for words having a low frequency in the English language. Given that phonology plays a much greater role in the reading performance of less skilled readers (M. Adams, 1990), Jared and Seidenberg suggest that the transition to skilled reading is marked by a shift from phonologically mediated to direct access of meaning.

Other evidence indicates the relative importance of orthographic information in skilled reading. For example, skilled readers are more sensitive to syllable boundaries than are less-skilled readers. This is illustrated by the finding that individuals who score high on vocabulary tests are less affected by word length when performing word naming or lexical decision tasks than are low scorers (Butler & Hains, 1979). Those who score low on vocabulary tests perform these tasks more slowly as the words (or nonwords) become larger. What is the reason for this difference in ability to process word information quickly? At some stage of processing affected by word length, high-vocabulary readers are faster. It has been proposed that high-vocabulary readers are better able to use the redundancy present in the English language to make their classifications (Butler et al., 1984). However, Jackson and McClelland (1975, 1979) found that skilled readers are relatively faster than nonskilled readers at any task requiring memory retrieval and suggested that the difference in speed depends on the complexity of the to-be-remembered memory code. Thus differences in word naming and lexical decision could be due either to speed differences between low- and high-ability readers in retrieving orthographic information during word processing or to speed differences during lexical retrieval.

Butler et al. (1984) tested these hypotheses by presenting low- and high-vocabulary readers with pseudowords varying in their approximation to English. For example, a zero-order approximation to English is a randomly ordered string of letters (e.g., kgtrjdi), whereas a fourth-order approximation is a pronounceable nonword (e.g., dinglect). Second-order approximations would lie between the two in terms of pronounceability. After viewing the letter strings for a brief (60-ms) period, as many as possible of the letters that had been presented were to be reported. Butler et al. found that high-vocabulary individuals recalled more letters in the fourth-order approximation strings than did low-vocabulary individuals but that the latter individuals recalled more letters in the zero-order approximation strings. It seems that the high-vocabulary readers are more sensitive to the structure of the letter strings and better able to use redundancy when it is present. From this finding, Butler et al. concluded that individual differences in lexical decision and naming tasks reflect differences in reading skill and the efficiency of letter sequence parsing prior to word recognition rather than speed differences in lexical retrieval. In a second experiment, they found that skilled readers were more sensitive to syllabic structure than were nonskilled readers. Nonskilled readers, on the other hand, were more affected by characteristics of the presentation that were unrelated to word boundaries. A generalization from this research is that skilled readers process letter strings in a more holistic fashion than do nonskilled readers.

Another concern in reading skill is how working memory might be used in the comprehension of text. Masson and Miller (1983) noted that the ability to store and process information in working memory is positively related to scores on standardized reading comprehension tests and to long-term encoding and retrieval of explicitly presented information as well as with the ability to integrate information for the purposes of making inferences. However, the ability to store information (without the requirement to process it) is not related to these abilities. Thus the ability to coordinate storage and processing functions in working memory may be an important determinant of text processing skill. As we saw in Chapter 7 in our discussion of the work of Carlson et al. (1989), storing and using information in short-term memory have different costs in terms of processing demand; it is not too surprising that the ability to process information is more predictive of the cognitive ability to draw inferences.

The evidence presented above suggests that skilled readers may process words more efficiently than do less skilled readers. However, there is an alternative explanation for why some readers are less skilled. We mentioned previously that reading skill is highly correlated with other verbal abilities such as listening comprehension. It is also correlated with the ability to comprehend nonverbal picture stories (Gernsbacher, Varner, & Faust, 1990). The apparent overlap in ability to perform a range of tasks has led some researchers to propose that all these behaviors depend on the same underlying mechanisms. Gernsbacher (1993) has proposed that one such underlying mechanism is the ability to suppress unwanted or inappropriate mental representations. The basic idea is that when reading or performing other cognitive tasks much stored information may be activated automatically or retrieved unconsciously. That is, along with the appropriate representations, related but task-inappropriate representations are activated. To illustrate this, read the following sentence: "While placing her bet, she glanced at the spade held in her hand." Most likely, the sentence brought to mind the image of a playing card, perhaps the ace of spades. It is also possible that you thought of a different sort of spade—one used for digging the garden. Successful reading depends on the determination of the appropriate meaning of ambiguous words and the suppression of inappropriate meanings, just as successful execution of an action depends on selecting one motor program and suppressing all others.

An impressive array of experiments has been conducted that shows that less skilled readers have more trouble suppressing inappropriate meanings than do skilled readers (Gernsbacher, 1993). For example, immediately after reading a sentence such as "He dug with the spade," both skilled and unskilled readers have trouble determining whether the word "ace" fits into the sentence context relative to the time it takes to make the judgment after reading a sentence with an unambiguous word such as shovel. However, if they are asked to make such a judgment 1 s after reading the sentence, the unskilled readers have much more trouble rejecting the inappropriate word than do skilled readers (see Figure 10.6). This difference suggests that more skilled readers are better able to suppress irrelevant representations than are less skilled readers. Similar differences are obtained for latencies to reject homophones (e.g., reject *patients* after reading the sentence "She treated the dog with great patience") and words related to pictures that were to be ignored (Gernsbacher, 1993).

The hypothesis that suppression of irrelevant or inappropriate information is a general cognitive function gains some support from the finding of individual differences in the ability to suppress information in different populations. For example, Connelly and Hasher (1993) found that elderly adults showed less suppression of distracting information than did young adults. However, whereas elderly adults showed less suppression of object information, they showed normal or above-average suppression of location information. This difference in suppression suggests that separate mechanisms of suppression might act on the neural systems that process object and location information. Thus, although suppression may be important for different kinds of information processing, there may be different mechanisms of suppression at work in different types of tasks. More support that the same mechanism of suppression is at work in reading as

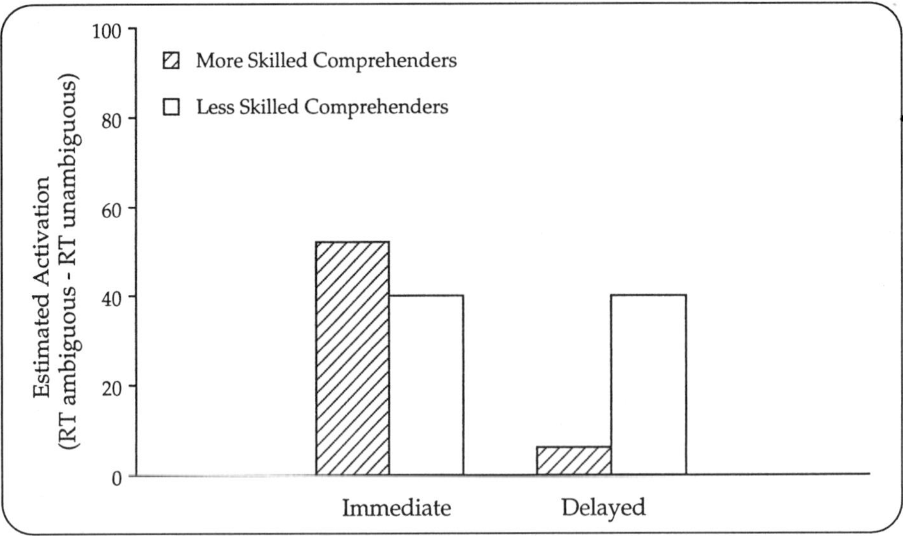

Figure 10.6. Estimated activation of the inappropriate meaning of an ambiguous word by skilled and unskilled comprehenders when tested immediately after the presentation of a sentence prime or after a 1-s delay.
SOURCE: Adapted from Gernsbacher (1993).

in other information processing tasks could be gained by showing that the same individuals who show deficits in suppression of irrelevant meanings show similar deficits in the suppression of other characteristics, such as visual features or the locations of objects. This is a fascinating area for future research and one that is likely to receive elucidation from studies in cognitive neuroscience that examine the performance of brain-damaged and normal individuals.

Skill and Aging

Sooner or later, all of us will be faced with the prospect of changes in our abilities to perform certain tasks simply because of our ages. Some of the changes in our abilities will be due to physical deterioration, such as failing eyesight and loss of strength. But evidence is accumulating to indicate that changes in information processing ability also occur, such as changes in inhibitory mechanisms as mentioned in the preceding section. In this section, we review what is known about changes in the ability to perform simple information processing tasks and the implications of these changes for skill maintenance and acquisition. Unfortunately, there are few definitive answers to questions about skill and aging; thus, there are limits to the conclusions that can be drawn.

In earlier chapters, we examined in some detail the operations and procedures that underlie performance of many tasks. For example, a problem solver must perceive the elements of the problem, construct a representation of the problem space, and, most likely, apply some heuristic strategy to reach a solution. Success may depend on the ability to detect similarities to other problems, to infer relationships, and to coordinate information in working memory. The consideration of complex tasks in terms of more basic abilities suggests that the ability to perform basic information processing tasks should be predictive of more complex task performance. This reasoning underlies many attempts to understand aging processes by determining the relationship between age and the efficiency of elementary cognitive processes (e.g., Salthouse, 1985).

The general finding regarding the relationship between age and basic cognitive processing is that the two things are negatively related. That is, older persons generally perform less well on basic cognitive tests than do younger persons. One study demonstrating this negative relation was conducted by Salthouse, Kausler, and Saults (1988). Salthouse et al. administered a set of cognitive test batteries to groups of 129 and 233 adults who ranged in age from 20 to 79 years. Table 10.4 summarizes the results of correlating chronological age with performance of the various tests administered. On several measures of ability, including speed of information processing (e.g., time to make a true-false decision), storage of information in memory (visual and spatial memory measures), and formation and recollection of simple associations (e.g., paired associates task), increased age was associated with poorer performance. The important question, then, is to what degree do decreases in the efficiency or effectiveness of basic cognitive processing interfere with the acquisition and performance of skills?

The relationship between skill and aging is not as clear-cut as the relationship between aging and basic cognitive processing. Even though the supposed constituent elements of skill seem to degrade with age, skilled performance does not necessarily suffer (Salthouse, 1989). To examine the relation between aging and cognitive components of skill, it is necessary to first control for other factors (e.g., physical changes, initial skill proficiency). One approach to doing so has been termed the **molar equivalence-molecular decomposition** strategy (Salthouse, 1984). This

Table 10.4 Summary Correlations Between Tests of Elementary Cognitive Processes and Chronological Age

Age Correlation	*Measure/Ability*	*Task Description*
–0.55	Digit symbol speed/Speed of information processing	Rate of determining whether symbols and digits match according to a specified code
–0.36	Number comparison speed/ Speed of information processing	Rate of determining whether two strings of digits are identical
–0.38	Verbal memory/Capacity for temporarily retaining information	Accuracy of recalling the identities of target letters from a matrix
–0.43	Spatial memory/Capacity for temporarily retaining information	Accuracy of recalling the location of target letters from a matrix
–0.34	Paired associates/Efficiency in forming associations	Accuracy of recalling the response word associated with a stimulus word
–0.43	Geometric analogies/Infer or abstract relationships	Accuracy of determining the truth or falsity of geometric analogies

SOURCE: Adapted from Salthouse (1989).

strategy involves selecting individuals who have the same level of skill and then analyzing the effects of age on the efficiency of the processes that are the components of that skill. Thus the question that is asked concerns whether people of different ages rely on the efficiency of the same component processes when performance is at equivalent levels.

The outcome of the limited amount of research that has been conducted using this strategy suggests that older individuals rely less on domain-related memory skills but are still able to achieve the same performance levels as younger persons. For example, in the domain of chess, Charness (1981) found that older players were less accurate in recalling meaningful game configurations (see Chapter 7) and had a different recall organization. Specifically, older players used a smaller number of chunks than did younger players. Older players were also faster at selecting a next move than were younger players. Analyses of players' protocols suggested that this was because fewer alternative moves were considered by the older players (perhaps because of memory limitations but more likely due to a different criterion for move selection: namely, that older players tended to select the first acceptable move). It is not clear whether the ability of older players to match that of younger players despite some lower basic cognitive abilities is due to compensation of deficient abilities by some other age-related or experience-based factor, or if it is due to a different task composition. That is, with experience, a skill may be encapsulated or compiled in such a way that it no longer directly depends on basic processes but has a form that is automated or somehow independent of other abilities. It will be interesting to see more research on the intriguing possibility that skilled performance can become somehow independent of basic abilities.

The other important question regarding aging and skill is "How does aging affect the ability to acquire new skills?" Based on the finding that older persons are more limited in basic cognitive abilities, it might be expected that skill acquisition ability would also be limited. However, there is little evidence for this (Salthouse, 1989). The lack of evidence is in large part due to the paucity of studies of skill acquisition in older persons but is also due to difficulties in controlling for experience-related factors. One study that examined the acquisition of a perceptual-motor skill found that the acquisition functions for young and old persons were about the same (Salthouse & Somberg, 1982). Older persons did not perform as well as younger persons either at the outset of the task or after 50 hours of practice, but the acquisition curves for both groups were similar. Somewhat earlier, Thorndike, Bregman, Tilton, and Woodward (1928) reported several studies showing a greater degree of improvement in older persons for tasks such as left-hand writing (using right-handed individuals) and learning Esperanto (an artificial language). These somewhat contradictory results are not resolved by any more recent studies, so the question of how aging affects skill acquisition remains an open one.

SUMMARY

Psychologists have been interested in measuring individual differences since the 19th century, and this interest has led to the development of many different conceptions of human abilities. One of the most controversial areas in the study of individual differences is the extent to which an "ability to learn" exists separate from general ability. In fact, learning ability is often equated with intelligence. Apart from general intelligence, different abilities have been shown to correlate with task performance. Much research has been concerned with the extent to which measures of specific abilities can be used to predict performance early and late in practice. The research evidence on this question is mixed; the predictive ability of different measures seems to depend on the type of criterion task and the nature of the measures of component abilities.

The joint study of individual differences and skill acquisition can lead to new understanding of particular skills as the abilities that correlate with that skill are discovered. For example, in reading, the view that there is both phonologically mediated and direct access of lexical knowledge receives support from the finding that skilled readers are less sensitive to phonological information and more sensitive to orthographic information than are less skilled readers. Although the efficiency of basic cognitive processes tends to decline with age, similar declines in skill are not always seen. Moreover, the ability to acquire new skills may or may not be limited by increasing age. Continued study of skill and aging is certainly warranted both to understand age-related performance problems and to better understand the nature of skill. Apparent dissociations between basic cognitive abilities and level of skill suggest possible hypotheses regarding the building blocks of skill and the eventual structure of skilled behavior.

Arousal and Performance

Circadian Rhythms

Sleep Deprivation and Fatigue

Stressful Physical Environments

Drug Use and Performance

Summary

CHAPTER **11**

Situational Influences on Skilled Performance

Skills often have to be performed under extreme environmental conditions. A skilled firefighter must make quick decisions and take appropriate actions while operating in extreme heat and under the stress imposed by the potential for loss of life and property if mistakes are made. A pianist entering a competition must perform in front of a critical audience, with the knowledge that the performance is being evaluated in relation to that of other skilled pianists. A baseball player may be placed in the situation of coming to bat at a crucial point in a championship game. Whether the player hits safely may determine not only the outcome of the game but also whether the team wins the season championship. The stress imposed by situations such as these often leads to performances that differ from those that would occur in less stressful circumstances.

A good example is provided by the former professional baseball player, Reggie Jackson, who was inducted into the Baseball Hall of Fame during his first year of eligibility in 1993. The magnitude of this honor becomes apparent when it is noted that only 28 players prior to him had been elected during their first year of eligibility. Jackson played as an outfielder from 1967 to 1987, and his regular season credentials were good but not outstanding. During his career, he hit 563 home runs and batted in 1,702 runs, both of which are considered to be excellent statistics. However, he also struck out a record number of 2,597 times, and his career batting average of .262 is lower than that of any other outfielder in the Hall of Fame. So, why was Jackson elected so quickly? In his words, "I think all the great moments I had put me over the top" ("Jackson in Hall of Fame," 1993, AP wire service). Among these great moments were 10 home runs in 27 World Series games, including three in a single game, a feat matched only by the great ballplayer Babe Ruth. Moreover, Jackson's batting average in the series games was .357, almost 100 points higher than his regular season average. His performances "when the chips were down" in the World Series and other playoff games were so outstanding that they earned Jackson the title of "Mr. October," in reference to the month in which the series is played.

Any sports fan can probably think of many examples of the opposite case, in which an athlete was known for *not* performing well in crucial situations. What distinguishes a "clutch player" like Reggie Jackson from a "choke artist"? This is one of the questions that has been of interest to researchers who study the effects of environmental factors on skilled performance. Other topics studied include how performance varies as a function of time of day, the influence of sleep deprivation and fatigue on performance, and effects of other environmental factors, such as noise, extreme temperatures, and drugs.

The starting point for most contemporary research on performance-moderating factors is arousal, or activation, theory. **Arousal** as a construct is supposed to represent a unitary dimension of activation varying from the low levels associated with sleeping to the extremely high levels associated with stressful situations. Arousal is presumed to be reflected in the intensive dimension of behavior (i.e., the intensity of responding) rather than in the direction of behavior (i.e., the particular activity in which the person engages), which is determined by purposes and goals. Although variants of the construct of arousal were suggested as far back as the 1920s, the notion that there is a unidimensional continuum of arousal reflecting the intensive aspect of behavior did not become widely accepted until the 1950s and 1960s (e.g., Duffy, 1962; Malmo, 1959). Its acceptance was based largely on the discovery that the reticular formation of the brain stem, which receives input from all of the senses and is connected to the cerebral cortex, produces a diffuse activation pattern in the electroencephalogram (Lindsley, 1951; Moruzzi & Magoun, 1949), with higher levels of activation presumably corresponding to higher levels of arousal. With regard to performance, the general idea behind arousal theory is that factors such as time of day, sleep deprivation, incentives, drug use, and so forth can be thought to exert their effects on performance by influencing arousal level. As we shall see, it has become apparent that the concept of a unitary construct of arousal is an oversimplification, although there is disagreement among researchers as to whether the unitary construct still serves a useful role.

Arousal and Performance

The construct of a unidimensional, overall arousal level leads naturally to the question of what relation exists between arousal and performance. Any discussion of this relation must begin with the work of Yerkes and Dodson (1908). They conducted a series of experiments in which mice had to learn to make a brightness discrimination, avoiding the darker of two boxes in a chamber and entering the lighter box. If a mouse entered the darker box, it received an electrical shock. Yerkes and Dodson conducted three experiments that differed in the difficulty of the discrimination to be learned. Difficulty was increased by decreasing the difference in brightness between the two boxes. Within each experiment, different mice learned the discrimination under different intensities of shock. Each mouse was tested until a criterion of 30 correct trials in a row was attained. For the simplest discrimination, the rate of learning was an increasing function of the shock intensity. However, for the more difficult discriminations, the learning rate was an inverted U-shaped function of intensity, with learning being slower for high- and low-intensity shocks than for intermediate values (see Figure 11.1). Moreover, the shock intensity associated with the fastest learning was of lower magnitude for the most difficult task than for the task of intermediate difficulty.

The concept of a unidimensional construct of arousal had not yet been developed, so Yerkes and Dodson (1908) did not interpret their results in terms of arousal. However, once the arousal construct became popular and researchers collected additional data suggesting that the relation between arousal and performance might have an inverted U-shape (see, e.g., Hebb, 1955), Yerkes and Dodson's inverted U-shaped functions for shock intensity and learning were noted and generalized as functions relating arousal and performance. The generalization that performance is an inverted U-shaped function of arousal and that the optimal arousal

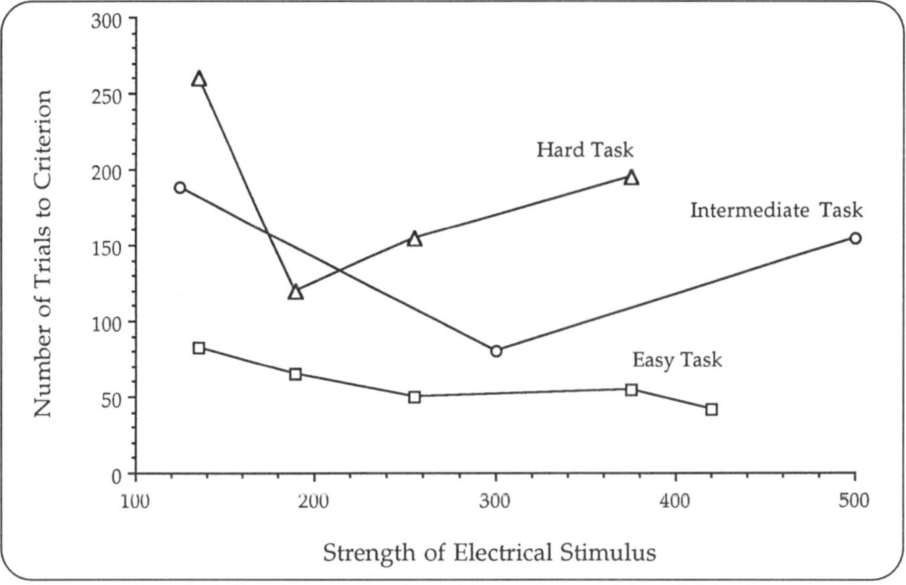

Figure 11.1. Yerkes and Dodson's results for learning (number of trials to criterion) as a function of strength of electrical stimulus for three levels of task difficulty. Note that learning rate is the inverse of performance.

level is a decreasing function of task complexity came to be called the **Yerkes-Dodson law** (see Figure 11.2). In terms of the Yerkes-Dodson law, one might attribute Reggie Jackson's superior performance in playoff games to his having a lower baseline level of arousal than most people, such that the increase in arousal that accompanies big games moves his arousal level closer to the optimum rather than beyond the optimum. Of course, without corroborating evidence this is all conjecture.

There currently is considerable debate about the status and value of the Yerkes-Dodson law, with opinions ranging from the view that "substantial evidence supports this law" (Anderson, Revelle, & Lynch, 1989, p. 2) to the view that "the Yerkes-Dodson law has served out its role in psychology and is no longer needed" (Christianson, 1992, p. 298). Researchers who hold the first view have attempted to develop psychological theories to explain the inverted U-shaped relation between arousal and performance, whereas those who hold the latter view have criticized the law itself and questioned the value of developing theories based on it. We will first review explanations of the relation between arousal and performance based on the Yerkes-Dodson law and then discuss the criticisms that have been raised.

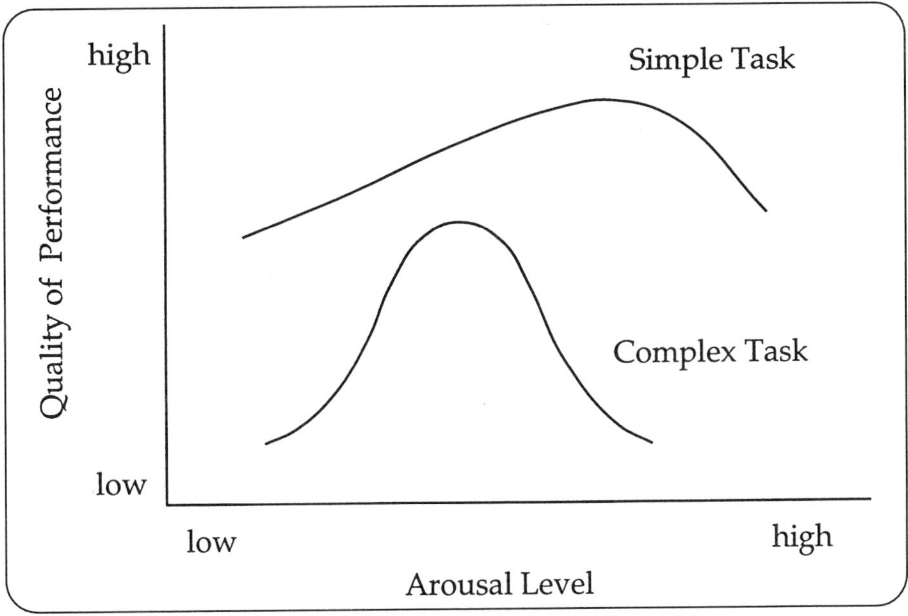

Figure 11.2. The Yerkes-Dodson law. Quality of performance is an inverted U-shaped function of arousal level, with the optimal arousal level being lower for complex tasks than for simple tasks.

Accounts of the Yerkes-Dodson Law

Even if correct, the Yerkes-Dodson law is just a description of the relation between arousal and performance and not an explanation. The inverted U-shaped function might occur as a direct consequence of the general activation levels within the nervous system, as suggested by Schreter (1990), who recently demonstrated that the Yerkes-Dodson law can be generated from a neural network model of performance by including an arousal node that changes the overall level of activation within the network. However, most authors have proposed that arousal exerts its influence on performance only indirectly by altering the nature of information processing. Two prominent accounts of this type are the cue utilization hypothesis and the multiple resources hypothesis.

The Cue Utilization Hypothesis

The best known account of the Yerkes-Dodson law is that of Easterbrook (1959), who proposed a **cue utilization** hypothesis to explain these relations. This hypothesis is based on the idea that the range of cues that a person can observe, maintain an orientation toward, respond to, or associate with responses changes as a function of arousal. According to Easterbrook, as arousal increases, the range of cues to which the person attends is reduced (or, in other words, attention narrows). The cue utilization hypothesis accounts for the inverted U-shaped function by assuming that at low levels of arousal both task-relevant (or central) and task-irrelevant (or peripheral) cues are used and the task-irrelevant cues interfere with performance to some extent. As arousal increases, the peripheral or irrelevant cues are excluded from the range of cue utilization. Because the range is increasingly restricted to the task-relevant cues, performance improves. However, when the point is reached at which all of the remaining cues being used are task relevant, any further increase in arousal will result in some relevant cues being excluded. Consequently, performance will decline at high arousal levels. Assuming that difficult tasks have a higher proportion of task-relevant cues than do easy tasks, the fact that performance deteriorates at a lower level of arousal for complex tasks than for simple tasks is also explained.

Support for Easterbrook's (1959) cue utilization hypothesis has come primarily from evidence for attentional narrowing (i.e., a restriction in the range of cues used) in dual-task contexts. For example, when people performed 1-minute trials of a continuous tracking task, with the requirement to turn out lights that occurred occasionally in the peripheral visual field or to respond to an occasional deflection of a pointer of a peripherally located dial, performance on the tracking task depended on whether a bonus was offered for high combined scores on the central tracking task and the peripheral tasks (Bahrick, Fitts, & Rankin, 1952). When the bonus was in effect, performance on the central tracking task improved but performance on the peripheral tasks declined. Assuming that the influence of the bonus is to increase arousal, these results suggest that increasing arousal causes the range of cue utilization to be restricted to the central cues. Similar results have been obtained for other manipulations assumed to affect arousal, such as shocks administered randomly during performance of the tracking task (Bacon, 1974).

The Multiple Resources Hypothesis

Humphreys and Revelle (1984) proposed an alternative to Easterbrook's cue utilization account of the Yerkes-Dodson law that is based on the multiple resources view of attention. Their **multiple resources** hypothesis attributes the law to opposing effects of arousal on two distinct information processing components. The first of these components is **sustained information transfer,** which encompasses all of the processes involved in identifying a stimulus and selecting and executing a response to it. Humphreys and Revelle liken this component to the concept of sustained attention and propose that the resources available for information transfer increase monotonically as a function of arousal level. The second component is **short-term memory,** which encompasses the processes required to retain and retrieve information in the short-term store. In contrast to sustained information transfer, the resources for short-term memory are presumed to decrease monotonically as arousal increases.

Humphreys and Revelle's (1984) multiple resources model makes different predictions for the influence of arousal on performance as a function of the relative demands that a task places on both information transfer and short-term memory resources. For tasks with little or no short-term memory demands, such as choice reactions, vigilance (monitoring displays for signals that rarely occur), and letter cancellation, performance should be solely a function of the sustained information transfer component and hence should be an increasing function of arousal. For tasks that have significant short-term memory demands as well, such as digit span and running memory tasks, performance should be a combination of the increasing and decreasing functions and thus an inverted U-shaped function of arousal (see Figure 11.3). Moreover, as the task demands for short-term memory resources increase relative to the demands for information transfer resources, the arousal level at which optimal performance is obtained should decrease. Because complex tasks typically draw more on short-term memory resources than do simple tasks, the optimal arousal level for performing complex tasks should be less.

The explanations for the inverted U-shaped function proposed by Easterbrook (1959) and Humphreys and Revelle (1984) both attribute the function to two factors (irrelevant and relevant cues in the first case; information transfer and short-term memory in the second case) and assume that the primary limitation is on controlled information processing. This makes it difficult to test between the explanations. For example, the cue utilization hypothesis has been tested by comparing performance decrements associated with arousal for single- and dual-task situations. Consistent with the view that a wider range of cues is relevant in the dual-task situation, the decrement is usually greater for dual-task performance than for single-task performance (e.g., Bacon, 1974). However, it can also be argued that the dual-task situation usually imposes a greater

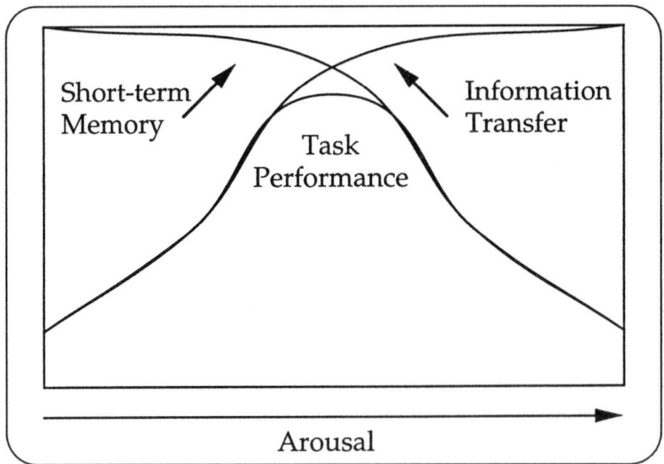

Figure 11.3. Humphreys and Revelle's multiple-resources model. The increasing function for information transfer and decreasing function for short-term memory combine to produce an inverted U-shaped function for performance of tasks in which both resources are demanded.
SOURCE: From Humphreys and Revelle (1984).

short-term memory load, which makes the results also consistent with Humphreys and Revelle's model. In fact, Bacon (1974) interpreted the greater decrement for dual- as compared to single-task performance as showing that the ability to exclude peripheral cues from processing is a function of short-term memory demands.

One way to test between the cue utilization and multiple resources hypotheses is to vary both short-term memory demands and the range of task-relevant cues. Anderson et al. (1989) conducted an experiment intended to provide such a test. Three types of memory search tasks were performed; in all cases, the members of the memory set were category names that varied from trial to trial. For the physical match task, the probe on a trial was also a category name that was either in the memory set (positive trials) or not (negative trials). For the category match task, the probe was an exemplar of one of the memory set categories (positive trials) or of another category (negative trials). For the dual task, the probe on any trial could be either a category name or an exemplar (i.e., the performer did not know prior to the trial whether the trial would involve physical match or category match). Memory-set size was varied from 1 to 4 for all three tasks, and individuals performed the task after ingesting either caffeine (which has been shown to increase arousal) or a placebo. As predicted by the Humphreys and Revelle (1984) model, caffeine increased the slope of the functions relating reaction time to set size (thought to reflect short-term memory demands) but decreased the intercept (thought to reflect information transfer). Assuming that a wider range of cue utilization is required for the dual task than for either single task, the cue utilization hypothesis predicts that caffeine should have a greater effect on dual-task performance, which it did not. Thus, although far from conclusive, the results of this experiment are more consistent with the multiple resources hypothesis than with the cue utilization hypothesis.

Challenges to the Yerkes-Dodson Law

Criticisms of the interpretation of the Yerkes-Dodson arousal function as a psychological law have focused on many perceived deficiencies, with the most serious being its reliance on the construct of arousal. It was during the 1950s and 1960s, when arousal theory was in its heyday, that the inverted U-shaped relation between arousal and performance came to be regarded as a law. However, the construct of arousal has since come under severe criticism because at least one neural system in addition to the reticular activation system (i.e., the hypothalamic-limbic system involved in emotional arousal) contributes to arousal; moreover, many of the criterion measures that are supposed to reflect arousal do not correlate highly with each other (Lacey, 1967; Neiss, 1988). Such findings led Lacey (1967) to conclude that, contrary to the view of arousal as a unidimensional intensive dimension of behavior, "activation or arousal processes are not unidimensional but multidimensional and . . . activation processes do not reflect just the intensive dimension of behavior but also the intended aim or goal of the behavior" (p. 25).

One of the strongest critics of the status of the Yerkes-Dodson function as a law has been Näätänen (1973), who has focused on Lacey's concerns about the importance of behavioral goals. According to Näätänen, it is the pattern of physiological response rather than its intensity that is of most importance for performance. Specifically, he argued that if this pattern is appropriate to the task in question, performance will be a negatively accelerated function of the intensity of activation. Näätänen proposed that the downturn in performance often observed at high arousal levels is an artifact caused by the specific patterns of activation being inappropriate for directing behavior toward the task at hand, in part because most laboratory tasks are not representative of those encountered in the natural environment. Although Näätänen described his account as inconsistent with the Yerkes-Dodson law, it is similar to Humphreys and Revelle's (1984) multiple resources hypothesis. For both, performance is not expected to degrade at high levels of arousal for all tasks.

As is evident from the many explanations for the Yerkes-Dodson law, the law is essentially irrefutable (Neiss, 1988). There are many instances in the literature in which the inverted U-shaped function has not been obtained, but additional ad hoc assumptions make the results appear consistent with the law. Neiss (1988) concluded that the Yerkes-Dodson law is correct only in the trivial sense that "subjects with incentive will outperform either those with none or those responding to a serious plausible threat" (p. 345), or, in stronger terms, that "the motivated outperform the apathetic and terrified" (p. 355). Perhaps the most serious criticism that Neiss leveled against the Yerkes-Dodson law is that it largely obscures individual differences in performance under conditions in which threats or incentives are high, which Neiss regarded as the most salient feature of such situations. Specifically, with the exception of ad hoc conjectures of the type that we presented as a possible reason for why Reggie Jackson performed well in championship games, the construct of arousal level does not provide much insight into why some individuals enter a facilitative state in threatening situations whereas others enter a debilitative state. Even in life-threatening situations, for which arousal should be extremely high, 12% to 25% of people show appropriately organized responses (Tyhurst, 1951). So, it seems that high arousal itself does not preclude successful performance of complex tasks; perhaps cognitive and affective factors as well as biological factors should also be considered to enable better understanding of such individual differences (Neiss, 1988).

In conclusion, it seems that in many cases, although not always, performance is an inverted U-shaped function of such variables as drug use, incentives, and so on, as described by the Yerkes-Dodson law. The breakdown in performance that is often observed at high levels of these variables apparently reflects to a large extent processes involved in maintaining appropriate information in working memory and directing behavior toward the task being performed. It is clear, however, that the Yerkes-Dodson law is an oversimplification that does not adequately capture the complex, interactive effects that many variables have on performance.

Circadian Rhythms

Almost everyone is aware that personal performance is not constantly efficient across the day and that the time of day for which performance is optimal for one person may differ from that for another. For example, the first author of this book is a "morning" person who is able to accomplish work that requires considerable concentration (such as writing book chapters) more efficiently in the morning than in the afternoon or evening. However, a colleague of his dislikes working in the morning and has had to make major adjustments in his preferred schedule to hold classes before 3 p.m. Cyclical influences on performance such as time of day have been investigated by researchers since the latter part of the 19th century (e.g., Lombard, 1887).

Human biological and performance rhythms can be characterized in terms of their period (length of time for completion of one cycle), amplitude (the range of oscillation during the cycle), and phase (the relative location, with respect to the maximum and minimum values, of the rhythm in time) (Hockey, 1986). Rhythmic changes with a period of approximately 24 hours, which are of primary concern in the present chapter, are called **circadian rhythms.** Circadian rhythms are well established for many physiological functions, with a distinction made between endogenous rhythms, those that result primarily from natural bodily functions, and exogenous rhythms, those that are a function primarily of external environmental cues. Both endogenous and exogenous rhythms typically have a natural periodicity of longer than 24 hours but become entrained to 24-hour periods by time-giving cues, often called by their German name *zeitgebers* (Aschoff, 1954). Time of day provided by clocks is an example of a time-giving cue. When such cues are removed, most rhythms will deviate from 24-hour periods. If the deviations are large, the rhythms are classified as exogenous.

Body Temperature and Performance

The most widely studied biological rhythm is body temperature. Temperature usually reaches a minimum around 5 a.m. and then increases throughout the day until about 10 p.m., at which point it starts to drop again (see Figure 11.4). It is regarded as endogenous because it will shift only slightly to a period of 25 hours when a person is isolated from time-giving cues. Like the results described by the Yerkes-Dodson law, diurnal variations in performance have often been interpreted in terms of

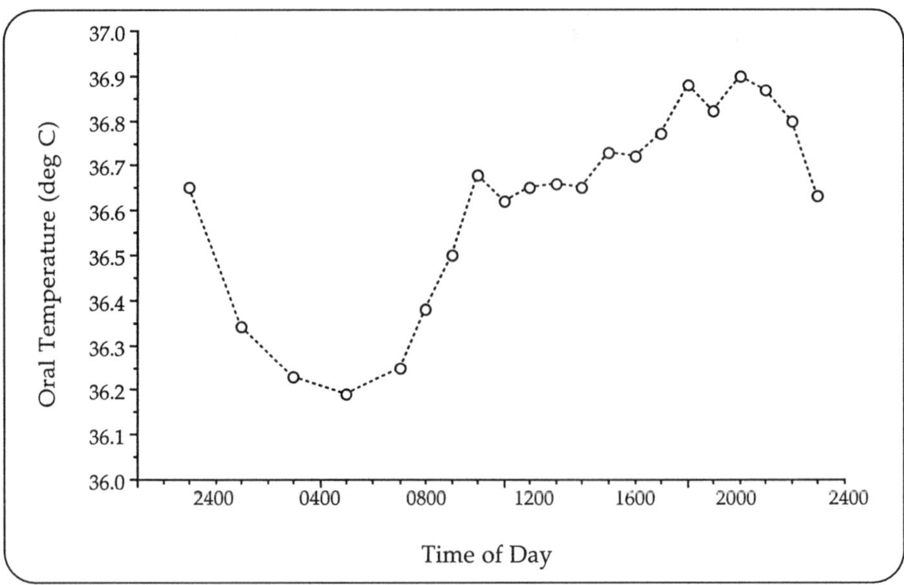

Figure 11.4. Circadian rhythm for oral temperature.

changes along a single dimension of arousal, which the circadian rhythm for temperature is supposed to reflect. Kleitman and Jackson (1950) provided evidence for such a proposal by showing a relatively strong parallel throughout the day between body temperature and performance efficiency for rapidly naming series of color patches, making odd/even choice reactions regarding the number of lights illuminated, and operation of a flight simulator under conditions that required vigilance and attention to many details. The parallel between body temperature and performance, illustrated in Figure 11.5, which shows performance as a function of time of day for visual search tasks, has been found for performance of many perceptual-motor tasks, although often a deviant "postlunch dip" occurs in the performance function. Based on findings from his and other labs, Kleitman (1938/1963) concluded that "most of the curves of performance can be brought into line with the known 24-hr body temperature curves" (p. 161).

Memory and Cognitive Tasks

Kleitman's general conclusion about a close relation between temperature and performance turned out to be erroneous, in part because the

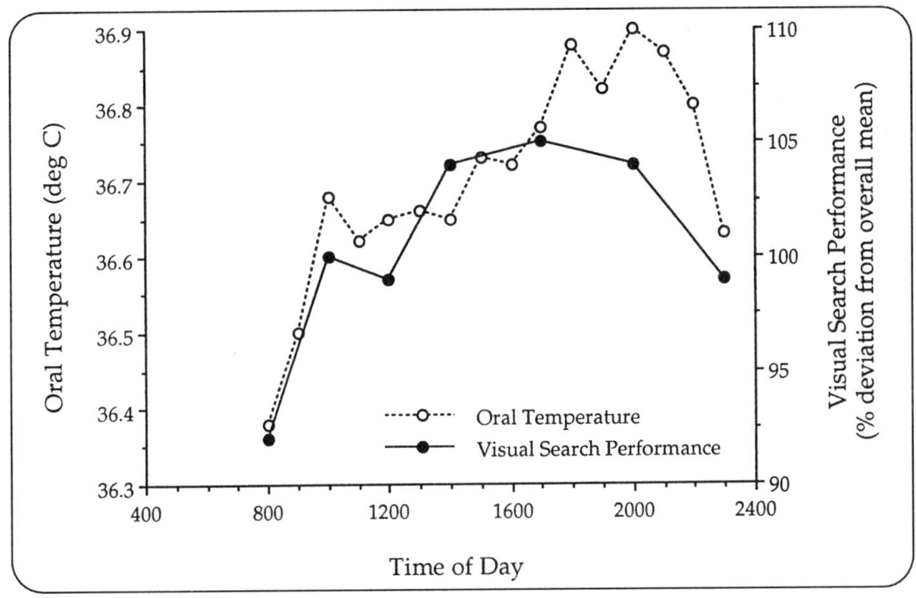

Figure 11.5. Performance as a function of time of day for visual search tasks, averaged across four separate studies.
SOURCE: Adapted from Smith (1992).

conclusion was based largely on perceptual-motor tasks that required minimal cognitive effort and placed little demand on short-term memory. When tasks with significant short-term memory components are considered, such as verbal reasoning and mental arithmetic, performance typically is better in the morning than later in the day, peaking around midmorning (e.g., Folkard, 1975). Moreover, when immediate memory is tested, performance is usually best early in the morning and deteriorates progressively throughout the rest of the day. For example, Folkard and Monk (1980) had people read short articles and then immediately answer multiple-choice questions about the contents. Immediate memory performance decreased throughout the day (see Figure 11.6). The data thus suggest that the peak performance for tasks varies from late in the day (for tasks with minimal short-term memory demands) to early in the day (for tasks with heavy short-term memory demands). If we assume that arousal increases throughout the day, we can account for such results in terms of Humphreys and Revelle's (1984) multiple resources model. The implication is that information transfer resources increase throughout the day while short-term memory resources decrease.

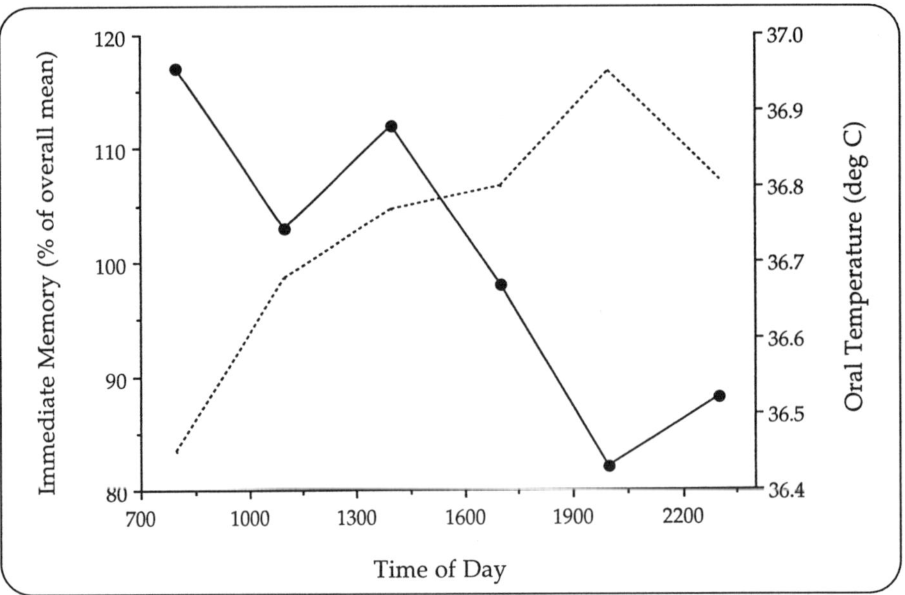

Figure 11.6. Immediate memory performance as a function of time of day, with oral temperature shown by the dotted line.
SOURCE: Adapted from Smith (1992).

The morning advantage for tasks with a substantial short-term memory component seems to be due at least in part to changes in cognitive strategy that occur during the day. For example, Folkard and Monk (1979) proposed that people have a tendency to engage in relatively more maintenance rehearsal (e.g., repeating words silently) in the morning and relatively more elaborative rehearsal (e.g., attempting to establish meaningful relations among items) in the afternoon. These researchers evaluated strategy use by looking at performance curves for the recall of lists of 15 items. They found a morning advantage for immediate recall of items at all except the last few positions in the lists. However, when the participants were required to perform an articulatory suppression task (counting repeatedly from 1 to 10 at two digits per second in time with a metronome) while the lists were presented, immediate recall performance decreased in the morning but was unaffected in the afternoon. That is, under conditions of articulatory suppression, the difference between morning and afternoon performances was eliminated. Because articulatory suppression typically is thought to prevent maintenance rehearsal, this finding suggests that the morning advantage can be attributed to a maintenance rehearsal strategy. Oakhill (1988) has obtained more direct evidence for this proposition, showing that when textual material is used, the superior immediate memory in the morning is attributable to better verbatim recall.

Because elaborative rehearsal is thought to be better than maintenance rehearsal for long-term retention, an evening advantage should be apparent for delayed recall. Indeed, Folkard and Monk (1980) obtained an evening advantage in experiments in which recall was delayed by several days. Moreover, other studies have found that people spend more time integrating text as they are reading in the afternoon than in the morning (Oakhill, 1988) and show better delayed recall of more important information in the evening, with text structure influencing evening recall but not morning recall (Marks & Folkard, 1988). Thus, whereas it may be best to perform tasks that benefit from maintenance rehearsal early in the day, learning of materials that requires elaborative rehearsal is best later in the day.

Speed-Accuracy Trade-Off

Even for perceptual-motor tasks that do not have significant short-term memory demands, performance does not always peak late in the day. Monk and Leng (1982) proposed that the tendency for speed of perceptual-motor performance to peak late in the day as well as the deviations from this pattern might also be accountable in terms of a strategy shift—in this case, from one emphasizing accuracy of responding early in the day to one emphasizing speed of responding later in the day. To support this proposal, Monk and Leng provided evidence from several speeded response tasks that the increase in speed of responding that occurs as the day progresses is accomplished at least in part through the cost of being less accurate. Monk and Leng noted that the peak performance speed for tasks in which poor accuracy has deleterious effects, such as placing pegs in holes, occurs earlier in the day than the peak speed for tasks on which accuracy has little effect. This suggests that there is an increasing tendency to make disruptive errors later in the day. More important, a relatively difficult task involving serial rhyme decisions showed the typical increase in performance speed throughout the day, but this speedup was accompanied by an increasing number of incorrect decisions.

Smith (1991) evaluated the hypothesis that the differences in speed of responding across the day can be attributed to a strategy shift by explicitly manipulating the speed-accuracy criterion during both early morning and early evening sessions. His reasoning was that differences in performance due to such strategies should be eliminated by instructions that explicitly encourage a specific speed-accuracy strategy (e.g., high speed or high accuracy) to be adopted. In his experiment, individuals had to perform a self-paced serial reaction task. When one of three red lights came on, they were to move their preferred hand from a center touch plate to the corresponding one of three relatively distant touch plates. This task was performed under three instructional sets: accuracy emphasis, speed emphasis, and neutral. This manipulation of the speed-accuracy criterion was effective, but it did not interact with time of day. Responding was faster and less accurate in the evening under all three criteria conditions. Because the instructions to adopt specific strategies emphasizing speed or accuracy did not eliminate the difference between morning and evening performances, Smith concluded that the shift in the speed-accuracy criterion that occurs across the day most likely is not due to intentional strategies.

Adaptation

Because the phases of the circadian rhythm cycle typically are set to coincide with an activity cycle of working during the day and sleeping at night, any change that is inconsistent with the cycle can be disruptive. The "jet lag" that some people suffer when they fly to a locale in a new time zone is a good example of this disruption. If the shift in time is very great, as, for example, on a flight from Chicago to Paris, the body may be entering the normal nighttime phase during the day and vice versa, tending to make the person sleepy during the day and wakeful at night. Over a period of several days, the feeling of jet lag gradually disappears. What this indicates is that the circadian rhythms adapt to the changes. This adaptation occurs because the new physical and social time cues entrain the rhythms and shift their periods.

Disruption and adaptation are evident in performance measures as well as in physiological measures. For example, people who performed symbol cancellation and addition tasks after eastward or westward transzonal flights of 6-hour displacement showed gradual shifts in the phase of the circadian rhythm on both tasks that eventually coincided with the new time zone (see Figure 11.7; Klein, Wegman, & Hunt, 1972). Klein et al. (1972) also obtained the standard finding that adaptation of physiological rhythms, in this case temperature, occurs more rapidly for flights from east to west than from west to east. This asymmetry likely has its basis in the fact that the normal period is longer than 24 hours when time-giving

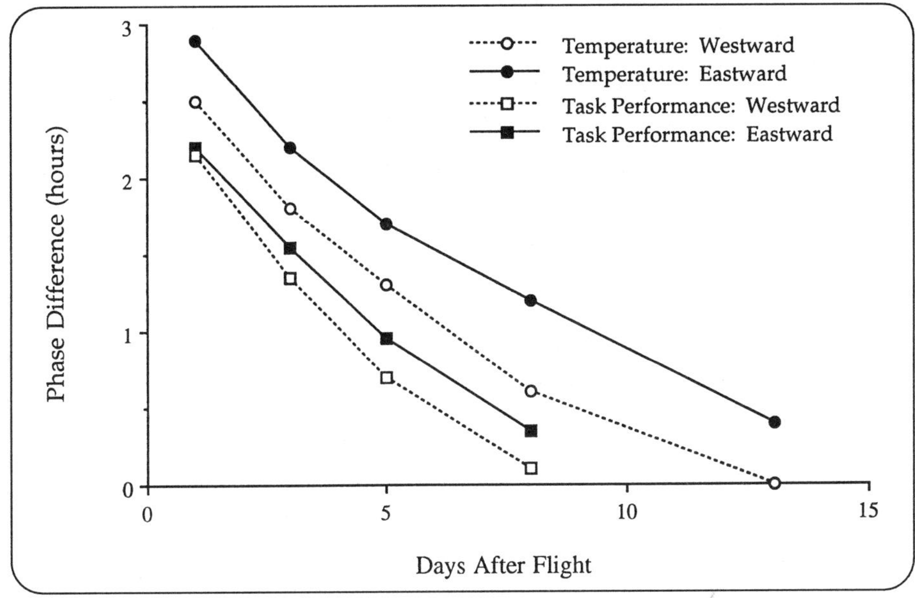

Figure 11.7. Adaptation of the circadian rhythms for temperature and task performance after westward or eastward flights of 6-hour tranzonal displacement.
SOURCE: Adapted from Hockey (1986).

cues are not present. Consequently, the adjustment necessary for a lengthened day (east-to-west flight) is more natural than the adjustment for a shortened day (west-to-east flight). Klein et al. found a similar pattern for performance of the symbol cancellation and addition tasks.

Individual Differences

Individual differences have been found in the circadian rhythms for both biological and performance measures. Research has confirmed the notion that there is a distinction between morning types and evening types. Body temperature for those who prefer working in the morning runs higher in the morning and lower at night than that of the evening types. More important, major differences in performance across times of day occur on perceptual-motor tasks. For example, whereas evening types show the typical increase in performance speed throughout the day on a visual detection task, morning types show the reverse function (Horne, Brass, & Pettit, 1980). Another individual difference that has been implicated in working preference is that of introversion-extroversion. Extroverts who are high in impulsivity (i.e., who tend to act spontaneously) show the performance pattern associated with evening types, whereas introverts who are low in impulsivity perform more like the morning types (Revelle, Humphreys, Simon, & Gilliland, 1980).

Sleep Deprivation and Fatigue

The diurnal changes in performance described in the previous section occur in people who are receiving a normal amount of sleep each night. Skilled performance can additionally be affected by sleep deprivation. Students in college often pull "all nighters" to learn material in preparation for final exams. Although such a strategy may increase a student's knowledge of the material that is to be tested, the sleep-deprived state in which the exams are taken often has the undesired consequence of adversely affecting performance. The first author remembers as an undergraduate studying all night for two final exams the next day. At the second of the two finals, an English essay examination, his pen periodically drifted from the line on which he was writing as he fought to stay awake. As we shall see, such intermittent lapses of attention are a major contributor to performance decrements associated with sleep deprivation.

A wide variety of tasks show impairment when performed after periods of sleep deprivation of 24 hours or longer (Dinges & Kribbs, 1991). Performance deficits will be more apparent on tasks that are of long duration than on short-duration tasks. This point is evident in a study by Dinges and Powell (1988), in which an auditory simple-reaction task was performed for 10-minute periods after a normal night's sleep or one or two nights of sleep deprivation. As shown in Figure 11.8, although some decrement in performance associated with sleep deprivation was evident in the first minute of testing, the decrement increased across the 10-minute period, particularly when the task was performed after two nights of sleep deprivation.

Why does performance deteriorate when a person is sleep deprived? The most widely accepted explanation for the majority of the effect is the **lapse hypothesis,** first proposed by Williams, Lubin, and Goodnow (1959). According to this hypothesis, a sleep-deprived person periodically falls asleep for a few seconds, creating a lapse in information processing. These lapses are presumed to increase in frequency and duration with increasing sleep loss and with increasing time on task. Williams et al. noted that in

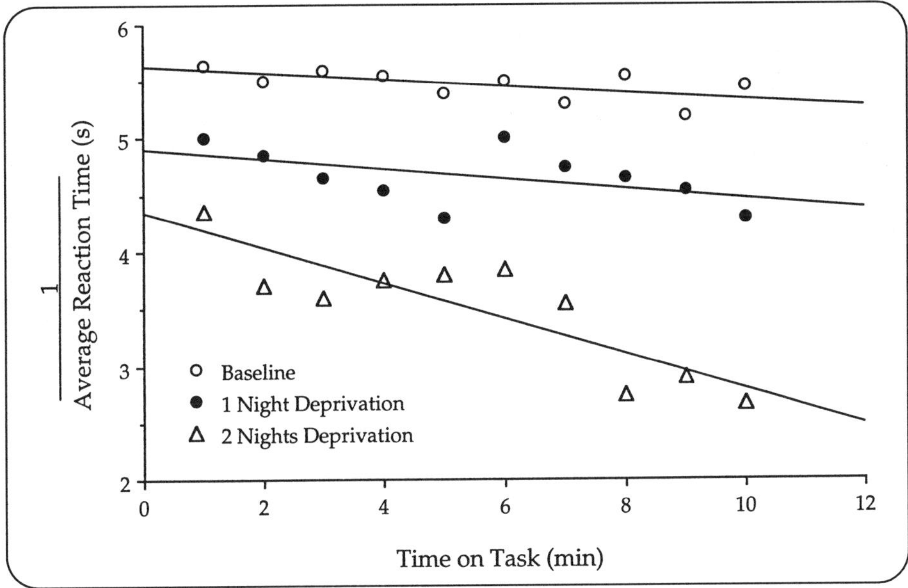

Figure 11.8. Performance of a simple reaction task as a function of amount of sleep deprivation and minutes on task.
SOURCE: Adapted from Dinges and Kribbs (1991).

self-paced tasks the lapses show up primarily in slower reaction times. They found that in such tasks the variability as well as the mean of the reaction times increases progressively as sleep deprivation increases. That is, although some reaction times are about as fast as in undeprived conditions, an increasing number of extremely slow reactions are mixed in. In experimenter-paced tasks, the lapses show up primarily in the accuracy of performance. In other words, experimenter pacing removes the option of maintaining accuracy by delaying responding, and so errors occur.

Although there is considerable evidence that lapses account for a significant part of the performance decrement due to sleep loss, there also seems to be a reduction in processing efficiency during the nonlapse periods (Kjellberg, 1977). One line of evidence to this effect is that the reaction times for the fastest responses, which should be reflecting performance between lapses, also show increases during sleep deprivation (Dinges & Kribbs, 1991). The findings of Dinges and Powell (1988), cited earlier to illustrate the role of time on task, also provide evidence of decreased efficiency during nonlapse periods. The data plotted in Figure

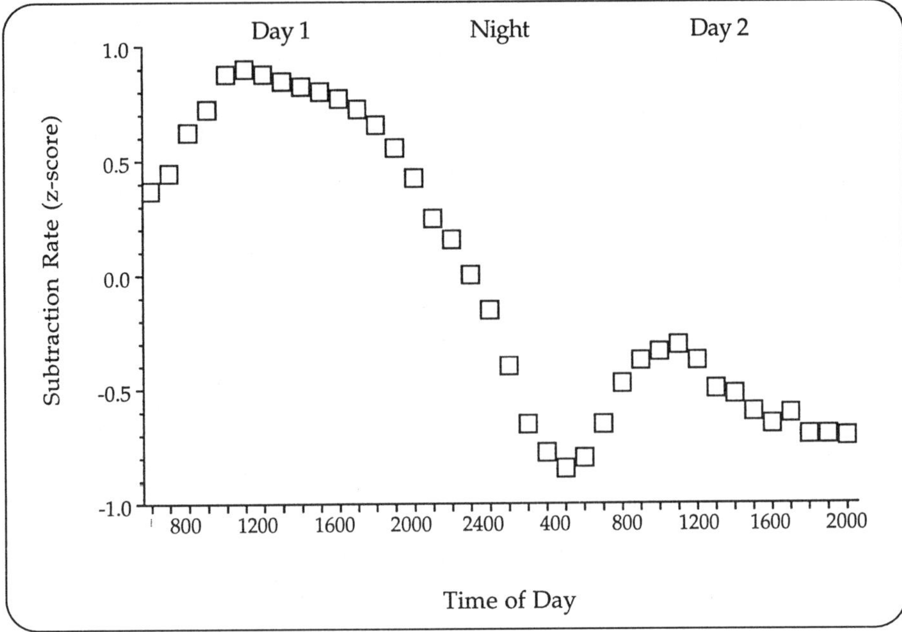

Figure 11.9. Subtraction rate as a function of time of day for a 5-minute, iterative, descending subtraction task during 36 hours without sleep. The performance profile on this task is one of linear decline superimposed on the circadian performance rhythm.
SOURCE: Adapted from Tilley and Brown (1992).

11.9 have been transformed in a way that removes the disproportionate contribution of the lapses to the overall mean reaction times. Even though the contribution of lapses has been removed, both an overall performance decrement and its increase as a function of time on task are still present.

Other factors, such as circadian rhythms, may moderate the effects of sleep deprivation (Tilley & Brown, 1992). Basically, the circadian rhythm for task performance can be superimposed onto the sleep-deprivation function. That is, a similar cycle will be apparent each day of sleep deprivation but with a progressively lower mean. For example, Figure 11.9 shows performance on a mental arithmetic task, for which the peak is typically around mid-morning, over a period of two days without sleep. The mid-morning peak is apparent on both days but at a considerably lower level of performance on Day 2 than on Day 1. Another moderating variable is modest exercise, which tends to reduce the sleep loss decrement when performed immediately prior to testing. Tilley and Bohle (1988) illustrated the apparent benefit of exercise in combating the harmful effects of sleep deprivation by testing high school students taking part in an all-night disco dancing marathon. Every 2 hours, each of 8 students performed a simple reaction time task for 20 minutes. For a control condition, performance was measured in a similar manner on another night in which the students were allowed to engage in activities with a minimum of physical activity, such as watching television and playing board games. Reaction times were significantly faster overall and less variable during the dancing marathon, with the difference being particularly pronounced for the late-night hours in which performance is normally poorest. Tilley and Bohle concluded that the exercise provided by the dancing likely increased the arousal levels of the students, making them less drowsy and better able to concentrate, but you can probably think of other factors associated with dancing that might also have resulted in increased arousal!

Effects similar to those observed when a person is sleep deprived can also be observed when the person is fatigued from continually engaging in an activity (Craig & Cooper, 1992). In particular, lapses of attention increase in frequency when a person is fatigued, much as they do under sleep deprivation (Bills, 1931). This results in occasional extremely long response times, which increase the variability of performance. These effects of fatigue are evident not only on the continued performance of the fatiguing task itself but also on the performance of other tasks performed afterward, as illustrated by two studies that examined pilots engaged in the fatiguing task of flying simulated or real aircraft. Drew (1979) studied the performance of pilots controlling a flight simulator over periods of 2 hours or longer. Control of the aircraft worsened by as much as 50% during the flight. Errors, particularly those involving timing, increased during the flight, and the pilots tolerated progressively larger deviations from target values for such things as airspeed. Lapses of attention were also evident in responses to changes in gauges. Not only did performance of the individual tasks decrease but the task as a whole lost its integrity and was perceived more in terms of its elements. That the fatigue that accumulates during a lengthy flight also has deleterious effects on tasks performed after completion of the flight was shown through experiments conducted on civilian air crews immediately upon return from a trip and after not having flown for 8 days (Welford, Brown, & Gabb, 1950). Performance at solving an electrical problem and at plotting location on a grid was impaired for the pilots who had just returned from trips, particularly for those whose flight routes were regarded as hard (e.g., routes for which there was little time on the ground between legs of the flight).

Stressful Physical Environments

In many situations, people have to perform in physical environments that are less than ideal. Performance will suffer in most cases, and it is important to know the basis for such performance decrements. In the present section, we discuss two aspects of the environment that are considered to be stressful and deleterious to skilled performance—those of noise and extreme temperatures.

Effects of Noise

Noise is generally regarded as unwanted sound that has no direct bearing to the task at hand. In contemporary society, noise of varying magnitude and frequency composition is present in virtually every work and domestic setting. Loud noise levels can affect perception of auditory stimuli through masking of the signals and through temporary elevation of hearing thresholds (Jones, 1983). Our concern, however, is with whether noise exerts any effects above and beyond those associated with hearing in the performance of tasks that do not depend on auditory perception. Because noise is usually thought of as a stressor that increases arousal level, we would expect noise to have effects on performance that extend beyond its influence on auditory information processing.

Most tasks that tap basic information processing functions show little effect of continuous noise (Smith & Jones, 1992). Sensory functions (e.g., visual accommodation), motor skills, and simple reaction times (when sufficient warning is provided) all show little impairment by noise. However, noise does seem to have a major influence on attentional control. For example, when multiple tasks are performed in noise, attentional narrowing of the type described by Easterbrook's cue utilization hypothesis often occurs. Hockey (1970) found that when a central tracking task was paired with a peripheral light detection task (as in the task used by Bahrick et al., 1952), performance of the tracking task improved under noisy conditions relative to quiet conditions, whereas responses to the occasional light stimuli became slower.

Noise can also affect higher-order processes such as the use of strategies (Smith & Jones, 1992). First, the strategies selected to perform a task may be different when noise is present versus when it is not. For memory studies, noise leads to less use of elaborative rehearsal and more maintenance rehearsal (Daee & Wilding, 1977) and to relatively more emphasis in recall on local detail than on global structure (Smith, 1985). Second, noise reinforces the use of a single dominant strategy and leads to inflexibility in switching from one strategy to another when conditions change to make a new strategy more appropriate. When past experiences or instructions indicate an obvious strategy, this strategy will tend to be relied on more exclusively in noisy environments (e.g., Wilding, Mohindra, & Breen-Lewis, 1982). Third, noise reduces the efficiency of processes used to monitor behavior and change performance. One such process that we discussed in Chapter 3 is that of setting the speed-accuracy criterion in choice-reaction tasks. Recall that to perform efficiently, a criterion for responding must be set that leads to fast responding but minimal errors. Rabbitt (1979) has proposed that noise decreases the efficiency with which this criterion is determined and controlled.

Effects of Extreme Temperatures

Another physical stressor common to many work environments is temperature. High temperature levels have been shown to produce only minor effects on performance of simple perceptual-motor tasks (Ramsey, 1983). As is the case under noise, attentional narrowing tends to occur under heat stress. For example, Bursill (1958) found that high ambient temperatures increased the number of misses of peripheral light stimuli that occurred during performance of a central tracking task. Consistent with the view that attentional focus narrows, this deleterious effect of heat was an increasing function of lateral eccentricity at which the stimuli were presented.

Heat seems to have two opposing effects on skilled performance. Mackworth (1961) found that more skilled performers on a physical push-pull task showed a greater decrement in performance from an increased heat load than did less skilled performers. In contrast, skilled telegraph operators showed less of a decrement from heat than did less skilled operators. The apparent resolution of these seemingly paradoxical findings is that the people who were performing better on the push-pull task were doing so because they were exerting more effort and thus had a greater mental and physical load than those who were performing less well, whereas the mental load most likely is less for skilled telegraphers than for unskilled ones. In other words, the group with the most mental load to begin with showed the largest decrement when heat was increased.

Extreme cold can also affect performance. Skills requiring manual dexterity deteriorate when the skin temperature goes below approximately 20° C. Clark and Jones (1962) showed that the magnitude of a cold decrement of this type for the time to tie sets of knots remained relatively constant as skill at knot tying increased across three weeks of practice. Moreover, people who practiced for the first two weeks under warm conditions (hand skin temperature of 32° C) and then transferred to cold conditions (skin temperature of 7° C) in the last week performed worse in the cold than did those who practiced under the cold conditions or who alternated between warm and cold conditions on successive days. To explain these results, Clark and Jones proposed that the thermal conditions become part of the stimulus complex that controls the manual response or, in other words, that people learn to perform the task specifically with warm or cold hands. This proposal is consistent with the notion of transfer-appropriate processing discussed in earlier chapters in the book.

Besides reducing physical dexterity, cold temperatures induce performance decrements on a variety of tasks for which dexterity is not a factor (Brooke & Ellis, 1992). One possibility for these decrements is that extreme cold is distracting and induces lapses of attention, much like drowsiness and fatigue. Another possibility is that arousal becomes sufficiently high that performance deteriorates. Ellis (1982) tested between these possibilities by measuring errors and lag trials (responses taking more than twice the normal reaction time) as a serial choice-reaction task was performed in which digits were classified as odd or even. As shown in Figure 11.10, the mean number of errors increased when the task was performed in the cold. However, the number of lag trials decreased, contrary to the outcome expected if the participants were becoming more distracted under cold conditions. Moreover, Ellis, Wilcock, and Zaman (1985) showed that these effects of cold on performance were much greater for a difficult eight-choice-reaction task than for an easier four-choice task. Thus the deleterious effect of cold temperatures on performance does not seem to involve lapses of attention of the type that occur when the performer is sleep deprived or fatigued.

Drug Use and Performance

Everyone is aware of the fact that drug use can influence skilled performance. If nothing else, the widespread incidence of automobile

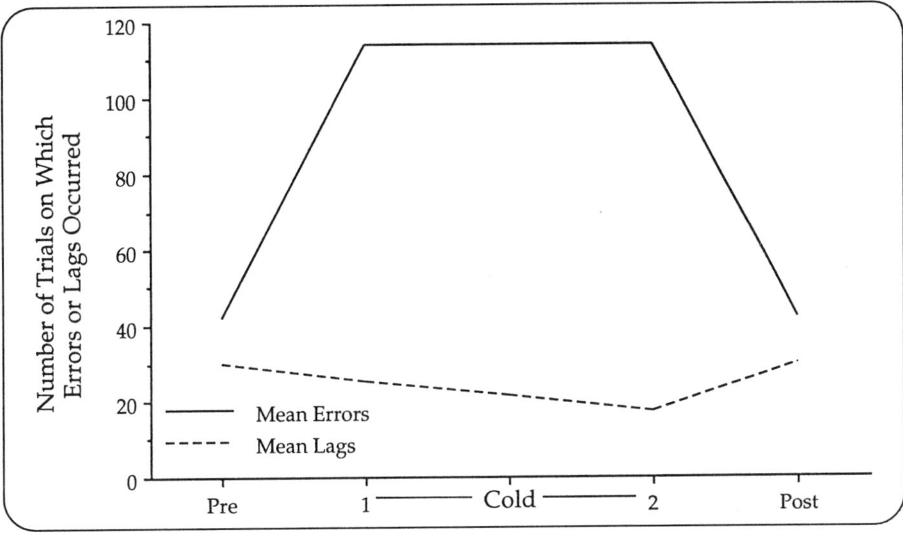

Figure 11.10. Mean errors and mean number of lag trials for a serial choice-reaction task performed twice under cold and moderate temperatures.
SOURCE: Adapted from Brooke and Ellis (1992).

accidents while driving under the influence of alcohol attests to this fact. Many other drugs, both legal and illegal, medicinal and recreational, influence performance as well. In this chapter, we restrict consideration to the three most widely used legal drugs: caffeine, nicotine, and alcohol.

Effects of Caffeine

Caffeine occurs naturally in coffee, tea, and chocolate, is added to many soft drinks, and is found in certain medications. It is a stimulant that can help prevent drowsiness and maintain alertness when engaging in activities such as studying late into the night or driving on a long trip. Caffeine produces an increase in activity of the central nervous system by blocking a naturally occurring modulator of neural activity called adenosine (Snyder, 1984). In humans, the peak blood levels of caffeine occur 15-45 minutes after ingestion, and the half-life is 5-6 hours (Lieberman, 1992).

As you might expect, ingestion of caffeine has been found to increase self-reported alertness and to reduce fatigue. Such effects have been obtained for doses as low as 64 mg (Lieberman, Wurtman, Emde, Roberts, & Coviella, 1987), which is equivalent to a weak cup of coffee. Consistent with such self-reports, caffeine has also been shown to increase performance on tasks requiring vigilance. For example, Hauty and Payne (1955) demonstrated a beneficial effect of caffeine on monitoring performance in an aviation training device, and Baker and Theologus (1972) showed that it enhanced performance on a visual monitoring task.

Caffeine is often used to increase alertness when driving an automobile. Is there any evidence that it improves driving performance? Direct evidence to that effect comes from a study by Regina, Smith, Keiper, and McKelvey (1974). Drivers who were moderate coffee drinkers performed two 90-minute driving periods in an automobile-driving simulator after ingesting 200 mg of caffeine or a placebo. The simulator, constructed around the chassis of a 1965 Rambler, presented a realistic driving situation that corresponded to driving along a straight, flat road in a rural environment at twilight. The driver interacted with a lead car by accelerating, decelerating, or braking in response to the lead car's actions. In addition, the high beam light periodically came on, requiring a response to shut it off. Performance of all aspects of the task was improved by caffeine. Response times to lead car accelerations and decelerations were substantially faster, as were those to the high beam signal. Moreover, substantially fewer of the high beam signals were missed. The results of this study thus seem to confirm in a simulated driving environment both the folklore belief that caffeine enhances driving performance and the implication from monitoring tasks in other environments that it should do so.

A recent finding of considerable interest is that even small amounts of caffeine may benefit performance. Lieberman, Wurtman, Emde, and Coviella (1987) had people perform a vigilance task, in which they were to respond by pressing a key whenever a 330-ms tone occurred within a stream of 400-ms tones, for an hour after ingesting either a placebo or 32, 64, 128, or 256 mg of caffeine in capsule form. Even as little as 32 mg of caffeine, which is typically thought to be below the level at which behavioral effects will be observed, increased the number of target tones that were detected relative to the placebo (see Figure 11.11) without affecting false alarm rates. Lieberman et al. (1987) similarly found reaction times to be reduced, without an accompanying increase in error rates, at all dosage levels for a four-choice-reaction task in which individuals responded to the location of a visual stimulus by pressing the corresponding key. This study suggests that even amounts of caffeine equivalent to those found in a 12-oz cola drink or a cup of tea may be sufficient to improve performance efficiency.

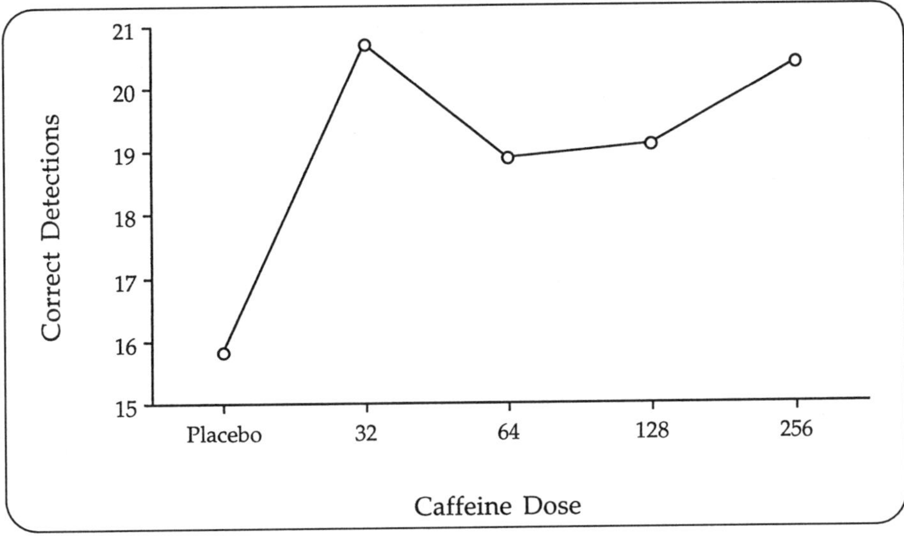

Figure 11.11. Number of Target Tones Detected as a Function of Amount of Caffeine Consumed.
SOURCE: Adapted from Lieberman (1992).

Effects of Nicotine

Nicotine is present in tobacco and is most often ingested by smoking. When a puff of cigarette smoke is inhaled into the lungs, brain nicotine levels become high within 10 s and then decline rapidly (Wesnes & Parrott, 1992). Plasma levels of nicotine have a half-life of approximately 2 hours. Smokers typically show beneficial effects of nicotine on a range of performance measures. However, because nicotine is an addictive drug, these benefits may only be with respect to impaired performance for smokers deprived of nicotine and not with respect to the performance of nonsmokers. This point is illustrated by a study of Heimstra, Bancroft, and DeKock (1967) in which individuals were tested in a driving simulator for 6 hours. Smokers who were allowed to smoke performed throughout the period at a level comparable to that of nonsmokers. However, smokers who were not allowed to smoke performed significantly worse than either of the other two groups.

Effects of nicotine on the performance of other sustained vigilance tasks suggest that it may have a true facilitative effect. Wesnes and Warburton (1978) had smokers smoke either regular cigarettes or nicotine-free cigarettes at 20-minute intervals during both auditory and visual vigilance tasks. The decline in performance that usually occurs in the latter part of the vigil for nonsmokers was largely absent for the smokers who smoked the nicotine-containing cigarettes but not for those who smoked the placebo cigarettes. Because nonsmokers would be expected to show a vigilance decrement, this outcome suggests that the benefit for the smokers who were allowed to smoke normal cigarettes was over and above any decrements in performance for the smokers who were deprived of nicotine. Wesnes and Warburton (1984) obtained similar results for nonsmokers when nicotine was administered in tablets, providing further evidence that nicotine has a facilitative effect relative to the baseline performance of nonsmokers.

Nicotine has also been found to influence performance on a range of other basic and complex tasks that require high levels of concentration. Wesnes and Parrott (1992) suggested that the general benefit of nicotine in such tasks is due to an increase in processing resources. However, this general benefit is not apparent on tasks involving short- or long-term retention of verbal materials, suggesting that if nicotine has any effect on learning and memory, that effect is negative. In terms of Humphreys and Revelle's (1984) model, the effects of nicotine would seem to be on the information transfer resources and not the short-term memory resources.

Effects of Alcohol

Alcohol is a depressant that tends to have a relatively widespread deleterious effect on performance. Substantial individual differences exist in the relation of alcohol intake to peak blood alcohol level, the time at which this peak is reached, and the elimination rate. For example, Finnigan and Hammersley (1992) described a study in which 16 persons received an alcohol dose designed to achieve a peak blood alcohol level of 80 mg% (mg of alcohol per 100 ml of blood). Actual peak levels ranged from 47 to 81 mg%, with the peak occurring anywhere between 20 and 60 minutes after consuming the alcohol and the elimination rates varying from 4 to 40 mg% per hour. Moreover, there was little correlation between these three measures. Because of these substantial individual differences in the physiological effects of alcohol, the extent to which and the time at which alcohol affects performance can also be expected to vary widely across individuals.

Alcohol impairs performance in a variety of tasks, decreasing the accuracy of tracking, slowing decision making, reducing memory performance, and increasing body sway. The best explanation for the widespread effects of alcohol on performance is that it produces a general slowing in the speed of information processing. Whether the impairment shows up primarily in increased reaction times or in decreased accuracy is in part a function of whether the performer can detect that errors are being made. Maylor, Rabbitt, Sahgal, and Wright (1987) had people perform a serial choice-reaction task and a visual search task with and without alcohol. For the choice-reaction task, alcohol produced slower reaction times for both correct and incorrect responses but had virtually no effect on the error rate. In contrast, for the visual search task, alcohol decreased accuracy but had no effect on search speed. The crucial difference between the two tasks was that errors in the choice task involved overt responses that could be detected, whereas errors in the search task involved misses of targets and thus could not be detected by the performers. When performers were aware of having made errors, they apparently altered their speed-accuracy criteria to maintain their accuracy at the level that it would be if alcohol had not been consumed; when they were not aware of their errors, such an adjustment could not be made.

It is obvious from the inordinate numbers of automobile accidents associated with alcohol that people do not always adjust their speed-accuracy criteria to minimize errors even when errors are detectable. Other factors likely come into play, with one factor being beliefs about alcohol. McMillen and Wells-Parker (1987) found that persons who believed that they had ingested a moderate amount of alcohol prior to performing a simulated driving task (regardless of whether or not they had actually ingested alcohol) showed greater risk-taking behavior, as measured by time spent at high speed and number of cars passed. In a follow-up study, this pattern was found to hold only for individuals classified as high sensation seekers; low sensation seekers showed more cautious behavior when they thought that they had ingested alcohol (McMillen, Smith, & Wells-Parker, 1989). It should be apparent that the tendency of some individuals to take greater risks when consuming alcohol, along with the reduced rate of information processing, can have serious consequences.

At least three possible predictions have been suggested for how consumption of alcohol might interact with level of practice as skill is acquired. First, alcohol might have less of a disruptive effect on the performance of a highly practiced task than on a less well-practiced task. This proposal arises in part from attentional models in which processing becomes automatized and the role of attention decreases as performance becomes well practiced (e.g., Schneider & Shiffrin, 1977). If automatic processes are less susceptible to disruption by alcohol, then the influence of alcohol on performance should be reduced at higher levels of practice. Although this argument is plausible, there is little support for it. For example, Maylor and Rabbitt (1988) had individuals perform word categorization and visual search tasks for several days. Alcohol impaired performance to a similar extent both early and late in practice and under both consistent-mapping conditions (which should promote the development of automaticity) and varied-mapping conditions (for which attentional demands should remain high). They obtained similar results for performance in a video game in which the task was to destroy a tank by dropping a bomb onto it from a plane moving horizontally across the screen (Maylor & Rabbitt, 1987) and of a dual task involving visual tracking and auditory detection (Maylor, Rabbitt, James, & Kerr, 1990).

A second possible interaction of alcohol and practice is on learning. Specifically, alcohol ingested prior to practice might be expected to slow the rate of learning. Maylor and Rabbitt's (1987, 1988) findings have also run counter to this possibility. They had people perform either the categorization task, the visual search task, or the bombing task for 4 days under the influence of alcohol and then for a fifth day without ingesting alcohol. Performances in the last session showed improvement and were similar to those of individuals who had performed without alcohol all along, suggesting that learning occurred to a similar extent regardless of whether alcohol had been consumed during the practice sessions.

Finally, another possibility is that alcohol may produce state-dependent learning, such that a task practiced while under the influence of alcohol will be performed better when it later must be performed under the influence than will a task that was initially practiced while not under the influence. Again, Maylor and Rabbitt (1987, 1988) found no support for this proposition. For the tasks described above, participants performed in a second session after having practiced either with or without alcohol in the first session. Those who had practiced previously under the influence of alcohol performed no better in the second session than did those who had not.

It has also been suggested that the disruptive effect of alcohol on performance is greater for tasks that require divided attention, such as driving, than for tasks that do not. Evidence to this effect was provided by Brewer and Sandow (1980), who conducted an investigation of metropolitan automobile accidents and found that drivers who were intoxicated were more likely than unintoxicated drivers to have been engaged in some activity at the time of an accident that was secondary to the driving task. However, there does not seem to be any unique deficit in the ability to divide attention that is associated with alcohol impairment. Maylor et al. (1990) had persons perform visual tracking task and auditory tone detection tasks in both single- and dual-task contexts. Although speed of responding for the detection task was influenced more by alcohol in the dual-task context, an analysis showed no effect of alcohol on relative divided-attention costs but did show a strong effect of practice. The absolute effect of alcohol in the dual-task context was not reduced with practice, even though the decrease in relative divided-attention costs with practice suggested decreasing attentional involvement. This outcome is consistent with the view that the disruptive effect of alcohol is not moderated by the attentional requirements of the task.

In short, the primary effect of alcohol seems to be to produce a decrease in the rate of information processing. This shows up as decrements in speed or accuracy of performance, or both, for virtually any task that is performed under the influence of alcohol. Because of the greater demands imposed by more complex tasks, the absolute amount of performance decrement is an increasing function of task complexity. However, alcohol does not seem to impair control processes, such as the ability to judge response speed and to coordinate dual tasks, so its effects are relatively independent of those induced by practice.

SUMMARY

The central theme of this chapter is that the quality of human performance at any given level of skill is a function of many variables that influence stress and arousal. Performance of any task suffers if the performer's arousal level is too low. For many tasks, performance also deteriorates at high levels of arousal. There is not complete agreement regarding why this deterioration occurs, but the accounts focus primarily on a reduced capacity of processing resources and a reduced ability to control the allocation of these resources. These reductions are often accompanied by strategy changes. Moreover, the specific effects of the variables that induce different arousal levels are not equivalent.

Performance varies systematically throughout the day. The speed at which simple perceptual-motor tasks are performed typically increases from morning until late in the evening (as does body temperature), whereas immediate memory tasks usually show performance peaks early in the day. These two performance patterns are consistent with the hypothesis of the multiple resources model that information transfer resources increase but short-term memory resources decrease as arousal increases. However, these performance patterns reflect, at least in part, changes in speed-accuracy criteria and rehearsal strategies. Sleep deprivation and fatigue also exert effects on performance, to a large extent through lapses in processing that result in exceedingly long response times to or misses of target events.

Aspects of the physical environment, such as loud noise and extreme temperature, also affect the quality of performance. Noise not only interferes with the processing of auditory stimuli but also decreases attentional capacity and control of its allocation, which show up in inappropriate and less flexible selection of strategies for performing tasks. Extreme temperatures produce similar decreases in processing resources, with cold temperatures causing additional problems for performing tasks that require manual dexterity.

Drugs can have both positive and negative impacts on performance. Caffeine can offset the low levels of arousal that accompany sleep deprivation and fatigue, having a facilitative effect on the performance of tasks that require continuous monitoring of displays. Likewise, nicotine has a facilitative effect on the performance of many tasks, although this effect is at least in part due to its offsetting impairments in performance that occur for nicotine-deprived smokers. Finally, alcohol causes an across-the-board debilitative effect on performance that is best characterized as a reduction in the speed at which information is processed. Because self-monitoring skills are little affected, people who have consumed alcohol can slow their performance speed to maintain accuracy if feedback is available.

Although much of the research in this chapter was conducted from the perspective of a unidimensional construct of arousal, virtually all researchers agree that this construct has deficiencies. A fuller understanding of how to optimize performance in various situations will emerge as the specific influences of various stressors and arousing variables as well as the strategies used by individuals who perform well in the various situations come to be better understood.

CHAPTER 12

Modeling the Characteristics of Skill

The range of studies of skilled performance conducted from the late 1800s to the present is immense, and it can be difficult to summarize the important findings of these studies to create a coherent picture of skill. In this book our goal has been to organize these studies in a form that conveys the central characteristics of skill and the methods used to discover them. We have taken several approaches in our attempt to converge on a unified conception of skill. For example, we discussed historical foundations and general frameworks of skill acquisition to provide a foundation for evaluating more recent work on skill. We also organized much of the research on skill according to the information processes—perception, response selection, and response programming and execution—most affected by practice in particular task domains. One of our purposes in taking this information processing approach was to identify several themes regarding skilled performance that recur throughout the book. Finally, we illustrated how basic information processing characteristics contribute to skilled performance in a variety of domains and identified underlying similarities in how skill is acquired across different task types. In this final chapter, we summarize the fundamental characteristics of skill identified in previous chapters and elaborate our account of the unifying role that formal modeling can serve in characterizing performance.

Characteristics of Skill

Our survey of the skills and characteristics associated with the basic information processes (Chapters 2, 3, and 4) identified several recurrent themes:

1. Learning is often enhanced by increasing the salience of distinctive features.
2. The context in which a task is practiced partially determines what is learned.
3. Stimuli are not remembered independently of the operations performed on them.
4. Conditions of practice that promote relatively good acquisition performance do not always produce effective learning and transfer (see Schmidt & Bjork, 1992, for more extensive discussion of this point).
5. Consistent practice conditions lead to performance that shows many characteristics of automaticity.
6. There are degrees of automaticity, rather than an all-or-none shift to an alternative mode of performance—as evidenced in part by the lack of fundamental changes in the representations used for response selection and continued reliance on feedback for movement execution.
7. Most acquired skills show surprisingly good long-term retention.

Chapters 5 and 6 dealt more directly with the role of attention in the acquisition and coordination of the components of skilled performance by examining dual-task performance (Chapter 5) and the learning of relations incidental to the stated goals of task performance (Chapter 6). Among the points made in these chapters are the following:

8. No single model of attention is adequate for capturing the primary findings from focused- and divided-attention tasks, although in many cases response conflict is a major factor.
9. Two tasks can be time-shared with little or no cost when the performance of one of the tasks has become relatively automatic and attention is devoted to the remaining task.

10. Time-sharing seems to be a skill that can be taught and that is a factor in efficient dual-task performance.
11. Matching the form in which multidimensional information is displayed (as integral or separable display attributes) to the task demands can benefit performance.
12. Much learning of subtle environmental regularities occurs incidentally as a function of performing a task.
13. Learning of these regularities may be hindered by intentional, selective strategies if the pertinent stimulus features are not salient.

The latter part of Chapter 6 and Chapter 7 reviewed research on the high-level cognitive skills of operating complex devices and solving problems and illustrate the following:

14. The problem space hypothesis, with its emphasis on representation and search, provides a good framework for analyzing complex tasks into goals and the operations and strategies for accomplishing those goals.
15. The closely related concept of a mental model, with its emphasis on dynamic mental simulation, also is useful for understanding problem-solving performance.
16. Analogical transfer from a source problem to a target problem requires many subprocesses, any one of which may be a source of difficulty.
17. Production system models have value for characterizing performance, learning, and transfer in higher-level cognitive tasks.
18. The principles underlying higher-level cognition seem to be similar in many respects to those underlying skill in perceptual-motor tasks.

Most of the emphasis in Chapters 1 through 7 was on the acquisition of skill in laboratory tasks that allow relatively tight control but for which the amount of practice that can be given is restricted. Chapter 8 highlighted comparisons of the performance of experts to that of novices:

19. Approximately 10 years of deliberate practice seem necessary for a person to attain a level of performance that would be characterized as "expert."
20. Experts in a variety of domains show the ability to encode large chunks of information and recognize the information contained in them effortlessly.

21. Experts spend more time relative to novices planning how to solve a problem and do so based on underlying principles, rather than surface features.
22. The skills of experts do not typically transfer broadly beyond the specific domain of expertise.

Finally, Chapters 9, 10, and 11 built on the general background provided in the earlier chapters to illustrate both applications and extensions of much of the basic research being conducted in different domains. The points demonstrated in these chapters include the following:

23. The development of any training program should begin with a task analysis.
24. A variety of part-task training methods can be effective if they take into account the relations among task components.
25. High fidelity is not necessary for a simulator to be effective, but functional equivalence of the simulated environment to the environment being simulated is.
26. The study of skill acquisition and individual differences can aid in the understanding of particular skills.
27. Individual differences often play differing roles in performance early and late in skill acquisition.
28. Individual differences in the ability to suppress irrelevant information may influence performance on a variety of tasks.
29. The decline in cognitive efficiency that occurs with increasing age is not always accompanied by similar decreases in skills.
30. The quality of human performance at any level of skill is a complex function of the many variables that affect stress and arousal.

Modeling Skill Acquisition and Skilled Performance

Throughout the text, we stressed that progress in the understanding of skilled behavior occurs through the interplay between data and theory. The theories that we considered ranged from general frameworks to verbally stated accounts of specific phenomena to formalized models. Among the more significant recent events in the study of skill has been the development of numerous quantitative and computational models that capture various aspects of skill acquisition and skilled performance. As described in Chapter 1, two classes of models—production systems and connectionist networks—are currently receiving the most attention. We have already described a variety of models from each class in varying degrees of detail as well as numerous models that do not fall within either of these classes. However, because formal models will likely play an ever increasing role in future work on skill, it seems fitting to end the book by focusing directly on issues in modeling.

Formal models are valuable tools because they enable the formulation and testing of exact predictions. In the process of developing models, inadequacies of verbal theoretical accounts may be revealed, and relations may be discovered that would not be apparent otherwise. However, there are also potential drawbacks associated with the use of formal models. For example, discrepancies between a computational model and the theory on which it is based may be introduced inadvertently as additional assumptions are made to implement the model. Perhaps the biggest danger is that too much importance may be placed on models that fit the relevant data but in relatively uninformative ways (Lewandowsky, 1993). As we have done at different times throughout the book, we use the information processing stages of perception, response selection, and response programming and execution as a framework for discussing some models and their implications in more detail. We also include discussion of a skill that is not so easily classified—analogical problem solving.

Modeling Perceptual Skill

Several micromodels of specific aspects of perceptual skill were introduced in Chapter 2, as was a general view of learning and transfer—procedural learning (also discussed as transfer-appropriate processing). The specific models we introduced tended to deal with some restricted subset of relatively basic behavior, such as the integration of perceptual features, rather than capturing more generally the dynamics of skill development, and were not formally developed mathematically or as computer simulations. One exception was Schneider and Detweiler's (1987) connectionist/control architecture, which simulates a shift from controlled to automatic processing in visual search tasks by means of a control structure that comes to be bypassed.

The relative lack of formal models for perceptual learning is somewhat puzzling, since many models have been developed for perceptual tasks such as visual search and word recognition. The most influential of the latter type of model in recent years has been McClelland and Rumelhart's (1981) interactive activation model. This model is an instance of the kind of model shown in Figure 2.7c, in which letter and word units are activated in parallel. It is a local rather than distributed connectionistic model in that each different feature, letter, and word is signaled by the activity of a distinct node rather than by a pattern of activation distributed across the entire network. The key feature of the model is that nodes at the word level send feedback to the letter level for visual stimuli and to the phoneme (i.e., the auditory equivalent of letters) level for auditory stimuli (see Figure 12.1). This additional input to the lower levels by the higher-level word units can increase the perceptibility of letters or phonemes. For bimodal stimuli, interactions can also occur between visual and auditory information through connections between the letter nodes and the phoneme nodes.

McClelland and Rumelhart conducted simulations showing that the model can produce the word superiority effect and the pseudoword superiority effect, both of which were described in Chapter 2, through the influence of the word level on the letter level. However, as with most other models of pattern recognition, McClelland and Rumelhart's model has no learning mechanism and so has not been developed as an account of performance at different skill levels.

Pattern recognition models can be extended to take into account perceptual skill, as demonstrated in a study by Massaro, Cohen, and Gesi (1993). Massaro et al. showed that the **fuzzy logical model of perception** (Massaro, 1987) can account for improvements in bimodal speech perception (i.e., perception of speech when the spoken sound can be heard and the speaker's lip movements seen) as people become practiced at lipreading. In the model, "fuzzy logic" refers to the fact that the logical operations performed to make decisions are based on relative, rather than absolute, truth values regarding the match of stimulus information to stored representations of phonemes. As illustrated in Figure 12.2, multiple sources of information—in this case auditory and visual cues—are evaluated independently of each other to determine the extent to which each source matches each of the possible alternative phonemes represented in memory. These independent evaluations (in the form of "degrees of match") are then combined to provide an overall degree of support for each alternative representation. The overall value in favor of each possible alternative is then evaluated relative to the evidence in favor of every other alternative, and the response alternative with the best evaluation is selected. Thus, in this model, unlike the interactive activation model, independent sources of information contribute to perception as a function of their information values. That is, sources of information do not influence each other (e.g., visual information does not increase the value of auditory information); rather, the independent sources are summed.

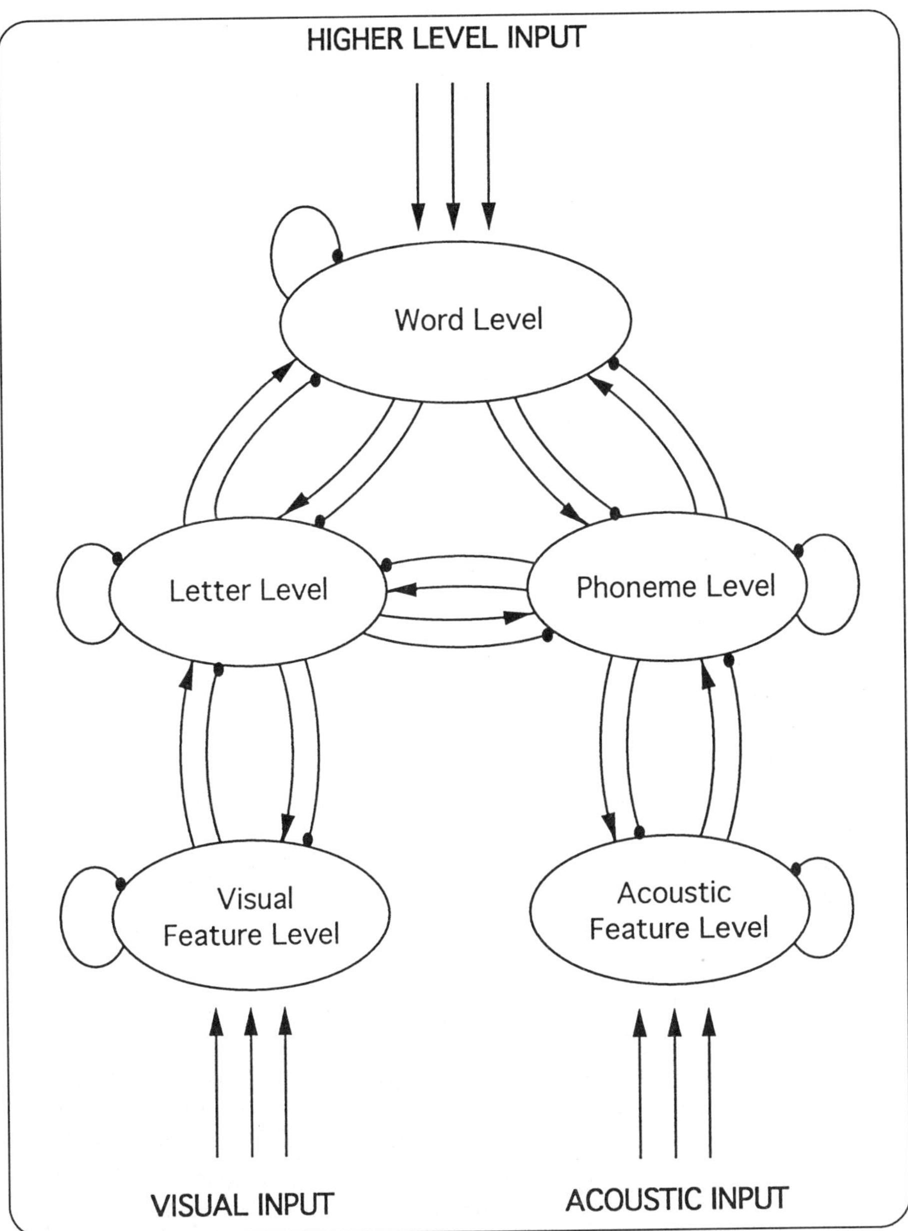

Figure 12.1. The interactive-activation model. Arrows indicate excitatory connections, and circles indicate inhibitory connections. The links from each level back to that level indicate that items within each level are inhibitory with respect to each other.
SOURCE: From McClelland and Rumelhart (1981).

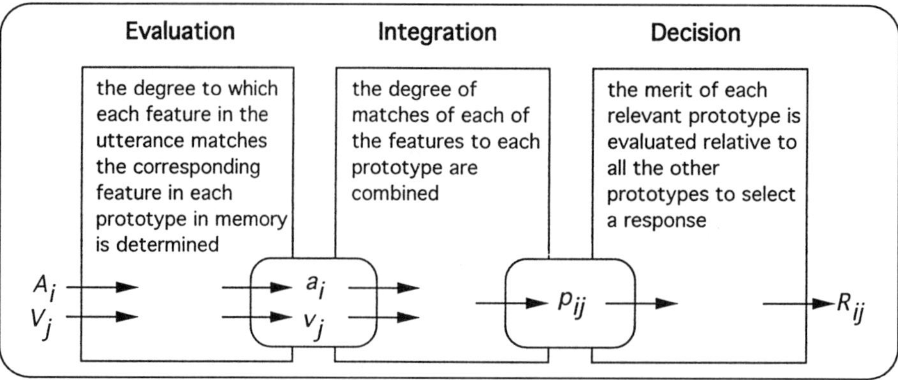

Figure 12.2. Schematic representation of the three operations of the fuzzy logical model of perception.

There are numerous demonstrations that the visual information provided by a speaker's lip movements contributes to speech perception and influences what is perceived. According to the fuzzy logical model, if lipreading can be taught, the information value of the visual information should increase with training at lipreading and so should contribute more to the overall evaluation of response alternatives even when both visual and auditory information are present. To test this prediction, Massaro et al. (1993) provided participants with training at lipreading and assessed both unimodal and bimodal speech perception at several points during training. Lipreading performance improved over practice for judgments involving syllables, words, and sentences. As with most other skills, this improvement in lipreading performance was retained well, with little loss between the last test of the initial training session and a retention session conducted 7.5 weeks later.

The fuzzy logical model was fit to the confusion matrixes (i.e., matrixes showing how often particular stimuli were misidentified as others) obtained for unimodal and bimodal speech perception, and the fit of the model was compared to that of the **prelabeling integration model** (Braida, 1991). In the prelabeling integration model, the bimodal information is integrated without the information from each modality first being evaluated separately. The fuzzy logical model was found to provide a fit to the matrixes that was both good in an absolute sense and better than that of the prelabeling integration model. As predicted, the contribution of the visual information to bimodal speech perception increased with practice at lipreading, and the fuzzy logical model accounted well for the joint improvement in unimodal and bimodal speech perception. If the assumption of the interactive activation model that cross talk occurs between auditory and visual sources of information were correct—such that the contribution of visual information alone would not equal the effect of the same visual information when auditory information is also present—it is not likely that the fuzzy logical model, which assumes independence, would have provided a good fit to the confusion matrixes.

This study thus used modeling to test a fundamental assumption about how bimodal information sources are evaluated while addressing how processing might change as skill is acquired. As Massaro et al. (1993) emphasize, without quantitative models of the type that they evaluated, it would be difficult to address the question of how bimodal speech perception is influenced by improved skill at lipreading.

Modeling Response Selection Skill

Relatively more models of the nature and mechanisms of changes with practice have been developed for response selection, as introduced in Chapter 3. Models of response selection skill range from the very specific (e.g., adjustment of speed-accuracy trade-off setting; Rabbitt & Vyas, 1970) to more general descriptions of possible changes (e.g., transitory speedup or bypassing of response selection when stimuli or responses are repeated from one trial to the next; Pashler & Baylis, 1991b). Perhaps the most notable development in the modeling of response selection skill is Rosenbloom and Newell's (1987) work on stimulus-response compatibility and practice. As discussed in Chapter 3, Rosenbloom and Newell developed a production-system model of stimulus-response compatibility from which they were able to generate the relative compatibility of particular stimulus-response mappings across a variety of tasks, as well as changes in the speed of response selection that occur with practice as the productions for performing a task are chunked.

A different approach was taken by Cohen, Dunbar, and McClelland (1990), who developed a local connectionist model to explain the Stroop effect (described in Chapter 5) and related phenomena. The model, shown in Figure 12.3, has two independent pathways for the processing of Stroop color stimuli: one for word information and the other for color information. Each possible stimulus color and color word is represented by an input unit, and the input units in the respective pathways are each connected to hidden units, which in turn are connected to the shared response

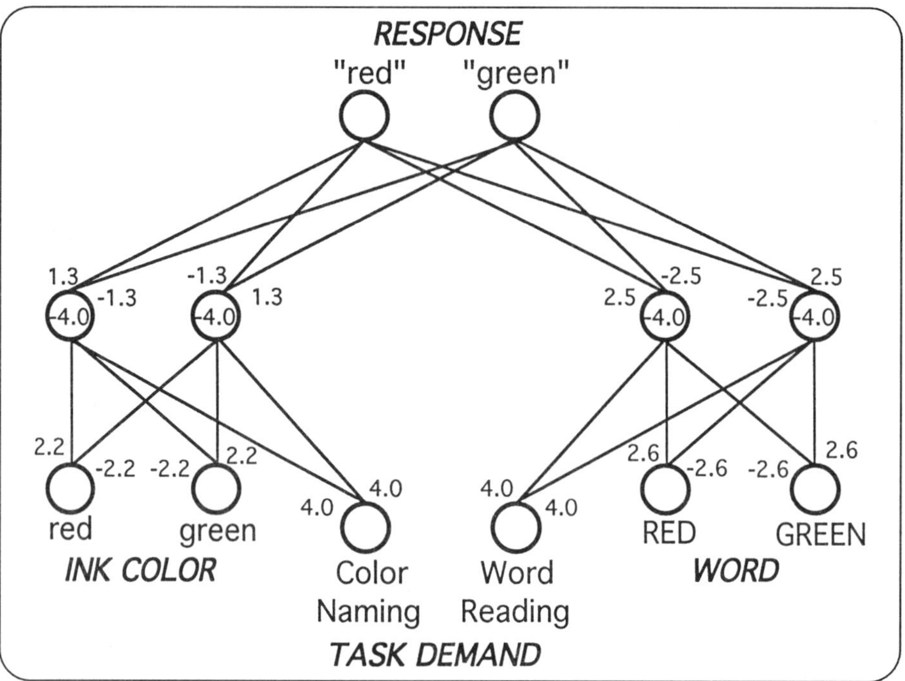

Figure 12.3. Diagram of network used to simulate performance in the Stroop task. The connection weights are those acquired after training on the word-reading and color-naming tasks, except for the weights on connections between the task demand and hidden units, which are set by the experimenter.
SOURCE: From Cohen, Dunbar, and McClelland (1990).

units. Separate task demand units, corresponding to the intention to name colors or words, are used to allocate attention to one or the other pathway. Activation of the appropriate task demand unit (e.g., color naming) adjusts the resting levels of activation of the units in the two pathways, setting the task-appropriate units (e.g., those in the ink color pathway for the color-naming task) at a higher resting level than the inappropriate units (e.g., the units in the word pathway). As discussed below, this adjustment makes the appropriate units more responsive to stimulus input.

The growth of activation in the network in response to a stimulus is characterized by a cascade process: Input is presented as a pattern of activation at the input nodes, and this activation propagates through the system, with the activation of each node being a running average of its net input over time. This process continues until a response unit reaches a

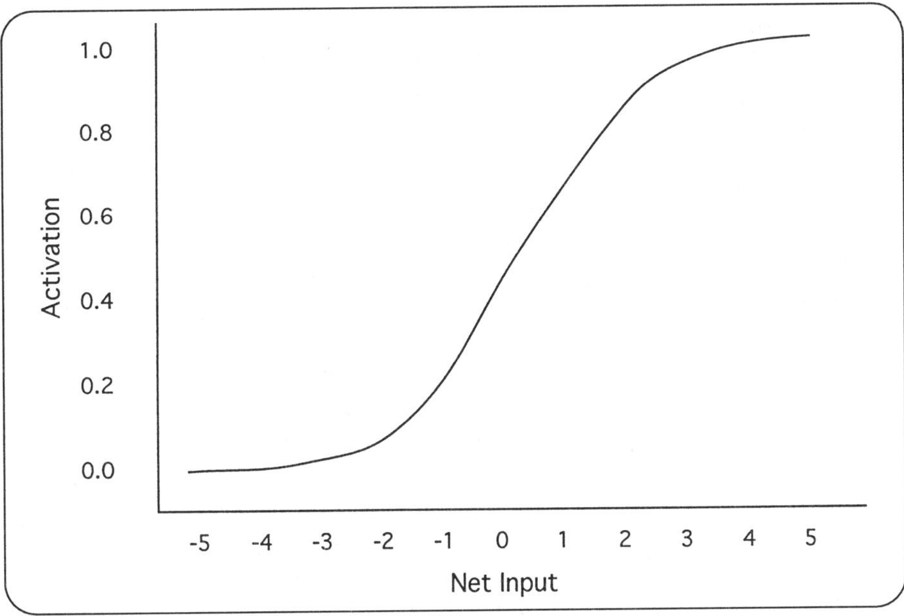

Figure 12.4. The relation between net input and activation in the Cohen, Dunbar, and McClelland (1990) model.

threshold level of activation and the response is executed. A logistic, sigmoid activation function (see Figure 12.4), in which the units are more responsive when they are in the middle, more linear part of their dynamic ranges rather than at either extreme of activation, is used. One consequence of this function is that the task demand unit not only increases the resting level activations for the units in the task-appropriate pathway but also puts them into a more responsive state.

This network, unlike that of McClelland and Rumelhart's (1981) interactive activation model, described previously, has no interactions between pathways or feedback from higher-level nodes onto lower-level nodes. Moreover, the network has the capacity to learn through the backpropagation learning algorithm, in which the connection strengths are adjusted incrementally after each trial, with the sizes of the changes made being proportional to the difference between the output pattern produced by the network and that desired in response to the input pattern. The changes will be larger early in learning than later because as the output pattern becomes closer to that desired, due to an appropriate set of connection strengths being developed, the computed difference between the target and output patterns will be smaller. Moreover, as the units approach the target positive or negative values, they enter less responsive regions on the activation function.

Cohen, Dunbar, and McClelland (1990) showed, through simulations of word reading alone (i.e., input was provided only to the word pathway), that the network generates the power-law relation between reaction time and practice that has become a benchmark test for models intended to account for skill acquisition. To simulate the basic Stroop effect, the network was first trained with color stimuli paired with the color-naming task demand unit and, separately, with word stimuli paired with the word reading task demand unit. More training was given on words than on colors to reflect the fact that word reading is more highly practiced than color naming. The trained network simulated many characteristics of the mean reaction times for conditions in the Stroop task, including that (a) irrelevant color words interfere with color naming but irrelevant ink colors do not interfere with word reading even when the color is presented several hundred milliseconds before the word, and (b) the interference that occurs when the word conflicts with the to-be-named color is much larger than is the facilitation that occurs when the word and color are congruent.[1]

In Cohen, Dunbar, and McClelland's (1990) model, automaticity is not all-or-none but is a function of the relative strengths of the competing pathways. This property enabled the network to account for the fact that color naming, which is not regarded as automatic in the typical Stroop task, appears to be so when novel forms are used instead of words (MacLeod & Dunbar, 1988). That is, responding to novel forms with assigned color names shows interference from incongruent ink colors, but naming the ink colors shows no interference from incongruent forms. This outcome was simulated in the model by adding a new pathway for shape naming that received no training prior to the Stroop simulation. Because the connections in the color-naming pathway were stronger initially than those in the shape-naming pathway, incongruent ink colors interfered with shape naming. The model also accounted for the fact that this pattern of interference reverses after the shape-naming task has been practiced extensively (MacLeod & Dunbar, 1988). Practice at shape naming increases the strengths of the connection weights for the shape-naming pathway, with the pattern of interference reversing when the weights for that pathway exceed those for the color-naming pathway.

At present, there is disagreement as to whether rule-based models or network models are more appropriate for characterizing response selection skill. This disagreement is apparent even among proponents of production rule models for higher-level cognition. For example, Newell (1990) places emphasis on the fact that *Soar*, which was developed for learning and performance in problem-solving tasks, has been extended to the domain of response selection processes that take place within less than 1 second after stimulus presentation. In contrast, Anderson (1993) notes that the time per production in his most recent version of ACT theory, ACT-R, is typically longer than 1 s and concludes that response selection "is a level of processing that is best modeled in nonsymbolic terms," with the processes having "ultimately connectionistic implementations" (p. 119).

Modeling Motor Skill

Disagreement about the best way to model skilled behavior is nowhere more apparent than in the area of motor control and learning. A number of very distinct models have been proposed, often based on different fundamental assumptions. In Chapter 4, we discussed the motor programming perspective, which describes growth in motor skill in terms of the development of parameterized motor programs and of schemas that specify the parameter values for the programs, as well as the dynamical perspective, which describes skill in terms of the interactions between characteristics of the physical system (the body) and behavioral information (task instructions and environmental constraints). Attempts have been made to integrate the two perspectives, however, as in the work of Jordan (1990, 1992; Jordan & Rosenbaum, 1989) that has addressed two of the fundamental problems in motor learning: the serial order and degrees of freedom problems.

As discussed in Chapter 4, the serial order problem concerns how series of actions can be learned and executed smoothly and efficiently. One aspect of this problem is how the context in which a movement is performed (i.e., the sequence in which it is produced) affects the execution of that movement (Jordan & Rosenbaum, 1989). For example, it is clear that we cannot pronounce the words "free" and "Ontario" at the same time. But what happens when the word "Ontario" is pronounced after the word "free" rather than in some other context? In this case, the muscular movements that allow the pronunciation of the nasal */n/* begin during the pronunciation of the */i/* in "free." Such **coarticulation** illustrates the integration of different actions across time and reflects the context sensitivity of pronunciation. Essentially, the serial order problem is one of satisfying temporal constraints regarding how a movement is integrated with other movements to be produced in the same sequence. Thus the problem regards the relationships between outputs produced at different points in time. The major constraint on the movements is that actions produced close together in time be produced in nonconflicting ways. In other words, actions should blend together smoothly while still satisfying the configural constraint that the appropriate actions be performed.

The degrees of freedom problem is one of selecting just a single manner of performing an action from an infinite number of possible ways. Both the generalized motor program and the dynamical systems perspectives have provisions to account for the solving of the degrees of freedom problem. The motor programs and associated schemas postulated in the generalized motor programming approach reduce the degrees of freedom for a given action by providing, in effect, a template for the action. The dynamical systems approach, with its emphasis on the interaction between biomechanical and environmental variables, uses the constraint that behavior should be characterized by stability and efficiency. Characteristics of both of these approaches can be found in Jordan's (1990) "dynamical systems approach to describing the flow through parameter space" (p. 797), in which motor programs are learned dynamically and used to guide movement selection.

Solving the Serial Order Problem

Models of serial ordering that account for context sensitivity are of two major types: **symbolic hierarchical** and **parallel activation.** Examples of hierarchical models were discussed in both Chapters 4 (Povel & Collard, 1982) and 6 (Cohen, Ivry, & Keele, 1990), and one parallel model of sequencing, Rumelhart and Norman's (1982) typing model, was described in Chapter 8. Jordan's (1990) model of sequential control is a parallel activation connectionist network capable of learning and executing sequences of actions.

In the network, illustrated in Figure 12.5, an action is represented as a pattern of activation across the output units. The learning of sequences of actions is reflected in changes in the weights between the layers of the network. The model shown in Figure 12.5 has three layers of units—input, hidden, and output—with the input units divided into two types: **plan**

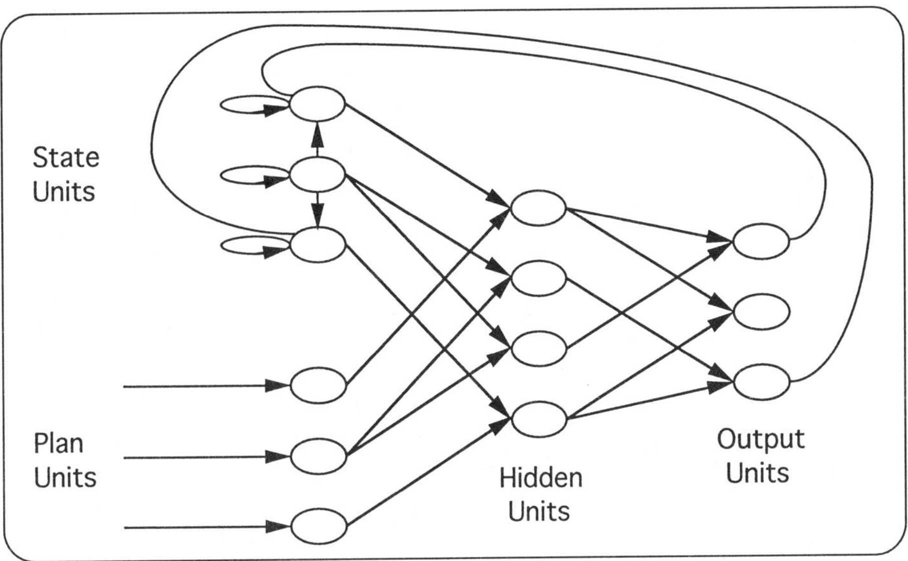

Figure 12.5. The basic architecture of Jordan's (1990) sequential network. During learning, the desired activations of the output units are fed back to the state units. During performance, the actual activations are fed back.

and **state**. The plan units encode the external input to the network, that is, the specification of the movement sequence that is to be performed. Input to the plan units remains constant throughout the execution of the specified movement sequence. The state units also contribute input to the network, but this input varies in time due to the presence of **recurrent connections** from the output units back to the state units and from each state unit back to itself. The recurrent connections provide a time-varying input to the network and allow temporal constraints to be dealt with by comparing values of the output units across time.

During the learning of a movement sequence, the desired activations of the output units are fed back to the state units, whereas the actual activations of the output units are fed back during performance of the sequence. Learning occurs as the backpropagation algorithm is applied to the differences between the desired outcome specified by the plan units and the actual outcome (i.e., the current activation of the output units). Sequential constraints are learned by comparing the activations of the output units on the previous trial with the activations on the current trial.

This difference represents the distance between effector positions at the two time points and thus the minimization of this difference ensures a smooth transition between successive movements.

Solving the Degrees of Freedom Problem

In Jordan's (1990) network model, learning is treated as the solution of an optimization problem in which some function, such as the difference between desired and actual movement outcomes, is minimized. This minimization requirement acts as a constraint that allows the system to select an efficient means of performing an action. The solution of the degrees of freedom problem thus depends on the ability to make predictions. To do this, a so-called **forward model** that allows a particular output to be predicted from the current input is required. In Jordan's network, the forward model is a learned internal mapping that allows prediction of the movement outcome expected to obtain for a given motor program output in the current environmental state. Interestingly, the forward model that allows the prediction of output from input conditions is the key to solving the inverse problem of selecting the appropriate input (i.e., particular movements) to achieve the desired output.

As can be seen in Figure 12.6, the network that incorporates the forward model has two auxiliary layers in addition to those for the network described previously. One of these layers is another layer of hidden units, but the other layer contains what are called **task units.** The task units represent movement outcomes, whereas the output (articulatory) units represent the signals to the effectors (i.e., the motor output).

There are three key components of the framework:

1. A vector, z, which is a function of the environmental state and the motor program output (which is in turn a function of the internal state of the performer, a plan, and a set of structural parameters that describe the current configuration of the motor program)
2. A cost functional that is the weighted sum of squares of the difference between the desired result, z^*, and the actual result, z
3. A learning rule that finds the set of parameters that will minimize the cost functional.

In this network, the learning rule for the forward model is based on a function that relates small changes in the motor output to small changes in the task space (i.e., the vector space in which environmental specifica-

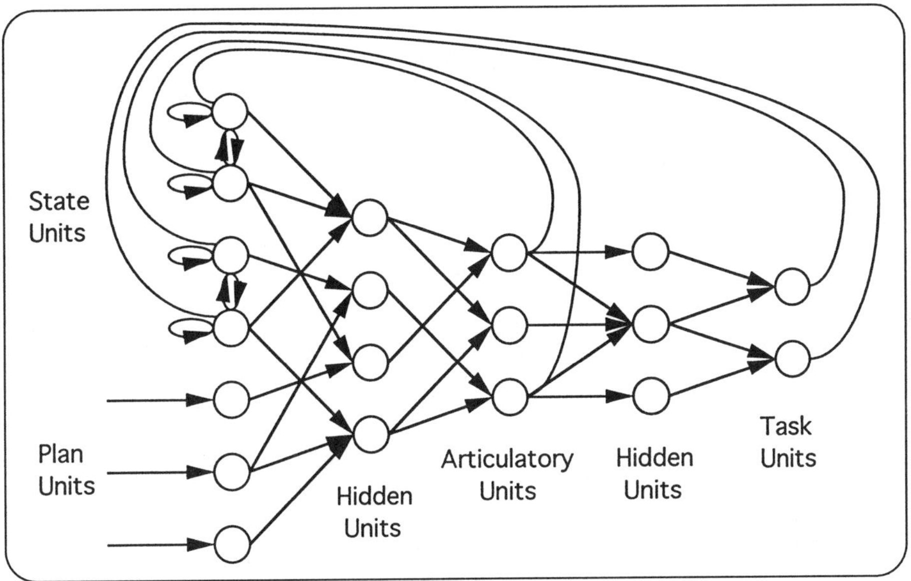

Figure 12.6. The sequential network conjoined with an auxiliary network. The articulatory units are the output units of the network.

tions of tasks are given to the learner). The top half of Figure 12.7 illustrates how the forward model is acquired.

An important aspect of this approach is that the learning operator can work even when there are excess degrees of freedom. As with other approaches to the degrees of freedom problem (e.g., Morasso, 1981), Jordan's (1990) approach depends on the specification of constraints on the movements to be selected. What are the constraints that affect how skill is acquired? Jordan and others have described two types of constraints. **Task constraints** are the minimal constraints, such as timing or trajectory requirements, that must be provided by the environment, whereas **intrinsic constraints** refer to the dynamic characteristics of movement control. The most germane of the intrinsic constraints are those that reflect the principle of optimization, as they are clearly related to the cost functional. These constraints include **smoothness,** which implies that targets nearby in time should be achieved with similar articulatory configurations (as discussed for the serial order problem); **distinctiveness,** which states that actions be distinct so that they can be easily interpreted; and **rest configuration,** which corresponds to associating a greater cost to articulatory

Modeling

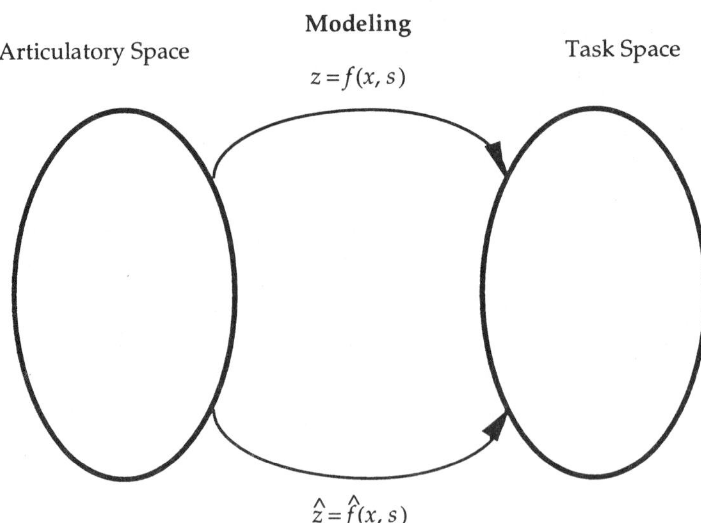

The relationship between the environment and the forward model: The model is adjusted on the basis of the discrepancy between the actual result z and the predicted $\hat{z}$.

Optimization

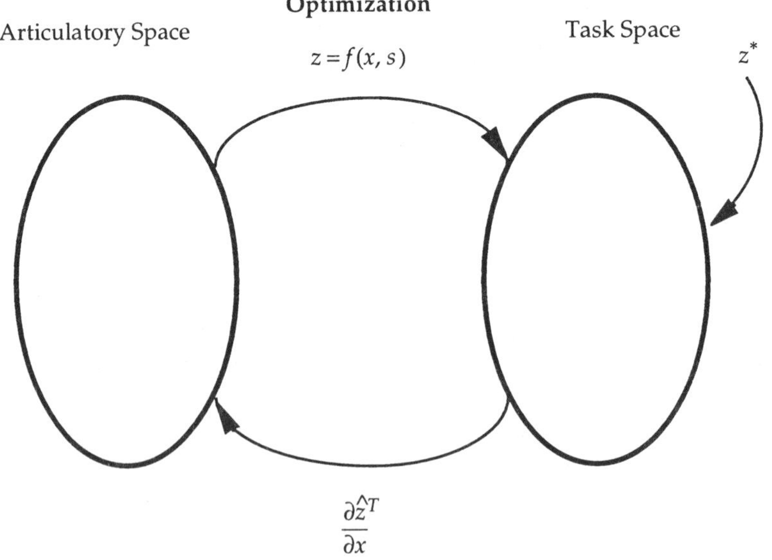

The learning of the motor program: The discrepancy between the desired result **z*** *and the actual result z is transformed by the learning operator, $\partial\hat{z}/\partial x$, obtained by differentiating the forward model.*

Figure 12.7. The transformations proposed by the forward modeling approach. For Modeling, the top arrow represents the transformation performed by the environment and the bottom arrow represents the internal forward model; for Optimization, the top arrow represents the transformation performed by the environment and the bottom arrow represents the internal learning operator.

configurations that deviate from configurations that the system adopts when at rest. All of these constraints contribute terms to the cost functional.

Once an accurate forward model is discovered that relates motor output in the articulatory space (the vector space of all possible control signals to the effectors) to the movement outcome in the task space, its derivatives provide a learning operator that allows the system to use task space error to determine errors in the articulatory space and thereby to change the motor program. The bottom half of Figure 12.7 illustrates this optimization process. The same learning algorithm used to learn the forward model is used to take into account the various constraints on the motor program by transforming the task space error vector backward from the task units to the articulatory units. This propagation of the error vector continues back from the articulatory units to the state units, which represent the motor program. If no constraints exist to guide the system, that is, if learning is unsupervised, the forward model is learned by random exploration of the parameter space. However, as implied by the optimization process illustrated in Figure 12.7, the forward model must be at least partially learned before the motor program can be learned.

Jordan's work provides an illustration of how modeling techniques can provide insight into fundamental issues of motor control and learning. In this case, elements of the seemingly disparate viewpoints of the motor programming and dynamical perspectives are combined in a coherent approach to motor skill. Moreover, because supervised learning algorithms such as backpropagation are widely used in connectionist models applied to a range of psychological problems, his work makes the more general contribution of showing how problems associated with the "teacher" in supervised learning may be solved with learned internal models of the environment (Jordan & Rumelhart, 1992).

Modeling Problem-Solving Skill

Problem solving and other higher-level cognitive processes, such as text comprehension, have been explained virtually exclusively in terms of production systems and other forms of models based on symbolic representation. These models reflect two relatively distinct generations of thought on problem-solving skill (Holyoak, 1991). The first generation, characterized by the work of Newell and Simon (1972) described in Chapter 7, was based on the problem space representation and general methods for heuristic search of the problem space. Expert problem solving was thought to reflect primarily the use of more efficient search heuristics. The second generation involved production system models, such as those of Anderson (1983) and Newell (1990) and his colleagues, that rely heavily on the knowledge of the problem solver and include mechanisms for acquiring that knowledge.

Models of problem solving and reasoning have been primarily symbolic because the fundamental characteristics of thought seem to require relational knowledge that is not implemented readily within connectionist models. For example, the proposition "Scott hit Matt" requires not only that the constituents (i.e., Scott and Matt) be activated but also that their roles be represented and assigned to the appropriate individuals.

Although connectionist models seem to be unable to adequately capture the phenomena of higher-level thought, they have certain appealing properties. One such property is **soft constraint satisfaction.** Specifically, connectionist models can generate a stable global pattern of activity as a consequence of several, sometimes conflicting constraints operating in parallel. The fact that symbolic representation seems necessary but that connectionist models have some appealing properties has led some researchers to develop **symbolic connectionist** models that combine the properties of the two. Such hybrid models possibly signal the beginning of a third generation of models for problem solving and expertise (Holyoak, 1991). The basic idea behind symbolic connectionist models is that the units do not have to be restricted to subsymbolic "microfeatures" but can represent complex, symbolic information. The symbolic information represented by the units can be connected in networks that allow this information to be processed in the manner of connectionist models.

An example of a symbolic connectionist model is one developed by Holyoak and Thagard (1989) for mapping the elements of a source analog onto a target analog, one of the basic processes in the use of analogies (see Chapter 7). The target and source analogs are input to the model, called ACME (*A*nalogical *C*onstraint *M*apping *E*ngine), in structural descriptions consisting of objects (e.g., Iraq, Kuwait), predicates (e.g., attack), and propositions that bind predicates to arguments (e.g., Iraq attacked Kuwait). The model then generates a network of units that represent possible mappings between the elements of the analogs (see Figure 12.8). Information pertinent to three constraints is built into the network. The first is a **structural constraint** that mappings should be one-to-one and structurally consistent (i.e., if a target proposition maps to a specific source proposition, then the objects and predicates should also match). This constraint is implemented by establishing excitatory connections among elements of

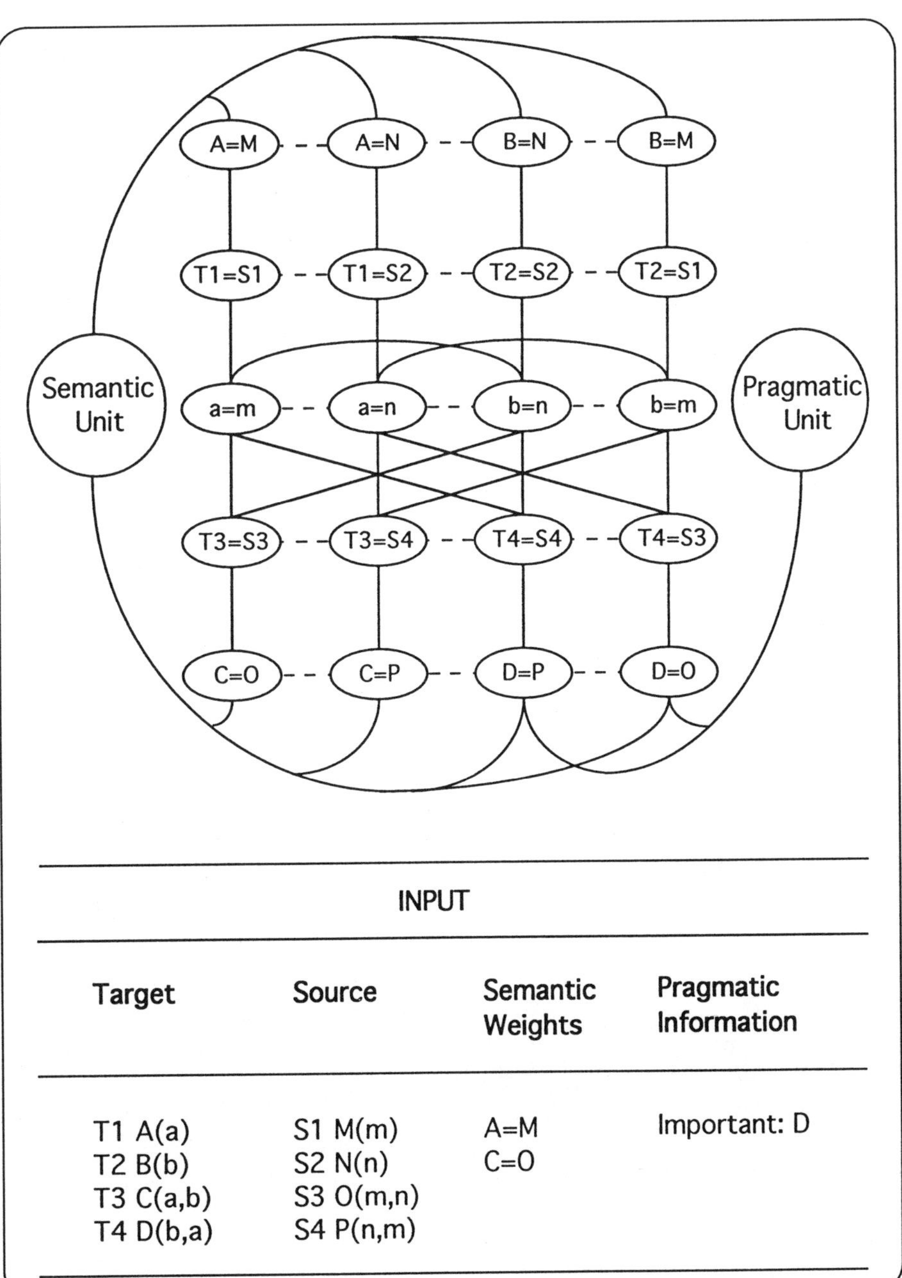

INPUT

Target	Source	Semantic Weights	Pragmatic Information
T1 A(a)	S1 M(m)	A=M	Important: D
T2 B(b)	S2 N(n)	C=O	
T3 C(a,b)	S3 O(m,n)		
T4 D(b,a)	S4 P(n,m)		

Figure 12.8. The network produced by the ACME model of analogical mapping. The numbered capital letters indicate target (T) or source (S) propositions (i.e., the subject matter of the analog fragment), unnumbered capital letters represent predicates (i.e., whatever is stated about the subject of the proposition), and lowercase letters represent objects. Excitatory connections are shown by solid lines and inhibitory connections by dotted lines.

the proposition, whereas all units that represent alternative mappings of the same element have inhibitory connections.

The remaining two constraints, **semantic similarity** (a preference for mappings of predicates with similar or identical meanings) and **pragmatic centrality** (a preference for correspondences that are pragmatically important to the problem solver) are represented respectively by two special units, the **semantic unit** and the **pragmatic unit.** Excitatory connections are placed between the semantic unit and all units that represent mappings between predicates, with the weights being proportional to the degree of semantic similarity between the mapped concepts. Connections of the pragmatic unit to the mapping units are determined in the same manner, only with the weights reflecting relative pragmatic importance to the problem solver.

A cooperative algorithm that allows parallel satisfaction of the three interacting constraints is then applied, and the network is allowed to settle into a stable state. The asymptotic activations of units reflect the degree of confidence in the possible mappings. Holyoak and Thagard (1989) demonstrated that the ACME model provides a good account of several phenomena regarding mapping of analogies, including those associated with convergence analogies of the type described in Chapter 7.

In one test of ACME, the model was applied to the analogical relation between the 1991 Persian Gulf War and World War II. Spellman and Holyoak (1992) showed that the roles constructed for the participants in these wars followed the structural constraint embodied in ACME. Namely, most people who mapped the United States in 1991 to the United States in World War II also mapped George Bush to Franklin D. Roosevelt, whereas most people who mapped the United States in 1991 to Great Britain in World War II mapped George Bush to Winston Churchill. These structurally consistent mappings were produced even when "histories" biased toward inconsistent, crossed mappings were presented, and simulations produced by ACME fit the data well.

The hybrid nature of ACME gives it the capability of simulating a broader range of data regarding human analogical mapping than is typical for either symbolic or connectionist models. It can simulate the mapping of relatively complex, naturalistic target and source scenarios, which typically create difficulty for symbolic models, and of simpler, artificial scenarios, which are not treated readily within connectionist models. Similar successful applications of a symbolic connectionist model to text comprehension (Kintsch, 1988) and levels of expertise in planning computing tasks (Mannes & Kintsch, 1991) suggest that much future modeling of higher-level cognition will involve integration of the symbolic and connectionist paradigms.

Role of Modeling in Theory Development

It should be clear from our discussion of models in the respective areas covered in this book that there is little agreement as to which type of modeling is best. In the areas of perception, response selection, and response preparation and execution, symbolic models—often in the form of production systems—can be found as well as connectionist models. Even in problem solving, which has long been the province of production systems and other symbolic models, models that incorporate network properties have been used with some success.

The debate about the relative merits of alternative approaches to modeling is one that is ongoing and for which no resolution is in sight (see, e.g., Massaro, 1988, and McCloskey, 1991, for relatively negative views regarding connectionist models and McClelland, 1988, and Seidenberg, 1993, for relatively positive views). In this book, then, we have not advocated one type of model over another but discussed models of any type that seemed to provide insight into issues pertaining to skill. The fundamental point is that, when used judiciously, models provide powerful tools that aid in our understanding of cognition in general and skill in particular.

Concluding Remarks

These are exciting times for researchers interested in skill. Although skill has been investigated systematically since the latter part of the 19th century, recent developments in research methodologies, conceptual systems, and modeling techniques have produced a rapid growth of new findings and a better understanding of the nature of skill acquisition and skilled performance. It has been our intent to convey this excitement and the recent advances in skills research by providing a coherent overview of several distinct areas of research.

We hope that you have learned how researchers go about investigating skilled behavior and that we have convinced you that an integrated approach to understanding skill is not only feasible but also necessary. While there is still much to be learned about skilled performance, the progress made to date is quite substantial.

NOTE

1. Although the model predicts the correct mean response times for these conditions, the distributions of response times that are predicted for the different conditions are not the same as those observed in human data (Mewhort, Braun, & Heathcote, 1992).

References

Aasman, J., & Michon, J. A. (1992). Multitasking in driving. In J. A. Michon & A. Akyurek (Eds.), *Soar: A cognitive architecture in perspective* (pp. 169-198). Dordrecht: Kluwer.

Abrams, R. A., & Pratt, J. (1993). Rapid aimed limb movements: Differential effects of practice on component submovements. *Journal of Motor Behavior, 25,* 288-298.

Ackerman, P. L. (1987). Individual differences in skill learning: An integration of psychometric and information processing perspectives. *Psychological Bulletin, 10,* 3-27.

Ackerman, P. L. (1988). Components of individual differences during skill acquisition: Cognitive abilities and information processing. *Journal of Experimental Psychology: General, 117,* 288-318.

Ackerman, P. L. (1992). Predicting individual differences in complex skill acquisition: Dynamics of ability determinants. *Journal of Applied Psychology, 77,* 598-614.

Ackerman, P. L., & Kyllonen, P. C. (1991). Trainee characteristics. In J. E. Morrison (Ed.), *Training for performance: Principles of applied human learning* (pp. 193-229). London: Wiley.

Adams, J. A. (1953). *The prediction of performance at advanced stages of training on a complex psychomotor task* (Res. Bull. No. 53-49). Lackland Air Force Base, TX: Perceptual and Motor Skills Research Laboratory, Human Resources Research Center.

Adams, J. A. (1960). Part trainers. In G. Finsh (Ed.), *Educational and training media: A symposium* (Publication No. 789). Washington, DC: National

Academy of Science, National Research Council.

Adams, J. A. (1987). Historical review and appraisal of research on the learning, retention, and transfer of human motor skills. *Psychological Bulletin, 101,* 41-74.

Adams, M. J. (1990). *Beginning to read: Thinking and learning about print.* Cambridge: MIT Press.

Adamson, R. E., & Taylor, D. W. (1954). Functional fixedness as related to elapsed time and to set. *Journal of Experimental Psychology, 47,* 122-126.

Adelson, B. (1981). Problem solving and the development of abstract categories in programming languages. *Memory & Cognition, 9,* 422-433.

Ahlum-Heath, M. E., & Di Vesta, F. J. (1986). The effect of conscious controlled verbalization of a cognitive strategy on transfer in problem solving. *Memory & Cognition, 14,* 281-285.

Allport, D. A., Antonis, B., & Reynolds, P. (1972). On the division of attention: A disproof of the single channel hypothesis. *Quarterly Journal of Experimental Psychology, 24,* 225-235.

Allport, D. A., & Styles, E. A. (1990). *Multiple executive functions, multiple resources? Experiments in shifting attentional control of tasks.* Unpublished manuscript, University of Oxford.

Alluisi, E. A., & Muller, P. F., Jr. (1958). Verbal and motor responses to seven symbolic visual codes: A study in S-R compatibility. *Journal of Experimental Psychology, 55,* 247-254.

Alm, H., & Brehmer, B. (1982). Hypotheses about cue-criterion relations in linear and random inference tasks. *Umeå Psychological Reports,* No. 164, 1-20.

Anderson, J. A., & Rosenfeld, E. (Eds.). (1988). *Neurocomputing: Foundations of research.* Cambridge: MIT Press.

Anderson, J. R. (1982). Acquisition of cognitive skill. *Psychological Review, 89,* 369-406.

Anderson, J. R. (1983). *The architecture of cognition.* Cambridge, MA: Harvard University Press.

Anderson, J. R. (1987). Skill acquisition: Compilation of weak-method problem solutions. *Psychological Review, 94,* 192-210.

Anderson, J. R. (1989). Practice, working memory, and the ACT* theory of skill acquisition: A comment on Carlson, Sullivan, and Schneider (1989). *Journal of Experimental Psychology: Learning, Memory, and Cognition, 15,* 527-530.

Anderson, J. R. (1993). *Rules of the mind.* Hillsdale, NJ: Lawrence Erlbaum.

Anderson, J. R., Farrell, R., & Sauers, R. (1984). Learning to program in LISP. *Cognitive Science, 8,* 87-129.

Anderson, K. J., Revelle, W., & Lynch, M. J. (1989). Caffeine, impulsivity, and memory scanning: A comparison of two explanations for the Yerkes-Dodson effect. *Motivation and Emotion, 13,* 1-20.

Annett, J. (1991). Skill acquisition. In J. E. Morrison (Ed.), *Training for performance: Principles of applied human learning* (pp. 13-51). New York: John Wiley.

Anzai, Y. (1987). Doing, understanding, and learning in problem solving. In D. Klahr, P. Langley, & R. Neches (Eds.), *Production system models of learning and development* (pp. 55-97). Cambridge: MIT Press.

Anzola, G. P., Bertoloni, G., Buchtel, H. A., & Rizzolatti, G. (1977). Spatial compatibility and anatomical factors in simple and choice reaction time. *Neuropsychologia, 15,* 295-302.

Aschoff, J. (1954). Zeitgeber der tierischen tagesperiodik [Zeitgeber of animals' daily periodicity]. *Naturwissenshaft, 41,* 40-56.

Ash, D. W., & Holding, D. H. (1990). Backward versus forward chaining in the acquisition of a keyboard skill. *Human Factors, 32,* 139-146.

Atwood, M. E., & Polson, P. G. (1976). A process model for water jug problems. *Cognitive Psychology, 8,* 191-216.

Bacon, S. J. (1974). Arousal and the range of cue utilization. *Journal of Experimental Psychology, 102,* 81-87.

Bahrick, H. P., Fitts, P. M., & Rankin, R. E. (1952). Effect of incentives upon reactions to peripheral stimuli. *Journal of Experimental Psychology, 44,* 400-406.

Baker, W. J., & Theologus, G. C. (1972). Effects of caffeine on visual monitoring. *Journal of Applied Psychology, 56,* 422-427.

Barfield, W. (1986). Expert-novice differences for software: Implications for problem-solving and knowledge acquisition. *Behaviour and Information Technology, 5,* 15-29.

Barnett, B. J., & Wickens, C. D. (1988). Display proximity in multicue information integration: The benefits of boxes. *Human Factors, 30,* 15-24.

Baron, J., & Thurston, I. (1973). An analysis of the word superiority effect. *Cognitive Psychology, 4,* 207-228.

Bartlett, F. (1958). *Thinking: An experimental and social study.* New York: Basic Books.

Battig, W. F. (1979). The flexibility of human memory. In L. S. Cermak & F.I.M. Craik (Eds.), *Levels of processing in human memory* (pp. 23-44). Hillsdale, NJ: Lawrence Erlbaum.

Baudhuin, E. S. (1987). The design of industrial and flight simulators. In S. M. Cormier & J. D. Hagman (Eds.), *Transfer of learning: Contemporary research and applications* (pp. 217-237). San Diego: Academic Press.

Bennett, K. B., & Flach, J. M. (1992). Graphical displays: Implications for divided attention, focused attention, and problem solving. *Human Factors, 34,* 513-533.

Bernstein, I. H., Chu, P. K., Briggs, P., & Schurman, D. L. (1973). Stimulus intensity and foreperiod effects in intersensory facilitation. *Quarterly Journal of Experimental Psychology, 25,* 171-181.

Bernstein, N. (1967). *The coordination and regulation of movements.* New York: Pergamon.

Berry, D. C. (1991). The role of action in implicit learning. *Quarterly Journal of Experimental Psychology, 43A,* 881-906.

Berry, D. C., & Broadbent, D. E. (1984). On the relationship between task performance and associated verbalizable knowledge. *Quarterly Journal of Experimental Psychology, 36A,* 209-231.

Berry, D. C., & Broadbent, D. E. (1988). Interactive tasks and the implicit-explicit distinction. *British Journal of Psychology, 79,* 251-272.

Berry, D. C., & Dienes, Z. (1991). The relationship between implicit memory and implicit learning. *British Journal of Psychology, 82,* 359-373.

Bertelson, P. (1963). S-R relationships and reaction times to new versus repeated signals in a serial task. *Journal of Experimental Psychology, 65*, 478-484.

Bertelson, P. (1967). The time course of preparation. *Quarterly Journal of Experimental Psychology, 19*, 272-279.

Bethell-Fox, C. E., & Shepard, R. N. (1988). Mental rotation: Effects of stimulus complexity and familiarity. *Journal of Experimental Psychology: Human Perception and Performance, 14*, 12-23.

Biederman, I., & Shiffrar, M. M. (1987). Sexing day-old chicks: A case study and expert systems analysis of a difficult perceptual-learning task. *Journal of Experimental Psychology: Learning, Memory, and Cognition, 13*, 640-645.

Bills, A. G. (1931). A new principle of mental fatigue. *American Journal of Psychology, 43*, 230-245.

Binet, A., & Henri, V. (1896). La psychologie individuelle. *L'Anee Psychologique*, 2(81), 411-463.

Bizzi, E., & Mussa-Ivaldi, F. A. (1989). Geometrical and mechanical issues in movement planning and control. In M. I. Posner (Ed.), *Foundations of cognitive science* (pp. 769-792). Cambridge: MIT Press.

Blaxton, T. A. (1989). Investigating dissociations among memory measures: Support for a transfer-appropriate processing framework. *Journal of Experimental Psychology: Learning, Memory, and Cognition, 15*, 657-668.

Bloom, B. S. (1985). Generalizations about talent development. In B. S. Bloom (Ed.), *Developing talent in young people* (pp. 507-549). New York: Ballantine.

Book, W. F. (1908). *The psychology of skill: With special reference to its acquisition in typewriting.* University of Montana Publications in Psychology, Bulletin No. 53, Psychological Series No. 1.

Bovair, S., Kieras, D. E., & Polson, P. G. (1990). The acquisition and performance of text-editing skill: A cognitive complexity analysis. *Human-Computer Interaction, 5*, 1-48.

Bower, G. H., Black, J. B., & Turner, T. (1979). Scripts in memory for text. *Cognitive Psychology, 11*, 177-220.

Braida, L. D. (1991). Crossmodal integration in the identification of consonant segments. *Quarterly Journal of Experimental Psychology, 43A*, 647-677.

Brewer, N., & Sandow, B. (1980). Alcohol effects on driver performance under conditions of divided attention. *Ergonomics, 23*, 185-190.

Broadbent, D. E. (1958). *Perception and communication*. Oxford: Pergamon.

Broadbent, D. E. (1977). Levels, hierarchies, and the locus of control. *Quarterly Journal of Experimental Psychology, 29*, 181-201.

Broadbent, D. E., & Aston, B. (1978). Human control of a simulated economic system. *Ergonomics, 21*, 1035-1043.

Broadbent, D. E., Fitzgerald, P., & Broadbent, M.H.P. (1986). Implicit and explicit knowledge in the control of complex systems. *British Journal of Psychology, 77*, 33-50.

Brooke, S., & Ellis, H. (1992). Cold. In A. P. Smith & D. M. Jones (Eds.), *Handbook of human performance: Vol. 1. The physical environment* (pp. 105-130). San Diego: Academic Press.

Bruce, D. (1994). Lashley and the problem of serial order. *American Psychologist, 49,* 93-103.

Brunswick, E. (1955). Representative design and probabilistic theory in a functional psychology. *Psychological Review, 62,* 193-217.

Bryan, W. L., & Harter, N. (1897). Studies in the physiology and psychology of the telegraphic language. *Psychological Review, 4,* 27-53.

Bryan, W. L., & Harter, N. (1899). Studies on the telegraphic language: The acquisition of a hierarchy of habits. *Psychological Review, 6,* 345-375.

Bursill, A. E. (1958). The restriction of peripheral vision during exposure to hot and humid conditions. *Quarterly Journal of Experimental Psychology, 10,* 113-129.

Butler, B. E., & Hains, S. (1979). Individual differences in word recognition. *Memory & Cognition, 7,* 68-76.

Butler, B. E., Jared, D., & Hains, S. (1984). Reading skill and the use of orthographic knowledge by mature readers. *Psychological Research, 46,* 337-353.

Campbell, K. C., & Proctor, R. W. (1993). Repetition effects with categorizable stimulus and response sets. *Journal of Experimental Psychology: Learning, Memory, and Cognition, 19,* 1345-1362.

Campbell, R. L., Brown, N. R., & Di Bello, L. A. (1992). The programmer's burden: Developing expertise in programming. In R. R. Hoffman (Ed.), *The psychology of expertise* (pp. 269-294). New York: Springer-Verlag.

Card, S. K., Moran, T. P., & Newell, A. (1983). *The psychology of human-computer interaction.* Hillsdale, NJ: Lawrence Erlbaum.

Carlson, R. A., Khoo, B. H., Yaure, R. G., & Schneider, W. (1990). Acquisition of a problem-solving skill: Levels of organization and use of working memory. *Journal of Experimental Psychology: General, 119,* 193-214.

Carlson, R. A., Sullivan, M. A., & Schneider, W. (1989). Practice and working memory effects in building procedural skill. *Journal of Experimental Psychology: Learning, Memory, and Cognition, 15,* 517-526.

Carlson, R. A., & Yaure, R. G. (1990). Practice schedules and the use of component skills in problem solving. *Journal of Experimental Psychology: Learning, Memory, and Cognition, 16,* 484-496.

Caro, P. W. (1979). The relationship between flight simulator motion and training requirements. *Human Factors, 21,* 493-501.

Carr, T. H., & Pollatsek, A. (1985). Recognizing printed words: A look at current models. In D. Besner, T. G. Waller, & E. M. McKinnon (Eds.), *Reading research: Advances in theory and practice* (Vol. 5, pp. 1-82). San Diego: Academic Press.

Carroll, J. B. (1989). Factor analysis since Spearman: Where do we stand? What do we know? In R. Kanfer, P. L. Ackerman, & R. Cudeck (Eds.), *Abilities, motivation, and methodology: The Minnesota symposium on learning and individual differences* (pp. 43-67). Hillsdale, NJ: Lawrence Erlbaum.

Carroll, J. M., & Carrithers, C. (1984). Training wheels in a user interface.

Communications of the ACM, 27, 800-806.

Carron, A. V. (1969). Performance and learning in a discrete motor task under massed vs. distributed practice. *Research Quarterly, 40,* 481-489.

Casey, S. (1993). *"Set phasers on stun" and other true tales of design, technology, and human error.* Santa Barbara, CA: Aegean.

Catrambone, R., & Carroll, J. M. (1987). Learning a word processing system with training wheels and guided explorations. In *Proceedings of CHI + GI 1987* (pp. 169-174). New York: ACM Press.

Catrambone, R., & Holyoak, K. J. (1989). Overcoming contextual limitations on problem-solving transfer. *Journal of Experimental Psychology: Learning, Memory, and Cognition, 15,* 1147-1156.

Cattell, J. McK. (1890). Mental tests and measurements. *Mind, 15,* 373-381.

Challis, B. H., & Brodbeck, D. R. (1992). Level of processing affects priming in word fragment completion. *Journal of Experimental Psychology: Learning, Memory, and Cognition, 18,* 595-607.

Charness, N. (1981). Aging and skilled problem solving. *Journal of Experimental Psychology: General, 110,* 21-38.

Chase, W. G., & Ericsson, K. A. (1982). Skill and working memory. In G. H. Bower (Ed.), *The psychology of learning and motivation* (Vol. 16, pp. 1-58). New York: Academic Press.

Chase, W. G., & Simon, H. A. (1973). Perception in chess. *Cognitive Psychology, 4,* 55-81.

Chi, M.T.H., Feltovich, P. J., & Glaser, R. (1981). Categorization and representation of physics problems by experts and novices. *Cognitive Science, 5,* 121-152.

Christianson, S.-A. (1992). Emotional stress and eyewitness memory: A critical review. *Psychological Bulletin, 112,* 284-309.

Clark, R. E., & Jones, C. E. (1962). Manual performance during cold exposure as a function of practice level and the thermal conditions of training. *Journal of Applied Psychology, 46,* 276-280.

Cleeremans, A., & McClelland, J. L. (1991). Learning the structure of event sequences. *Journal of Experimental Psychology: General, 120,* 235-253.

Cohen, A., Ivry, R. I., & Keele, S. W. (1990). Attention and structure in sequence learning. *Journal of Experimental Psychology: Learning, Memory, and Cognition, 16,* 17-30.

Cohen, J. D., Dunbar, K., & McClelland, J. L. (1990). On the control of automatic processes: A parallel distributed processing account of the Stroop effect. *Psychological Review, 97,* 332-361.

Coltheart, M. (1978). Lexical access in simple reading tasks. In G. Underwood (Ed.), *Strategies of information processing* (pp. 151-216). San Diego: Academic Press.

Connelly, S. L., & Hasher, L. (1993). Aging and the inhibition of spatial location. *Journal of Experimental Psychology: Human Perception and Performance, 19,* 1238-1250.

Cooper, L. A., & Podgorny, P. (1976). Mental transformations and visual comparison processes: Effects of complexity and similarity. *Journal of Experimental Psychology: Human Perception and Performance, 2,* 503-514.

Cormier, S. M. (1987). The structural processes underlying transfer of training. In S. M. Cormier & J. D. Hagman (Eds.), *Transfer of learning: Contemporary research and applications* (pp. 152-182). San Diego: Academic Press.

Craig, A., & Cooper, R. E. (1992). Symptoms of acute and chronic fatigue. In A. P. Smith & D. M. Jones (Eds.), *Handbook of human performance: Vol. 3. State and trait* (pp. 289-339). San Diego: Academic Press.

Craik, K.J.W. (1943). *The nature of explanation.* Cambridge: Cambridge University Press.

Craik, K.J.W. (1948). Theory of the human operator in control systems: II. Man as an element in a control system. *British Journal of Psychology, 38,* 142-148.

Cronbach, L. J. (1990). *Essentials of psychological testing* (3rd ed.). New York: Harper & Row. (Original work published 1970)

Cronbach, L. J., & Snow, R. E. (1977). *Aptitudes and instructional methods: A handbook for research on interactions.* New York: Irvington.

Crossman, E.R.F.W. (1959). A theory of the acquisition of speed-skill. *Ergonomics, 2,* 153-166.

Crutcher, R. J., Ericsson, K. A., & Wichura, C. A. (1994). Improving the encoding of verbal reports using MPAS: A computer-aided encoding system. *Behavior Research Methods, Instruments, & Computers, 26,* 167-171.

Cuqlock-Knopp, V. G., Wilkins, C. A., & Torgerson, W. S. (1991). Multiple cue probability learning and the design of information displays for multiple tasks. In D. L. Damos (Ed.), *Multiple-task performance* (pp. 139-152). London: Taylor & Francis.

Curran, T., & Keele, S. W. (1993). Attentional and nonattentional forms of sequence learning. *Journal of Experimental Psychology: Learning, Memory, and Cognition, 19,* 189-202.

Daee, S., & Wilding, J. (1977). Effects of high intensity white noise on short-term memory for position in a list and sequence. *British Journal of Psychology, 68,* 335-349.

Dalrymple-Alford, E. C., & Budayr, B. (1966). Examination of some aspects of the Stroop color-word test. *Perceptual and Motor Skills, 23,* 1211-1214.

Davis, R. (1957). The human operator as a single channel information system. *Quarterly Journal of Experimental Psychology, 9,* 119-129.

de Groot, A. (1978). *Thought and choice in chess.* The Hague: Mouton. (Original work published 1946)

De Jong, R. (1993). Multiple bottlenecks in overlapping task performance. *Journal of Experimental Psychology: Human Perception and Performance, 19,* 965-980.

Desor, J. A., & Beauchamp, G. K. (1974). The human capacity to transmit olfactory information. *Perception & Psychophysics, 16,* 551-556.

Deutsch, J. A., & Deutsch, D. (1963). Attention: Some theoretical considerations. *Psychological Review, 70,* 80-90.

Dinges, D. F., & Kribbs, N. B. (1991). Performing while sleepy: Effects of experimentally-induced sleepiness. In T. H. Monk (Ed.), *Sleep, sleepiness,* *and performance* (pp. 97-128). New York: John Wiley.

Dinges, D. F., & Powell, J. W. (1988). Sleepiness is more than lapsing. *Sleep Research, 17,* 84.

Donchin, E., & Coles, M.G.H. (1988). Is the P300 component a manifestation of context updating? *Behavioral and Brain Research, 11,* 357-374.

Donchin, E., Fabiani, M., & Sanders, A. (Eds.). (1989). The learning strategies program: An examination of the strategies in skill acquisition [Special issue]. *Acta Psychologica, 71.*

Donders, F. C. (1969). On the speed of mental processes. In W. G. Koster (Ed. and Trans.), *Attention and performance II* (pp. 412-431). Amsterdam: North-Holland. (Original work by Donders published 1868)

Drew, G. C. (1979). An experimental study of mental fatigue. In E. J. Dearnaley & P. B. Warr (Eds.), *Aircrew stress in wartime operations* (pp. 135-177). New York: Academic Press. (Original work by Drew published 1940)

Drewnowski, A., & Healy, A. F. (1977). Detection errors on *the* and *and*: Evidence for reading units larger than the word. *Memory & Cognition, 5,* 636-647.

Drury, C. G., Paramore, B., Van Cott, H. P., Grey, S. M., & Corlett, E. N. (1987). Task analysis. In G. Salvendy (Ed.), *Handbook of human factors* (pp. 370-401). New York: John Wiley.

Duffy, E. (1962). *Activation and behavior.* New York: John Wiley.

Dulaney, C. L., & Rogers, W. A. (1994). Mechanisms underlying reduction in Stroop interference with practice for young and old adults. *Journal of Experimental Psychology: Learning, Memory, and Cognition, 20,* 470-484.

Duncan, J. (1977). Response selection rules in spatial choice reaction tasks. In S. Dornic (Ed.), *Attention and performance VI* (pp. 49-61). Hillsdale, NJ: Lawrence Erlbaum.

Duncker, K. (1945). On problem solving. *Psychological Monographs, 58,* No. 270.

Dutta, A., & Proctor, R. W. (1992). Persistence of stimulus-response compatibility effects with extended practice. *Journal of Experimental Psychology: Learning, Memory, and Cognition, 18,* 801-809.

Dyck, J. L., Abbott, D. W., & Wise, J. A. (1993). HCI in multi-crew aircraft. In M. J. Smith & G. Salvendy (Eds.), *Human-computer interaction: Applications and case studies* (pp. 151-156). Amsterdam: Elsevier.

Dyer, F. N. (1973). The Stroop phenomenon and its use in the study of perceptual, cognitive, and response processes. *Memory & Cognition, 1,* 106-120.

Easterbrook, J. A. (1959). The effect of emotion on cue utilization and the organization of behavior. *Psychological Review, 66,* 183-201.

Ebbinghaus, H. (1964). *Memory: A contribution to experimental psychology.* New York: Dover. (Original work published 1885)

Elio, R. (1986). Representation of similar well-learned cognitive procedures. *Cognitive Science, 10,* 41-73.

Elliott, D., & Jaeger, M. (1988). Practice and visual control of manual aiming movements. *Journal of Human Movement Studies, 14,* 279-291.

Ellis, H. D. (1982). The effects of cold on the performance of serial choice reaction time and various discrete tasks. *Human Factors, 24,* 589-598.

Ellis, N. R., & Dulaney, C. L. (1991). Further evidence for cognitive inertia in persons with mental retardation. *American Journal on Mental Retardation, 95,* 613-621.

Ellis, N. R., Wilcock, S. E., & Zaman, S. A. (1985). Cold and performance: The effects of information load, analgesics, and the rate of cooling. *Aviation, Space, and Environmental Medicine, 61,* 399-405.

Engen, T., & Pfaffman, C. (1960). Absolute judgment of odor quality. *Journal of Experimental Psychology, 59,* 214-219.

English, H. B. (1942). How psychology can facilitate military training: A concrete example. *Journal of Applied Psychology, 26,* 3-7.

Ericsson, K. A., Krampe, R. Th., & Tesch-Romer, C. (1993). The role of deliberate practice in the acquisition of expert performance. *Psychological Review, 100,* 363-406.

Ericsson, K. A., & Polson, P. G. (1988). A cognitive analysis of exceptional memory for restaurant orders. In M.T.H. Chi, R. Glaser, & M. J. Farr (Eds.), *The nature of expertise* (pp. 23-70). Hillsdale, NJ: Lawrence Erlbaum.

Ericsson, K. A., & Simon, H. A. (1980). Verbal reports as data. *Psychological Review, 87,* 215-251.

Ericsson, K. A., & Simon, H. A. (1993). *Protocol analysis* (2nd ed.). Cambridge: MIT Press.

Ericsson, K. A., & Smith, J. (1991). Prospects and limits of the empirical study of expertise: An introduction. In K. A. Ericsson & J. Smith (Eds.), *Toward a general theory of expertise: Prospects and limits* (pp. 1-38). New York: Cambridge University Press.

Fabiani, M., Buckley, J., Gratton, G., Coles, M.G.H., Donchin, E., & Logie, R. (1989). The training of complex task performance. *Acta Psychologica, 71,* 259-299.

Fel'dman, A. G. (1966). Functional tuning of the nervous system with control of movement or maintenance of steady posture—III: Mechanographic analysis of the execution by man of the simplest motor tasks. *Biophysics, 19,* 766-771.

Fendrich, D. M., Healy, A. F., & Bourne, L. E., Jr. (1991). Long-term repetition effects for motoric and perceptual procedures. *Journal of Experimental Psychology: Learning, Memory, and Cognition, 17,* 137-151.

Finnigan, F., & Hammersley, R. (1992). The effects of alcohol on performance. In A. P. Smith & D. M. Jones (Eds.), *Handbook of human performance: Vol. 2. Health and performance* (pp. 73-126). San Diego: Academic Press.

Fisher, C. (1988). Advancing the study of programming with computer-aided protocol analysis. In G. Olson, E. Soloway, & S. Sheppard (Eds.), *Empirical studies of programmers: 1987 workshop.* Norwood, NJ: Ablex.

Fisk, A. D., Lee, M. D., & Rogers, W. A. (1991). Recombination of automatic processing components: The effects of transfer, reversal, and conflict situations. *Human Factors, 33,* 267-280.

Fitts, P. M. (1964). Perceptual-motor skill learning. In A. W. Melton (Ed.), *Categories of human learning* (pp. 243-285). New York: Academic Press.

Fitts, P. M. (1990). Factors in complex skill training. In M. Venturino (Ed.),

Selected readings in Human Factors (pp. 275-295). Santa Monica, CA: Human Factors Society. (Original work by Fitts published 1962)

Fitts, P. M., Bahrick, H. P., Noble, M. E., & Briggs, G. E. (1961). *Skilled performance.* New York: John Wiley.

Fitts, P. M., & Deininger, R. L. (1954). S-R compatibility: Correspondence among paired elements within stimulus and response codes. *Journal of Experimental Psychology, 48,* 483-492.

Fitts, P. M., & Posner, M. I. (1967). *Human performance.* Belmont, CA: Brooks/Cole.

Fitts, P. M., & Seeger, C. M. (1953). S-R compatibility: Spatial characteristics of stimulus and response codes. *Journal of Experimental Psychology, 46,* 199-210.

Flach, J. M. (1993, April). *Perception-action relations in system control.* Talk presented at the Human Factors Colloquium series, Purdue University.

Fleishman, E. A. (1978). Relating individual differences to the dimensions of human tasks. *Ergonomics, 21,* 1007-1019.

Fleishman, E. A., & Hempel, W. E., Jr. (1954). Changes in factor structure of a complex psychomotor test as a function of practice. *Psychometrika, 19,* 239-252.

Fleishman, E. A., & Quaintance, M. K. (1984). *Taxonomies of human performance: The description of human tasks.* Orlando, FL: Academic Press.

Fleishman, E. A., & Rich, S. (1963). Role of kinesthetic and spatial-visual abilities in perceptual motor learning. *Journal of Experimental Psychology, 66,* 6-11.

Flexman, R. E., & Stark, E. A. (1987). Training simulators. In G. Salvendy (Ed.), *Handbook of human factors* (pp. 1012-1038). New York: John Wiley.

Folkard, S. (1975). Diurnal variation in logical reasoning. *British Journal of Psychology, 66,* 1-8.

Folkard, S., & Monk, T. H. (1979). Time of day and processing strategy in free recall. *Quarterly Journal of Experimental Psychology, 31,* 461-475.

Folkard, S., & Monk, T. H. (1980). Circadian rhythms in human memory. *British Journal of Psychology, 71,* 295-307.

Foss, M. A., Fabiani, M., Mané, A. M., & Donchin, E. (1989). Unsupervised practice: The performance of the control group. *Acta Psychologica, 71,* 23-51.

Frederiksen, J. R., & White, B. Y. (1989). An approach to training based upon principled task decomposition. *Acta Psychologica, 71,* 89-146.

Fuchs, A. H. (1962). The progression-regression hypothesis in perceptual-motor skill learning. *Journal of Experimental Psychology, 63,* 177-182.

Gagné, R. M. (1985). *The conditions of learning and theory of instruction* (4th ed.). New York: Holt, Rinehart & Winston.

Gagné, R. M., & Briggs, L. J. (1974). *Principles of instructional design.* New York: Holt, Rinehart & Winston.

Gagné, R. M., Foster, H., & Crowley, M. E. (1948). Measurement of transfer of training. *Psychological Bulletin, 45,* 97-130.

Gaines, B. R. (1967). Teaching machines for perceptual motor skills. In D. Irwin & J. Leedham (Eds.), *Aspects of education technology: The proceed-*

ings of the Programmed Learning Conference held at Loughboughy 1966 (pp. 337-358). London: Methuen.

Galton, F. (1869). *Hereditary genius: An inquiry into its laws and consequences.* London: Macmillan.

Galton, F. (1883). *Inquiry into human faculty and its development.* New York: Macmillan.

Gardner, G. T. (1973). Evidence for independent parallel channels in tachistoscopic perception. *Cognitive Psychology, 4,* 130-155.

Garner, W. R. (1974). *The processing of information and structure.* Hillsdale, NJ: Lawrence Erlbaum.

Garvey, W. D. (1960). A comparison of the effects of training and secondary tasks on tracking behavior. *Journal of Experimental Psychology, 44,* 370-375.

Geiger, S., & Reeves, B. (1993). The effects of scene changes and semantic relatedness on attention to television. *Communication Research, 20,* 155-175.

Gentner, D. R., Larochelle, S., & Grudin, J. (1988). Lexical, sublexical, and peripheral effects in skilled typewriting. *Cognitive Psychology, 20,* 524-548.

Gernsbacher, M. A. (1993). Less skilled readers have less efficient suppression mechanisms. *Psychological Science, 4,* 294-298.

Gernsbacher, M. A., Varner, K. R., & Faust, M. (1990). Investigating differences in general comprehension skill. *Journal of Experimental Psychology: Learning, Memory, and Cognition, 12,* 430-445.

Gibson, E. J. (1969). *Principles of perceptual learning and development.* New York: Academic Press.

Gibson, J. J. (Ed.). (1947). *Motion picture testing and research* (Army Air Forces Aviation Psychology Program Research Reports, Report No. 7). Washington, DC: U.S. Government Printing Office.

Gick, M. L., & Holyoak, K. J. (1980). Analogical problem solving. *Cognitive Psychology, 12,* 306-355.

Gick, M. L., & Holyoak, K. J. (1983). Schema induction and analogical transfer. *Cognitive Psychology, 15,* 1-38.

Gillan, D. J., Breedin, S. D., & Cooke, N. J. (1992). Network and multidimensional representations of the declarative knowledge of human-computer interface design experts. *International Journal of Man-Machine Studies, 36,* 587-615.

Glaser, R., & Chi, M.T.H. (1988). Overview. In M.T.H. Chi, R. Glaser, & M. J. Farr (Eds.), *The nature of expertise* (pp. xv-xxviii). Hillsdale, NJ: Lawrence Erlbaum.

Gopher, D. (1982). A selective attention test as a predictor of success in flight training. *Human Factors, 24,* 173-183.

Gopher, D. (1993). The skill of attention control: Acquisition and execution of attention strategies. In D. E. Meyer & S. Kornblum (Eds.), *Attention and performance XIV* (pp. 299-322). Cambridge: MIT Press.

Gopher, D., Brickner, M., & Navon, D. (1982). Different difficulty manipulations interact differently with task emphasis: Evidence for multiple resources. *Journal of Experimental Psychology: Human Perception and Performance, 8,* 146-157.

Gopher, D., Karis, D., & Koenig, W. (1985). The representation of movement schemas in long-term memory:

Lessons from the acquisition of transcription skill. *Acta Psychologica, 60*, 105-134.

Gopher, D., & Kimchi, R. (1989). Engineering psychology. *Annual Review of Psychology, 40*, 431-455.

Gopher, D., Weil, M., & Siegel, D. (1989). Practice under changing priorities: An approach to training of complex skills. *Acta Psychologica, 71*, 147-177.

Gottsdanker, R., & Stelmach, G. E. (1971). The persistence of psychological refractoriness. *Journal of Motor Behavior, 3*, 301-312.

Gould, S. J. (1981). *The mismeasure of man*. New York: Norton.

Graf, P., Shimamura, A. P., & Squire, L. R. (1985). Priming across modalities and category levels: Extending the domain of preserved function in amnesia. *Journal of Experimental Psychology: Learning, Memory, and Cognition, 11*, 386-396.

Green, D. M., & Swets, J. A. (1974). *Signal detection theory and psychophysics*. Huntington, NY: Krieger. (Original work published 1966)

Greenberg, S. N., & Koriat, A. (1991). The missing-letter effect for common function words depends on their linguistic function in the phrase. *Journal of Experimental Psychology: Learning, Memory, and Cognition, 17*, 1051-1061.

Grudin, J. T. (1983). Error patterns in novice and skilled transcription typing. In W. E. Cooper (Ed.), *Cognitive aspects of skilled typewriting* (pp. 121-143). New York: Springer-Verlag.

Grudin, J. T., & Larochelle, S. (1982). *Digraph frequency effects in skilled typing* (Tech. Rep. CHIP 110). La Jolla: University of California, San Diego, Center for Human Information Processing.

Haier, R. J., Siegel, B. V., Jr., Nuechterlein, K. H., Hazlett, E., Wu, J. C., Paek, J., Browning, H. L., & Buchsbaum, M. S. (1988). Cortical glucose metabolic rate correlates of abstract reasoning and attention studied with positron emission tomography. *Intelligence, 12*, 199-217.

Halff, H. M., Hollan, J. D., & Hutchins, E. L. (1986). Cognitive science and military training. *American Psychologist, 41*, 1131-1139.

Hancock, P. A., & Meshkati, N. (Eds.). (1988). *Human mental workload*. Amsterdam: North-Holland.

Hasbroucq, T., Guiard, Y., & Ottomani, L. (1990). Principles of response determination: The list-rule model of S-R compatibility. *Bulletin of the Psychonomic Society, 28*, 327-330.

Hauty, G. T., & Payne, R. B. (1955). Mitigation of work decrement. *Journal of Experimental Psychology, 49*, 60-67.

Hayes, N. E., & Broadbent, D. E. (1988). Two modes of learning for interactive tasks. *Cognition, 28*, 249-276.

Healy, A. F. (1976). Detection errors on the word *the*: Evidence for reading units larger than letters. *Journal of Experimental Psychology: Human Perception and Performance, 2*, 235-242.

Healy, A. F., & Drewnowski, A. (1983). Investigating the boundaries of reading units: Letter detection in misspelled words. *Journal of Experimental Psychology: Human Perception and Performance, 9*, 413-426.

Healy, A. F., Fendrich, D. W., & Proctor, J. D. (1990). Acquisition and retention of a letter-detection skill. *Journal of Experimental Psychology: Learning, Memory, and Cognition, 16,* 270-281.

Hebb, D. O. (1955). Drives and the C.N.S. (conceptual nervous system). *Psychological Review, 62,* 243-254.

Heimstra, N. W., Bancroft, N. R., & DeKock, A. R. (1967). Effects of smoking upon sustained performance in a simulated driving task. *Annals of the New York Academy of Science, 142,* 295-307.

Hick, W. E. (1952). On the rate of gain of information. *Quarterly Journal of Experimental Psychology, 4,* 11-26.

Higginson, G. (1931). *Fields of psychology: A study of man and his environment.* New York: Holt.

Hirst, W., & Kalmar, D. (1987). Characterizing attentional resources. *Journal of Experimental Psychology: General, 116,* 68-81.

Hirst, W., Spelke, E. S., Reaves, C. C., Caharack, G., & Neisser, U. (1980). Dividing attention without alternation or automaticity. *Journal of Experimental Psychology: General, 109,* 98-117.

Hockey, G.R.J. (1970). Signal probability and spatial location as possible bases for increased selectivity in noise. *Quarterly Journal of Experimental Psychology, 22,* 37-42.

Hockey, G.R.J. (1986). Changes in operator efficiency as a function of environmental stress, fatigue, and circadian rhythms. In K. R. Boff, L. Kaufman, & J. P. Thomas (Eds.), *Handbook of human perception and performance: Vol. II. Cognitive processes and performance* (chap. 4, pp. 1-49). New York: John Wiley.

Holding, D. H. (1965). *Principles of training.* Oxford: Pergamon.

Holding, D. H. (1985). *The psychology of chess skill.* Hillsdale, NJ: Lawrence Erlbaum.

Hollan, J. D., Hutchins, E. L., & Weitzman, L. (1984). STEAMER: An interactive inspectable simulation-based training system. *AI Magazine,* 5(2), 15-27.

Holland, J. H., Holyoak, K. J., Nisbett, R. E., & Thagard, P. R. (1986). *Induction.* Cambridge: MIT Press.

Holyoak, K. J. (1991). Symbolic connectionism: Toward third-generation theories of expertise. In K. A. Ericsson & J. Smith (Eds.), *Toward a general theory of expertise* (pp. 301-335). New York: Cambridge University Press.

Holyoak, K. J., & Thagard, P. (1989). Analogical mapping by constraint satisfaction. *Cognitive Science, 13,* 295-355.

Horne, J. A., Brass, C. G., & Pettit, A. N. (1980). Circadian performance differences between morning and evening "types." *Ergonomics, 23,* 29-36.

Howard, J. H., & Ballas, J. A. (1980). Syntactic and semantic factors in the classification of nonspeech transient patterns. *Perception & Psychophysics, 28,* 431-439.

Humphreys, M. S., & Revelle, W. (1984). Personality, motivation, and performance: A theory of the relationship between individual differences and information processing. *Psychological Review, 91,* 153-184.

Hunt, E. B. (1978). Mechanics of verbal ability. *Psychological Review, 85,* 109-130.

Hyman, R. (1953). Stimulus information as a determinant of reaction time. *Journal of Experimental Psychology, 45*, 188-196.

Jackson, M. D., & McClelland, J. L. (1975). Sensory and cognitive determinants of reading speed. *Journal of Verbal Learning and Verbal Behavior, 14*, 565-574.

Jackson, M. D., & McClelland, J. L. (1979). Processing determinants of reading speed. *Journal of Experimental Psychology: General, 108*, 151-181.

"Jackson in Hall of Fame; lives up to own prediction." (1993, August 2). Associated Press wire service.

Jacobs, R. S., & Roscoe, S. N. (1975). Simulator cockpit motion and the transfer of initial flight training. In *Proceedings of the Human Factors Society 19th Annual Meeting* (pp. 218-226). Santa Monica, CA: Human Factors Society.

Jacoby, L. L., & Dallas, M. (1981). On the relationship between autobiographical memory and perceptual learning. *Journal of Experimental Psychology: General, 110*, 306-340.

Jagacinski, R. J., & Hah, S. (1988). Progression-regression effects in tracking repeated patterns. *Journal of Experimental Psychology: Human Perception and Performance, 14*, 77-88.

Jared, D., & Seidenberg, M. S. (1991). Does word identification proceed from spelling to sound to meaning? *Journal of Experimental Psychology: General, 120*, 358-394.

Jeannerod, M., & Marteniuk, R. G. (1992). Functional characteristics of prehension: From data to artificial neural networks. In L. Proteau & D. Elliott (Eds.), *Vision and motor control* (pp. 197-232). Amsterdam: North-Holland.

John, B. E., & Newell, A. (1990). Toward an engineering model of S-R compatibility. In R. W. Proctor & T. G. Reeve (Eds.), *Stimulus-response compatibility: An integrated perspective* (pp. 427-479). Amsterdam: North-Holland.

Johnson-Laird, P. N. (1989). Mental models. In M. I. Posner (Ed.), *Foundations of cognitive science* (pp. 469-499). Cambridge: MIT Press.

Jones, D. M. (1983). Noise. In R. Hockey (Ed.), *Stress and fatigue in human performance* (pp. 61-95). New York: John Wiley.

Jonides, J., & Gleitman, H. (1972). A conceptual category effect in visual search: O as letter or as digit. *Perception & Psychophysics, 12*, 457-460.

Jordan, M. I. (1990). Motor learning and the degrees of freedom problem. In M. Jeannerod (Ed.), *Attention and performance XIII* (pp. 796-836). Hillsdale, NJ: Lawrence Erlbaum.

Jordan, M. I. (1992). Constrained supervised learning. *Journal of Mathematical Psychology, 36*, 396-425.

Jordan, M. I., & Rosenbaum, D. A. (1989). Action. In M. I. Posner (Ed.), *Foundations of cognitive science* (pp. 727-767). Cambridge: MIT Press.

Jordan, M. I., & Rumelhart, D. E. (1992). Forward models: Supervised learning with a distal teacher. *Cognitive Science, 16*, 307-354.

Kahneman, D. (1973). *Attention and effort.* Englewood Cliffs, NJ: Prentice-Hall.

Kaiser, M. K., Jonides, J., & Alexander, J. (1986). Intuitive reasoning about abstract and familiar physics problems. *Memory & Cognition, 14*, 308-312.

Kaiser, M. K., McCloskey, M., & Proffitt, D. R. (1986). Development of intuitive theories of motion: Curvilinear motion in the absence of external forces. *Developmental Psychology, 22*, 67-71.

Kantowitz, B. H., & Sorkin, R. D. (1987). Allocation of functions. In G. Salvendy (Ed.), *Handbook of human factors* (pp. 355-369). New York: John Wiley.

Karlin, L., & Kestenbaum, R. (1968). Effects of number of alternatives on the psychological refractory period. *Quarterly Journal of Experimental Psychology, 20*, 167-178.

Keele, S. W. (1968). Movement control in skilled motor performance. *Psychological Bulletin, 70*, 387-403.

Keller, F. S. (1958). The phantom plateau. *Journal of the Experimental Analysis of Behavior, 1*, 1-13.

Kelso, J.A.S. (1984). Phase transitions and critical behavior in human bimanual coordination. *American Journal of Physiology: Regulatory, Integrative, and Comparative Physiology, 15*, R1000-R1004.

Kerr, B. (1973). Processing demands during mental operations. *Memory & Cognition, 1*, 401-412.

Kieras, D. E. (1988). Towards a practical GOMS model methodology for user interface design. In M. Helander (Ed.), *The handbook of human-computer interaction* (pp. 135-158). Amsterdam: North-Holland.

Kieras, D. E., & Bovair, S. (1984). The role of a mental model in learning to operate a device. *Cognitive Science, 8*, 255-273.

Kieras, D. E., & Bovair, S. (1986). The acquisition of procedures from text: A production-system analysis of transfer of training. *Journal of Memory and Language, 25*, 507-524.

Kieras, D., & Polson, P. G. (1985). An approach to the formal analysis of user complexity. *International Journal of Man-Machine Studies, 22*, 365-394.

Kintsch, W. (1988). The role of knowledge in discourse comprehension: A construction-integration model. *Psychological Review, 95*, 163-182.

Kirsner, K., Speelman, C., & Schofield, P. (1993). Implicit memory and skill acquisition: Is synthesis possible? In P. Graf & M.E.J. Masson (Eds.), *Implicit memory: New directions in cognition, development, and neuropsychology* (pp. 119-139). Hillsdale, NJ: Lawrence Erlbaum.

Kjellberg, A. (1977). Sleep deprivation and some aspects of performance: II. Lapses and other attentional effects. *Waking and Sleeping, 1*, 145-148.

Klein, K. E., Wegman, H. M., & Hunt, B. I. (1972). Desynchronization of body temperature and performance circadian rhythm as a result of outgoing and homegoing transmeridian flights. *Aerospace Medicine, 43*, 119-132.

Kleitman, N. (1963). *Sleep and wakefulness* (rev. ed.). Chicago: University of Chicago Press. (Original work published 1938)

Kleitman, N., & Jackson, D. P. (1950). Body temperature and performance under different routines. *American Journal of Applied Psychology, 3*, 309-328.

Kohl, R. M., & Shea, C. H. (1992). Pew (1966) revisited: Acquisition of hierarchical control as a function of observational practice. *Journal of Motor Behavior, 24*, 247-260.

Kolers, P. A. (1975a). Memorial consequences of automatized encoding. *Journal of Experimental Psychology: Human Learning and Memory, 1,* 689-701.

Kolers, P. A. (1975b). Specificity of operations in sentence recognition. *Cognitive Psychology, 7,* 289-306.

Kolers, P. A. (1976). Reading a year later. *Journal of Experimental Psychology: Human Learning and Memory, 2,* 554-565.

Kolers, P. A., & Roediger, H. L., III. (1984). Procedures of mind. *Journal of Verbal Learning and Verbal Behavior, 23,* 425-449.

Kornblum, S. (1969). Sequential determinants of information processing in serial and discrete choice reaction time. *Psychological Review, 76,* 113-131.

Kornblum, S. (1973). Sequential effects in choice reaction time: A tutorial review. In S. Kornblum (Ed.), *Attention and performance IV* (pp. 259-288). New York: Academic Press.

Kornblum, S. (1975). An invariance in choice reaction time with varying numbers of alternatives and constant probability. In P. Rabbitt & S. Dornic (Eds.), *Attention and performance V* (pp. 366-382). San Diego: Academic Press.

Kornblum, S., Hasbroucq, T., & Osman, A. (1990). Dimensional overlap: Cognitive basis for stimulus-response compatibility—A model and taxonomy. *Psychological Review, 97,* 253-270.

Krueger, L. E. (1984). The category effect in visual search depends on physical rather than conceptual differences. *Perception & Psychophysics, 35,* 558-564.

Kundel, H. L., & LaFollette, P. S. (1972). Visual search patterns and experience with radiological images. *Radiology, 103,* 523-528.

Kundel, H. L., & Nodine, C. F. (1975). Interpreting chest radiographs without visual search. *Radiology, 116,* 527-532.

LaBerge, D. (1973). Attention and the measurement of perceptual learning. *Memory & Cognition, 1,* 268-276.

Lacey, J. I. (1967). Somatic response patterning and stress: Some revisions of activation theory. In M. H. Appley & R. Trumbull (Eds.), *Psychological stress* (pp. 14-42). New York: Appleton-Century-Crofts.

Laird, J. E., Rosenbloom, P. S., & Newell, A. (1986). *Universal subgoaling and chunking.* Dordrecht: Kluwer.

Landy, F. J. (1985). *Psychology of work behavior* (3rd ed.). Chicago: Dorsey Press.

Lashley, K. S. (1951). The problem of serial order in behavior. In L. A. Jeffress (Ed.), *Cerebral mechanisms in behavior: The Hixon symposium* (pp. 112-131). New York: John Wiley.

Laughery, K. R., Sr., & Laughery, K. R., Jr. (1987). Analytic techniques for function analysis. In G. Salvendy (Ed.), *Handbook of human factors* (pp. 329-354). New York: John Wiley.

Lavery, J. J. (1962). Retention of simple motor skills as a function of type of knowledge of results. *Canadian Journal of Psychology, 16,* 300-311.

Leavitt, J. (1979). Cognitive demands of skating and stick handling in ice hockey. *Canadian Journal of Applied Sport Sciences, 4,* 46-55.

Lee, T. D., & Genovese, E. D. (1988). Distribution of practice in motor skill acquisition: Learning and performance effects reconsidered. *Research Quarterly for Exercise and Sport, 59*, 277-287.

Lee, T. D., & Genovese, E. D. (1989). Distribution of practice in motor skill acquisition: Different effects for discrete and continuous tasks. *Research Quarterly for Exercise and Sport, 60*, 59-65.

Lee, T. D., & Magill, R. A. (1983). The locus of contextual interference in motor-skill acquisition. *Journal of Experimental Psychology: Learning, Memory, and Cognition, 9*, 730-746.

Leonard, J. A. (1958). Advance information in sensorimotor skills. *Quarterly Journal of Experimental Psychology, 5*, 141-149.

Lesgold, A., Rubinson, H., Feltovich, P., Glaser, R., Klopfer, D., & Wang, Y. (1988). Expertise in a complex skill: Diagnosing X-ray pictures. In M.T.H. Chi, R. Glaser, & M. J. Farr (Eds.), *The nature of expertise* (pp. 311-342). Hillsdale, NJ: Lawrence Erlbaum.

Lewandowsky, S. (1993). The rewards and hazards of simulation. *Psychological Science, 4*, 236-243.

Lewicki, P., Czyzewska, M., & Hoffman, H. (1987). Unconscious acquisition of complex procedural knowledge. *Journal of Experimental Psychology: Learning, Memory, and Cognition, 13*, 523-530.

Lieberman, H. R. (1992). Caffeine. In A. P. Smith & D. M. Jones (Eds.), *Handbook of human performance: Vol. 2. Health and performance* (pp. 49-72). San Diego: Academic Press.

Lieberman, H. R., Wurtman, R. J., Emde, G. G., & Coviella, I.L.G. (1987). The effects of caffeine and aspirin on mood and performance. *Journal of Clinical Psychopharmacology, 7*, 315-320.

Lieberman, H. R., Wurtman, R. J., Emde, G. G., Roberts, C., & Coviella, I.L.G. (1987). The effects of low doses of caffeine on human performance and mood. *Psychopharmacology, 92*, 308-312.

Lindsley, D. B. (1951). Emotion. In S. S. Stevens (Ed.), *Handbook of experimental psychology* (pp. 473-516). New York: John Wiley.

Lintern, G. (1989). The learning strategies program: Concluding remarks. *Acta Psychologica, 71*, 301-309.

Lintern, G. (1991). An informational perspective on skill transfer in human-machine systems. *Human Factors, 33*, 251-256.

Lintern, G., & Gopher, D. (1978). Adaptive training of perceptual-motor skills: Issues, results, and future directions. *International Journal of Man-Machine Studies, 10*, 521-551.

Lintern, G., Roscoe, S. N., & Sivier, J. (1990). Display principles, control dynamics, and environmental factors in pilot performance and transfer of training. *Human Factors, 32*, 299-317.

Lintern, G., Sheppard, D. J., Parker, D. L., Yates, K. E., & Nolan, M. D. (1989). Simulator design and instructional features for air-to-ground attack: A transfer study. *Human Factors, 31*, 87-99.

Logie, R., Baddeley, A., Mané, A., Donchin, E., & Sheptak, R. (1989). Working memory in the acquisition of complex cognitive skills. *Acta Psychologica, 71*, 53-87.

Lombard, W. P. (1887). The variants of the normal knee jerk and their relation to the activity of the central nervous system. *American Journal of Psychology, 1,* 5-71.

Luchins, A. S. (1942). Mechanization in problem solving. *Psychological Monographs, 54,* No. 6 (Whole No. 248).

Lunn, J. H. (1948). Chick sexing. *American Scientist, 36,* 280-287.

Mackworth, N. H. (1961). Researches on the measurement of human performance. In H. W. Sinaiko (Ed.), *Selected papers on human factors in the design and use of control systems* (pp. 174-331). New York: Dover.

MacLeod, C. M. (1991). Half a century of research on the Stroop effect: An integrative review. *Psychological Bulletin, 109,* 163-203.

MacLeod, C. M., & Dunbar, K. (1988). Training and Stroop-like interference: Evidence for a continuum of automaticity. *Journal of Experimental Psychology: Learning, Memory, and Cognition, 14,* 126-135.

Macmillan, N. A., & Creelman, C. D. (1991). *Detection theory: A user's guide.* New York: Cambridge University Press.

Magill, R. A., & Hall, K. G. (1990). A review of the contextual interference effect in motor skill acquisition. *Human Movement Science, 9,* 241-289.

Maier, N.R.F. (1930). Reasoning in humans. *Journal of Comparative Psychology, 10,* 115-143.

Malmo, R. B. (1959). Activation: A neuropsychological dimension. *Psychological Review, 66,* 367-386.

Mané, A., Adams, J. A., & Donchin, E. (1989). Adaptive and part-whole training in the acquisition of a complex perceptual-motor skill. *Acta Psychologica, 71,* 179-196.

Mané, A., & Donchin, E. (1989). The space fortress game. *Acta Psychology, 71,* 17-22.

Mannes, S. M., & Kintsch, W. (1991). Routine computing tasks: Planning as understanding. *Cognitive Science, 15,* 305-342.

Marks, M., & Folkard, S. (1988). The effects of time of day on recall from expository text. In M. Gruneberg, P. Morris, & R. Sykes (Eds.), *Practical aspects of memory: Current research and issues* (pp. 471-476). New York: John Wiley.

Marshalek, B., Lohman, D. F., & Snow, R. E. (1983). The complexity continuum in the radex and hierarchical models of intelligence. *Intelligence, 7,* 107-127.

Massaro, D. W. (1987). *Speech perception by ear and eye: A paradigm for psychological inquiry.* Hillsdale, NJ: Lawrence Erlbaum.

Massaro, D. W. (1988). Some criticisms of connectionist models of human performance. *Journal of Memory and Language, 27,* 213-234.

Massaro, D. W., Cohen, M. M., & Gesi, A. T. (1993). Long-term training, transfer, and retention in learning to lipread. *Perception & Psychophysics, 53,* 549-562.

Masson, M.E.J. (1986). Identification of typographically transformed words: Instance-based skill acquisition. *Journal of Experimental Psychology: Learning, Memory, and Cognition, 12,* 479-488.

Masson, M. E., & Miller, J. A. (1983). Working memory and individual differences in comprehension and memory of text. *Journal of Educational Psychology, 75,* 314-318.

Mathews, R. C., Buss, R. R., Stanley, W. B., Blanchard-Fields, F., Cho, J. R., & Druhan, B. (1989). Role of implicit and explicit processes in learning from examples: A synergistic effect. *Journal of Experimental Psychology: Learning, Memory, and Cognition, 15,* 1083-1100.

Matthews, G., Jones, D. M., & Chamberlain, A. G. (1992). Predictors of individual differences in mail-coding skills and their variation with ability level. *Journal of Applied Psychology, 77,* 406-418.

Matthews, G., & Margetts, I. (1991). Self-report arousal and divided attention: A study of performance operating characteristics. *Human Performance, 4,* 107-125.

Maylor, E. A., & Rabbitt, P.M.A. (1987). Effects of practice and alcohol on performance of a perceptual-motor task. *Quarterly Journal of Experimental Psychology, 39A,* 777-795.

Maylor, E. A., & Rabbitt, P.M.A. (1988). Amount of practice and degree of attentional control have no influence on the adverse effect of alcohol in word categorization and visual search tasks. *Perception & Psychophysics, 44,* 117-126.

Maylor, E. A., Rabbitt, P.M.A., James, G. H., & Kerr, S. A. (1990). Effects of alcohol and extended practice on divided-attention performance. *Perception & Psychophysics, 48,* 445-452.

Maylor, E. A., Rabbitt, P.M.A., Sahgal, A., & Wright, C. (1987). Effects of alcohol on speed and accuracy in choice reaction time and visual search. *Acta Psychologica, 65,* 147-163.

McCann, R. S., & Johnston, J. C. (1992). Locus of the single-channel bottleneck in dual-task interference. *Journal of Experimental Psychology: Human Perception and Performance, 18,* 471-484.

McClelland, J. L. (1979). On the time relations of mental processes: An examination of systems of processes in cascade. *Psychological Review, 86,* 287-330.

McClelland, J. L. (1988). Connectionist models and psychological evidence. *Journal of Memory and Language, 27,* 107-123.

McClelland, J. L., & Rumelhart, D. E. (1981). An interactive activation model of context effects in letter perception: Part 1. An account of basic findings. *Psychological Review, 88,* 375-407.

McClelland, J. L., Rumelhart, D. E., & PDP Research Group. (1986). *Parallel distributed processing: Explorations in the microstructure of cognition. Vol. 1: Foundations.* Cambridge: MIT Press.

McCloskey, M. (1991). Networks and theories: The place of connectionism in cognitive science. *Psychological Science, 2,* 387-395.

McCormick, E. J. (1979). *Job analyses: Methods and applications.* New York: Amacon.

McCusker, L. X., Hillinger, M. L., & Bias, R. G. (1981). Phonological recoding and reading. *Psychological Bulletin, 89,* 217-245.

McKeithen, K. B., Reitman, J. S., Reuter, H. H., & Hirtle, S. C. (1981). Knowledge organization and skill differences in computer programmers. *Cognitive Psychology, 13,* 307-325.

McKelvie, S. J. (1984). Relationship between set and functional fixedness:

A replication. *Perceptual and Motor Skills, 58,* 996-998.

McKelvie, S. J. (1985). Einstellung: Still alive and well. *Journal of General Psychology, 112,* 313-315.

McMillen, D. L., Smith, S. M., & Wells-Parker, E. (1989). The effects of alcohol, expectancy, and sensation seeking on driving risk taking. *Addictive Behaviors, 14,* 477-483.

McMillen, D. L., & Wells-Parker, E. (1987). The effect of alcohol consumption on risk-taking while driving. *Addictive Behaviors, 12,* 241-247.

Meijer, O. G., & Roth, K. (Eds.). (1988). *Complex movement behaviour: The motor-action controversy.* Amsterdam: North-Holland.

Mertens, H. W. (1981). Perception of runway image shape and approach angle magnitude by pilots in simulated night landing approaches. *Aviation, Space, and Environmental Medicine, 52,* 373-386.

Mewhort, D.J.K., Braun, J. G., & Heathcote, A. (1992). Response time distributions and the Stroop task: A test of the Cohen, Dunbar, and McClelland (1990) model. *Journal of Experimental Psychology: Human Perception and Performance, 18,* 872-882.

Miller, G. A., & Isard, S. (1963). Some perceptual consequences of linguistic terms. *Journal of Verbal Learning and Verbal Behavior, 2,* 212-228.

Miller, J. (1982). Discrete versus continuous models of human information processing: In search of partial output. *Journal of Experimental Psychology: Human Perception and Performance, 8,* 273-296.

Monk, T. H., & Leng, V. C. (1982). Time of day effects in simple repetitive tasks: Some possible mechanisms. *Acta Psychologica, 51,* 207-221.

Morasso, P. (1981). Spatial control of arm movements. *Experimental Brain Research, 42,* 223-227.

Moray, N. (1959). Attention in dichotic listening: Affective cues and the influence of instructions. *Quarterly Journal of Experimental Psychology, 11,* 56-60.

Moray, N. (1987). Intelligent aids, mental models, and the theory of machines. *International Journal of Man-Machine Studies, 27,* 619-629.

Morin, R. E., & Grant, D. A. (1955). Learning and performance on a key-pressing task as a function of the degree of spatial stimulus-response correspondence. *Journal of Experimental Psychology, 49,* 39-47.

Moruzzi, G., & Magoun, E. W. (1949). Brain-stem reticular formation and activation of the EEG. *Electroencephalography and Clinical Neurophysiology, 1,* 455-473.

Mowbray, G. H., & Rhoades, M. V. (1959). On the reduction of choice reaction times with practice. *Quarterly Journal of Experimental Psychology, 11,* 16-23.

Myers, G. L., & Fisk, A. D. (1987). Training consistent task components: Application of automatic and controlled processing theory to industrial task training. *Human Factors, 29,* 255-268.

Näätänen, R. (1973). The inverted-U relationship between activation and performance: A critical review. In S. Kornblum (Ed.), *Attention and performance IV* (pp. 155-174). New York: Academic Press.

Navon, D. (1984). Resources—A theoretical soupstone? *Psychological Review, 91,* 216-234.

Navon, D., & Gopher, D. (1979). On the economy of the human-processing system. *Psychological Review, 86,* 214-255.

Navon, D., & Miller, J. (1987). Role of outcome conflict in dual-task interference. *Journal of Experimental Psychology: Human Perception and Performance, 13,* 435-448.

Neill, W. T. (1977). Inhibitory and facilitatory processes in attention. *Journal of Experimental Psychology: Human Perception and Performance, 3,* 444-450.

Neiss, R. (1988). Reconceptualizing arousal: Psychobiological states in motor performance. *Psychological Bulletin, 103,* 345-366.

Neisser, U. (1963). Decision-time without reaction-time: Experiments in visual scanning. *American Journal of Psychology, 76,* 376-385.

Neisser, U., Novick, R., & Lazar, R. (1963). Searching for ten targets simultaneously. *Perceptual and Motor Skills, 17,* 955-961.

Neumann, O. (1987). Beyond capacity: A functional view of attention. In H. Heuer & A. F. Sanders (Eds.), *Perspectives on perception and action* (pp. 361-394). Hillsdale, NJ: Lawrence Erlbaum.

Neves, D. M., & Anderson, J. R. (1981). Knowledge compilation: Mechanisms for the automatization of cognitive skills. In J. R. Anderson (Ed.), *Cognitive skills and their acquisition* (pp. 57-84). Hillsdale, NJ: Lawrence Erlbaum.

Newell, A. (1980). Reasoning, problem solving, and decision processes: The problem space as a fundamental category. In R. S. Nickerson (Ed.), *Attention and performance VIII* (pp. 693-718). Hillsdale, NJ: Lawrence Erlbaum.

Newell, A. (1990). *Unified theories of cognition.* Cambridge, MA: Harvard University Press.

Newell, A., & Rosenbloom, P. S. (1981). Mechanisms of skill acquisition and the law of practice. In J. R. Anderson (Ed.), *Cognitive skills and their acquisition* (pp. 1-55). Hillsdale, NJ: Lawrence Erlbaum.

Newell, A., & Simon, H. A. (1972). *Human problem solving.* Englewood Cliffs, NJ: Prentice-Hall.

Newell, K. M. (1991). Motor skill acquisition. *Annual Review of Psychology, 42,* 213-237.

Newell, K. M. (1992). Preface to the theme issue on dynamical approaches to motor skill acquisition. *Journal of Motor Behavior, 24,* 2.

Newell, K. M., Carlton, M. J., Fisher, A. T., & Rutter, B. G. (1989). Whole-part training strategies for learning the response dynamics of microprocessor driven simulators. *Acta Psychologica, 71,* 197-216.

Newell, K. M., Sparrow, W. A., & Quinn, J. T., Jr. (1985). Kinetic information feedback for learning isometric tasks. *Journal of Human Movement Studies, 11,* 113-123.

Newell, K. M., & Walter, C. B. (1981). Kinematic and kinetic parameters as information feedback in motor skill acquisition. *Journal of Human Movement Studies, 7,* 235-254.

Nissen, M. J., & Bullemer, P. (1987). Attentional requirements of learning: Evidence from performance measures. *Cognitive Psychology, 19,* 1-32.

Norman, D. A. (1968). Toward a theory of memory and attention. *Psychological Review, 75,* 522-536.

Norman, D. A., & Bobrow, D. J. (1975). On data-limited and resource-limited processes. *Cognitive Psychology, 7,* 44-64.

Norman, D. A., & Shallice, T. (1985). Attention to action: Willed and automatic control of behavior. In R. J. Davidson, G. E. Schwartz, & D. Shapiro (Eds.), *Consciousness and self-regulation: Advances in research* (Vol. 4, pp. 1-17). New York: Plenum.

Novick, L. R., & Holyoak, K. J. (1991). Mathematical problem solving by analogy. *Journal of Experimental Psychology: Learning, Memory, and Cognition, 17,* 398-415.

Oakhill, J. (1988). Effects of time of day on text memory and inference. In M. Gruneberg, P. Morris, & R. Sykes (Eds.), *Practical aspects of memory: Current research and issues* (pp. 465-470). New York: John Wiley.

Olson, J. R., & Biolsi, K. J. (1991). Techniques for representing expert knowledge. In K. A. Ericsson & J. Smith (Eds.), *Toward a general theory of expertise: Prospects and limits* (pp. 240-285). New York: Cambridge University Press.

Olson, J. R., & Olson, G. M. (1990). The growth of cognitive modeling in human-computer interaction since GOMS. *Human-Computer Interaction, 5,* 221-265.

Osgood, C. E. (1949). The similarity paradox in human learning: A resolution. *Psychological Review, 56,* 132-143.

Parkin, A. J., Reid, T. K., & Russo, R. (1990). On the differential nature of implicit and explicit memory. *Memory & Cognition, 18,* 507-514.

Pashler, H. A. (1984). Processing stages in overlapping tasks: Evidence for a central bottleneck. *Journal of Experimental Psychology: Human Perception and Performance, 10,* 358-377.

Pashler, H., & Baylis, G. C. (1991a). Procedural learning: 1. Locus of practice effects in speeded choice tasks. *Journal of Experimental Psychology: Learning, Memory, and Cognition, 17,* 20-32.

Pashler, H., & Baylis, G. C. (1991b). Procedural learning: 2. Intertrial repetition effects in speeded-choice tasks. *Journal of Experimental Psychology: Learning, Memory, and Cognition, 17,* 33-48.

Patrick, J. (1992). *Training: Research and practice.* London: Academic Press.

Payne, S. J. (1988). Metaphorical instruction and the early learning of an abbreviated-command computer system. *Acta Psychologica, 69,* 207-230.

Payne, S. J., Squibb, H. R., & Howes, A. (1990). The nature of device models: The yoked state space hypothesis and some experiments with text editors. *Human-Computer Interaction, 5,* 415-444.

Pear, T. H. (1927). Skill. *Journal of Personnel Research, 5,* 478-489.

Pear, T. H. (1948). Professor Bartlett on skill. *Occupational Psychology, 22,* 92-93.

Pellegrino, J. W., Doane, S. M., Fischer, S. C., & Alderton, D. (1991). Stimulus complexity effects in visual comparisons: The effects of practice and learning context. *Journal of Experimental Psychology: Human Perception and Performance, 17,* 781-791.

Perruchet, P., & Amorim, M.-A. (1992). Conscious knowledge and changes in performance sequence learning: Evidence against dissociation. *Journal of Experimental Psychology: Learning, Memory, and Cognition, 18,* 785-800.

Perry, D. H., & Naish, J. M. (1964). Flight simulation for research. *Journal of the Royal Aeronautical Society, 68,* 645-662.

Petre, M. (1991). What experts want from programming languages. *Ergonomics, 34,* 1113-1127.

Pew, R. W. (1966). Acquisition of hierarchical control over the temporal organization of a skill. *Journal of Experimental Psychology, 71,* 764-771.

Pew, R. W. (1974). Levels of analysis in motor control. *Brain Research, 71,* 393-400.

Pew, R. W., & Rosenbaum, D. A. (1988). Human movement control: Computation, representation, and implementation. In R. C. Atkinson, R. J. Herrnstein, G. Lindzey, & R. D. Luce (Eds.), *Stevens' handbook of experimental psychology* (pp. 473-509). New York: John Wiley.

Pick, A. D. (1965). Improvement of visual and tactual form discrimination. *Journal of Experimental Psychology, 69,* 331-339.

Polich, J. (1993). Cognitive brain potentials. *Current Directions in Psychological Science, 2,* 175-179.

Pollatsek, A., & Rayner, K. (1989). Reading. In M. I. Posner (Ed.), *Foundations of cognitive science* (pp. 401-436). Cambridge: MIT Press.

Posner, M. I. (1978). *Chronometric explorations of mind.* Hillsdale, NJ: Lawrence Erlbaum.

Posner, M. I., & Boies, S. J. (1971). Components of attention. *Psychological Review, 78,* 391-408.

Posner, M. I., Klein, R., Summers, J., & Buggie, S. (1973). On the selection of signals. *Memory & Cognition, 1,* 2-12.

Posner, M. I., & Mitchell, R. F. (1967). Chronometric analysis of classification. *Psychological Review, 74,* 392-409.

Postman, L., & Underwood, B. J. (1973). Critical issues in interference theory. *Memory & Cognition, 1,* 19-40.

Poulton, E. C. (1957). On prediction in skilled movements. *Psychological Bulletin, 54,* 467-478.

Povel, D.-J., & Collard, R. (1982). Structural factors in patterned finger tapping. *Acta Psychologica, 52,* 107-123.

Priest, A. G., & Lindsay, R. O. (1992). New light on novice-expert differences in physics problem solving. *British Journal of Psychology, 83,* 389-405.

Proctor, R. W., & Dutta, A. (1993). Do the same stimulus-response relations influence choice reactions initially and after practice? *Journal of Experimental Psychology: Learning, Memory, and Cognition, 19,* 922-930.

Proctor, R. W., & Reeve, T. G. (1985). Compatibility effects in the assignment of symbolic stimuli to discrete finger responses. *Journal of Experimental Psychology: Human Perception and Performance, 11,* 623-639.

Proctor, R. W., & Reeve, T. G. (1986). Salient-feature coding operations in spatial precuing tasks. *Journal of Experimental Psychology: Human Perception and Performance, 12,* 277-285.

Proctor, R. W., & Reeve, T. G. (1988). The acquisition of task-specific productions and modification of declarative representations in spatial-precuing tasks. *Journal of Experimental Psychology: General, 117,* 182-196.

Proctor, R. W., & Reeve, T. G. (1991). The prevalence of salient-features coding in choice-reaction tasks. In J. Requin & G. E. Stelmach (Eds.), *Tutorials in motor neuroscience* (pp. 17-26). Dordrecht: Kluwer.

Proctor, R. W., Reeve, T. G., Weeks, D. J., Dornier, L., & Van Zandt, T. (1991). Acquisition, retention, and transfer of response selection skill in choice reaction tasks. *Journal of Experimental Psychology: Learning, Memory, and Cognition, 17,* 497-506.

Proteau, L. (1992). On the specificity of learning and the role of visual information for movement control. In L. Proteau & D. Elliott (Eds.), *Vision and motor control* (pp. 65-101). Amsterdam: North-Holland.

Proteau, L., & Cournoyer, J. (1990). Vision of the stylus in a manual aiming task. *Quarterly Journal of Experimental Psychology, 42A,* 811-828.

Proteau, L., Marteniuk, R. G., & Levesque, L. (1992). A sensorimotor basis for motor learning: Evidence indicating specificity of practice. *Quarterly Journal of Experimental Psychology, 44A,* 557-575.

Quastler, H. (Ed.). (1955). *Information theory in psychology: Problems and methods.* Glencoe, IL: Free Press.

Quinlan, P. T. (1991). *Connectionism and psychology: A psychological perspective on new connectionist research.* Chicago: University of Chicago Press.

Rabbitt, P.M.A. (1968). Repetition effects and signal classification strategies in serial choice-response tasks. *Quarterly Journal of Experimental Psychology, 20,* 232-240.

Rabbitt, P.M.A. (1979). Current paradigms and models in human information processing. In V. S. Hamilton & D. Warburton (Eds.), *Human stress and cognition* (pp. 115-140). New York: John Wiley.

Rabbitt, P.M.A. (1989). Sequential reactions. In D. H. Holding (Ed.), *Human skills* (2nd ed., pp. 147-170). New York: John Wiley.

Rabbitt, P.M.A., & Banerji, N. (1989). How does very prolonged practice improve decision speed? *Journal of Experimental Psychology: General, 118,* 338-345.

Rabbitt, P.M.A., & Vyas, S. M. (1970). An elementary preliminary taxonomy for some errors in laboratory choice RT tasks. *Acta Psychologica, 33,* 56-76.

Rabbitt, P.M.A., & Vyas, S. (1979). Signal recency effects can be distinguished from signal repetition effects in serial CRT tasks. *Canadian Journal of Psychology, 33,* 88-95.

Rabin, M. D. (1988). Experience facilitates olfactory quality discrimination. *Perception & Psychophysics, 44,* 532-540.

Ramsey, J. D. (1983). Heat and cold. In R. Hockey (Ed.), *Stress and fatigue in human performance* (pp. 33-60). New York: John Wiley.

Rasmussen, J. (1983). Skills, rules, and knowledge: Signals, signs, and symbols, and other distinctions in human performance models. *IEEE Transactions on Systems, Man, and Cybernetics, SMC-13,* 257-266.

Rasmussen, J. (1986). *Information processing and human-machine interaction: An approach to cognitive engineering.* Amsterdam: North-Holland.

Reber, A. S. (1967). Implicit learning of artificial grammars. *Journal of Verbal Learning and Verbal Behavior, 77,* 317-327.

Reber, A. S. (1976). Implicit learning of synthetic languages: The role of instructional set. *Journal of Experimental Psychology: Human Learning and Memory, 2,* 88-94.

Reber, A. S. (1989). Implicit learning and tacit knowledge. *Journal of Experimental Psychology: General, 118,* 219-235.

Reber, A. S., Kassin, S. M., Lewis, S., & Cantor, G. W. (1980). On the relationship between implicit and explicit modes in the learning of a complex rule structure. *Journal of Experimental Psychology: Human Learning and Memory, 6,* 492-502.

Reeve, T. G., & Proctor, R. W. (1984). On the advance preparation of discrete finger responses. *Journal of Experimental Psychology: Human Perception and Performance, 10,* 541-553.

Regina, E. G., Smith, G. M., Keiper, C. G., & McKelvey, R. K. (1974). Effects of caffeine on alertness in simulated automobile driving. *Journal of Applied Psychology, 59,* 483-489.

Reicher, G. M. (1969). Perceptual recognition as a function of meaningfulness of stimulus material. *Journal of Experimental Psychology, 81,* 275-280.

Reitman, J. S., & Reuter, H. R. (1980). Organization revealed by recall orders and confirmed by pauses. *Cognitive Psychology, 12,* 554-581.

Rescorla, R. A., & Wagner, A. R. (1972). A theory of Pavlovian conditioning: Variations in the effectiveness of reinforcement and nonreinforcement. In A. H. Black & W. F. Prokasy (Eds.), *Classical conditioning II: Current research and theory* (pp. 64-99). New York: Appleton-Century-Crofts.

Revelle, W., Humphreys, M. S., Simon, L., & Gilliland, K. (1980). The interactive effect of personality, time of day, and caffeine: A test of the arousal model. *Journal of Experimental Psychology: General, 109,* 1-31.

Robinson, J. S. (1955). The effect of learning verbal labels for stimuli on their later discrimination. *Journal of Experimental Psychology, 49,* 112-114.

Roediger, H. L., III (1990). Implicit memory: Retention without remembering. *American Psychologist, 45,* 1043-1056.

Roediger, H. L., III, & McDermott, K. B. (1993). Implicit memory in normal human subjects. In H. Spinnler & F. Boller (Eds.), *Handbook of neuropsychology* (Vol. 8, pp. 63-131). Amsterdam: Elsevier.

Rosenbaum, D. A. (1987). Successive approximations to a model of human motor programming. In G. H. Bower (Ed.), *The psychology of learning and motivation* (Vol. 21, pp. 153-182). San Diego: Academic Press.

Rosenbloom, P. S., & Newell, A. (1987). An integrated computational model of stimulus-response compatibility and practice. In G. H. Bower (Ed.), *The psychology of learning and motivation* (Vol. 21, pp. 1-52). San Diego: Academic Press.

Ross, B. H. (1987). This is like that: The use of earlier problems and the separation of similarity effects. *Journal of Experimental Psychology: Learning, Memory, and Cognition, 13,* 629-639.

Rumelhart, D. E., & Norman, D. A. (1982). Simulating a skilled typist: A study of skilled cognitive-motor performance. *Cognitive Science, 6,* 1-36.

Saariluoma, P. (1984). *Coding problem spaces in chess: A psychological study.* Helsinki: Societas Scientarium Fennica.

Saariluoma, P. (1992). Visuospatial and articulatory interference in chess players' information intake. *Applied Cognitive Psychology, 6,* 77-89.

Salmoni, A. W., Schmidt, R. A., & Walter, C. B. (1984). Knowledge of results and motor learning: A review and critical reappraisal. *Psychological Bulletin, 95,* 355-386.

Salthouse, T. A. (1984). Effects of age and skill in typing. *Journal of Experimental Psychology: General, 113,* 345-371.

Salthouse, T. A. (1985). *A theory of cognitive aging.* Amsterdam: North-Holland.

Salthouse, T. A. (1986). Perceptual, cognitive, and motoric aspects of transcription typing. *Psychological Bulletin, 99,* 303-319.

Salthouse, T. A. (1989). Aging and skilled performance. In A. M. Colley & J. R. Beech (Eds.), *Acquisition and performance of cognitive skills* (pp. 247-264). Chichester: Wiley.

Salthouse, T. A., Kausler, D. H., & Saults, J. S. (1988). Investigation of student status, background variables, and the feasibility of standard tasks in cognitive aging research. *Psychology and Aging, 3,* 29-37.

Salthouse, T. A., & Saults, J. S. (1987). Multiple spans in transcription typing. *Journal of Applied Psychology, 72,* 187-196.

Salthouse, T. A., & Somberg, B. L. (1982). Skilled performance: Effects of adult age and experience on elementary processes. *Journal of Experimental Psychology, General, 111,* 176-207.

Saltzman, E. L., & Munhall, K. G. (1992). Skill acquisition and development: The roles of state-, parameter-, and graph-dynamics. *Journal of Motor Behavior, 24,* 49-57.

Salvendy, G., & Pilitsis, J. (1980). The development and validation of an analytical training program for medical suturing. *Human Factors, 22,* 753-770.

Sanders, A. F. (1975). The foreperiod effect revisited. *Quarterly Journal of Experimental Psychology, 27,* 591-598.

Sanders, A. F. (1990). Issues and trends in the debate on discrete versus continuous processing of information. *Acta Psychologica, 74,* 123-167.

Sanderson, P. M., James, J. M., & Seidler, K. S. (1989). SHAPA: An interactive software environment for protocol analysis. *Ergonomics, 32,* 1271-1302.

Schacter, D. L. (1987). Implicit memory: History and current status. *Journal of Experimental Psychology: Learning, Memory, and Cognition, 13,* 501-518.

Schmidt, R. A. (1975). A schema theory of discrete motor skill learning. *Psychological Review, 82,* 225-260.

Schmidt, R. A. (1988). *Motor control and learning: A behavioral emphasis* (2nd ed.). Champaign, IL: Human Kinetics.

Schmidt, R. A., & Bjork, R. A. (1992). New conceptualizations of practice: Common principles in three paradigms suggest new concepts for training. *Psychological Science, 3,* 207-217.

Schmidt, R. A., & Young, D. E. (1991). Methodology for motor learning: A paradigm for kinematic feedback. *Journal of Motor Behavior, 23,* 13-24.

Schmidt, R. A., Young, D. E., Swinnen, S., & Shapiro, D. C. (1989). Summary knowledge of results for skill acquisition: Support for the guidance hypothesis. *Journal of Experimental Psychology: Learning, Memory, and Cognition, 15,* 352-359.

Schneider, W. (1985). Training high-performance skills: Fallacies and guidelines. *Human Factors, 27,* 285-300.

Schneider, W. (1989). *Getting smart quicker: Training more skills in less time.* Transcript of Science and Public Policy Seminar presented by the Federation of Behavioral, Psychological, and Cognitive Sciences, April 7, Washington, DC.

Schneider, W., & Detweiler, M. (1987). A connectionist/control architecture for working memory. In G. H. Bower (Ed.), *The psychology of learning and motivation* (Vol. 21, pp. 53-119). San Diego: Academic Press.

Schneider, W., & Detweiler, M. (1988). The role of practice in dual-task performance: Toward workload modeling in a connectionist/control architecture. *Human Factors, 30,* 539-566.

Schneider, W., & Fisk, A. D. (1982a). Concurrent automatic and controlled visual search: Can processing occur without resource cost? *Journal of Experimental Psychology: Learning, Memory, and Cognition, 8,* 261-278.

Schneider, W., & Fisk, A. D. (1982b). Degree of consistent training: Improvements in search performance and automatic process development. *Perception & Psychophysics, 31,* 160-168.

Schneider, W., & Shiffrin, R. M. (1977). Controlled and automatic human information processing: I. Detection, search, and attention. *Psychological Review, 84,* 1-66.

Schneider, W., Vidulich, M., & Yeh, Y.-Y. (1982). Training spatial skills for air-traffic control. In *Proceedings of the Human Factors Society 26th annual meeting* (pp. 10-14). Santa Monica, CA: Human Factors Society.

Schneiderman, B. (1976). Exploratory experiments in programmer behavior. *International Journal of Computer and Information Sciences, 5,* 123-143.

Schreter, Z. (1990). Neural networks and the Yerkes-Dodson law. *Cognitive Systems, 2,* 345-358.

Schuyler, Jr., E. (1992, August 2). *Problems with the scoring system contribute to Griffin's defeat.* Associated Press wire service.

Schvaneveldt, R. W. (Ed.). (1990). *Pathfinder associative networks: Studies in knowledge organization.* Norwood, NJ: Ablex.

Schweickert, R. (1983). Latent network theory: Scheduling of processes in sentence verification and the Stroop effect. *Journal of Experimental Psychology: Learning, Memory, and Cognition, 9,* 353-383.

Schweickert, R., Fisher, D. L., & Goldstein, W. M. (1992). *General latent network theory: Structural and quantitative analysis of networks of cognitive processes.* Purdue Mathematical Psychology Program Technical Report No. 92-1. Purdue University, West Lafayette, IN.

Seger, C. A. (1994). Implicit learning. *Psychological Bulletin, 115,* 163-196.

Seibel, R. (1963). Discrimination reaction time for a 1,023-alternative task.

Journal of Experimental Psychology, 66, 215-226.

Seidenberg, M. S. (1993). Connectionist models and cognitive theory. *Psychological Science, 4,* 228-235.

Shallice, T. (1988). *From neuropsychology to mental structure.* New York: Cambridge University Press.

Shannon, C. E., & Weaver, W. (1949). *The mathematical theory of communication.* Urbana: University of Illinois Press.

Shapiro, K. L., & Raymond, J. E. (1989). Training of efficient oculomotor strategies enhances skill acquisition. *Acta Psychologica, 71,* 217-242.

Shea, J. B., & Morgan, R. L. (1979). Contextual interference effects on the acquisition, retention, and transfer of a motor skill. *Journal of Experimental Psychology: Learning, Memory, and Cognition, 5,* 179-187.

Shea, J. B., & Wright, D. L. (1991). When forgetting benefits motor retention. *Research Quarterly for Exercise and Sport, 62,* 293-301.

Shiffrin, R. M., Dumais, S. T., & Schneider, W. (1981). Characteristics of automatism. In J. Long & A. Baddeley (Eds.), *Attention and performance IV* (pp. 223-238). Hillsdale, NJ: Lawrence Erlbaum.

Shiffrin, R. M., & Schneider, W. (1977). Controlled and automatic human information processing: II. Perceptual learning, automatic attending, and a general theory. *Psychological Review, 84,* 127-190.

Shrager, J., & Klahr, D. (1986). Instructionless learning about a complex device: The paradigm and observations. *International Journal of Man-Machine Studies, 25,* 153-189.

Simon, H. A., & Chase, W. G. (1973). Skill in chess. *American Scientist, 61,* 394-403.

Singley, M. K., & Anderson, J. R. (1989). *The transfer of cognitive skill.* Cambridge, MA: Harvard University Press.

Smith, A. P. (1985). The effects of noise on the processing of global shape and local detail. *Psychological Research, 47,* 103-108.

Smith, A. P. (1991). Strategy choice and time of day: An investigation of diurnal variation in speed and accuracy. In E. J. Lovesey (Ed.), *Contemporary ergonomics 1991* (pp. 44-48). London: Taylor & Francis.

Smith, A. P. (1992). Time of day and performance. In A. P. Smith and D. M. Jones (Eds.), *Handbook of human performance: Vol. 3. State and trait* (pp. 217-235). San Diego: Academic Press.

Smith, A. P., & Jones, D. M. (1992). Noise and performance. In A. P. Smith & D. M. Jones (Eds.), *Handbook of human performance: Vol. 1. The physical environment* (pp. 1-28). San Diego: Academic Press.

Smith, M. C. (1967). Theories of the psychological refractory period. *Psychological Bulletin, 67,* 202-213.

Smith, M. D., & Chamberlin, C. J. (1992). Effects of adding cognitively demanding tasks on soccer skill performance. *Perceptual and Motor Skills, 75,* 955-961.

Sniezek, J. A., & Naylor, J. C. (1978). Cue measurement scale and functional hypothesis testing in cue probability learning. *Organizational Behavior and Human Performance, 22,* 366-374.

Snoddy, G. S. (1926). Learning and stability: A psychophysiological analysis of a case of motor learning with clinical applications. *Journal of Applied Psychology, 10,* 1-36.

Snyder, S. H. (1984). Adenosine as a mediator of the behavioral effects of xanthines. In P. B. Dews (Ed.), *Caffeine: Perspectives from recent research* (pp. 119-128). New York: Springer.

Soloway, E., Adelson, B., & Ehrlich, K. (1988). Knowledge and processes in the comprehension of computer programs. In M.T.H. Chi, R. Glaser, & M. J. Farr (Eds.), *The nature of expertise* (pp. 129-152). Hillsdale, NJ: Lawrence Erlbaum.

Soloway, E., & Ehrlich, K. (1984). Empirical studies of programming knowledge. *IEEE Transactions on Software Engineering, SE-10,* 595-609.

Sparrow, W. A., & Summers, J. J. (1992). Performance on trials without knowledge of results (KR) in reduced relative frequency presentations of KR. *Journal of Motor Behavior, 24,* 197-209.

Spearman, C. (1904). "General intelligence," objectively determined and measured. *American Journal of Psychology, 15,* 201-293.

Spearman, C. (1927). *The abilities of man.* New York: Macmillan.

Spears, W. D. (1983). *Processes of skill acquisition: A foundation for the design and use of training equipment* (navtraequipcen 78-CO113-4). Orlando, FL: Naval Training Equipment Center.

Spelke, E., Hirst, W., & Neisser, U. (1976). Skills of divided attention. *Cognition, 4,* 215-230.

Spellman, B. A., & Holyoak, K. J. (1992). If Saddam is Hitler, then who is George Bush? Analogical mapping between systems of social roles. *Journal of Personality and Social Psychology, 62,* 913-933.

Sperandio, J.-C. (1978). The regulation of working methods as a function of work-load among air traffic controllers. *Ergonomics, 21,* 195-202.

Spitz, G. (1988). Flexibility in resource allocation and the performance of time-sharing tasks. In *Proceedings of the Human Factors Society 32nd annual meeting* (pp. 1466-1470). Santa Monica, CA: Human Factors Society.

Squire, L. R. (1987). *Memory and brain.* New York: Oxford University Press.

Squire, L. R. (1992). Memory and the hippocampus: A synthesis from findings with rats, monkeys, and humans. *Psychological Review, 99,* 195-231.

Srinivas, K. (1993). Perceptual specificity in nonverbal priming. *Journal of Experimental Psychology: Learning, Memory, and Cognition, 19,* 582-602.

Stadler, M. A. (1989). On learning complex procedural knowledge. *Journal of Experimental Psychology: Learning, Memory, and Cognition, 15,* 1061-1069.

Stanley, W. B., Mathews, R. C., Buss, R. R., & Kotler-Cope, S. (1989). Insight without awareness: On the interaction of verbalization, instruction and practice in a simulated process control task. *Quarterly Journal of Experimental Psychology, 41A,* 553-577.

Sternberg, R. J. (1977). *Intelligence, information processing and analogical reasoning: The componential analysis of human abilities.* Hillsdale, NJ: Lawrence Erlbaum.

Sternberg, R. J. (1979). The nature of mental abilities. *American Psychologist, 34,* 214-230.

Sternberg, R. J. (1988). Intelligence. In R. J. Sternberg & E. E. Smith, *The psychology of human thought* (pp. 267-308). New York: Cambridge University Press.

Sternberg, S. (1969). The discovery of processing stages: Extensions of Donders' method. In W. G. Koster (Ed.), Attention and performance II [Special issue]. *Acta Psychologica, 30,* 276-315.

Stroop, J. R, (1992). Studies of interference in serial verbal reactions. *Journal of Experimental Psychology: General, 121,* 15-23. (Original work published 1935)

Subcommittee on Administration of the ASME. (1912). The present state of the art of industrial management. *Transactions of the ASME, 34,* 1197-1198.

Swift, E. J. (1904). The acquisition of skill in typewriting; A contribution to the psychology of learning. *Psychological Bulletin, 1,* 295-305.

Swift, E. J. (1910). Learning to telegraph. *Psychological Bulletin, 7,* 149-153.

Swinnen, S. P. (1990). Interpolated activities during the knowledge-of-results delay and the post-knowledge-of-results interval: Effects on performance and learning. *Journal of Experimental Psychology: Learning, Memory, and Cognition, 16,* 692-705.

Swinnen, S. P., Schmidt, R. A., Nicholson, D. E., & Shapiro, D. C. (1990). Information feedback for skill acquisition: Instantaneous knowledge of results degrades learning. *Journal of Experimental Psychology: Learning, Memory, and Cognition, 16,* 706-716.

Taub, E., & Berman, A. J. (1968). Movement and learning in the absence of sensory feedback. In S. J. Freedman (Ed.), *The neuropsychology of spatially oriented behavior* (pp. 173-192). Homewood, IL: Dorsey Press.

Teichner, W. H., & Krebs, M. J. (1974). Laws of visual choice reaction time. *Psychological Review, 81,* 75-98.

Telford, C. W. (1931). Refractory phase of voluntary and associative responses. *Journal of Experimental Psychology, 14,* 1-35.

Thorndike, E. L., Bregman, E. O., Tilton, J. W., & Woodward, E. (1928). *Adult learning.* New York: Macmillan.

Thorndike, E. L., & Woodworth, R. S. (1901a). The influence of improvement in one mental function upon the efficiency of other functions, I. *Psychological Review, 8,* 247-261.

Thorndike, E. L., & Woodworth, R. S. (1901b). The influence of improvement in one mental function upon the efficiency of other functions, II: The estimation of magnitudes. *Psychological Review, 8,* 384-395.

Thorndike, E. L., & Woodworth, R. S. (1901c). The influence of improvement in one mental function upon the efficiency of other functions, III: Functions involving attention, observation, and discrimination. *Psychological Review, 8,* 553-564.

Thurstone, L. L. (1935). *The vectors of mind.* Chicago: University of Chicago Press.

Thurstone, L. L. (1947). *Multiple factor analysis.* Chicago: University of Chicago Press.

Tilley, A. J., & Bohle, P. (1988). Twisting the night away: The effects of all-night disco dancing on reaction time. *Perceptual and Motor Skills, 66,* 107-112.

Tilley, A., & Brown, S. (1992). Sleep deprivation. In A. P. Smith & D. M. Jones (Eds.), *Handbook of human performance: Vol. 3. State and trait* (pp. 237-259). San Diego: Academic Press.

Townsend, J. T. (1974). Issues and models concerning the processing of a finite number of inputs. In B. H. Kantowitz (Ed.), *Tutorials in performance and cognition* (pp. 133-185). Hillsdale, NJ: Lawrence Erlbaum.

Townsend, J. T., & Ashby, G. (1983). *Stochastic modeling of elementary psychological processes.* New York: Cambridge University Press.

Treisman, A. M. (1964). Verbal cues, language, and meaning in selective attention. *American Journal of Psychology, 77,* 206-219.

Treisman, A. M., & Davies, A. (1973). Divided attention to ear and eye. In S. Kornblum (Ed.), *Attention and performance IV* (pp. 101-117). New York: Academic Press.

Treisman, A. M., & Gelade, G. (1980). A feature-integration theory of attention. *Cognitive Psychology, 12,* 97-136.

Tsang, P. S., & Wickens, C. D. (1988). The structural constraints and resource control of resource allocation. *Human Performance, 1,* 45-72.

Tyhurst, J. S. (1951). Individual reactions to community disaster. *American Journal of Psychiatry, 107,* 764-769.

Umiltà, C., & Nicoletti, R. (1990). Spatial stimulus-response compatibility. In R. W. Proctor & T. G. Reeve (Eds.), *Stimulus-response compatibility: An integrated perspective* (pp. 89-116). Amsterdam: North-Holland.

Underwood, G. (1974). Moray vs. the rest: The effects of extended shadowing practice. *Quarterly Journal of Experimental Psychology, 26,* 368-372.

Van Orden, G. C. (1987). A ROWS is a ROSE: Spelling, sound, and reading. *Memory & Cognition, 15,* 181-198.

VanLehn, K. (1989). Problem solving and cognitive skill acquisition. In M. I. Posner (Ed.), *Foundations of cognitive science* (pp. 527-579). Cambridge: MIT Press.

Vereijken, B., van Emmerik, R.E.A., Whiting, H.T.A., & Newell, K. M. (1992). Free(z)ing degrees of freedom in skill acquisition. *Journal of Motor Behavior, 24,* 133-142.

Virzi, R. A., & Egeth, H. E. (1985). Toward a translational model of Stroop interference. *Memory & Cognition, 13,* 304-319.

Viviani, P., & Mounoud, P. (1990). Perceptuo-motor compatibility in pursuit tracking. *Journal of Motor Behavior, 22,* 407-443.

Viviani, P., & Stucchi, N. (1992). Biological movements look uniform: Evidence of motor-perceptual interactions. *Journal of Experimental Psychology: Human Perception and Performance, 18,* 603-623.

Voss, J. F., & Post, T. A. (1988). On the solving of ill-structured problems. In M.T.H. Chi, R. Glaser, & M. J. Farr (Eds.), *The nature of expertise* (pp. 261-285). Hillsdale, NJ: Lawrence Erlbaum.

Wallace, R. J. (1971). S-R compatibility and the idea of a response code. *Journal of Experimental Psychology, 88,* 354-360.

Warrington, E. K., & Weiskrantz, L. (1974). The effect of prior learning on subsequent retention in amnesic patients. *Neuropsychologia, 12,* 419-428.

Weeks, D. J., Lee, T. D., & Elliott, D. (1987). Differential forgetting and spacing effects in short-term motor retention. *Journal of Human Movement Studies, 13,* 309-321.

Weldon, M. S., & Roediger, H. L., III. (1987). Altering retrieval demands reverses the picture superiority effect. *Memory & Cognition, 15,* 269-280.

Welford, A. T. (1952). The "psychological refractory period" and the timing of high-speed performance: A review and a theory. *British Journal of Psychology, 43,* 2-19.

Welford, A. T. (1968). *Fundamentals of skill.* London: Methuen.

Welford, A. T. (1976). *Skilled performance: Perceptual and motor skills.* Glenview, IL: Scott, Foresman.

Welford, A. T., Brown, R. A., & Gabb, J. E. (1950). Two experiments on fatigue as affecting skilled performance in civilian aircrew. *British Journal of Psychology, 40,* 195-211.

Wesnes, K. A., & Parrott, A. C. (1992). Smoking, nicotine, and human performance. In A. P. Smith & D. M. Jones (Eds.), *Handbook of human performance: Vol 2. Health and performance* (pp. 127-167). San Diego: Academic Press.

Wesnes, K., & Warburton, D. M. (1978). The effects of cigarette smoking and nicotine tablets upon human attention. In R. E. Thornton (Ed.), *Smoking behaviour: Physiological and psychological influences* (pp. 131-147). London: Churchill Livingstone.

Wesnes, K., & Warburton, D. M. (1984). Effects of scopolamine and nicotine on human rapid information processing performance. *Psychopharmacology, 82,* 147-150.

Wickens, C. D. (1984). Processing resources in attention. In R. Parasuraman & D. R. Davies (Eds.), *Varieties of attention* (pp. 63-102). New York: Academic Press.

Wickens, C. D. (1992). *Engineering psychology and human performance* (2nd ed.). New York: HarperCollins.

Wightman, D. C., & Lintern G. (1985). Part-task training for tracking and manual control. *Human Factors, 27,* 267-283.

Wilding, J., Mohindra, N., & Breen-Lewis, K. (1982). Noise effects in free recall with different orienting tasks. *British Journal of Psychology, 73,* 479-486.

Williams, H. L., Lubin, A., & Goodnow, J. J. (1959). Impaired performance with acute sleep loss. *Psychological Monographs: General and Applied, 73,* 1-26.

Williams, M., Hollan, J., & Stevens, A. (1981). An overview of STEAMER: An advanced computer-assisted instruction system for propulsion engineering. *Behavior Research Methods & Instrumentation, 12,* 85-90.

Willingham, D. B., Nissen, M. J., & Bullemer, P. (1989). On the development of procedural knowledge. *Journal of Experimental Psychology: Learning, Memory, and Cognition, 15,* 1047-1060.

Winstein, C. J., & Schmidt, R. A. (1989). Sensorimotor feedback. In D. H. Holding (Ed.), *Human skills* (2nd ed., pp. 17-47). New York: John Wiley.

Winstein, C. J., & Schmidt, R. A. (1990). Reduced frequency of knowledge of results enhances motor skill learning. *Journal of Experimental Psychology: Learning, Memory, and Cognition, 16,* 677-691.

Wolfe, J. M., Cave, K. R., & Franzel, S. L. (1989). Guided search: An alternative to the feature integration model for visual search. *Journal of Experimental Psychology: Human Perception and Performance, 15,* 419-433.

Woodrow, H. (1946). The ability to learn. *Psychological Review, 53,* 147-158.

Woodworth, R. S. (1899). The accuracy of voluntary movement. *Psychological Review, 3*(Monograph Suppl.), 1-119.

Woodworth, R. S. (1938). *Experimental psychology.* New York: Holt.

Wulf, G., & Schmidt, R. A. (1989). The learning of generalized motor programs: Reducing the relative frequency of knowledge of results enhances memory. *Journal of Experimental Psychology: Learning, Memory, and Cognition, 15,* 748-757.

Yerkes, R. M., & Dodson, J. D. (1908). The relation of strength of stimulus to rapidity of habit formation. *Journal of Comparative Neurology and Psychology, 18,* 459-482.

Young, D. E., & Schmidt, R. A. (1992). Augmented kinematic feedback for motor learning. *Journal of Motor Behavior, 24,* 261-273.

Young, R. M. (1981). The machine inside the machine: Users' models of pocket calculators. *International Journal of Man-Machine Studies, 15,* 51-85.

Zanone, P. G., & Kelso, J.A.S. (1992). Evolution of behavioral attractors with learning: Nonequilibrium phase transitions. *Journal of Experimental Psychology: Human Perception and Performance, 18,* 403-421.

Author Index

Subject Index

About the Authors

Robert W. Proctor (Ph.D., University of Texas at Arlington, 1975) is Professor of Psychology at Purdue University. His research interests include the relation between perception and action, issues of mental representation in response selection, how and why information that is defined as irrelevant influences task performance, models of human information processing, skill acquisition, and philosophical issues pertaining to psychological research. He is currently editor of *Behavior Research Methods, Instruments, and Computers* and served as associate editor of *Memory & Cognition* from 1986 to 1993. He serves as a consulting editor for *Perception & Psychophysics* and as associate editor in cognitive sciences for the *International Journal of Human-Computer Interaction.* He is coeditor, with T. G. Reeve, of *Stimulus-Response Compatibility: An Integrated Perspective,* and coauthor, with T. Van Zandt, of *Human Factors in Simple and Complex Systems.*

Addie Dutta (Ph.D., Purdue University, 1993) is Assistant Professor of Psychology at Rice University. Her research interests include most aspects of human information processing, with a focus on skill acquisition and response selection. She also conducts research in information display and human-machine interaction and is collaborating in the development of interactive, computer-based tutorials in engineering psychology. She is coauthor, with Kathryn C. Campbell and Robert W. Proctor, of *Workbook in Human Factors for Simple and Complex Systems.*